Modeling and Analysis of Enterprise Information Systems

Angappa Gunasekaran
University of Massachusetts, USA

IGI PUBLISHING

Hershey • New York

Acquisition Editor: Kristin Klinger
Senior Managing Editor: Jennifer Neidig
Managing Editor: Sara Reed
Assistant Managing Editor: Sharon Berger
Development Editor: Kristin Roth
Copy Editor: Amanda Appicello
Typesetter: Amanda Appicello
Cover Design: Lisa Tosheff
Printed at: Yurchak Printing Inc.

Published in the United States of America by
        IGI Publishing (an imprint of IGI Global)
        701 E. Chocolate Avenue
        Hershey PA 17033
        Tel: 717-533-8845
        Fax: 717-533-8661
        E-mail: cust@idea-group.com
        Web site: http://www.idea-group.com

and in the United Kingdom by
        IGI Publishing (an imprint of IGI Global)
        3 Henrietta Street
        Covent Garden
        London WC2E 8LU
        Tel: 44 20 7240 0856
        Fax: 44 20 7379 0609
        Web site: http://www.eurospanonline.com

    Library of Congress Cataloging-in-Publication Data

Modeling and analysis of enterprise information systems / Angappa Gunasekaran, editor.
       p. cm. -- (Advances in enterprise information systems series ; v. 1)
    Summary: "This book presents comprehensive coverage and understanding of the organizational and techno-
logical issues of enterprise information systems. It covers current trends such as enterprise resource planning
and electronic commerce, and their implications on supply chain management and organizational competitiveness"--Provided by publisher.
    Includes bibliographical references and index.
    ISBN 978-1-59904-477-4 (hardcover) -- ISBN 978-1-59904-479-8 (ebook)
    1. Management information systems. 2. Information technology--Management. I. Gunasekaran, A.
    HD30.213.M63 2007
    658.4'038011--dc22
                        2006039665

British Cataloguing in Publication Data
A Cataloguing in Publication record for this book is available from the British Library.

All work contributed to this book is new, previously-unpublished material. The views expressed in this book
are those of the authors, but not necessarily of the publisher.

Modeling and Analysis of Enterprise Information Systems

Table of Contents

Preface

Enterprise information system(s) (EIS) such as the enterprise resource planning (ERP) and electronic commerce (EC) play a major role in the 21st century organizations. These systems will have a significant impact on organizational productivity and competitiveness in the increasingly global markets of the 21st century, and they warrant the attention of researchers. Globalization of markets and operations is closely related to the success of a company. This paradigm heightens the importance of sharing information and thus, the critical role of EIS in enhancing organizational effectiveness and competitiveness. ERP systems are the software tools used to manage enterprise data and provide information to those who need it, when they need it. These systems help organizations manage their supply chains: receiving, inventory management, customer order management, production planning and control, shipping, accounting, human resource management, and all other activities that take place in a modern business.

Global markets and competition have forced companies to operate in a physically distributed environment to take the advantage of benefits of strategic alliances between partnering firms. Earlier, information systems such as material requirements planning (MRP), computer-aided design (CAD), and computer-aided manufacturing (CAM) have widely been used for functional integration within an organization. With global operations are in place, there is a need for suitable enterprise information systems (EIS) such as enterprise resource planning (ERP) and e-commerce (EC) for the integration of extended enterprises along the supply chain with the objective of achieving flexibility and responsiveness. Companies all over the world spend billions of dollars in the design and implementation of EIS in particular

ERP systems such as Oracle, Peoplesoft, SAP, JD Edwards, and BAAN with the objective of achieving an integrated global supply chain. Inter-organizational information systems play a major role in improving communication and integration between partnering firms to achieve an integrated global supply chain. There is a growing demand for research and applications that will provide insights into issues, challenges, and solutions related to the successful applications and management aspects of EIS. *Modeling and Analysis of Enterprise Information Systems* provides researchers, scholars, professionals, and educators with the most current research on modeling and analysis of enterprise information systems. This volume presents new concepts in enterprise information systems.

Chapter I, "Implementation of Enterprise Resource Planning (ERP) Systems: Issues and Challenges", by Subramanian and Hoffer reviews the literature on ERP implementation and presents the results of a case study on ERP implementation. Using the case study, the chapter indicates the presence of four phases in ERP implementation through the support from qualitative interviews. Using t-tests, the results confirm the presence of a positive feeling of users towards the four ERP implementation phases.

Chapter II, "Research Issues of the IT Productivity Paradox: Approaches, Limitations, and a Proposed Conceptual Framework", by Law and Ngai proposed a research model to address the issues and problems of IT and its role in productivity. With expectation to mitigate the shortcomings of some of the prior studies, this model incorporates improvements in business process as an independent construct in parallel to the capabilities of IT and enterprise systems. Competitive capabilities are included as an intermediate construct to help conceptualize the linkage between the independent constructs and the dependent construct of organizational performance. Theories and empirical evidence are drawn from associated management disciplines such as operations management and from a resources-based view of the firm to illustrate and explain that investment in IT and business processes will eventually contribute to organizational performance through the creation and enhancement of competitive capabilities. Finally, the theoretical and managerial implications of this research model are highlighted.

Chapter III, "The Effects of Uncertainty on ERP-Controlled Manufacturing Supply Chains", by Koh and Gunasekaran presents the developmental and experimental work on modelling uncertainty within an ERP multi-product, multi-level dependent demand manufacturing supply chain in a simulation model developed using ARENA/ SIMAN. To enumerate how uncertainty affects the performance of an ERP-controlled manufacturing supply chain, the percentages of finished products delivered late and parts delivered late (PDL) are measured. Sensitivity analysis shows that PDL gives a more accurate effect. Simulations results are analysed using analysis of variance, which identifies four uncertainties namely late delivery from suppliers, machine breakdowns, unexpected/urgent changes to machine assignments, and customer design changes significantly affect PDL. Some uncertainties are found significantly interactive in two and three-way. They produce either knock-on and/or compound effects, a factor not generally recognized as a criterion for decision-making.

Chapter IV, "Software Architecture and Requirements for a Web-Based Survey System", by Baldwin and Chalasani briefly reviews literature regarding Web-based surveys and describes a software architecture for a Web-based survey system. The architecture for the survey system is based on three tiers comprised of a Web server, Web application server, and database server. The Web application server hosts the application modules that display and process the surveys. The application software consists of packages for establishing connections to the database and for reading static and dynamic data from the database. The processed surveys are written to the database with the survey responses. This system allows for anonymous survey responses and maintains user confidentiality. At the University of Wisconsin-Parkside, they have implemented this Web-based survey system, and used it to conduct three different surveys. This survey system is easily extensible to new surveys, and is used for instructional purposes to teach server-side programming. In this chapter, they discuss the key ideas behind the design and implementation of the extensible survey system, and provide results on its application.

Chapter V, "Identity Theft and E-Fraud Driving CRM Information Exchanges", by Smith and Lias deals with an empirical study of 75 managerial employees and/or knowledge workers in five large organizations in Pittsburgh, PA, revealed a number of interesting concepts to find out how much information they share with others, what the likelihood is that they will conduct business online, and whether or not they take steps to protect their personal identity and credit. Model construction and implications were generated concerning steps that employees and customers may take to avoid identity theft.

Chapter VI, "Pricing Outcomes in Dual Channel Monopoly and Partial Duopoly", by Sheikh, Amin, and Amin studies the pricing strategies first, of a monopolist selling a product through stores in two channels, but under single management (or coordinated management) and then propose a framework for a model for a partial duopoly market conditions. They find that the monopolist generally charges a higher price in the brick and mortar store than the price charged in the Internet store. If, however, there is a sufficiently large fraction of buyers who would strictly prefer to buy the product from the Internet store instead of the physical store at any given price, the monopolist might charge the same price in both the stores. They also find that physical store price of a dual-channel monopoly is higher than the physical store price of a single channel monopoly; the price charged in the Internet store is generally lower than the single channel monopoly price. The chapter concludes with an identification of parameters for channel pricing strategies under partial duopoly market conditions.

Chapter VII, "Enterprise Information Systems and B2B E-Commerce: Exchanging Secure Transactions Using XML", by Baker reviews the objectives of using XML in B2B e-commerce, reviews the technical structure of XML, and discusses ways that security and privacy can be enhanced while engaging in B2B e-commerce.

Chapter VIII, "Unleashing the Potential of SCM: The Adoption of ERP in Large Danish Enterprises", by Møller argues that with the present state of enterprise resource planning (ERP) adoption by the companies, the potential benefits of supply chain management (SCM) and integration is about to be unleashed. This chapter presents the results and the implications of a survey on ERP adoption in the 500 largest Danish enterprises. The study is based on telephone interviews with ERP managers in 88.4% of the "top 500" enterprises in Denmark. Based on the survey, the chapter suggests the following four propositions: (1) ERP has become the pervasive infrastructure; (2) ERP has become a contemporary technology; (3) ERP adoption has matured; and (4) ERP adoption is converging toward a dominant design. Finally, the chapter discusses the general implications of the surveyed state of practice on the SCM research challenges. Consequently, the author argues that research needs to adjust its conceptions of the ERP concept towards ERP II in order to accommodate to the emerging practices.

Chapter IX, "Using Simulation to Evaluate Electronic Data Interchange", by Truong identifies prescriptive and evaluative methodologies for analyzing investment in EDI: non-financial methods, purely financial methods, and financial and strategic consideration methods. The author also shows how computer simulation can be used as a tool for assessing EDI. Evaluating the benefits resulting from EDI implementation was illustrated through the well-known Beer Game. Their analysis and review also identifies difficulties involved in assessing the benefits of EDI in supply chains.

Chapter X, "Vertical Application Service Provision: An SME Perspective", by Lockett and Brown discusses the importance of e-business in SMEs by conducting quantitative surveys of four aggregations of SMEs using these applications (users) and comparing these results with similar enterprises who are not (non-users) the research takes a deliberately SME perspective.

Chapter XI, "Planning and Designing an Enterprise-Wide Database System for E-Business", by Yap presents a case study that involves a multi-national conglomerate that is in the process of integrating and Web-enabling their enterprise database systems. The objective of the system was to help engineers sift through millions of components offered by various suppliers and component manufacturers, where the end result was to improved the integration and efficiency of the product development, engineering design, e-sourcing, and e-procurement processes. This research is a qualitative action research study on how different organizational, social, political, and technical forces influenced the social construction of an enterprise-wide information system. Understanding the dynamics and power of these socio-technical forces in shaping the development environment and change process of enterprise systems is the focal point of this chapter's discussion.

Chapter XII, "Toward Always-On Enterprise Information Systems", by Bajgoric presents a framework for implementation of continuous computing technologies for improving business continuity. The framework is presented within a systemic view of developing an "always-on" enterprise information system.

Chapter XIII, "The Financial Appraisal Profile (FAP) Model for Evaluation of Enterprise-Wide Information Technology: A Case Example", by Lefley and Sarkis argues that one of the important reasons for these failures is inappropriate project evaluation and selection. In order to reduce the level of project failures, they introduce an innovative methodology, the financial appraisal profile (FAP) model, which seeks to address some of the issues and limitations posed by standard appraisal and evaluation approaches for strategic technologies and programs. By making the right decision in the first place and involving senior managers in the appraisal process, the organization will be better placed to achieve project success. The adoption of a management team approach to investment appraisals will not only enhance the information base but will also result in greater managerial commitment to a project. They believe by adopting the FAP model greater awareness to strategic issues and goals will also be achieved, which should lead to a more focused top management team—with all members pulling in the same direction.

Chapter XIV, "An Investigation of the Existence of Levels of Enterprise Integration", by Grant and Tu discusses six levels of enterprise integration and the ability of ERP to satisfy each of them. They analyzed six case studies that included IBM, Cisco, Tecktronic, Vandelay, China Holdings, and APD Manufacturing. They found evidence to support the existence of the six levels of integration. APD and China Holding did not exhibit evidence of global integration while the others did. System-user (level–II) integration was missing from all except APD. Islands-of-technology integration is no longer the dominant integration issue it was in the 80's. The dominant integration issues are functional integration, customer relationship management, and supply chain management.

Chapter XV, "Analyzing Different Strategies to Enterprise System Adoption: Re-Engineering-Led vs. Quick Deployment", by Newell, Cooprider, David, Edelman, and Logan explores how different strategies, such as the re-engineering of business processes up-front, employ a quick deployment on the assumption that organizational change plays out in practice and also consider the factors that influence which approach is taken. They use exploratory data from interviews with consultants from XYZ who have been involved in multiple ES implementations in external companies as well as interviews with project members involved in an internal ES implementation in XYZ. Analysis of the data suggests that some level of re-engineering is an inevitable outcome of ES implementation. However, attempts to re-engineer up-front is difficult and can be problematic. Much of this stems from how the ES is actually used versus its envisioned (or planned) use. The implications for post-implementation exploitation opportunities are explored.

Enterprise information systems have become a key component of 21st century organizations. It is hard to imagine an integrated supply chain without the application of ERP systems. Effective management of ERP will make a great difference in organizational performance and competitiveness. Nevertheless, design, development, and implementation of ERP become a necessary goal for all, and this may be accomplished by learning from the research and advances of others with ERP systems. An outstanding collection of the latest research associated with the effective development and implementation of ERP systems, *Modeling and Analysis of Enterprise Information Systems,* Volume I of the *Advances in Enterprise Information Systems Series*, provides insight and assistance in learning how to successfully implement ERP systems in companies.

My sincere thanks go to all the authors in this edited book whose timely submissions and revisions of chapters have made this book possible. I am thankful to Mehdi Khosrow-Pour, president of IGI Global, and Kristin Roth, development editor, for their constant support throughout editing the book.

I am grateful to my wife, Latha Parameswari and son, Rangarajan Gunasekaran, for their support and understanding during this book project.

Angappa Gunasekaran, PhD
Editor-in-Chief
Modeling and Analysis of Enterprise Information Systems
Volume I, Advances in Enterprise Information Systems Series

Chapter I

Implementation of Enterprise Resource Planning (ERP) Systems:
Issues and Challenges

Girish H. Subramanian, Penn State Harrisburg, USA

Christopher S. Hoffer, Penn State Harrisburg, USA

Abstract

Enterprise resource planning (ERP) systems are a growing area of research in business information systems. The primary purpose of this research is to review the literature on ERP implementation and to present results of a case study on ERP implementation. An exploratory case study was conducted to study these research issues. The case study consisted of a survey and interview of 25 employees at one organization. The results provide data analysis findings from the survey and qualitative findings from the interview. Using this case study, the chapter indicates the presence of four phases in ERP implementation through the support from qualitative interviews. Using t-tests, the results confirm the presence of a positive feeling of users toward the four ERP implementation phases.

Introduction

ERP software essentially organizes, codes, and standardizes an enterprise's business processes and data. The software converts transactional data into useful information and collates the data so that it can be analyzed. In this way, all of the collected transactional data becomes information that companies can use to support business decisions.

The first major step to collect the information flow of the manufacturing process occurred during the 1960s when materials requirement planning (MRP) software was developed. Efforts continued in the 1980s to make MRP applications more useful by being able to generate information based on a more realistic set of assumptions. As a result, manufacturing resource planning (MRP II) software was developed. Finally, in the 1990s, ERP applications evolved into applications capable of linking all internal transactions (Hiquet & Kelly, 1998).

An ERP system is an integrated commercial off-the-shelf (COTS) software package that can perform all the major business functions of an organization. These functions generally include all elements of the value chain from raw material purchases, inventory management, production, goods shipments, invoicing, accounting, and human resource management. ERP systems had their roots in manufacturing, including material resource planning, but quickly grew to include all the other related business functions. They now serve as the basic business systems for most of the large and mid-size organizations in the world today. The key elements of an ERP system according to Miller (2003) are: one large real-time database which reduces data redundancy and improves accuracy; integrated business process that cut across business functions such as supply chain management; and seamless transitions between business transactions.

ERP software is not intrinsically strategic; rather, it is an enabling technology, an application of integrated software modules that coordinates all internal transaction processing. Implementing ERP requires large-scale changes to organizational, cultural, and business processes. Many of the ERP products developed have enabled companies to re-design their business processes and eliminate non-value-adding work. As a result, employees could focus on value-adding activities that have dramatically increased productive capacity. One focus of process re-design is to improve the company's financial performance by improving operational performance. Long-term financial success occurs when a company delivers increasing customer value while simultaneously lowering the cost of delivering that value (Hiquet & Kelly, 1998).

The perspective that ERP software is simply a means of cutting cost is still prevalent. As a result, organizational resistance to ERP implementation has often been high, and not all ERP implementation programs delivered the promised enterprise improvements. The key to change is the willingness of individuals throughout the company to adopt new technology and new ways of working. It is estimated that ERP systems will exceed $11.9 billion in sales in 2007 (ARC Advisory Group, 2003). According to Bingi, Sharma, and Godla (1999), 70% of the Fortune 1000 have or will have ERP systems. There have been many difficult and costly implementations of ERP systems that have adversely impacted many organizations including FoxMeyer Drug, Dell Computer, Applied Materials, and Dow Chemical (Davenport, 1998). Over half of ERP implementations end in failure (Banker, Davis, & Slaughter, 1988). Hong and Kim (2002) suggest even poorer results with 75% of "ERP projects judged to be unsuccessful." Scott and Vessey (2002) believe that 90% of ERP projects are late. As a result, it is extremely important to understand factors that can influence success or failure of an ERP implementation.

A phased implementation approach for ERP implementation is highlighted in Robey, Ross, and Boudreau (2002). It is important to have a structured approach, similar to systems development, for the implementation and maintenance of ERP systems. Parr and Shanks (2000) review different models of ERP implementation and suggest a PPM/CSF hybrid model that incorporates a project phase model (PPM) with critical success factors (CSF). The phases included in their model include planning, project, and enhancement. Peslak, Subramanian, and Clayton (2006) show that preparation and training, transition, performance and usefulness, and maintenance phases exist in ERP implementation and maintenance activity of organizations, and these phases positively influence the preferred use of ERP system.

The purpose of this chapter is to review the literature on ERP implementation and to present results of a case study on ERP implementation. Using this case study, the chapter indicates the presence of four phases in ERP implementation through the support from qualitative interviews. Using t-tests, the results confirm the presence of a positive feeling of users towards the four ERP implementation phases.

Literature Review

ERP Implementation Studies

Hong and Kim (2002) study the "organizational fit of ERP". They define the concept of organizational fit of ERP and examine its impact on ERP implementation. Based on a field survey of 34 organizations, they show that ERP implementation success significantly depends on the organizational fit of ERP and certain implementation contingencies. Rajagopal (2002) also shows that ERP implementation was found to follow the Kwon and Zmud (1987) stage model. In their study, the findings from the process model were used to develop the items for the causal model and in identifying appropriate constructs to group those items. Sarker and Lee (2003) point to three key social enablers—strong and committed leadership, open and honest communication, and a balanced and empowered implementation team as necessary conditions/precursors for successful enterprise resource planning implementation. They also show that strong and committed leadership can only be empirically established as a necessary condition for ERP implementation.

Benders, Batenburg, and van Der Blonk (2006) point to the fact that competitive and institutional pressures play a role in ERP adoption. They point to the role of technical isomorphism in ERP implementation and show how it manifests itself in the enactment of blueprints for centralization and standard working procedures that are embedded in the ERP software. A case study of a Dutch publishing company is used in their study to illustrate how coercive and technical isomorphism jointly lead to adaptation of the organization to the system, although the firm aimed to differentiate itself from its competitors.

Gattiker and Goodhue (2004) study interdependence and differences between divisions of the same organizations in ERP implementation and observe the following. High interdependence among organizational sub-units contributes to the positive ERP-related effects because of ERPs' ability to coordinate activities and facilitate information flows. However, when differentiation among sub-units is high, organizations may incur ERP-related compromise or design costs.

ERP Implementation Models and Phases

Boudreau and Robey (2005), as noted, suggest a vital importance to acceptance of ERP systems. Currently they note that if not successfully implemented, users may work around the system and otherwise doom the project to costly duplication of effort, or worse, system failure. A phased implementation approach is highlighted in Robey et al. (2002). It is important to have a structured approach, similar to systems development, for the implementation and maintenance of ERP systems.

Systems development theory uses the concept of a life cycle and stages in the life cycle to indicate development of information systems. The waterfall model, incremental model, RAD (rapid application development) model, and spiral model are some of the systems development methods prevalent in the literature (Pressman, 2004). Newer approaches to systems development address component-based development using off-the-shelf packages, agile development, and the unified process for object-oriented software development (Pressman, 2004). The newer approaches have fewer stages in the development of systems. For example, the unified process which draws upon the best practices of conventional software process models (Pressman, 2004) has inception, elaboration, construction, and transition phases. A common aspect of all these models is that they focus little attention on implementation and the post-implementation of the system.

Empirical research has addressed issues that organizations face on and after implementation of systems. Specifically, several studies have looked at ERP implementation (Akkermans & van Helden, 2002; Hong & Kim, 2002; Robey et al., 2002). The implementation and performance stage model (Cooper & Zmud, 1990; Kwon & Zmud, 1987) is a useful tool for understanding the implementation of the ERP technology and provides six stages: initiation, adoption, adaptation, acceptance, routinization, and infusion. This six-stage model sets the framework to investigate the implementation and performance issues of utilizing an ERP system within an organization. The initiation stage analyzes the factors that influence the decision to utilize an ERP system such as incompatibility, need for connectivity, top management vision, and need to change. Implementation issues are addressed in the adoption and adaptation stages including: investment decisions, cost/benefit analysis, and choice of appropriate technology. Implementation and performance measures such as system modifications, training, integration of functional units, enhanced performance, user acceptance, flaws corrected, and organizational integration realized, are identified during the acceptance and routinization stages. Finally, the infusion stage addresses future innovations including IT integration at global levels and future opportunities.

Parr and Shanks (2000) review different models of ERP implementation and suggest a PPM/CSF hybrid model that incorporates a project phase model (PPM) with critical success factors (CSF). The phases included in their model include planning, project, and enhancement. Our work is both an extension and a testing of their project phase model for ERP implementation. Parr and Shanks (2000) are the first to suggest that "there is justification for creating a project phase model (PPM) of ERP implementation which is centered on the individual, discrete phases of the implementation project itself rather than one which treats the project as just another phase in the whole implementation enterprise."

What happens after ERP implementation, and the benefits derived from ERP implementation, is specifically addressed by Gattiker and Goodhue (2005). The model by these researchers looks at the sub-unit level of the organization, similar to our study, and looks at determinants of ERP benefits. Task efficiency, coordination improvements, and data quality explain a large amount of the ERP benefits of the sub-unit (Gattiker & Goodhue, 2005).

Literature Support for the Four Phases in ERP Implementation

An organization has to *prepare* itself for ERP implementation much before the actual ERP decision is taken (Bagchi, Kanungo, & Dasgupta, 2003) and these researchers believe that such preparation is key to ERP success. It may take years of build-up and requisite preparation with IT diffusion and infusion to determine, in large part, whether users demonstrate a combination of a positive predisposition to a new system when they view it from the standpoint of their work. Additional support for such requisite build-up comes from Bresnahan and Brynjolfsson (2000), who use the phrase "complementary investment". *User training* that included both technical and business processes, along with a phased implementation approach, helped firms to overcome assimilation knowledge barriers (Robey et al., 2002) noting the importance of training and a phased approach to ERP implementation. Gupta (2000) and Umble and Umble (2002) saw training as one of the most important factors in ERP success. Training is also noted as an important factor by Gallivan, Spitler, and Koufaris (2005) and Barker and Frolick (2003).

Nah, Zuckweiler, and Lau (2003) in their survey of Fortune 1000 CIOs found *performance* as a major factor in ERP success. Siau (2004) sees quality of service as essential in ERP implementations. *Usefulness* is also related to performance. Perceived usefulness looks at productivity, job effectiveness, and ease of doing the job (Segars & Grover, 1993; Subramanian, 1994), which could be argued as performance-related variables. For example, our performance phase also looks at productivity and use of information from the ERP system by the user. Extensive research supports the notion that usefulness and ease of use are primary drivers of user intentions to adopt new technology (Davis, 1989; Davis, Bagozzi, & Warshaw, 1989; Subramanian, 1994; Venkatesh & Davis, 2000).

Al-Mashari, Al-Mudimigh, and Zairi (2003) note the importance of *transition* suggesting that "it is important that an organization approaches the transition of legacy system carefully and with a comprehensive plan." Boudreau and Robey (2005) identified transition as a key factor in ERP implementation. Transition is also an important phase in the unified process model (Pressman, 2004).

"The problem of maintaining integrated applications is no means a simple one and requires an interdisciplinary approach" (Mookerjee, 2005). "Without the understanding of how the system is implemented, and how to maintain the efficiencies and functionality of that [ERP] system, it will be useless to the organization" (Banker et al., 1988). The use of packaged software is shown to result in decreased software complexity and software enhancement effort (Banker et al., 1988) and so it is expected that ERP packages would have reduced maintenance in comparison to traditional development. So, *maintenance* is the final phase in ERP implementation.

Having established the importance of these four phases in ERP implementation, we now present the results of a case study to show initial support to the existence of these four phases and related issues in ERP implementation.

Figure 1 shows the four ERP implementation and maintenance phases of our research model. Our research model explores preference for a new system based on Parr and Shanks (2000) model but the third phase of project is broken into two separate phases—transition and performance to better understand what truly influences project acceptance.

Figure 1. ERP implementation and maintenance phases

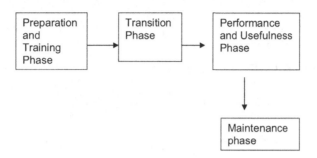

Research Study

Exploratory Case Study at ABC Company

A case study was conducted at ABC Company. ABC is a major manufacturer involved in SAP implementation. The survey population included employees in the areas of management, production, human resources, engineering, administration, quality, and maintenance who were employed at ABC Company during the SAP implementation and who used the SAP system. A cover letter and survey questionnaire were distributed to employees who were employed during the ERP implementation and also used the ERP system in their day-to-day job. Twenty-five surveys were completed. In addition, interviews of the employees were conducted by the investigator. Additional details can be obtained from Subramanian and Hoffer (2004).

Research Propositions Studied

The first proposition looks at the existence of two phases—preparation and training and transition through questions 1 through 5 next from the survey.

Proposition 1: *There is the existence of preparation and training, and transition phases and respondents have a positive feeling about these two phases.*

The survey questions used for testing this proposition are as follows.

1.   I feel that I understand why our company implemented SAP as our information system. (understand)

2.   I was provided with on-the-job training before we went live with SAP. (training)

3.   On the day we went live with SAP, I felt prepared to work on SAP. (prepared to work)

4.   Everyone worked together to help the transition to SAP be successful. (team work)

5.   From my perspective, the transition to SAP went smoothly. (smooth transition)

The second proposition relates to the performance and usefulness phase where questions on the use of information from ERP systems are posed to the users.

The research proposition 2 states:

Proposition 2: *There is the existence of performance and usefulness phase in the implementation of ERP systems and respondents have a positive feeling about this phase.*

The survey questions used for testing this proposition are as follows.

6.   I am able to be more productive with SAP than I was before SAP. (productivity)

7.   I can access information easier with SAP than I could before SAP. (access information)

8.   SAP provides me with information that was previously unavailable to me. (new information)

9.   With SAP, there is less entering of data than before SAP. (data entry)

10.   With SAP, the data I use is more accurate than before SAP. (data accuracy)

The final proposition is related to the maintenance phase. The questions posed all concern the maintenance activity that needs to be done regularly on the ERP systems.

The research proposition states:

Proposition 3: *There is the existence of maintenance phase in the implementation of ERP systems and respondents have a positive feeling about this phase.*

The survey questions used for testing this proposition are as follows.

11. I understand what is expected of me to maintain/update/confirm the information in SAP. (expectations)

12. I understand how the information I input/change/confirm in SAP is relevant to our company. (relevancy)

13. I feel confident that the information I input/change/confirm in SAP is accurate and correct. (accuracy)

14. The information I use from SAP makes sense to me. (understandability)

15. I would rather use SAP than our previous system. (preference)

The survey is shown in the Appendix. In addition to the survey questions, interviews were also conducted. First, we present the interview findings to show the presence of the four phases of Figure 1. Then, we present the results of the t-tests to assess the presence of a positive feeling about the four phases.

Qualitative Analysis of Interview Questions

We had the opportunity to conduct interviews. The interview helps us have a deeper understanding of ERP implementation issues. We prepared an interview script that had four open-ended queries. They are:

1. From your perspective, briefly describe the ERP implementation process.

2. How has SAP improved your job?

3. How has SAP made your job more difficult?

4. Describe your work experience with SAP.

For each of these queries, we provide some of the responses (in quotes) as provided by the respondents. Then, we summarize the responses.

From your perspective, briefly describe the ERP implementation process.

1. "Implementation went pretty smooth."

2. "Received good training."

3. "Was not bad. Still able to ship, just slower. Had some product back-up, but not close to shutting down."

4. "Process of mapping information over to SAP was difficult. First couple of weeks, nothing worked right. We did testing, but when they threw the switch, it didn't work right."

5. "The first implementation of SAP did not go very well. However, with the upgrade from 3.0 to 4.6, the SAP transition went very well."

6. "Shipping was not a problem from the plant but from the DC's. The DC's were backed up and this resulted in the whole pipeline backing up."

7. "System was so different from what we had previously been on."

8. "Not totally prepared. Training was too far ahead of implementation. Delayed actual start so by the time we went live, it was hard to recall what you learned in training".

This question seeks to provide qualitative information for Proposition 1. As in the earlier-noted responses, it is clear that ERP implementation (especially SAP) is very difficult. Problems will be present during implementation and appropriate planning for dealing with implementation problems should be done as part of implementation pre-planning. As ERP implementation often involves a new paradigm for integrating and using information across the organization seamlessly, there is a considerable adjustment, learning, and training needed for the users. Similarly, ERP developers and installers need to understand that real-life systems would behave quite differently from the planned way in which the computerized ERP systems expect them to behave. Hence, preparation and training and planning for a smooth transition are key phases in ERP implementation.

How has SAP™ improved your job?

1. "Easier to track inventory. Inventory confirmation is easier. The process of loading trucks is easier. Can track information that could not be accessed before."

2. "SAP makes ordering parts easier and reduces inventory. SAP is light years ahead of our old system."

3. "Upgrade to 4.6 provided a lot better front end, more user friendly. Can make shortcuts to reports you use most."

4. "Process is easier, can see more information. Can find more information by using links. Easier to search the system. Do not need to go through lots of papers as we previously did. Everything is in the system and can see the changes made and who made the changes. Easier to search history. Ex. can see how much we used of a certain product last year very easily."

5.   "SAP is better at recording and tracking purchases. Better documentation to see what was purchased. I can see different locations within the company. SAP saves time gathering information."

6.   "SAP has improved my job because now I can go in and see the schedule and plan testing accordingly around the production schedule. Visibility of the production schedule was a big help. Also, visibility of Bill of Materials was very helpful. I don't have to always contact someone else to obtain schedule information or BOM information; I can see it myself. These features make my job easier to do."

This question provides qualitative information for Proposition 2 and addresses the performance and usefulness phase of the ERP implementation model. It is clear that SAP has indeed contributed positively in improving the job of the respondents. All the responses to this question were positive. Even though the implementation and adjustment to the new SAP system was difficult, the respondents were unanimous in their approval of the contribution of SAP in improving the way they performed their job.

How has SAP™ made your job more difficult?

1.   "I'm on the computer more with SAP and less visible on the plant floor.

2.   "Can track information better with SAP, however, I'm not on plant floor while I'm looking up information."

3.   "More time-consuming to maintain information in system. Some processes require you to wait until certain other things are in the system due to all the checks and balances in SAP."

4.   "More inventory counts are required due to SAP being so dependent on real-time data and making adjustments right away instead of doing inventory counts twice a year."

5.   "Big learning curve."

6.   "Some training classes that should be a couple days were shortened to 1 day. Lots of people struggled with SAP because it was unfamiliar to them. Had to do things in SAP that you were never trained to do."

7.   "Has not made my job more difficult at all."

8.   "Originally SAP made job more difficult."

This question provides qualitative information for Proposition 2. Job and organization re-design through SAP (and other ERP systems) is a key factor in influencing user attitudes towards the new system. Users who do not like the job re-design (as in the inventory example responses earlier) do find that the system gets in their way. The learning curve and training effort involved seem to be underestimated as seen in these responses. So, it is important to provide sufficient training and learning to effectively use the new system. So, to an extent preparation and training phase is linked to the performance and usefulness phase of ERP implementation.

Describe your work experience with SAP.

1. "More precision with SAP. Less hand written issues (legibility). Now everything is confirmed electronically. Bill of ladings are more accurate, they are all stored in system: weight, count, product."

2. "The warehouse management system was changed. Different actions had to be completed than before. Ex. workflow was not in previous system. SAP is so exact with inventory that you get errors if you don't return the exact amount of material from the floor. If material is moved, it has to match the quantity that SAP has in the system for it or else you get a work flow error."

3. "Processes are better, you can see the future requirements for future production. Everything is in the MRP system, not looking through paperwork."

4. "Links are new. In a purchase order you can drill down to the material master, instead of going through menus to get there."

5. "SAP has a document overview. Before you only had a printed list of requisitions that were requested. Now you are able to bring up the list of requisitions in the system and select and transfer information over automatically."

6. "SAP's purchasing system has a screen with tabs and you can find all the information you need. Previously you had to go to different screens to find information."

7. "Part of implementation was because legacy system was not Y2K compatible. As a result, the SAP implementation project was pushed through faster than the company was ready."

8. "SAP has a very good ability to market itself to upper management. Ask anyone at the plants or in corporate middle management if they have ever been contacted by SAP. The answer will be no. If you ask the same question to corporate upper management. The answer will be yes. CFO's and CEO's have to look far ahead in the business world and are not concerned with micro-management. SAP know this and is very good at marketing and selling CEO's on the concept of SAP. It sounds very good and the potential is great. Once upper management is sold on SAP, then the rest of the company will follow. At that point, it's the plants and distribution centers that have to worry about integrating the operations of the company with SAP and all the difficulties that entails. As a result, you are going to run into issues during the implementation

process. Issues that were not addressed at the time the decision was made to implement SAP."

9. "User interface is not that user friendly. The Germans do not see any drawbacks with setting up their system in 3 letter abbreviations."

This question addresses the maintenance phase and provides qualitative flavor to Proposition 3. When the system becomes routine and incorporated as part of the user's job, the users are in a position to see the benefits of an ERP system. Users are also able to reflect on some of the shortcomings of implementation more objectively.

The interview responses clearly show that the users do consider the four phases (Figure 1) and issues associated with these phases in answering the questions. This qualitative analysis provides initial support to the existence of preparation and training, transition, performance and usefulness, and maintenance phases in ERP implementation.

Hypotheses Testing and Data Analysis

Now, each of the survey questions for each proposition was tested using one sample t-test with the null hypothesis being the sample mean is less than or equal to three (neutral, midpoint of the Likert scale in the Appendix). The alternate hypothesis (at a significance level of 0.025 for one-tail t-test) states that the sample mean is greater than three and the respondents agree with the survey questions. Please refer to Levine, Berenson, and Stephan (1999) for t-tests. The results for Proposition 1 questions are shown in Table 1.

Table 1. Proposition 1 results

Survey Questions	Mean	Standard Deviation	t-value	P(t-value) for One-tail test	Result
Understand	4.08	0.862	6.263	8.9E-07	Reject null hyp. Support proposition
Training	4.04	0.735	6.945	2.2E-07	Reject null hyp. Support proposition
Prepared	3.5	0.957	2.558	0.008	Reject null hyp. Support proposition
Team Work	4.12	0.881	6.354	7.1E-07	Reject null hyp. Support proposition
Smooth Transition	3.67	0.986	3.312	0.0015	Reject null hyp. Support proposition

As the results in Table 1 indicate, respondents agreed with the survey questions and a positive climate was fostered during the preparation and training, and transition phases. Tables 2 and 3 provide the results for Propositions 2 and 3, respectively. Proposition 2 is supported except for the data entry question as shown in Table 2. The amount of data to be entered is not impacted by the conversion to SAP. Hence, there is improved performance and usefulness through the use of ERP system. Proposition 3 is also supported as evidenced in Table 3.

Table 2. Proposition 2 results

Survey Questions	Mean	Standard Deviation	t-value	P(t-value) for One-tail test	Result
Productivity	3.6	0.764	3.928	0.0003	Reject null hyp. Support proposition
Access Information	3.68	1.069	3.179	0.002	Reject null hyp. Support proposition
New Information	3.72	0.89	4.04	0.0002	Reject null hyp. Support proposition
Data Entry	3.24	1.011	1.186	0.124	Do not Reject null hyp. No Support for proposition
Data Accuracy	3.68	0.748	4.543	6.63E-05	Reject null hyp. Support proposition

Table 3. Proposition 3 results

Survey Questions	Mean	Standard Deviation	t-value	P(t-value) for One-tail test	Result
Expectations	4.2	0.588	10.063	3.3E-10	Reject null hyp. Support proposition
Data Relevancy	4.16	0.565	10.122	3.03E-10	Reject null hyp. Support proposition
Accuracy	4.25	0.608	10.073	3.3E-10	Reject null hyp. Support proposition
Understandability	4.04	0.539	9.656	7.3E-10	Reject null hyp. Support proposition
SAP Preference	3.96	0.678	6.948	2.2E-07	Reject null hyp. Support proposition

Conclusion

The installation of an ERP system can be one of the most costly and critical projects that an organization undertakes. Generally, all other information technology projects pale in comparison to ERP systems. ERP systems are used to run all standard business processes in an organization. The success or failure of the implementation can be vitally important to both current profits and the future viability of a business. As a result, understanding the processes and phases involved in the implementation of this endeavor can pay major dividends. In this research, an exploratory case study was conducted. The case study consisted of a survey and interview of 25 employees at one organization.

This exploratory case study shows initial evidence from the interviews for the existence of four phases—preparation and training, transition, performance and usefulness, and maintenance in ERP implementation. Using t-tests, the presence of a positive feeling towards the four phases is confirmed. A limitation of the study is the small sample size. Though the results are based on a small sample size of a real-world implementation of SAP software, results may not be applicable to all SAP R/3 implementations. This study is just the beginning. A more detailed study involving more participants in more industries is a fruitful avenue for further research.

Specifically, future research needs to empirically confirm the existence of the four phases of ERP implementation as alluded to in Figure 1. By collecting more data, future studies need to use structural equation modeling to test the reliability and validity of the survey in the Appendix and confirm the presence of these four phases. In addition, data from multiple sites needs to be used for this purpose. Further, detailed qualitative analysis using interviews from a larger multi-site sample is needed. Moreover, differences in ERP implementation between sites using ERP software needs to be studied. Employee acceptance of ERP systems, return on investment, and future technology integration are other areas for future research in ERP implementation.

References

Akkermans, H., & van Helden, K. (2002). Vicious and virtuous cycles in ERP implementation: A case study of interrelations between critical success factors. *European Journal of Information Systems, 11*, 35-46.

Al-Mashari, M., Al-Mudimigh, A., & Zairi, M. (2003). ERP: A taxonomy of critical factors. *European Journal of Operational Research, 146*, 352-364.

ARC Advisory Group. (2003). *ERP market opportunities change while remaining strong overall at $8.9 billion.* Retrieved March 12, 2006, from http://www. arcweb.com/Community/arcnews/arcnews.as p?ID=328

Bagchi, S., Kanungo, S., & Dasgupta, S. (2003). Modeling use of enterprise resource planning systems: A path analytic study. *European Journal of Information Systems, 12*(2), 142.

Banker, R., Davis, G. B., & Slaughter, S. A. (1988). Software development practices, software complexity, and software maintenance performance: A field study. *Management Science, 44*(4), 433-451.

Barker, T., & Frolick, M. (2003). ERP implementation failure: A case study. *Information Systems Management, 20*(4), 43-49.

Benders, J., Batenburg, R., & van Der Blonk, H. (2006, March). Sticking to standards: Technical and other isomorphic pressures in deploying ERP-systems. *Information & Management, 43*(2), 194-203.

Bingi, P., Sharma, M., & Godla, J. (1999). Critical issues affecting an ERP implementation. *Information Systems Management, 16*(3), 7-14.

Boudreau, M., & Robey, D. (2005). Enacting integrated information technology: A human agency perspective. *Organization Science, 16*(1), 3-18.

Bresnahan, T. F., & Brynjolfsson, E. (2000). Information technology, workplace organization, and the demand for skilled labor: Firm-level evidence. *Quarterly Journal of Economics, 117*(1), 339-376.

Cooper, R., & Zmud, R. (1990). Information technology implementation research: A technological diffusion approach. *Management Science, 36*(2), 123.

Davenport, T. (1998). Putting the enterprise into the enterprise system. *Harvard Business Review, 76*(4), 121-131.

Davis, F. D. (1989). Perceived usefulness, perceived ease of use, and user acceptance of information technology. *MIS Quarterly, 13*(3), 319-340.

Davis, F. D., Bagozzi, R. P., & Warshaw, P. R. (1989). User acceptance of computer technology: A comparison of two theoretical models. *Management Science, 35*, 982-1003.

Gallivan, M. J. , Spitler, V. K., & Koufaris, M. (2005, Summer). Does information technology training really matter? A social information processing analysis of coworkers' influence on IT usage in the workplace. *Journal of Management Information Systems, 22*(1), 153-192.

Gattiker, T. F., & Goodhue, D. L. (2004, March). Understanding the local-level costs and benefits of ERP through organizational information processing theory, *Information & Management, 41*(4), 431-443.

Gattiker, T., & Goodhue, D. (2005). What happens after ERP implementation: Understanding the impact of inter-dependence and differentiation on plant-level outcomes. *MIS Quarterly, 29*(3), 559-584.

Gupta, A. (2000). Enterprise resource planning: The emerging organizational value systems. *Industrial Management + Data Systems, 100*(3), 114+.

Hiquet, B., & Kelly, A. F. (1998). *SAP R/3 implementation guide: A manager's guide to understanding SAP*. Indiana: Macmillan Technical.

Hong, K. K., & Kim, Y. G. (2002). The critical success factors for ERP implementation: An organizational fit perspective. *Information and Management, 40*(1), 25-40.

Kwon, T., & Zmud, R. (1987). Unifying the fragmented models of information systems implementation. In R. J. Boland, Jr., & R. A. Hirschheim (Eds.), *Critical issues in information systems research*. New York: John Wiley.

Levine, D. M., Berenson, M., & Stephan, D. (1999). *Statistics for managers* (2nd ed.). NJ: Prentice Hall.

Miller, B. (2003). What is ERP? *CIO*. Retrieved January 3, 2005, from http://www2.cio.com/analyst/report2003.html

Mookerjee, R. (2005, November). Maintaining enterprise software applications. *Communications of the ACM, 48*(11), 75-79.

Nah, F., Zuckweiler, K., & Lau, J. (2003). ERP implementation: Chief information officers' perceptions of critical success factors. *International Journal of Human-Computer Interaction, 16*(1), 5-22.

Parr, A., & Shanks, G. (2000). A model of ERP project implementation. *Journal of Information Technology, 15*, 289-303.

Peslak, A., Subramanian, G. H., & Clayton, G. (2006). *The phases of ERP software implementation and maintenance: A model for predicting preferred ERP use*. Working Paper, Penn State Harrisburg.

Pressman, R. S. (2004). *Software engineering: A practitioner's approach* (6th ed.). McGraw-Hill.

Rajagopal, P. (2002, December). An innovation—diffusion view of implementation of enterprise resource planning (ERP) systems and development of a research model. *Information & Management, 40*(2), 87-114.

Robey, D., Ross, J. W., & Boudreau, M. C. (2002, Summer). Learning to implement enterprise systems: An exploratory study of the dialectics of change. *Journal of Management Information Systems, 19*(1), 17-46.

Sarker, S., & Lee, A. S. (2003, September). Using a case study to test the role of three key social enablers in ERP implementation. *Information & Management, 40*(8), 813-829.

Scott, J., & Vessey, I. (2002). Managing risks in enterprise implementations. *Communications of the ACM, 45*(4), 74-81.

Segars, A. H., & Grover, V. (1993). Re-examining perceived ease of use and usefulness: A confirmatory factor analysis. *MIS Quarterly*, 17, 517-525.

Siau, K. (2004). Enterprise resource planning (ERP) implementation methodologies. *Journal of Database Management, 15*(1), 1-6.

Subramanian, G. H. (1994). A replication of perceived usefulness and perceived ease of use measurement. *Decision Sciences, 25*(5/6), 863-873.

Subramanian, G. H., & Hoffer, C. S. (2005, January-March). An exploratory case study of enterprise resource planning implementation. *The International Journal of Enterprise Information Systems, 1*(1), 23-38.

Umble, E., & Umble, M. (2002). Avoiding ERP implementation failure. *Industrial Management, 44*(1), 25-34.

Venkatesh, V., & Davis, F. D. (2000). A theoretical extension of the technology acceptance model: Four longitudinal field studies. *Management Science, 46*(2), 186-204.

Appendix:
Survey Questions

1	2	3	4	5
Strongly Disagree	Disagree	Neutral	Agree	Strongly Agree

1. I feel that I understand why our company implemented SAP as our information system. (understand)

2. I was provided with on-the-job training before we went live with SAP. (training)

3. On the day we went live with SAP, I felt prepared to work on SAP. (prepared to work)

4. Everyone worked together to help the transition to SAP be successful. (team work)

5. From my perspective, the transition to SAP went smoothly. (smooth transition)

6. I am able to be more productive with SAP than I was before SAP. (productivity)

7. I can access information easier with SAP than I could before SAP. (access information)

8. SAP provides me with information that was previously unavailable to me. (new information)

9. With SAP, there is less entering of data than before SAP. (data entry)

10. With SAP, the data I use is more accurate than before SAP. (data accuracy)

11. I understand what is expected of me to maintain/update/confirm the information in SAP. (expectations)

12. I understand how the information I input/change/confirm in SAP is relevant to our company. (relevancy)

13. I feel confident that the information I input/change/confirm in SAP is accurate and correct. (accuracy)

14. The information I use from SAP makes sense to me. (understandability)

15. I would rather use SAP than our previous system. (preference)

Chapter II

Research Issues of the IT Productivity Paradox:
Approaches, Limitations, and a Proposed Conceptual Framework

Chuck C. H. Law, Chaoyang University of Technology, Taiwan

Eric W. T. Ngai, The Hong Kong Polytechnic University, PR China

Abstract

Although corporations in the western world, especially those in the United States, have spent generously on information technology (IT) and information systems (IS) in recent decades, many empirical studies have found limited evidence for the payoffs of surging IT expenditures. In some cases, measures of IT spending were found to be either uncorrelated, or negatively associated, with the productivity or financial performance of the sample firms. To the dismay of the researchers and business executives, the phenomenon of the IT productivity paradox lingers on to this day. A review of the literature on this subject has pointed out several possible reasons underlying such inconsistencies, which include data and methodological problems and limitations of research models. Moreover, many of these studies have been criticized as weak in theoretical underpinning when they simply fed data into statistical models for the independent (IT spending), and dependent (productivity or financial performance) measures in order to empirically ascertain the relationships that might exist. In this chapter, a research model is proposed. With expectation to mitigate the shortcomings of some of the prior studies, this model incorporates improvements in business process as an independent construct in parallel to the capabilities of IT and enterprise systems. Competitive capabilities are included as an intermediate construct to help conceptualize the linkage between the independent constructs and the dependent construct of organizational performance. Theories and empirical evidence are drawn from associated management disciplines such as operations management and from a resources-based view of the firm to illustrate and explain that investment in IT and business processes will eventually contribute to organizational performance through the creation and enhancement of competitive capabilities. Finally, the theoretical and managerial implications of this research model are highlighted.

Introduction

Business enterprises in the western world have invested generously in information technology (IT) since the 1970s. Among them, corporations in the United States are the leading spenders, whose total expenditure in IT within the 10-year period between the late 1980s and 1990s was estimated to be around U.S. $500 billion (Strassmann, 1997). Paradoxically, such a surge in IT spending has not been accompanied by a consistently measurable increase in productivity, especially in the service sectors (Brynjolfsson, 1993). Many micro-level studies conducted in the last decades showed that the IT spending of business firms seemed to be uncorrelated with productivity and profitability, and the term of IT productivity paradox was, therefore, coined to describe such a phenomenon (Strassmann, 2002). A review of the extant literature in this subject reveals several possible reasons for the contradictory findings, including data and methodological problems (Brynjolfsson, 1993; Hu & Plant, 2001; Strassmann, 1990). Some researchers criticized the theoretical weakness of the extant studies (Shin, 1999), and pointed out the incompleteness of research models that have neglected relevant contextual constructs (Grover, Teng, Segars, & Fiedler, 1998).

In view of the contradictory findings, two interesting research questions arise. Does IT genuinely contribute to performance at the firm level? Can the extant research models be remedied or enhanced to overcome the limitations just alluded to? Specifically, the objectives of this chapter are three-fold. First, a literature review is conducted to pinpoint possible shortcomings in the existing studies, with results presented in the next section. Second, a research model, to address the issues and problems identified, is proposed and illustrated in the third section. Third, the theories and empirical findings of other management disciplines are presented to support the conceptualization of the linkage between IT and systems capabilities, business processes, competitive capabilities, and organizational performance. The academic contribution and managerial implications of the proposed research model will be discussed in the fourth section.

A Review of IT Business Value Studies

Inconsistent Findings, Weaknesses, and Evolving Approaches

The literature of IT business value research is filled with inconsistent results. Among the early studies with positive findings are Cron and Sobol (1983), Bender (1986), and Harris and Katz (1991), which confirmed the association between IT and firm performance.

On the other hand, many such studies have yielded no evidence for the contribution of IT to productivity (Hu et al., 2001; Loveman, 1994) or negative findings for the relationship between IT and performance (Morrison & Berndt, 1990; Dasgupta, Sarkis, & Talluri, 1999; Roach, 1991). Roach (1991) pointed out that while services companies in the United States had invested heavily in IT, accounting for approximately 85% of the nation-wide installations of IT, it did not yield the expected productivity growth. Hu et al. (2001) found no evidence to support the contribution of IT investment in a prior year to reduction in operating costs, increase in productivity, and growth in sales and profitability in the following year. Instead, their findings showed reverse causality—that a year of robust sales would lead to growth in IT spending in the subsequent year. Similarly, Tam (1998) presented mixed findings for the relationship between IT hardware capital and firm-level financial performance, and no evidence for the effect of the former on total shareholder returns across four Asian countries. Thus, the phenomenon of the IT productivity paradox, a term coined in the previous decade (Brynjolfsson, 1993; Thatcher & Oliver, 2001) lingers on to this day (Dasgupta et al., 1999; Hu et al., 2001; Strassmann, 2002; Tam, 1998). To illustrate the discrepancies that exist across the extant studies, a summary of selected studies is provided in the Appendix.

Generally speaking, the inconsistency in the research findings has led to criticisms that the traditional evaluation approaches are inappropriate for the study of IT benefits. A review of the literature has pointed to several weaknesses in IT productivity paradox research, which are summarized in Table 1.

Table 1. The limitations identified in prior studies of IT business value studies

Category	Research Issues and Limitations	References
Data	Unavailability and inaccuracy	Mahmood & Mann (1993)
	Arbitrary classification of IT spending	Brynjolfsson (1993)
	Failure of central MIS budgets to include IT spending of end-user departments	Strassmann (1990)
	Failure to account for the time-lagged effects of IT investment	Shafer & Byrd (2000); Hu et al. (2001)
Methods and Measures	Failure of financial-based measures to capture intangible impacts of IT	Patel & Irani (1999); Serafeimidis & Smithson (1999)
	Lack of adequate measurement models	Brynjolfsson (1993); Hitt & Brynjolfsson (1996)
Generalizability	Studies focused on single business sector	Brynjolfsson (1993)
	Studies based on small sample	Brynjolfsson (1993)
Assumption and Model	Oversimplified assumption ignoring the risks of mismanagement of IT projects	Grover et al. (1998)
	Exclusion of other contextual variables from research model	Grover et al. (1998)
Theoretical Foundation	Lack of theoretical underpinning to support research model and to explain findings	Shin (1999)
	"Black box" approach	Chan (2000b)

The flaws in such studies, according to critics, possibly include data and measurement problems (Brynjolfsson, 1993), the inconsistent classification of IT expenditures (Strassmann, 1990, p. 25), the exclusion of intangible benefits that are difficult to capture using the traditional accounting-based methods (Counihan, Finnegan, & Sammon, 2002; Murphy & Simon, 2002; Patel & Irani, 1999; Serafeimidis & Smithson, 1999; Shang & Seddon, 2002; Suwardy, Ratnatunga, & Sohal, 2003), unclear causal relationships between dependent and independent constructs (Hu et al., 2001), and the fact that some research models, being oversimplified, have failed to take other organizational and contextual variables into account (Brynjolfsson, 1993; Byrd & Marshall, 1997; Grover et al., 1998; Patel et al., 1999; Serafeimidis et al., 1999). Many of these studies, attempting to uncover empirical evidence on the contribution of IT to performance by applying analysis techniques on IT spending and financial data, are weak in theoretical underpinning, and often fail to provide explanations for their research models and findings (Shin, 1999). In fact, the use of IT spending as a predictor construct may be questionable. The assumption that higher levels of IT spending, measured in monetary terms, will naturally result in improved individual and organizational performance is an over-simplification of the issue as it ignores the complexity and risks associated with the deployment of IT, from the point of planning the project and receiving approval for funding to implementation. Simply stated, what matters most is not how much funding is available, but whether the investment is successfully utilized to raise the capabilities of the individuals and organizations concerned (Grover et al., 1998). On the other hand, Strassmann (2000) pointed out that there might be no direct relationship between firm-level performance measures such as return on investment (ROI) and sales turnover, and IT spending figures. This is because the former are influenced largely by external cost elements, which are beyond the control of the firm, for instance, by costs incurred by suppliers.

In view of such criticisms, alternative approaches of evaluation have emerged in the arena of academic research, as shown in Table 2.

Studies have been operationalized with different research methods or analysis techniques (Chatterjee, Pacini, & Sambamurthy, 2002; Mahmood & Mann, 1993; Shafer & Byrd, 2000), different or additional organizational constructs (Gelderman, 1998; Li & Ye, 1999; Shin, 1999), or data collected to take into account the lagged effects of IT investment on organizational performance (Shafer & Byrd, 2000). Surrogates such as system usage and user satisfaction (Gelderman, 1998) are used in some studies, while others include contextual constructs such as the reporting relationship of the chief IS executives, "environmental dynamism", and "munificence" (Li & Ye, 1999). Grover et al. (1998) pointed out that Cron and Sobol's (1983) findings showing a bi-modal distribution of performance may be an indication of the existence of other relevant constructs that have often been ignored in the studies of IT investments. Researchers in the disciplines of IT and business process re-design have been keen to point out the intervening relationships between business process re-design and IT deployment (Grover et al., 1998; Wu, 2002). The effective utilization of IT requires that changes be made to business processes, while IT is an enabler of the latter (Brynjolfsson, 1993; Chan, 2000a; Chan & Land, 1999; Davenport, 1993; Hammer & Champy, 1993; Stoddard & Jarvenpaa, 1995). However, while many authors and researchers have discussed the intervening relationships between

Table 2. The approaches and methods for evaluating IT business value of selected prior studies

Approaches / Methods	Prior Studies
• Cost function approach	Alpar & Kim (1990); Morrison et al. (1990)
• Event-study methodology	Ng & Yiu (1995); Chatterjee et al. (2002)
• Data envelopment analysis (DEA)	Shafer et al. (2000); Ross (2002)
• Models with intermediate variables (2-stage approach)	Mahmood et al. (1993); Barua, Kriebel, & Mukhopadhyay (1995)
• Process-oriented approach and process-level measures	Mooney, Gurbaxani, & Kraemer (1995); Tallon, Kraemer, & Gurbaxani (1999, 2000)
• Impact of IT capability on financial performance from a resource-based perspective; Integrative model based on resourced-based view of the firm.	Bharadwaj (2000); Santhanam & Hartono (2003); Melville, Kraemer, & Gurbaxani (2004)
• IT impact on co-ordination costs	Shin (1999)
• Effects of organizational variables on IT business value	Li et al. (1999)
• Exploratory study using discriminant analysis	Pratipati & Mensah (1997)
• Quantitative study of ERP impact on firm performance	Hitt, Wu, & Zhou (2002)
• Qualitative study of tangible and intangible ERP benefits	Shang et al. (2002); Murphy et al. (2002)
• Intensity of global IT usage	Sakaguchi & Dibrell (1998)
• IT impacts at 4 levels of organizational objectives	Cline & Guynes (2001)
• Study of causal relationship using data with time-lag	Hu et al. (2001)
• IT value from 3 different perspectives (3 research questions)	Hitt et al. (1996)
• Qualitative studies and discussion of intangible IT benefits	Patel et al. (1999); Serafeimidis et al. (1999)
• Use of perceptual measures of user satisfaction and usage as surrogates	Gelderman (1988)

business process re-design and IT, there seems to be insufficient empirical evidence to support theoretical principles (Grover et al., 1998).

The Recent Trends in IT Business Value Research

A review of the more recent studies reflects that the approaches, methods, and constructs in IT business value research are still evolving. Barua et al. (1995) espoused an approach that measured the contribution of IT at the intermediate level, while others began to examine the benefits of IT in terms of improvement in coordination (Shin, 1999). Similarly, the so-called "process-oriented models" proposed by Kraemer and colleagues (Mooney et al., 1995; Tallon, et al., 1999, 2000) attempted to understand the value of IT by measuring its effects on the business processes of the value chain. This school of researchers believed that it is more appropriate to put the focus on business processes as they are the objects for which IT is being applied, and at which the impacts of IT occur. These studies seem to indicate a trend of IT business value studies that researchers are getting more aware of the limitations associated with the traditional firm-level (financial) measures, which are susceptible to the confounding effects of a plethora of external factors, and with the accounting-based evaluation approaches, which are not adequate in capturing intangible aspects of IT impacts. It is also reasonable to conclude that researchers are becoming more supportive of the view that IT impacts are multi-dimensional and should include both tangible and intangible aspects. Therefore, a comprehensive measurement scale should attempt to capture both tangible and intangible benefits of IT.

As traditional IT business value research was criticized as weak in theoretical underpinning, researchers have begun to augment the "black box" approach by sharing theories and experience of other management disciplines (Bharadwaj, 2000; Melville et al., 2004; Rivard, Raymond, & Verreault, 2006; Santhanam et al., 2003). Bharadwaj (2000), and Santhanam and Hartono (2003) used resource-based theories to explain their conceptual models. Melville et al. (2004) have also developed an "integrative model", and a set of propositions, based on resource-based theories to guide researchers in conceptualizing IT and its impacts. That Tallon et al. (2000) made use of Porter's (1985b) value chain concepts and model also demonstrates that theories and concepts developed in other management disciplines are applicable to MIS studies in many circumstances.

Porter discussed the competitive advantages for firms to survive the forces of the market place (Porter, 1985b), and the impacts of IT adoption on the business strategies of firms (Porter, 1985a; Porter & Millar, 1985). There is also an abundance of discussion of IT as a source of competitive advantages in the literature of MIS (Clemons & Row, 1991). In the literature of operations management, the concepts and empirical evidence regarding competitive capabilities of manufacturing firms have been extensively described. These are the capabilities possessed by firms to carry out vital business activities, for instance, innovation in products, delivery capability, and material handling, among others. Some of these studies have explored the impact of advance manufacturing technologies (AMT) on the competitive capabilities and performance of manufacturing firms (Chen, 1999; Tracey, Vonderembse, & Lim, 1999). On the other hand, resource-based theory espouses that firms have in their possession many types of resources, for instance, fixed assets, processes, organizational routines and culture, firm specific knowledge, and human resources, whose interaction would enhance or engender new capabilities (Amit & Schoemaker, 1993; Barney, 1986; Grant, 1991; Wernerfelt, 1984). The theory also emphasizes that sustainable competitive capabilities will be generated only if the resources possessed and used by the firms are valuable, rare, imperfectly imitable, and non-substitutable. These are the four critical characteristics of resources from the resource-based view of the firm. Resources that fall short of any of these characteristics would lead to no more than competitive parity, or temporary competitive capabilities (Barney, 1991; Mata, Fuerst, & Barney, 1995).

The preceding paragraphs have highlighted the changing approaches that are emerging in the IT business value research arena. That is, many studies are operationalized to capture intangible aspects of IT impacts, include intermediate variables, and measure IT impacts at the process level as opposed to at the firm level alone. Theories developed in other management disciplines are also utilized to help explain IT phenomena. In recognition of the relevance of these theories to MIS research, they are discussed briefly in this sub-section to highlight their potential contribution to IT business value studies. Researchers in the subject of IT productivity paradox should expand their perspectives and be prepared to share the theories and experience of other well established management disciplines (Chan, 2000b). The potential opportunities resulting from an extended perspective for addressing the limitations of traditional IT business value studies should not be ignored.

Consequently, the objectives of this chapter are to review the extant literature on this subject, and propose a research model for studying the contribution of IT to performance. This chapter attempts to contribute to research by strengthening the conceptualization and theoretical basis for the relationship between IT and other constructs, drawing upon theories and empirical evidence developed in other management disciplines such as operations management.

The Research Model

The proposed model, depicted in Figure 1, is comprised of five constructs: namely, the success of enterprise resource planning (ERP) systems, IT infrastructure capa-

Figure 1. The conceptual model

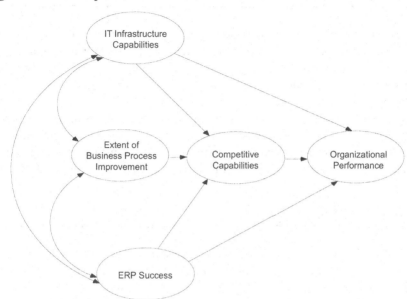

bilities, the extent of improvement in business processes, competitive capabilities, and organizational performance, all of which are to be measured using self-reported perceptual ratings.

Surrogates based on perceptual data are used for the constructs of IT infrastructure and ERP systems because of the absence of objective quantitative measures (McHaney, Hightower, & Pearson, 2002; Saarinen, 1996) and the lack of accurate data for investments and benefits in IT and IS (Brynjolfsson, 1993; Counihan et al., 2002; Murphy et al., 2002; Patel et al., 1999; Serafeimidis et al., 1999; Shang et al., 2002). This is consistent with the approach recommended by Dess and Robinson (1984). Although objective data on organizational performance is preferred, self-reported subjective data would be considered acceptable when the former is unavailable or unreliable (Dess et al., 1984).

Also noteworthy is the perspective underlying the formulation of this model, which takes into consideration the direct and indirect effects of the business processes, and those of the intermediate construct of competitive capabilities on organizational performance. With this perspective, we attempted to develop a model that measures IT impacts at a level closer to the business activities as opposed to measuring the benefits of IT only at the highest level of firm performance as many of the traditional IT business value studies did.

Information Technology Constructs

The IT constructs in this model include two aspects: namely, the success of ERP systems, and the capabilities of IT infrastructure. Both IS and IT infrastructure are important to an organization, as they are essential components of its information architecture (Allen & Boynton, 1991; Mudie & Schafer, 1985; Richardson, Jackson, & Dickson, 1990). In this context, the focus is placed on ERP systems instead of on a broad range of application software, as the strategic and operational contributions of ERP systems to organizations have been widely recognized, such as in the cross-boundary integration of organizational units, sharing of information, and automation of value chain workflows (Botta-Genoulaz & Millet, 2006; Shang et al., 2002).

The Success of ERP Systems

IS user satisfaction is to be used in this model as a surrogate measure of the success of ERP systems. In spite of the criticisms on its weak theoretical basis and lack of standardization in conceptual definitions (Melone, 1990; Sanders & Garrity, 1995), user satisfaction is often accepted in information systems (IS) research due to the lack of objective quantitative measures for the success of IS (Gelderman, 1998; Saarinen, 1996). In this proposed model, user satisfaction is to be measured by the Doll and Torkzadeh (1988) instrument, which includes multiple dimensions: namely the content, accuracy, format, and timeliness of information, and the ease of use of systems. This instrument was initially developed for the end-user computing environment and was subsequently adopted for, and validated in other systems settings such as data warehousing systems (Chen, Soliman, Mao, & Frolick, 2000), decision support systems (McHaney & Cronan, 1998) and ERP systems (Somers & Nelson, 2003; Zviran, Pliskin, & Levin, 2005). It was re-validated by Somers and Nelson (2003) using a sample of ERP system users. Using this instrument, Zviran et al. (2005) tested the relationships between user satisfaction and perceived usefulness in an ERP setting involving system users of different seniority levels. This instrument has also been validated in different cultural contexts (McHaney et al., 2002; Gelderman, 1998). For these reasons, we recommended its use as a surrogate measure for ERP success in this proposed research model.

IT Infrastructure Capabilities

Many authors take a broader view of IT infrastructure that includes multiple aspects beyond networking facilities (Broadbent, Weill, & St. Clair, 1999; Mitchell & Zmud, 1999; Weill & Broadbent, 1999). Mitchell et al. (1999) defined IT infrastructure capabilities to include information technologies, sourcing arrangements, and policies that form an overall system supporting information-related activities. Broadbent et al. (1999) and Weill et al. (1999) described the IT infrastructure capabilities of an organization as a portfolio of technologies and services that consists of network infrastructure and the supporting technical and management expertise required to provide connectivity and information sharing within and across organizational boundaries. In this model, in alignment with the preceding definitions (Broadbent et al., 1999; Mitchell et al., 1999; Weill et al., 1999), IT infrastructure capabilities include the capabilities of network infrastructure, messaging (electronic mail) systems, and supporting services, for which perceptual ratings will be collected from respondents.

Porter and Millar (1985) discussed how IT could contribute to the competitive advantages of firms, by automating activities of the value chain and facilitating control and decision functions. Many studies have empirically demonstrated the impact of IT on operating efficiency (Cline & Guynes, 2001; Mitra & Chaya, 1996), and coordination performance (Ross, 2002; Shin, 1999). Similarly, some studies have confirmed the positive impact of ERP systems on organizational performance (Gefen & Ragowsky, 2005; Hitt et al., 2002), and illustrated the tangible and intangible benefits associated with the adoption of enterprise systems, in terms of reducing inventory and operational costs, customer satisfaction (Murphy et al., 2002), and contributing to the fulfillment of different levels of organizational objectives (Shang et al., 2002). It is believed that together with IT infrastructure capabilities, successful ERP systems can contribute to the competitive capabilities of a firm, as stated in the following hypotheses:

$H_0 1$: *IS user satisfaction as a surrogate of the perceived success of ERP systems is positively associated with the perceived level of competitive capabilities of an organization.*

$H_0 2$: *The perceived quality of IT infrastructure capabilities is positively associated with the perceived level of competitive capabilities of an organization.*

The Extent of Improvement in Business Processes

In this context, the extent of improvement in business processes refers to any changes implemented for the simplification and betterment of work practices and processes through either evolutionary changes or radical re-engineering (Bhatt, 2000; Earl & Khan, 1994; Hammer et al., 1993; Harkness, Kettinger, & Segars, 1996; Stoddard et al., 1995). The re-engineering of business processes, as advocated by Hammer et al. (1993), is a radical approach that requires "rethinking" and drastic transformation of business, while the evolutionary approach attempts to achieve incremental improvement. Although the business process re-design or re-engineering (BPR) approach has many proponents, research has also shown that some companies adopted the more evolutionary approach in their process improvement projects (Harkness et al., 1996; Stoddard et al., 1995).

From a resource-based view, efficient and effective processes are among the difficult-to-imitate internal strengths that enable firms to compete in the market (Coates & McDermott, 2002). The reasons for improving processes are manifold, including the desire to reduce defects and production cycle times, raise the efficiency of internal processes, pursue technological improvements, and re-define business strategies (Chan & Peel, 1998; Paper, Rodger, & Pendharkar, 2001). Chan et al. (1998) also listed several external factors that motivated companies to embark on the re-engineering of business processes, such as evolving customer service requirements, competition, changing market conditions, new government regulations, and political pressure. Therefore, the improvement of business processes plays an important role in organizations. The pursuit of such improvements can cultivate a deeper understanding of business practices and processes among employees, thus laying the foundation for innovative practices. Consequently, by analyzing and pinpointing potential problems in its existing processes, an organization can effectively address fundamental problems by ameliorating or restructuring the processes (Bhatt, 2000).

Using a revised instrument based on the one developed by Bhatt (2000), the extent of business process improvement construct of this model measures the perceived degree of the changes in processes that were implemented, as reported by respondents, to achieve the objectives of enhancing process efficiency and effectiveness, reducing waste and defects, shortening cycle time, and improving logistics and customer services.

It is speculated that adequate efforts expended to improve business processes will contribute to the competitive capabilities of an organization, as stated in the following hypothesis:

$H_0 3$: *The extent of improvement in business processes is positively associated with the perceived level of competitive capabilities of an organization.*

The Interacting Effects of the Constructs for IT and Business Process Improvement

It is important to note the interacting relationship between the two IT constructs, namely IT infrastructure capabilities and the success of ERP systems that may exist in this research model. Both IT infrastructure and business applications are important to an organization, as they support each other in the overall information architecture (Allen et al., 1991; Mudie et al., 1985; Richardson et al., 1990) to yield the capacity, stability, and usability desired by users. It has also been widely discussed that automating inefficient processes without re-designing them would compromise the benefits of adopting IT (Hitt & Brynjolfsson, 1996; Petroni & Rizzi, 2001; Stoddard et al., 1995). On the other hand, the lack of or inflexibility of IT could inhibit the re-designing of business processes (Stoddard et al., 1995). Grover et al. (1998) has found that the re-designing of business processes was statistically significant as a mediator in the relationship between IT diffusion and perceived productivity gain for several types of information technologies such as electronic mail, relational database management systems, expert systems, imaging, and local area networks. Bhatt (2000, 2001) confirmed the impact of IT infrastructure, namely EDI, and network infrastructure on improvements in business processes. It is therefore theorized that the IT constructs in this model will contribute to improvements in business processes, which are to be assessed using a revised instrument based on those developed by Bhatt (2000, 2001). The hypotheses are stated as follows:

H$_0$4: *The interacting effects between IS user satisfaction as a surrogate for the success of ERP systems, and the perceived quality of IT infrastructure capabilities will contribute to higher levels of perceived improvement in business processes.*

H$_0$5: *The interacting effects among IS user satisfaction as a surrogate for the success of ERP systems, the perceived quality of IT infrastructure capabilities, and the perceived extent of business process improvements will contribute to higher levels of perceived competitive capabilities for an organization.*

Competitive Capabilities

The competitive capabilities of a firm can be defined as a set of attributes that represent a firm's capacity to fulfill business requirements in aspects such as order cycle times, order fulfillment, delivery frequencies, cost structures and pricing, and prompt product and order status information (Tracey et al., 1999). Noble (1997) described the following six composite variables of the capabilities of manufacturing firms: the quality of products, dependability of the handling of materials, logistics, and production control, reliable and quick delivery of products, competitive product costs, flexibility of production control and product changes, and innovativeness in introducing new products.

From a resource-based view, the capabilities of a firm are its "capacity to deploy" internal resources, tangible as well as intangible (Amit et al., 1993). These capabilities consist of assets, technology, business practices and processes, and human resources (Miller, 2001). Such capabilities resulting from the development and exploitation of internal resources must be regenerated regularly in order to protect an organization's competitive position in the market (Wernerfelt, 1984). Amit and Schoemaker's discussions are of significant theoretical relevance to the conceptualized linkage between the competitive capabilities possessed by a firm, and the use of IT and ERP systems addressed in this chapter. Amit and Schoemaker (1993) pointed out that the capabilities of a firm were often "information-based", and involved firm-specific processes developed over time. The acquisition and deployment of different combinations of resources would require managerial discretion in the handling of uncertainty, personal biases, complex interactions among various resources, and intra-organizational conflicts. This explains why unique and sustainable rent-producing capabilities exist within some firms, despite the fact that some of the resources are available in the market.

Resource-based theorists argue, from a traditional static perspective, that many information technologies are generic and therefore, high in transferability and imitability. This criticism directly places under closer scrutiny Porter's discussion, from a market-oriented perspective, on the contribution of IT to competitive advantages (Porter, 1985a). According to the traditional resource-based view, the capabilities resulting from the use of generic IT will be short-lived (Smith, Vasudevan, & Tanniru, 1996). Such technologies will cease to generate sustainable competitive capabilities as soon as they are adopted by competitors, and subsequently become necessities for market survival. However, from a dynamic perspective of the resource-based view, IT can facilitate organizational learning in the process of building new capabilities (Smith et al., 1996). IT will play a critical role in the creation of new sustainable capabilities through interaction with other resources (Smith et al., 1996; Teece, 1998). Smith et al. (1996) has cited cases to show how generic IT was coupled with unique internal methods and processes to facilitate the generation of competitive advantages. TWA Getaway Vacations, Inc. successfully pinpointed the needs of individual customers using database technologies. AES, an energy company, used such technologies in strategic planning (Smith et al., 1996). Teece (1998) also pointed out that IT has made the processing of many new transactional structures possible, leading to innovations such as new intermediate products in the financial market. From a knowledge management perspective, IT can easily be exploited for the distribution and sharing of highly structured or, in Teece's words, "well-codified" information, and in order to support the processes of managing tacit knowledge such as knowledge about customers and suppliers (Teece, 1998). Other studies have also re-iterated the contribution of IT to an organization's capabilities in marketing and operations by endowing it with the ability to collect, manage, and analyze huge volumes of data (Beckett, 2000; Plakoyiannaki & Tzokas, 2002).

Pereira (1999) argued that it was possible to create sustained competitive advantages in the deployment of SAP systems. SAP provides a vast number of tables and parameters for firms to configure. In many circumstances, firms may need to re-engineer their internal business processes to achieve an appropriate degree of mutual fit between systems and processes. However, this action may not preclude the creation of firm-specific and "imperfectly mobile" resources and capabilities. For instance, the objective of generating unique and sustainable capabilities can be achieved by making the deployment of SAP a job dependent on the skills and knowledge of the whole team, rather than those of an individual staff member or consultant, in order to deal with the mobility of such personnel. The firm should develop critical managerial capabilities that would set it apart from its competitors, and should minimize the turnover of SAP specialists by creating job-switching costs through appropriate means such as the development of a unique organizational culture (Pereira, 1999). The literature has time and again posited that human resources could be one of the sources of unique competitive capabilities. In the case of IT management, an IT manager's ability in understanding the needs of, and establishing relationships with, other business and functional managers would likely lead to better IT infrastructure and application systems that may set the firm apart from its competitors (Mata et al., 1995). Such a tacit ability may not be easily copied by other firms or acquired from the market, but often requires the IT manager to have the intimate knowledge of business practices, thorough understanding of organizational routines, and skills and experience in "socializing" and co-ordinating complex relationships (Grant, 1991). These attributes need to be developed gradually over time within a business enterprise.

Similarly, we argue that it may be more of fallacy than fact that employing generic IT and systems will not result in unique sustainable competitive capabilities. ERP systems, such as Oracle Applications, allow firms to choose from a large number of modules, functionality, and configurable parameters to meet their requirements. For instance, the deployment of Oracle ERP requires firm-specific business knowledge and decisions on such matters as the design of the chart of account structures, and deciding on the number of operating units, number of inventory organizations, inventory costing methods, pricing schemes, discount policies, and credit policies to be implemented (James, Russell, & Seibert, 2002). Therefore, the acquisition of an ERP package does not eliminate the needs of firm-specific knowledge and judgment. Critical decisions are to be made from time to time by various categories of personnel, ranging from project managers, functional specialists, and application architects, to fulfill business requirements in the face of uncertainty and to deal with trade-offs between competing technological and organizational objectives. This is an iterative and heuristic process in which a combination of internal and external resources, such as expertise in financial management, business operations, project management, and process design, are blended together to reach an optimal design that meets various business requirements, and yet is practical to implement. Consequently, although ERP packages are generic, ERP systems implemented across firms, incorporating firm-specific knowledge and practices, are not identical. This explains why some firms have reportedly benefited from adopting ERP, while others have suffered greatly. In summary, we posit that, although IT and systems by themselves may not generate sustained competitive capabilities, the enabling and facilitating roles that IT and systems play can lead to the creation of new sets of resources and capabilities, such as firm-specific business processes and customer management practices, that bear the characteristics of low imitability and transferability. The organization will gain sustainable competitive advantage over its competitors to the extent that this coupling of IT and internal processes will contribute to unique and non-imitable knowledge (Smith et al., 1996; Teece, 1998).

Unlike manufacturing capabilities resulting from the deployment of computer-based advanced manufacturing technologies (AMT), as described in the literature on operations management, information technologies enhance the capabilities of managing and controlling material requirements, production scheduling, logistics processes, and information processing and distribution across organizational boundaries (Kotha & Swamidass, 2000). Intra- and inter-organizational coordination has been recognized as critical to the success of modern organizations, as documented in the literature on supply chain networks, globally dispersed firms, and collaboration and knowledge-sharing among networks of firms (Gnyawali & Madhavan, 2001; Kogut, 1985; Stock, Greis, & Kasarda, 1998; Tsai, 2002). Capability in implementing the centralized coordination of global activities through the establishment of an integrated system is the key to the success of a globally dispersed firm (Kogut, 1985). Luo (2002) espoused a view of dynamic capabilities in which coordination and collaboration in knowledge sharing and learning among firms, coupled with internal resources, would be major contributing factors to the generation of new capabilities. The preceding perspectives are in alignment with the view in IT investment research that IT contributes to the efficiency of intra- and inter-organizational coordination, which involves the gathering, processing, and sharing of information for supporting the economic activities of organizations (Shin, 1999).

In this research model, the competitive capabilities construct is an intermediate construct between the independent constructs (namely, the capabilities of IT infrastructure, the success of ERP systems, and the extent of improvements in business processes) and the dependent construct (namely organizational performance), the existence of which helps conceptualize the linkage between the independent and dependent constructs. The adoption of IT and the implementation of IT-enabled processes will contribute to organizational performance through the creation or enhancement of competitive capabilities. An instrument will be developed on the basis of Tracey et al.'s (1999) questionnaire to capture perceptual ratings in such aspects as price and cost relative to competitors, product and service quality, reliability of delivery, knowledge sharing and learning, and flexibility in product and service offerings.

Empirical studies have confirmed the contribution of competitive capabilities to the performance of organizations (Barney, 1986; Tracey et al., 1999). It is therefore theorized that competitive capabilities will have a positive impact on organizational performance, as stated in the following hypothesis:

H$_0$6: *The perceived level of competitive capabilities of an organization is positively associated with its organizational performance.*

Organizational Performance

Organizational performance in this model is a firm-level measure based on the perceptual ratings of respondents. Objective financial data has often been used in studies on IT investment and organizational performance, in which relevant data was extracted from published financial databases (Bender, 1986; Cron & Sobol, 1983; Hitt et al., 2002; Hu et al., 2001; Mahmood et al., 1993; Tam, 1998) such as Standard and Poor's Compustat database. However, the accuracy and reliability of such secondary sources of financial data have been questioned (Dess et al., 1984; San Miguel, 1997). San Miguel (1977) pointed out that discrepancies found between the Compustat database and the Securities and Stock Exchange Commission's 10-K reports might also mean that potential errors existed in other financial databases. Dess et al. (1984) discussed the difficulties in obtaining objective performance measures for business units of multi-industry conglomerates. Although the audited financial data of such conglomerates is published, objective data for business units or divisions operating in individual industries is not available or unreliable due to inconsistent allocation methods being used. Certainly, reliable objective data is preferred, but the use of self-reported perceptual data will be acceptable if the former is unavailable (Dess et al., 1984).

Perceptual performance measures have been used in many empirical studies, for instance, on IS user satisfaction and performance (Gelderman, 1998), advanced manufacturing technologies (AMT) and performance (Das & Narasimhan, 2001; Kotha et al., 2000; Tracey et al., 1999), total quality management practices and operational performance (Samson & Terziovski, 1999), commitment to quality, vendor evaluation and organizational performance (Ebrahimpour & Johnson, 1992), and human resources issues and organizational performance (Delaney & Huselid, 1996).

Firm-level performance could include multiple dimensions, for instance sales growth, gain in market share, customer retention rate, customer's satisfaction with products (Tracey et al., 1999), delivery performance, cost reduction, product introduction time (Das et al., 2001), employee retention, management-employee relationships (Delaney et al., 1996), and after-tax return on total assets and total sales (Robinson & Pearce, 1988). In this model, Tracey et al.'s (1999) instrument will be adopted with some adjustments to capture perceptual ratings on profitability relative to competitors, reductions in operating costs, market share growth, sales growth, customer retention rate, and overall organizational performance.

Discussions

As previously discussed, the rationale underlying the proposed research model is to address the problems associated with IT business value studies: namely, the inadequacy of the traditional accounting-based appraisal approaches, the inaccuracy and unavailability of data, incomplete research models, and weak theoretical underpinnings. The lack of reliable objective data is believed to have adversely affected research findings as reported in the academic literature. Therefore, perceptual data is recommended as a substitute following the suggestions by other authors (Dess et al., 1984; Saarinen, 1996). This approach will make possible the capturing of the intangible benefits of IT and systems that are not quantifiable using traditional accounting-based appraisal methods. The use of perceptual ratings on IT and on systems capabilities based directly on the respondents' assessment of existing IT platforms will eliminate the need to use historical monetary measures on IT spending as predictor variables. This will shelter the evaluation model from the risk of project failures that may have occurred in the course of IT and systems deployment. It is hoped that the elimination of such a factor of uncertainty will contribute to a research model with a higher degree of predictability.

Intended as an improvement to the research models found among prior studies, the proposed model incorporates two major elements. First, business process improvement is incorporated in the model, since we believe that the impact of business processes should not be ignored, given the inter-relationship among business processes, IT, and systems (Al-Marshari, Irani, & Zairi, 2001; Grover et al., 1998; Hitt et al., 1996; Stoddard et al., 1999). The gist for the inclusion of business process is to model its contribution to, and the impact of its interaction with IT and IS capabilities on competitive capabilities and organizational performance. Second, the inclusion of competitive capabilities as an intermediate construct provides a conceptual linkage between IT capabilities, ERP systems, and business processes, on the one hand, and organizational performance on the other.

The inconsistent findings of prior studies are testimony to the elusiveness of the relationship between investment in IT and organizational performance. As Shin (1999) has pointed out, there lacks a theoretical underpinning to explain the linkage between IT spending and firm performance. This chapter supports the notion that there may exist a set of intermediate variables between IT investment and firm performance (Barua et al., 1995). It attempts to augment the traditional "black box" approach of IT business value research that has often been criticized by researchers over the past years (Chan, 2000b). It is hoped that this proposed model with competitive capabilities as the intermediate variable will improve the ability to model and explain the linkage between IT investment and performance, and help address the previously discussed issues (Barua et al., 1995; Chan, 2000b; Shin, 1999).

Future Research

Following an in-depth review of the literature, and the formulation of this research model, we have planned to conduct a postal survey of a significant scale in order to collect sufficient data for testing the model. Structural equation modelling (SEM) is a "large" sample technique that requires at least 200 observations (Andersen & Gerbing, 1984; Marsh, Balla, & MacDonald, 1988). The operationalization of the proposed research model calls for the testing of both the measurement and structural models (Anderson & Gerbing, 1988). The former would involve the specification and validation of a standardized IT infrastructure capabilities instrument that comprises the dimensions of network infrastructure, messaging systems, and supporting services.

Theoretical Implications

The proposed model is important to academic research in that its operationalization may potentially produce empirical evidence, which is scarce in the literature, for a relationship of interaction between IT and the re-designing of business processes, and the impact of this relationship on organizational performance.

One of the uses of the model is to generate relevant testable hypotheses for studies on the business value of IT. The proposed model will be used to model the infrastructural capabilities of IT, the re-designing of business processes, the success of ERP systems, and competitive capabilities, and the impact of these factors on organizational performance. The formulation of testable hypotheses is important, since the hypotheses determine the potential significance of a research effort.

The proposed study would lead to the development of a standardized instrument for measuring IT infrastructure capabilities, which would facilitate MIS research in a systematic and repeatable manner (Santhanam et al., 2003). Moreover, measurements of the constructs of business process improvement and competitive capabilities have not been previously tested in studies on MIS. Theories and empirical findings relating to such constructs will be of interest to MIS researchers and to researchers in other disciplines, who will be able to utilize them to strengthen their conceptualizations and theoretical foundations. As Chan (2000b) has pointed out, research on the value of IT is a relatively young branch of academic study, which may benefit from the experience of other academic disciplines.

Managerial Implications

The insight and understanding derived from operationalizing the proposed model will also have significant managerial implications for business and IS managers involved in IT investment and implementation. It will shed light on the importance of IT and business processes to organizational capabilities and performance. It is widely accepted that IT and improvements in business processes are inter-related. In practice, however, changes to business processes may not be implemented properly before systems are implemented, due to constraints in project costs and scheduling, or because of resistance from business units, thus limiting the success of the overall project. Empirical studies using this model may confirm or disprove generally accepted principles, and be used as guidelines for initiatives on the re-designing of business processes, IT infrastructure, and the deployment of ERP systems.

Limitations

While the operationalization of the proposed model may lead to many new elements of improvement in studies on the value of IT, and be conducted according to the guidelines of reliability and validity (Churchill, 1979; Nunnally, 1978), it is not free from potential limitations. First, as the exogenous and endogenous constructs rely on perceptual inputs from the same respondents, the operationalization may be subject to common method bias. Second, the effects of the time-lag between the implementation of IT and systems capabilities, and the outcomes (namely, the generation of competitive capabilities and organizational performance) would not be accounted for under this proposed model due to the use of perceptual data based on the respondents' assessment of "current" situations. In studies involving monetary IT spending and firm performance data, a time-lag between the former and the latter is recommended, so that its relationship of causality can be tested (Brynjolfsson, 1993; Hu et al., 2001). Logically thinking, there should be a time-gap from the time the investments in IT were made and the emergence of its effects. This period of time includes time spent on IT and system deployment, and on training and adapting staff to operating these newly available IT platforms for productivity improvement. In fact, the inconsistent findings of some early studies have been attributed to the failure to match data on IT spending with data on financial performance captured after an appropriate lapse of time, for instance, one or two years (Brynjolfsson, 1993; Hu et al., 2001). Conceptually, the emergence of IT capabilities must precede the outcomes in terms of competitive capabilities and organizational performance. Therefore, it is ideal that this temporal relationship can also be captured in the research model if the relationship of causality between IT and systems capabilities and the resulting gains in competitive capabilities and organizational performance is to be tested. Unfortunately, it would be very difficult in practice to identify and model this relationship. This is because the self-reported timing for the emergence of IT capabilities depends on the memories and subjective opinions of the respondents, and therefore lacks accuracy. However, we believe that the problem may be less serious in this case, since using the perceptual ratings on the existing IT and systems capabilities would exclude the time and uncertainty of the pre-commissioning periods of such IT platforms.

Given these potential limitations, it is necessary to reiterate that the proposed research model is not intended to be a panacea to address all of the problems associated with the paradox of IT productivity. Realistically speaking, our primary goal is to use the proposed model as an example of alternative approaches to studying the value of IT. This proposed model also shows how theories and findings of associated management disciplines can be used to enrich the theoretical underpinning of IT value research (Chan, 2000b).

As the last note, we would like to state that this study has made only limited use of some of the theories borrowed from other management disciplines. Therefore, there may exist opportunities for improving the theoretical justification for some of the constructs of the proposed model through a more thorough illustration and application of such theories as resources-based view of the firm and competitive capabilities.

Conclusion

Inconsistent findings on the contribution of IT to organizational performance have perplexed academics and practitioners alike, and the paradox has not yet been fully debunked. However, an extensive review of the studies conducted on this subject has pointed to several flaws in data and methodology that may possibly explain the inconsistent and inconclusive results. In view of such limitations, an alternative conceptual model is proposed. The aim is to address the problems associated with inaccurate data, an incomplete research model, and weak theoretical underpinning in IT value research. We plan to test the proposed conceptual model using empirical data to be collected by means of a large-scale postal survey, and will report the findings in future publications. We will verify and validate the proposed model, and test the relationships between the constructs using structural equation modeling (SEM) techniques. As stated in the previous sections, we hope that introducing the process improvement and competitive capabilities constructs into the research model, and supporting the model with theories and principles of other management disciplines would help address the inherent theoretical weakness of the studies in IT business value. The use of perceptual data allows the measuring of the intangible aspects in IT infrastructure capabilities, business process improvement, and organizational outcomes, hence overcoming the problems associated with the traditional accounting-based evaluation approaches. We also anticipate that the development of the instrument for measuring IT infrastructure capabilities would be a significant contribution to MIS research.

In summary, we believe that the research agenda we have put forward will be a workable means of helping provide better understanding of the business value of IT, its relationship with organizational performance, and its measures. Significant benefits could result from further work on both theories and empirical studies on the relationship between the business value of IT and organizational performance.

Acknowledgment

This chapter is an extension of an earlier paper written by the same authors: Law, C. H. C., & Ngai, W. T. E. (2005). IT business value research: A critical review and a research agenda. *International Journal of Enterprise Information Systems*, 1(3), 35-55.

References

Allen, B. R., & Boynton, A. C. (1991, December). Information architecture: In search of efficient flexibility. *MIS Quarterly, 15*(4), 435-445.

Al-Mashari, M., Irani, Z., & Zairi, M. (2001). Business process reengineering: A survey of international experience. *Business Process Management Journal, 7*(5), pp. 437-455.

Alpar, P., & Kim, M. (1990). A microeconomic approach to the measurement of information technology value. *Journal of Management Information Systems, 2*, 55-59.

Amit, R., & Schoemaker, P. J. H. (1993). Strategic assets and organization rent. *Strategic Management Journal, 14*, 33-46.

Andersen, J. C., & Gerbing, D. W. (1984). The effect of sampling error on convergence, improper solutions, and goodness-of-fit indices for maximum likelihood confirmatory factory analysis. *Psychometrika, 49*, 155-173.

Anderson, J. C., & Gerbing, D. W. (1988). Structural equation modeling in practice: A review and recommended two-step approach. *Psychological Bulletin, 103*, 411-423.

Barney, J. (1991). Firm resources and sustained competitive advantages. *Journal of Management, 17*(1), 99-120.

Barney, J. B. (1986). Types of competition and the theory of strategy: Toward an integrative framework. *Academy of Management Review, 11*, 791-800.

Barua, A., Kriebel, C. H., & Mukhopadhyay, T. (1995). Information technologies and business value: An analytic and empirical investigation. *Information Systems Research, 6*(1), 3-23.

Beckett, R. C. (2000). A characterization of corporate memory as a knowledge system. *Journal of Knowledge Management, 4*(4), 311-319.

Bender, D. H. (1986). Financial impact of information processing. *Journal of Management Information Systems, 3,* 22-32.

Bharadwaj, A. S. (2000). A resource-based perspective on information technology capability and firm performance: An empirical investigation. *MIS Quarterly, 24*(1), 169-196.

Bhatt, G. D. (2000). Exploring the relationship between information technology, infrastructure and business process re-engineering. *Business Process Management Journal, 6*(2), 139-163.

Bhatt, G. D. (2001). Business process improvement through electronic data interchange (EDI) systems: An empirical study. *Supply Chain Management: An International Journal, 6*(2), 60-73.

Botta-Genoulaz, V., & Millet, P. (2006). An investigation into the use of ERP systems in the service sector. *International Journal of Production Economics, 99,* 202-221.

Broadbent, M., Weill, P., & St. Clair, D. (1999). The implications of information technology infrastructure for business process redesign. *MIS Quarterly, 23*(2), 159-182.

Brynjolfsson, E. (1993). The productivity paradox of information technology. *Communications of the ACM, 36*(12), 67-77.

Byrd, T., & Marshall, T. (1997). Relating information technology investment to organizational performance: A causal model analysis. *Omega, 25*(1), 43-56.

Chan, P. S., & Land, C. (1999). Implementing reengineering using information technology. *Business Process Management Journal, 5*(4), 311-324.

Chan, P. S., & Peel, D. (1998). Causes and impact of reengineering. *Business Process Management Journal, 4*(1), 44-55.

Chan, S. L. (2000a). Information technology in business process. *Business Process Management Journal, 6*(3), 224-237.

Chan, Y. E. (2000b). IT value: The great divide between qualitative and quantitative and individual and organizational measures. *Journal of Management Information Systems, 16*(4), 225-261.

Chatterjee, D., Pacini, C., & Sambamurthy, V. (2002). The shareholder-wealth and trading-volume effects of information technology infrastructure investment. *Journal of Management Information Systems, 19*(2), 7-42.

Chen, L. D., Soliman, K. S., Mao, K. S., & Frolick, M. (2000). Measuring user satisfaction with data warehouses: An exploratory study. *Information & Management, 37*, 103-110.

Chen, W. H. (1999). The manufacturing strategy and competitive priorities of SMEs in Taiwan: A case survey. *Asia Pacific Journal of Management, 16*, 331-349.

Churchill, G. A., Jr. (1979). A paradigm for developing better measures of marketing constructs. *Journal of Marketing Research, 16*, 64-73.

Clemons, E. K., & Row, M. C. (1991). Information technology at Rosenbluth Travel: Competitive advantage in a rapidly growing global service company. *Journal of Management Information Systems, 8*(2), 53-79.

Cline, M. K., & Guynes, C. S. (2001). A study of the impact of information technology investment on firm performance. *The Journal of Computer Information Systems, 4*(3), 15-19.

Coates, T. T., & McDermott, C. M. (2002). An exploratory analysis of new perspectives: A resource based view perspective. *Journal of Operations Management, 20*, 435-450.

Counihan, A., Finnegan, P., & Sammon, D. (2002). Towards a framework for evaluating investments in data warehousing. *Information Systems Journal, 12*, 321-338.

Cron, W., & Sobol, M. (1983). The relationship between computerization and performance: A strategy for maximizing economic benefits of computerization. *Information and Management, 6*, 171-181.

Das, A., & Narasimhan, R. (2001). Process-technology fit and its implications for the manufacturing performance. *Journal of Operations Management, 19*, 521-540.

Dasgupta, S., Sarkis, J., & Talluri, S. (1999). Influence of information technology investment on firm productivity: A cross-sectional study. *Logistics Information Management, 12*(1/2), 120-129.

Davenport, T. (1993). *Process innovation*. Boston: Harvard Business School Press.

Delaney, J. T., & Huselid, M. A. (1996). The impact of human resources management practices on perceptions of organizational performance. *Academy of Management Journal, 39*(4), 949-969.

Dess, G., & Robinson, J. R. (1984). Measuring organizational performance in the absence of objective measures: The case of the privately-held firm and conglomerate business unit. *Strategic Management Journal, 5*, 265-273.

Doll, W. J., & Torkzadeh, G. (1998, June). The measurement of end-user computing satisfaction. *MIS Quarterly, 12*(2), 258-274.

Earl, M., & Khan, B. (1994). How new is business process redesign? *European Management Journal, 12*(1), 20-30.

Ebrahimpour, M., & Johnson, J. L. (1992). Quality, vendor evaluation and organizational performance: A comparison of U. S. and Japanese firms. *Journal of Business Research, 25,* 129-142.

Gefen, D., & Ragowsky, A. (2005). A multi-level approach to measuring the benefits of an ERP system in manufacturing firms. *Information Systems Management, 22*(1), 18-25.

Gelderman, M. (1998). The relation between user satisfaction, usage of information systems and performance. *Information and Management, 34,* 11-18.

Gnyawali, D. R., & Madhavan, R. (2001). Cooperative networks and competitive dynamics: A structural embeddedness perspective. *The Academy of Management Review, 26*(3), 431-445.

Grant, R. M. (1991, Spring). The resource-based theory of competitive advantage: Implications for strategy formulation. *California Management Review,* 114-135.

Grover, V., Teng, J., Segars, A. H., & Fiedler, K. (1998). The influence of information technology diffusion and business process change on perceived productivity: The IS executive's perspective. *Information and Management, 34,* 141-159.

Hammer, M., & Champy, J. (1993). *Reengineering the corporation: A manifesto for business revolution.* London: Nicholas Brealey Publishing.

Harkness, W. L, Kettinger, W. J., & Segars, A. H. (1996, September). Sustaining process improvement and innovation in the information services function: Lessons learned at the Bose Corporation. *MIS Quarterly, 20*(3), 349-368.

Harris, S. E., & Katz, J. (1991). Organization performance and information investment intensity in the insurance industry. *Organization Science, 2,* 263-295.

Hitt, L. M., & Brynjolfsson, E. (1996). Productivity, business profitability, and customer surplus: Three different measures of information technology value. *MIS Quarterly, 20*(2), 121-142.

Hitt, L. M., Wu, D. J., & Zhou, X. G. (2002). Investment in enterprise resource planning: Business impact and productivity measures. *Journal of Management Information Systems, 19*(1), 71-98.

Hu, Q., & Plant, R. (2001). An empirical study of the casual relationship between IT investment and firm performance. *Information Resources Management Journal, 14*(3), 15-26.

James, D., Russell, S., & Seibert, G. (2002). *Oracle e-business suite financials handbook.* New York: Oracle Press.

Kogut, B. (1985, Fall). Designing global strategies: Profiting from operational flexibility. *Sloan Management Review, 27*(1), 27-38.

Kotha, S., & Swamidass, P. M. (2000). Strategy, advanced manufacturing technology and performance: Empirical evidence from U. S. manufacturing firms. *Journal of Operations Management, 18*, 257-277.

Li, M. F., & Ye, L. R. (1999). Information technology and firm performance: Linking with environmental, strategic and managerial contexts. *Information and Management, 35,* 43-51.

Loveman, G. W. (1994). An assessment of the productivity impact of information technologies. In T. J. Allen, & M. S. Scott Morton (Eds.), *Information technology and the corporation of the 1990's* (pp. 84-110). New York: Oxford University Press.

Luo, Y. D. (2002). Capabilities exploitation and building in a foreign market: Implications for multinational enterprises. *Organizational Science, 13*(1), 48-63.

Mahmood, M. A., & Mann, G. J. (1993). Measuring the organizational impact of information technology investment: An exploratory study. *Journal of Management Information Systems, 10*(1), 97-122.

Marsh, H. W., Balla, J. R., & MacDonald, R. P. (1988). Goodness-of-fit indexes in confirmatory factor analysis: The effect of sample size. *Psychological Bulletin, 103*(3), 391-410.

Mata, F. J., Fuerst, W. L., & Barney, J. B. (1995). Information technology and sustained competitive advantage: A resource-based analysis. *MIS Quarterly, 19*(4), 487-505.

McHaney, R., & Cronan, T. P. (1998). Computer simulation success: On the use of the end-user computing satisfaction instrument: A comment. *Decision Sciences, 29*(2), 525-534.

McHaney, R., Hightower, R., & Pearson, J. (2002). A validation of the end-user computing satisfaction instrument in Taiwan. *Information and Management, 39,* 503-511.

Melone, N. P. (1990). A theoretical assessment of the user satisfaction construct in information systems research. *Management Science, 36*(1), 76-91.

Melville, N., Kraemer, K., & Gurbaxani, V. (2004). Information technology and organizational performance: An integrative model of IT business value. *MIS Quarterly, 28*(2), 283-322.

Miller, W. L. (2001). Innovation for business growth. *Research Technology Management, 44*(5), 26-41.

Mitchell, V. L., & Zmud, R. W. (1999). The effects of coupling IT and work process strategies in redesign projects. *Organization Science, 10*(4), 424-438.

Mitra, S., & Chaya, A. K. (1996). Analyzing cost-effectiveness of organizations: The impact of information technology spending. *Journal of Management Information Systems, 13*(2), 29-57.

Mooney, J. G., Gurbaxani, V., & Kraemer, K. L. (1995). *A process oriented framework for assessing the business value of information technology.* Working paper, Graduate School of Management, University of California, Irvine.

Morrison, C. J., & Berndt, E. R. (1990, January). *Assessing the productivity of information technology equipment in the U. S. manufacturing industries* (No. 3582). Working paper, National Bureau of Economic Research.

Mudie, M. W., & Schafer, D. J. (1985). An information technology architecture for change. *IBM Systems Journal, 24*(3/4), 307-305.

Murphy, K. E., & Simon, S. J. (2002). Intangible benefits valuation in ERP project. *Information Systems Journal, 12*, 301-320.

Ng, I. S. Y., & Yiu, K. (1995). An application of event-study methodology on evaluating information technology investments. *International Journal of Computer and Engineering Management, 3*(1), 1-13.

Noble, M. A. (1997). Manufacturing competitive priorities and productivity: An empirical study. *International Journal of Operations and Production Management, 17*(1), 85-99.

Nunnally, J. (1978). *Psychometric theory.* New York: McGraw-Hill.

Paper, D. J., Rodger, J. A., & Pendharkar, P. C. (2001). A BPR case study at Honeywell. *Business Process Management Journal, 7*(2), 85-99.

Patel, N. V., & Irani, Z. (1999). Evaluating information technology in dynamic environments. *Logistics Information Management, 12*(1/2), 32-99.

Pereira, R. E. (1999). Resource view theory analysis of SAP as a source of competitive advantage for firms. *The Data Base for Advances in Information Systems, 30*(1), 38-46.

Petroni, A., & Rizzi, A. (2001). Antecedents of MRP adoption in small and medium-sized firms. *Benchmarking: An International Journal, 8*(2), 144-156.

Plakoyiannaki, E., & Tzokas, N. (2002). Customer relationship management: A capabilities portfolio perspective. *Journal of Database Marketing, 9*(3), 228-237.

Porter, M. E. (1985a, Winter). Technology and competitive advantage. *Journal of Business Strategy*, 60-78.

Porter, M. E. (1985b). *Competitive advantage: Creating and sustaining superior performance.* New York: The Free Press.

Porter, M. E., & Millar, V. E. (1985, July-August). How information gives you competitive advantage. *Harvard Business Review, 63*(4), 149-160.

Pratipati, S. N., & Mensah, M. O. (1997). Information systems variables and management productivity. *Information and Management, 33*, 33-43.

Richardson, G. L., Jackson, B. M., & Dickson, G. W. (1990, December). A principles-based enterprise architecture: Lessons from Texaco and Star Enterprise. *MIS Quarterly, 14*(4), 385-403.

Rivard, S., Raymond, L., & Verreault, D. (2006). Resource-based view and competitive strategy: An integrated model of the contribution of information technology to firm performance. *Journal of Strategic Information Systems, 15*, 29-50.

Roach, S. S. (1991, September-October). Services under siege—the restructuring imperative. *Harvard Business Review, 69*(5), 82-92.

Robinson, R. B., Jr., & Pearce J. A., II. (1988). Planned patterns of strategic behaviour and their relationship to business-unit performance. *Strategic Journal Management, 9*, 43-60.

Ross, A. (2002). A multi-dimensional empirical exploration of technology investment, co-ordination, and firm performance. *International Journal of Physical Distribution and Logistics Management, 32*(7), 591-609.

Saarinen, T. (1996). An expanded instrument for evaluating information system success. *Information and Management, 31*, 103-118.

Sakaguchi, T., & Dibrell, C. C. (1998). Measurement of the intensity of global information technology usage: Quantitizing the value of a firm's information technology. *Industrial Management & Data Systems, 8*, 380-394.

Samson, D., & Terziovski, M. (1999). The relationship between total quality management practice and operational performance. *Journal of Operations Management, 17*, 393-409.

Sanders, G. L., & Garrity, E. J. (1995). *Dimensions of information system success.* Working paper, Jacobs School of Management, State University of New York at Buffalo.

San Miguel, J. G. (1997). The reliability of R&D data in Compustat and 10-K Reports. *The Accounting Review, 11*(3), 638-641.

Santhanam, R., & Hartono, E. (2003). Issues in linking information technology capability to firm performance. *MIS Quarterly, 27*(1), 125-143.

Serafeimidis, V., & Smithson, S. (1999). Rethinking the approaches to information systems investment evaluation. *Logistics Information Management, 12*(1/2), 94-107.

Shafer, S. M., & Byrd, T. A. (2000). A framework for measuring the efficiency of organizational investments in information technology using data envelopment analysis. *Omega, 28*, 125-141.

Shang, S., & Seddon, P. B. (2002). Assessing and managing the benefits of enterprise systems: The business manager's perspective. *Information Systems Journal, 12*, 271-299.

Shin, N. (1999). Does information technology improves co-ordination? An empirical study. *Logistics Information Management, 12*(1/2), 138-144.

Smith, K. A., Vasudevan, S. P., & Tanniru, M. R. (1996). Organizational learning and resource-based theory: An integrative model. *Journal of Organizational Change Management, 9*(6), 41-53.

Somers, T. M., & Nelson, K. G. (2003). The impact of strategy and integration mechanisms on enterprises system value: Empirical evidence from manufacturing firms. *European Journal of Operational Research, 146*, 315-338.

Stock, G. N., Greis, N. P., & Kasarda, J. D. (1998). Logistics, strategy and structure: A conceptual framework. *International Journal of Operations and Production Management, 18*(1), 37-52.

Stoddard, D. B., & Jarvenpaa, S. L. (1995). Business process redesign: Tactics for managing radical change. *Journal of Management Information Systems, 12*(1), 81-107.

Strassmann, P. A. (1990). *The business value of computers: An executive's guide.* New Canaan: Information Economic Press.

Strassmann, P. A. (1997, September 15). Computers have yet to make companies more productive. *Computerworld.* Retrieved January 20, 2005, from http://www.computerworld.com/news/1997/story/

Strassmann, P. A. (2000). *Assessment of productivity, technology and knowledge capital.* New Canaan: Information Economic Press.

Strassmann, P. A. (2002). *The persistence of the computer paradox: A critique of efforts to disprove the computer paradox.* New Canaan: The Information Economics Press.

Suwardy, T., Ratnatunga, J., & Sohal, A. S. (2003). IT project: Evaluation, outcomes, and impediments. *Benchmarking: An International Journal, 10*(4), 325-342.

Tallon, P. P., Kraemer, K. L., & Gurbaxani, V. (1999). *The development and application of a value-based thermometer of IT business value* (No. ITR-121). Working paper, Graduate School of Management, University of California, Irvine.

Tallon, P. P., Kraemer, K. L., & Gurbaxani, V. (2000). Executives' perceptions of the business value of information technology: A process-oriented approach. *Journal of Management Information Systems, 16*(4), 145-173.

Tam, K. Y. (1998). The impact of IT investment on firm performance and evaluation: Evidence from newly industrialized economies. *Information Systems Research, 9*(1), 85-98.

Teece, D. J. (1998). Capturing value from knowledge assets: The new economy markets for know-how, and intangible assets. *California Management Review, 40*(3), 55-79.

Thatcher, M. E., & Oliver, J. R. (2001). The impact of technology investments on a firm's production efficiency, product quality, and productivity. *Journal of Management Information Systems, 18*(7), 17-45.

Tracey, M., Vonderembse, M. A., & Lim, J. S. (1999). Manufacturing technology and strategy formulation: Keys to enhancing competitiveness and improving performance. *Journal of Operations Management, 17*, 411-428.

Tsai, W. P. (2002). Social structure of "cooperation" within a multiunit organization: Co-ordination, competition, and intraorganizational knowledge sharing. *Organization Science, 13*(2), 179-190.

Weill, P., & Broadbent, M. (1999). Four views of IT infrastructure: Implications for IT investment. In L. P. Willcocks, & S. Lester (Eds.), *Beyond the IT productivity paradox* (pp. 335-360). Chichester: John Wiley & Sons.

Wernerfelt, B. (1984). A resource-based view of the firm. *Strategic Management Journal, 5*(2), 171-180.

Wu, I. L. (2002). A model for implementing BPR based on strategic perspectives: An empirical study. *Information and Management, 39*, 313-324.

Zviran, M., Pliskin, N., & Levin, R. (2005). Measuring user satisfaction and perceived usefulness in the ERP context. *Journal of Computer Information Systems*, Spring, 43-52.

Appendix:
A Summary of Selected
Studies of IT Business Value

Study	Objectives	Methods and Data Sources	Dependent Measures	Independent Measures	Findings and Implications
Cron & Sobol (1983)	Examine the effects of computerization on the organizational performance of medical wholesalers.	Chi square analysis using the data of 138 medical wholesaling firms.	Return on assets, pretax profits, return on net worth, and a five-year sales growth rate.	Categorical variables of computer ownership, number of computer applications in use, and types of computer software.	Computerization was associated with performance. Small firms with average performance were less likely to use computers. Firms making extensive use of computers were either high or low performing.
Bender (1986)	Investigate and suggest a model for evaluating the impact of IT spending on firm performance.	Linear correlation based on the data of 132 life insurance firms supplied by LOMA.	Ratio of total general expense to premium income.	Ratio of information processing expenses to total general expenses.	IT spending is associated with operating efficiency. It has been found that an optimal level of IT investment seemed to be around 20% to 25% of total operating expenses.
Loveman (1994)	Investigate the impact of IT on productivity.	Used a production function model, and based on 60 business units of 20 manufacturing firms derived from MPIT database.	Difference of changes in sales and inventory, deflated by price index.	IT capital, non-IT capital, raw material expenditure, non-IT purchased services expenditures, and labour compensation.	No evidence was found to support the relationship between IT investment and improved productivity.

Appendix continued

Study	Objectives	Methods and Data Sources	Dependent Measures	Independent Measures	Findings and Implications
Alpar & Kim (1990)	Investigate the impact of IT investment on the performance of banks, and develop a methodology to measure the economic impact of IT on the cost of banking services.	Study based on microeconomic theory and the cost function approach using data collected during 1979 to 1986 by the Federal Reserve Bank of New York of mostly small banks, and a few large ones. The sample size varied from 624 to 759 banks since some banks did not respond every year during the data collection period. This study also repeated the key ratio approaches of Bender (1986), and Cron and Sobol (1983) using the dataset.	Outputs: demand deposits, installment loans, real estate mortgage loans, and commercial loans.	Inputs: Time deposits, labor, capital, IS expenses, IT index (i.e. number of ATMs and number of computerized bank functions).	An increase in IT spending was found to be significantly associated with a reduction in total cost. For every 10% increase in IT spending, there was a 1.9% decrease in total cost. The operationalization of the key ratio approaches of Bender, and Cron and Sobol did not yield conclusive results.

Appendix continued

Study	Objectives	Methods and Data Sources	Dependent Measures	Independent Measures	Findings and Implications
Harris & Katz (1991)	Examine the relationship between IT spending and firm performance.	Longitudinal study based on a sample of 40 insurance firms extracted from the LOMA database for the period of 1983 to 1986.	Operating cost efficiency ratio (i.e. total operating expenses to premium income).	IT expenses ratio (i.e. IT expenses to total operating expenses); IT cost efficiency ratio (i.e. IT expenses to premium income).	Top-performing firms spent a larger percentage of revenue on IT than did low-performing firms. Also, top performing firms were found to have a lower IT costs to premium income ratio.
Mahmood & Mann (1993)	(a) Explore what could be the significant measures in the relationship between IT investment and organizational performance, and (b) attempt to confirm the relationship among these measures.	Correlation analysis, and canonical correlation analysis based on the Computerworld Premier 100 database of 1989 and on a compact DISCLOSURE database.	Return on sales; growth in revenue; sales by total assets; return on investment; market to book value; sales per employee.	IT budget expressed as a percentage of revenue; value of IT expressed as a percentage of revenue; percentage of IT budget spent on staff; percentage of IT budget spent on training; and number of PCs as a percentage of total number of employees.	A weak relationship was found between individual dependent variables, and individual independent variables. A significant relationship was found between dependent variables and independent variables taken as groups respectively by canonical correlation analysis.

Appendix continued

Study	Objectives	Methods and Data Sources	Dependent Measures	Independent Measures	Findings and Implications
Pratipati & Mensah (1995)	Propose a different strategy for understanding IT productivity and gather supporting evidence for this strategy.	Exploratory approach; Discriminant Analysis of 86 cases in a sample derived from the Computerworld Premier 100 database, and on Information and Productivity Index rankings (Strassmann's).	Information Productivity Index (IPI).	IS budget, level of CIO; percentage of IS employees to total number of employees; number of years the CIO has been in the position; percentage change in the IS budget from 1992; percentage of IS budget spent outside the IS department; percentage of the software budget spent on new development; percentage of software development spent on client-server applications; number of desktop servers, percentage of networked desktop devices.	Years in the CIO position, percentage of software budget spent on developing new applications, percentage of software development spent on client-server applications were found to be the most significant. Shorter tenure of CIO was associated with higher levels of productivity.

Appendix continued

Study	Objectives	Methods and Data Sources	Dependent Measures	Independent Measures	Findings and Implications
Mitra & Chaya (1996)	Examine the effect of IT investment on various categories of costs.	ComputerWorld Premier 100, and Compustat databases.	Measures per unit of output: average total cost, average cost of production, average overhead cost, and average clerical labour cost.	Three-year average of IT (infrastructure) budgets expressed as a percentage of sales.	Firms with a higher level of IT spending would have lower production costs, lower total operating costs, and higher overhead costs. There was no evidence to support the relationship between IT spending and lower labour costs, confirming the authors' belief that IT's primary contribution was in control and monitoring rather than automating clerical tasks. Larger firms were also found to spend a larger percentage of total revenue on IT than smaller firms.
Gelderman (1998)	Investigate and test the influence of user satisfaction and use of IT on organizational performance.	Correlational analysis and ANOVA using data collected through a questionnaire survey using a pre-tested instrument on user satisfaction, a self-developed questionnaire for usage, and a modified Van de Ven and Ferry instrument to capture organizational performance.	Original measures in Van de Ven and Ferry, and additional measures for profitability and revenue.	Usage and user satisfaction (Doll & Torkzadeh) as surrogates.	User satisfaction was found to be significantly related to organizational performance while usage was not. Previous findings that usage was not significantly related to organizational performance were reconfirmed. This study using self-reported data from respondents is subject to the common method bias.

Appendix continued

Study	Objectives	Methods and Data Sources	Dependent Measures	Independent Measures	Findings and Implications
Tam (1998)	Conduct an empirical study across national settings in Asia (i.e., Hong Kong, Singapore, Malaysia, and Taiwan) on the relationship between IT investment and business performance.	OLS regression analysis based on the matched data of listed companies, derived from an ACD database (IT capital), a PACAP database, and a Global Vintage database. Used performance data with no time lag in the initial test, and a repeated test with a one-year lag.	Return on equity, return on sales, and total shareholder returns.	IT capital from ACD database, adjusted by annual obsolescence factor, and price deflator.	The study yielded mixed results across nations for hypothesis 1 (i.e., impact of IT on business performance), and found no effect for hypothesis 2 (i.e., impact of IT on total shareholder returns). The limitation of the study is associated with its use of only IT capital amounts in the research model without incorporating spending on computer applications.
Shin (1999)	Examine the relationship between IT spending and coordination costs.	OLS and TLS (Two-stage Least Squared) Regression based on firm level data between 1988 and 1992 of 549 observations (of 232 firms) derived from Compustat, and IDG databases.	Sales and administrative expenses less advertising, R&D, software, bad debt, and pension and retirements, deflated to the value of the 1987 dollar.	Market value of CPUs; total central IS budget; percentage of IS budget spent on labour expenses; and number of PCs and terminals.	It was confirmed that IT spending was related to decreased coordination costs in manufacturing and trade, but not in the transportation and utility sectors. This implies that intangible benefits were associated with IT spending beyond 'productivity' and 'profitability'.

Appendix continued

Study	Objectives	Methods and Data Sources	Dependent Measures	Independent Measures	Findings and Implications
Li & Ye (1999)	Examine and test the moderating effects of organizational contextual variables on the relationship between IT investment and firm-level performance.	OLS regression analysis using data on 513 observations (of 216 firms) carried out between 1992-1994, derived from the Information Week database (for IT investment, CEO/CIO reporting relationship), the US Industrial Outlook (1994) (for 'environmental dynamism' and 'munificence'), and the Compustat database (for firm performance).	Return on assets, and return on sales.	IT-strategy integration (CEO/CIO distance ratings); environmental dynamism (standardized variation in industry-level sales revenue over five years); IT budget divided by total assets. Control variable: size of firm; debt-to-equity ratio; and environmental munificence (derived using beta coefficients obtained by regressing industry-level revenue against time, which was divided by five-year average industry sales revenues).	The following relationships were found to be statistically significant: 1. Between the three-way interaction term of strategy, IT, and dynamism (i.e., strategy x IT x dynamism), and ROA; 2. between the two-way interaction term (IT x 'dynamism') and ROS; 3. between the interaction term between CEO/CIO distance and ROS. This implies that (1) a higher level of IT investment in 'a dynamic environment and with an externally oriented strategy' will lead to a higher level of profitability; (2) a greater distance of CIO from CEO will lead to lower performance; and (3) the impact of IT investment on firm performance depends on many contextual factors.

Appendix continued

Study	Objectives	Methods and Data Sources	Dependent Measures	Independent Measures	Findings and Implications
Bharadwaj (2000)	Illustrate a conceptual framework for the relationship between IT capability and firm performance from a resource-based perspective, and examine the relationship empirically using matched samples.	Used non-parametric Kolmogorov-Smirnov test on matched samples. The treatment sample contained 56 firms ranked by InformationWeek as IT leaders for at least any 2 years during1991 and 1996. The control firms (one per treatment firm), were selected based on 5-year average sales levels, to match the respective IT leader firms, from industries defined by the four-digit SIC code. Financial data for the sample firms was extracted from Compustat database.	Profit-related ratios (ROA, ROS, operating income to assets, operating income to sales, operating income to employees); Cost-related ratios (operating expenses to sales (OEXP/S), cost of goods sold to sales (COGS/S), selling, and general administrative expenses to sales (SG&A/S)).	A dummy variable was used with "1" to indicate the status of being in the treatment group, and "0" for being in the control group.	It was found that IT capability was related positively to firm performance. (The hypotheses that superior IT capabilities were related to higher profit, and lower cost ratios were supported.)

Appendix continued

Study	Objectives	Methods and Data Sources	Dependent Measures	Independent Measures	Findings and Implications
Shafer & Byrd (2000)	Propose a framework, for measuring IT investment and organizational performance, to overcome limitations found in previous studies.	Data envelopment analysis based on data extracted from the Computerworld Premier 100 and Stock Investor databases. The input has been averaged over three years.	Five-year compound annual income growth, and five-year compound annual revenue growth.	IS budget expressed as a percentage of sales; firm-level total processor value expressed as a percentage of sales; and percentage of IS budget allocated to training.	It demonstrated that the proposed framework could be used to compare IT investment efficiency in organizations while overcoming data measurement problems regarding the time-lag effect of investment in IT.

Appendix continued

Study	Objectives	Methods and Data Sources	Dependent Measures	Independent Measures	Findings and Implications
Tallon, Kraemer, & Gurbaxani (2000)	Investigate the relationships between the corporate goals of IT and perceived payoffs of IT, using a process-oriented approach; and examine the relationships between IT management practices and perceived payoffs of IT.	One-way analysis of variance; partial correlation based on perceptual inputs of a sample of 304 executives participating in a postal survey of Fortune 1,000 firms, and foreign firms.	Perceived "realized" IT payoffs: An average was computed for each of the 6 categories of business processes: (a) process planning & support (5 items); (b) supplier relations (5 items); (c) production & operations (5 items); (d) product and service enhancement (5 items); (e) sales & marketing (5 items); (f) customer relations (5 items).	(1). Corporate goals for IT: Sample firms were classified into 4 types of firms (dual focused; market focused; operations focused; and unfocused). (2). IT management practice: (a). strategic alignment: one question item (7-point Likert scale). (b) pre-implementation evaluation: 2 question items (7-point Likert scale) (c). post-implementation evaluation: 2 question items (7-point Likert scale).	It was found that the corporate goals for IT (namely, market-focused, operations-focused, dual-focused, and unfocused) for IT investment was associated with the "realized" payoffs perceived by the executives. Firms with a market focus were perceived to have realized better payoffs than firms with an operational or an undefined focus while firms with a dual focus were associated with the highest level of perceived payoffs than all others. Firms with an operational focus were perceived to have received better payoff only than those with an undefined focus. Management practice, namely strategic alignment, and IT evaluation was also found related to perceived payoffs in IT.

Appendix continued

Study	Objectives	Methods and Data Sources	Dependent Measures	Independent Measures	Findings and Implications
Andersen & Segars (2001)	Investigate empirically the impact of IT on the decentralization of decision structure, and financial performance of firms in the apparel and textile industry.	Longitudinal study involving regression analyses on data of 50 firms. Factor analyses were performed on measures before regression analyses. Questionnaires on IT use and decentralization were mailed to CIOs in 1995. Financial data were extracted from the Compustat database, Disclosure database, and annual reports for two periods: (1) pre-period (1992-1994), and (2) post-period (1994-1996). (Note: pre-period (1992-1994) performance data preceded the administering of the IT and decentralization questionnaire.)	Decentralization measures (for the authority, and participation constructs) were based on self-assessment ratings of CIOs. Financial measures included 3-year averages of net profit margin, operating margin, return on assets, and adjusted cash flow margin for the pre- and post-periods.	Measures on the use of IT were based on self-assessment ratings of CIOs.	The positive impact of IT on authority and participation was confirmed respectively. However, only authority was found to have positive effect on pre-period and post-period financial performance. The impact of participation on financial performance was found to be statistically insignificant. It was also found that IT did not directly affect financial performance but might be related to higher performance in larger firms (as shown by the interactive term of IT and size of firm assets).

Appendix continued

Study	Objectives	Methods and Data Sources	Dependent Measures	Independent Measures	Findings and Implications
Hu & Plant (2001)	Determine whether there is a causal relationship between IT investment and firm performance and the direction of such a relationship if it exists.	Least-square linear regression analysis using the Granger (1969) causal model. Sample data was derived from the Information Week and Compustat databases.	(1) Change in employee productivity (i.e., differences in sales per employee for two consecutive years); growth rate of annual sales; change in operating expenses between two consecutive years; and changes in ROA and ROE between two consecutive years.	Percentage change in IT investment between two consecutive years.	No evidence was found to support the view that IT investment contributed to a reduction in operating costs, an increase in productivity, sales growth, and profitability. A statistically significant relationship was found only between IT investment (1991-1992) and ROA (1993), but the authors concluded that this was not enough to confirm the impact between IT and firm performance. Instead, the evidence showed that the sales growth in a year was related to an increase in IT spending in the subsequent year. There was no evidence to support the (instantaneous) relationship between IT spending and performance in the same year.

Appendix continued

Study	Objectives	Methods and Data Sources	Dependent Measures	Independent Measures	Findings and Implications
Hitt, Wu, & Zhou (2002)	Examine the impact of the adoption of ERP systems on firm productivity and profitability.	Multiple regression analysis based on a SAP licenses database (for a list of organizations that have adopted SAP ERP), Standard and Poor's Compustat II database (for financial data), and the Computer Intelligence InfoCorp (CII) database (for data on information technology usage).	Profitability measures: labour productivity (per employee); return on assets; return on equity; profit margin; Activity measures: inventory turnover; asset turnover; accounts receivable turnover; Debt and solvency measure: debt-to-equity ratio; Market value: Market value / book value (Tobin's Q).	Adoption of ERP; IT capital; levels of ERP deployment.	It confirmed that the adoption of ERP contributed to firm performance, and that the benefits of using ERP varied according to levels of implementation. This study contributes to research through its consistent quantitative analysis of the benefits of adopting ERP. It is limited in generalizability, as it is based on a sample of SAP adopters, while firms using other brands of ERP systems are not included in the study.

Appendix continued

Study	Objectives	Methods and Data Sources	Dependent Measures	Independent Measures	Findings and Implications
Santhanam & Hartono (2003)	Examine empirically the impact of IT capabilities on financial performance of firms and investigate the issues surrounding the use of resource-based theories in IT business value research using the framework of Bharadwaj (2000).	Longitudinal firm level analysis involving Wilcoxon signed-ranked test, parametric t-test, and regression analysis using a sample of firms identified by Informationweek during 1991 and 1994 as IT leaders, and two control samples based on the 2- and 4-digit SIC codes. Financial data between 1991 and 1997 was extracted from Compustat database.	Profit ratios: ROS, ROA, operating income to assets, operating income to sales, and operating income to employees; Cost ratios: cost of goods sold to sales, selling, and general administrative expenses to sales, and operating expenses to sales.	Dummy variable (with values of 0 or 1) coded to indicate whether a firm was selected as IT leader; financial performance data of prior year was used in regression model to adjust for the effects of prior-year financial performance.	The hypotheses that firms with superior IT capability rating were associated with higher profit ratios, and lower cost ratios than their counterparts in their respective industries defined by 2- and 4-digit SIC codes. Similar hypotheses adjusting for the effects of prior-year financial performance were only partially supported, depending on the benchmark firms used (i.e. whether based on 2-digit or 4-digit SIC codes). The sustainability of the effects of IT capability on firm performance in subsequent years was also supported before and after adjusting for prior year financial performance.

Chapter III

The Effects of Uncertainty on ERP-Controlled Manufacturing Supply Chains

S. C. Lenny Koh, University of Sheffield, UK

Angappa Gunasekaran, University of Massachusetts, USA

Abstract

The use of enterprise resource planning (ERP) is becoming increasingly prevalent in many modern manufacturing supply chains. However, knowledge of their performance when perturbed by several significant uncertainties simultaneously is not as widespread as it should have been. This chapter presents the developmental and experimental work on modelling uncertainty within an ERP multi-product, multi-level dependent demand manufacturing supply chain in a simulation model developed using ARENA/SIMAN. To enumerate how uncertainty affects the performance of an ERP-controlled manufacturing supply chain, the percentages of finished products delivered late (FPDL) and parts delivered late (PDL) are measured. Sensitivity analysis shows that PDL gives a more accurate effect. Simulations results are analysed using analysis of variance (ANOVA), which identifies four uncertainties namely late delivery from suppliers, machine breakdowns, unexpected/urgent changes to machine assignments, and customer design changes significantly affect PDL. Some uncertainties are found significantly interactive in two and three-way. They produce either knock-on and/or compound effects, a factor not generally recognised as a criterion for decision-making.

Background and Literature

Modern manufacturing supply chains are facing increasing pressure to improve its responsiveness to market dynamics. Central to this are the issues addressed by production planning and scheduling system. Customer expectations for shorter delivery lead-times, greater agility, improved quality, and reduced costs have made the effective application of an appropriate system a significant determinant of survival for many manufacturing enterprises. Within a batch manufacturing supply chain, material requirements planning (MRP), manufacturing resource planning (MRPII), or enterprise resource planning (ERP) is the ideal system for producing work order (Enns, 2001). Since MRP logic is deployed within MRPII and ERP, when they are used for planning and scheduling, the planned order release (POR) schedule outputs are identical (Koh & Saad, 2002; Moon & Phatak, 2005). This research refers to the use of these systems in batch manufacturing enterprises as ERP-controlled manufacturing supply chains.

To elaborate the emergence of ERP and how this system yet is still incapable in tackling uncertainty, lets discuss the characteristics of this system. In the 1960s, Oliver Wight and Joseph Orlicky introduced MRP (Wight, 1981). It was designed and developed to operate within a stable and predictable batch manufacturing environment; and it was defined as a set of back scheduling techniques that uses bill of materials (BOM) data, inventory data, and a master production schedule (MPS) to calculate net requirements for materials. MRP run takes place by offsetting parts' due date with planned lead-time from the upper to the lower levels in the BOM. Output from the run is a POR schedule, which contains order number, part number, net requirement, release date, and due date for all orders in the MPS. The POR schedule is used to release order to the manufacturing supply chain and execute purchase or manufacture operations.

MRP assumes infinite capacity as no consideration is given to used and available resources capacity in generating the POR schedule. Both planned purchase and manufacture lead-times are pre-determined, which ignore variation in lead-times, for instance, delay resulting from late delivery from suppliers or machine breakdowns.

These uncertainties often distort the planned lead-times due to their unpredictability and the stochastic nature in manufacturing environment.

MRP release logic is used in MRPII to generate POR schedule. However, there is a feedback loop in MRPII, which considers used and available resources capacity. However, the feedback loop does not operate in real-time, hence whenever uncertainty is encountered, it is too late to plan for until the next MRP run. It is arguable that regenerative or net-change rescheduling can be carried out to update the POR schedule, but how frequent should we reschedule? The more frequent that we reschedule, the more nervous will the system become (Ho, Law, & Rampal, 1995). Different uncertainty might occur after the POR schedule is updated.

ERP is a more advanced version of MRPII that integrates sales, marketing, human resource, accounting, purchasing, and logistics modules altogether. Nevertheless, when ERP is used within batch manufacturing environment as a planning and scheduling system, the same problems in MRP and MRPII will be encountered. Although detailed analysis can be performed within ERP, for instance whether to assign three batches of orders using a shared route, provided that the logistics module is integrated, their inabilities to operate under uncertainty are still overwhelming. For this instance, delay might have already occurred in production and the affected orders might not be delivered on time.

Considerable amount of research showed many underperformance of ERP-controlled manufacturing supply chain ranging from the work by Duchessi, Schaninger, and Hobbs (1989), Yusuf and Little (1998), Tinham (1999), and Koh and Saad (2006). The main finding from their work is that MRP, MRPII, or ERP is an enabler (planner) rather than optimiser (executer), therefore under an unperturbed manufacturing environment without the effects of uncertainty the plan can be executed without revision. Otherwise the planner has to apply buffering or dampening techniques, for example, rescheduling or subcontract, to tackle the effects of uncertainty. This has led to extensive research to examine techniques to tackle the effects of uncertainty.

A study carried out by Mather (1977) examined changes to MPS and poor vendor performance, and recommended removal of uncertainty as a better approach than simply managing it. The results were derived from a planning heuristic and suggested that rescheduling is the main cause of uncertainty and by tackling the causes of rescheduling the effects of uncertainty could be reduced significantly. It was identified that most reschedules are not caused by reactions to customer requirements, but resulted from algorithms for calculating lot-sizes and lead-times and from poor execution of manufacturing plans.

Grasso and Taylor (1984) suggested allowing purchased parts to arrive late more frequently than allowing them to arrive early would be advantageous since it resulted in the lowest total costs of the system. The results of their simulation study showed that when buffering against variations in supply timing, it is more prudent to use safety stock instead of safety lead-time. New and Mapes (1984) studied the effect of process yield losses, using the measures of cost effectiveness and customer satisfaction. Their framework showed that mean yield rate and fixed buffer stocks techniques are appropriate in a continuous schedule, make-to-stock (MTS) environment. In a continuous schedule, make-to-order (MTO) environment, mean yield rate, fixed buffers, and a yield to finish monitoring system are suitable. The framework also suggested that for a single batch production MTO environment, it is more appropriate to use mean yield rate, fixed buffers, and a desired service level yield rate. If the enterprise has multiple batch production and operates in MTO environment, then they should use mean yield rate, fixed buffers, and a variable yield rate by batch.

Ho et al. (1995) developed a framework to dampen uncertainty caused by external demand and supply and system uncertainties. They proposed two types of techniques, known as the inventory-oriented and information-oriented techniques. The framework suggested that the inventory-oriented techniques of safety stock and safety capacity are appropriate to buffer external demand, external supply and system uncertainties, whereas the information-oriented techniques of safety lead-time and rescheduling are appropriate to dampen them.

For tackling quality uncertainty, an optimal over planning factor was suggested by Murthy and Ma (1996) as a dampening technique in the planning process. A mathematical model was used to measure the optimal over planning factor required to cope with scrap resulting from both supply and process failures. Further work by Ho and Carter (1996) simulated static dampening, automatic rescheduling, and cost-based dampening techniques to tackle external demand and systems uncertainties. The results indicated that the performance of dampening procedures depends on the operating environment within a manufacturing enterprise. The results also showed that a reduction in uncertainty, as measured by rescheduling frequency, does not necessarily lead to better system performance. Rather, it is the appropriate use of dampening techniques and lot-sizing rules that results in system improvement.

To tackle external demand uncertainty in forecast, Krupp (1997) proposed a statistical model that expressed deviations in units of time rather than quantity to provide safety stock calculations that are responsive to trend and/or seasonality in future forecasts. A forecast tracking signal was used to dampen forecast inaccuracy by adjusting safety stock calculations in cases where forecasts were consistently over-optimistic. A service factor multiplier was also designed to optimise the balance between safety stock carrying costs and recouped profit.

Through simulation modelling, Ho and Ireland (1998) found that scheduling instability or system uncertainty could be dampened using an appropriate lot-sizing rule. Their study concluded that economic order quantity (EOQ) and lot for lot (LFL) are less favoured than silver meal (SM) and part period balancing (PPB). Saad and Gindy (1998) proposed the use of resource elements (RE) technique to tackle lead-time and capacity uncertainties. Their simulation results suggested that the larger is the responsiveness; the better is the system performance.

Yang and Pei (1999) developed and proposed a standard for transfer and exchange product (STEP) model database integration environment to link design tasks with manufacturing planning and scheduling activities to tackle the effect of engineering changes uncertainty. For each engineering change activity, engineering (EBOM) data relating to the change and stored in a computer aided design (CAD) database will be extracted and transformed to a manufacturing (MBOM) data stored in the ERP database. The modified MRP record is generated and compared with the original data. Based on this information, the designer can determine an appropriate design alternative such that the effect on inventory can be minimised. To tackle material release time uncertainty, Homem-de-Mello, Shapiro, and Spearman (1999) suggested a real-time optimisation technique, which is measured by tardiness and flow time costs minimisation.

Despite research on techniques to tackle uncertainty, Brennan and Gupta (1993) studied the factors influencing enterprise performance under uncertainty. Using performance measures of cost and service level, analysis of variance (ANOVA) was applied to the simulation results and showed that lead-time and demand uncertainties are individually and interactively significant determinants of performance; the number of parts at a given level in the product structure and its shape are significant when lead-time and demand uncertainties are applied; the choice of lot-sizing rule has a significant effect on performance and the value of the ratio of set-up to holding cost has significant effect on performance when lead-time and demand uncertainties occur.

Koh and Tan (2006) examined the translation of knowledge of uncertainty into strategy and actions. The results suggested that capturing knowledge of uncertainty could be carried out using analytical tool, and hence it provides a basis for decision making. Following a similar concept, further research was performed by Koh and Gunasekaran (2006) through a proposed theory called management by value-added urgency. This theory suggested that managers should filter out less significant uncertainty, prioritise significant uncertainty management using a new knowledge management approach, and map tacit and explicit knowledge to manage uncertainty.

Geary, Disney, and Towill (2006) theorised bull-whip effect caused by uncertainty. A comprehensive review of the literature was carried out, and yet their review and this review show that considerable amount of past research in this area examined effectiveness and efficiencies of buffering or dampening techniques to tackle uncertainty. Little research study which uncertainty has significant effect on the performance of ERP-controlled manufacturing supply chain. Knowledge of their performance when perturbed by several significant uncertainties simultaneously is not as widespread as it should have been. As a result, many sub-optimal solutions to uncertainty were proposed because diagnosis on their effects to enterprise performance has not been performed.

To resolve this problem, research has been carried out to diagnose the significant uncertainty within ERP-controlled manufacturing supply chain. Findings from the previous study can be found in Koh and Saad (2002). This chapter presents the developmental and experimental work on modelling several uncertainties, which have been identified most likely to affect customer delivery performance in an ERP-controlled multi-product, multi-level dependent demand planning and scheduling system using simulation experiments, and analyses the effects of these uncertainties on delivery performance.

Simulation Model Development

To model an ERP-controlled manufacturing supply chain is to implement MRP release logic in a multi-product, multi-level dependent demand planning and scheduling environment. This research has developed a simulation model, which has modelled a manufacturing supply chain that is controlled by MRP release logic in its entirety. The simulation model is developed using SIMAN programming language within ARENA simulation software.

A concept known as parent and child is deployed. This concept mimics the logic within MRP, which defines child as parts at the lower level BOM chain that are required to make the part at the upper level BOM chain—defined as parent. A parent part can only be released when all child parts at the associated lower level BOM chain are available and its release date is reached. Multi-level dependency adheres this type of logic within an ERP system. Therefore, when MRP run is completed, a POR schedule that links all parts within a BOM by lead-times is generated to control purchase and manufacture activities.

Problems Formulation

Although the dependency between parts is integrated in the POR schedule, finite capacity within the simulation model does not assure the validity of the multi-level dependency when resource constraint, delay, and queue are applied. For instance, if a delay occurs at one of the child parts, the parent part should be released late. This lateness is caused by the delay of the child part unless some sort of slack exists in the system and is able to absorb the lateness.

In an infinite capacity environment, the parent part will be released according to its release date if no control rules are programmed. Then, the parent part will continue with its routing with child shortages and still fully complete the batch. In contrast, this phenomenon should result in child shortages and the associated parent part should be released late and never be completed until the remaining of its child part arrives. Without implementing such control rules in the simulation model, the dependency logic in the POR schedule will be flaw.

If the planned and actual lead-times are identical, then the release date will be valid in the simulation run and the order will be processed on time. If the planned lead-times are longer than the actual lead-times, then the parts will be completed early. In this case, early release may be resulted. In contrast, the parts will be completed late. Late release may be resulted. Under adherence to POR schedule condition, it is invalid to release an order earlier than its release date.

Solutions

To overcome these problems, additional control rules have been programmed. The control rules are divided into two divisions. The first division is the introduction

Figure 1. Sub-routines of multi-level dependency control rule

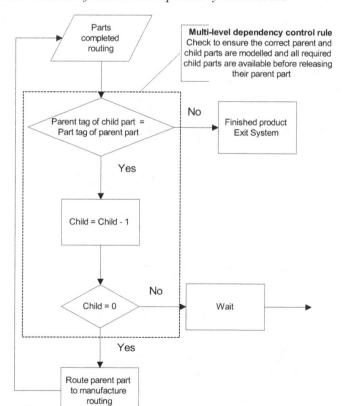

of additional attributes in the simulation model, to model multi-level dependency between parent and child parts. Hence, *parent tag, part tag,* and *child* are attributed. Figure 1 shows the implementation of the multi-level dependency control rule together with its sub-routines.

Parent tag and *part tag* define the parent and child relationship of the parts with an equal value. To identify whether the part is a child part of that parent part, comparison is made between *parent tag* of the child part and *part tag* of the parent part for matching value. The comparison between *parent tag* and *part tag* is not constrained by the levels in the BOM. Therefore, it accommodates condition when a parent part is also a child part for another parent part. *Child* defines the number of child parts of a parent part. *Child* for parts at the lowest level BOM will always be zero and for others will initially be set the number of child parts required according to its respective BOM.

The second division is the introduction of a conditional sub-routine in the simulation model in which parent part cannot be released until its release date is reached and all required child pars are present. Figure 2 shows the sub-routines of the release timeliness control rule.

To control release timeliness, Time Now (TNOW) variable is recorded when the last child part is completed. TNOW is a reserved variable defines the time now in the simulation run. TNOW is compared with the release date of the parent part. If TNOW = release date, an on-time release is achieved. If TNOW > release date, TNOW will be assigned to the release date to model late release. On the other hand,

Figure 2. Sub-routines of release timeliness control rule

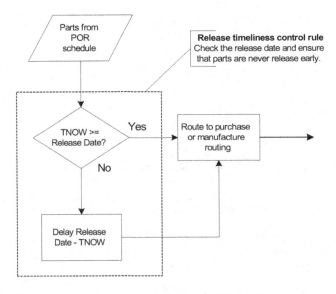

if TNOW < release date, a delay of release date – TNOW is executed to offset the time difference in order to prevent early release.

Simulation Model Logic

MRP release logic is modelled with the additional control rules being programmed in the simulation model. Figure 3 shows the programmed simulation model logic in a flow diagram.

The attributes in the POR schedule, namely order number, part number, net requirement, release date, and due date, together with *parent tag, part tag,* and *child* for all orders in the MPS are read into the simulation model entity-by-entity. In simulation term, an entity is defined as a unique part consisting of its associated attributes.

An evaluation is made to identify whether a parent part or a child part exists. If a parent part exists, it is routed to a holding bay to wait for its required child parts. If a child part exists, it is routed to its purchase or manufacture routings for operation. When completed, it searches its parent part in the holding bay. Another evaluation is then required to check whether all child parts are completed before the parent part can be released provided that its release date is reached. If these conditions are not met, the parent part remains in the holding bay. If the part fails to identify its parent part, this implies that it is a finished product and hence leaves the system. These evaluations recur until all entities are processed.

Figure 3. Simulation model logic

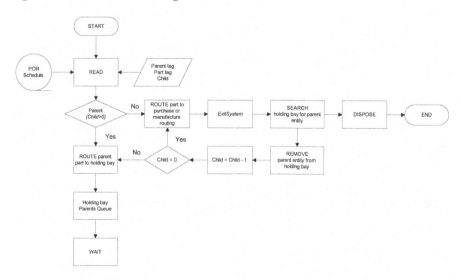

SIMAN uses model file to control the simulation logic and experiment file to define the policy (Pegden, Shannon, & Sadowski, 1995). This simulation model logic is programmed within the model file, while all associated resources capacity, queue, routing, and attributes are programmed within the experiment file. First-In-First-Out (FIFO) queuing rule is modelled. Three different resource states are designated, namely idle, working, and breakdown. For purchase parts, routings are sequenced through a station with a set-up time modelling the purchase lead-time and zero operation time. For manufacture parts, routings are sequenced by work centre with a set-up time per batch and operation time per unit.

Performance Measures

The most pertinent performance measures in assessing the effects of uncertainty in an ERP-controlled manufacturing supply chain are customer deliveries because ERP system itself is due date driven. FPDL was identified as a preferred industrial performance measure (Koh & Gunasekaran, 2006). Therefore, it is measured in the sensitivity study for the simulation model. FPDL is calculated as a percentage of finished products delivered late, that is TNOW > due date in any time period.

As the effect on FPDL is cumulative, in that it records the effect of all uncertainty within a product, it is relatively less sensitive to analyse the effect of particular uncertainty and its significance. To overcome this problem, a second performance measure, known as PDL is measured. PDL measures the effects of uncertainty on individual piece parts and is calculated as a percentage of all parts delivered late in any time period. The larger is the PDL, the greater is the effects of uncertainty.

To illustrate the sensitivity of FPDL and PDL, let's consider the simple BOM as shown in Figure 4. If part number 10006 is delivered late and no slack exists to recover the lateness, then it will also cause part numbers 10005, 10003, and the finished product 10001 to be late. The effect will be 44.4% PDL (as there are nine parts). If FPDL is measured, the measure is 100%. Thus, irrespective of the number of parts late in a single BOM, no increase in FPDL can result. If more than one finished product is considered, the incremental effect on FPDL will be inaccurate as compared to PDL because the denominator (number of parts) of FPDL is significantly less than of PDL.

FPDL is therefore seen to be a dampened measure and hence misleading when establishing which uncertainty is significant. PDL, on the other hand, measures the precise effect of uncertainty to a much higher level of sensitivity.

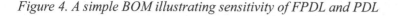

Figure 4. A simple BOM illustrating sensitivity of FPDL and PDL

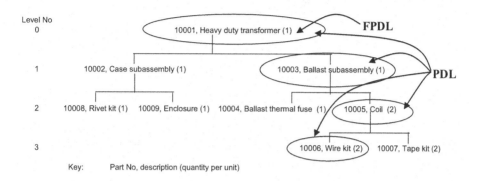

Experimental Design

Having recognised the appropriate performance measure, the next step is to design the experiments for the simulation study. There are several issues that need to be addressed in experimental design:

- How many factors to simulate?
- How many levels?
- What levels?

Koh and Saad (2002) have identified eight uncertainties, which are most likely to affect customer delivery performance. They are late delivery from suppliers (LDFS), insecure stores (INSC), planned set-up/changeover times exceeded (PSE), machines breakdown (BD), waiting for labour (WFL), waiting for tooling (WFT), unexpected/urgent changes to machine assignments (MA), and customer design changes (CDC). To examine their effects to PDL, simulation experiments for the eight factors are designed.

Number of levels per factor determines the total number of experiments. A half factorial design of eight factors at two levels requires a total of (0.5×2^8) 128 experiments. Two levels are considered sufficient in this study because the objective is to model uncertainty realistically at both end of the spectrum. Ten replications are run initially for each experiment to obtain a normal distributed response. Therefore, a minimum of 1,280 simulation run is required. A normal distributed response is measured by an acceptable half-width (h) value, considered to be less than 5% of the sample mean, which the confidence level is set in all experiments to 95%. The formula to calculate the h value is:

$$h = t_{1-\alpha/2, n-1} \frac{S(x)}{\sqrt{n}}$$ (1)

where

h = distribution half-width

$t_{1-\alpha/2, \, n-1}$ = standard deviate in t-distribution for α confidence level

$S(x)$ = an unbiased estimator of the standard deviation

n = number of replications

A 5% error from the sample mean would be calculated to yield the lower and upper confidence interval as the following:

$$Confidence \, \text{int} \, erval = \bar{x} \pm h$$ (2)

where

$\bar{x}$ = sample mean

If a normal distributed response is obtained, the computed confidence interval will lie within the calculated confidence interval and hence no further replications are required. Otherwise, to calculate the number of further replications, the following equation is used:

$$n^* \geq n \left(\frac{h}{h^*} \right)^2$$ (3)

where

n^* = total replications required

n = initial number of replications

h = initial calculated half-width for n replications

h^* = desired distribution half width

Recursion of the process of obtaining a normal distributed response has resulted in a total of 1,534 simulation run.

The levels set for each factor is determined by the sensitivity study on the responsiveness of the simulation model to small changes. A low and a high level are set to model uncertainty in the best and worst case scenario. This is dependent upon the simulation method to model uncertainty with reflects to how it would occur realistically. Table 1 shows the simulation method and levels set for each uncertainty.

Table 1. Simulation methods and levels

Uncertainty	Simulation methods	Code	Levels	
			Low	High
Late delivery from suppliers	Purchase lead-time increment	LDFS	Discrete probability distribution	
			Frequency = 2.00% Magnitude = 480mins	Frequency = 2.00% Magnitude = 1440mins
Insecure stores Planned set-up/change-over times exceeded	Purchase and manufacture lead-time increment Set-up time increment	INSC	Discrete probability distribution	
			Frequency = 2.00% Magnitude = 480mins	Frequency = 2.00% Magnitude = 1440mins
		PSE	Discrete probability distribution	
			Frequency = 5.00% Magnitude = 15mins	Frequency = 5.00% Magnitude = 240mins
Machine breakdowns	Machine failures defined by MTBF and MTTR	BD	MTBF: Exponential distribution	
			Brake press=60000mins Coiler=24000mins Weld=30000mins	Brake press=60000mins Coiler=24000mins Weld=30000mins
			MTTR: Gamma distribution	
			Brake press=(300mins, 2) Coiler = (120mins, 2) Weld = (150mins, 2)	Brake press=(1200mins,2) Coiler = (1200mins, 2) Weld = (1200mins, 2)
Waiting for labour	Lead-time increment at labour-oriented resources	WFL	Discrete probability distribution Frequency = 5.00% Magnitude = 15mins	Frequency = 5.00% Magnitude = 240mins
Waiting for tooling	Lead-time increment at tooling	WFT	Discrete probability distribution Frequency = 5.00% Magnitude = 30mins	Frequency = 5.00% Magnitude 480mins
Unexpected/ urgent changes to machine assignments	Batch size increment and number of orders affected	MA	Batch size multiplier = 100% Orders affected = 1	Orders affected = 10
Customer design changes	Alternative routing with additional operations	CDC	Discrete probability distribution Frequency = 4.00%	Frequency = 10.00%

LDFS, PSE, WFL, and WFT are intrinsically lead-time oriented in which delay can be used to model these uncertainties. Delay can either be discretely distributed by a specified proportion of parts or distributed within the operation time of their routings. Interviews with several ERP-controlled manufacturing enterprises have concluded that delay is often distributed discretely with a proportion of parts, therefore is used to model these uncertainties.

When applying discrete probability distribution, it is found that better robustness is achieved via varying magnitude of delay rather than frequency, and hence should be implemented in setting the levels for the factors. To illustrate this robustness, the sensitivity matrix for LDFS as shown in Figure 5 is used as an example.

It can be clearly seen that changing the frequency of LDFS for one day (480 mins) late produces very little effect on PDL. Detailed analysis showed this to be due to the existence of some slack in the simulation model. Increasing the lateness to three days (1,440 mins) causes a pronounced increase in PDL, which is directly proportional to the frequency. The response then levels off as lateness is increased. The conclusion is that for any level of LDFS, reducing magnitude of lateness is the key issue in improving customer delivery performance, accepting that any frequency of LDFS will produce a problem.

Based on these rules, the levels for these factors are chosen. The difference between their implementation is that LDFS is modelled on purchase parts, PSE on machine-oriented resources that involve set-up/change-over, WFL on labour-oriented resources such as manual assembly station and WFT on tools. INSC is also modelled using the

Figure 5. Sensitivity matrix for LDFS

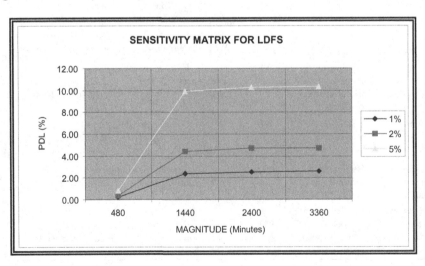

same distribution and rules assuming that delay will be resulted due to reordering for purchase and/or manufacture parts that have gone missing. However, CDC is modelled by varying frequency because delay as a result of engineering changes is modelled using alternative routings, which randomness is applied in the routings selection process.

BD is modelled with mean time between failure (MTBF) and mean time to repair (MTTR). MTBF models how frequent breakdown occurs and how reliable the machine is. MTTR models how long a breakdown will last and how quickly repair can be made. Pegden et al. (1995) suggest an exponential distribution to model MTBF and a gamma distribution for MTTR, and hence are implemented. Based on the same rules, MTBF is fixed and MTTR is varied. BD is only implemented on machine-oriented resources.

MA is modelled with a batch size multiplier assuming that batch size increment is the unexpected/urgent changes. A double batch size (100%) is modelled with variation in number of orders affected. Only orders requiring machine-oriented resources input are affected.

Results, Analysis, and Discussion

Data used for the simulation study is derived from a commercial transformer manufacturer who uses a proprietary ERP system for manufacturing planning and scheduling. Ten products are simulated, classified by order interval (Parnaby, 1988) as 3 runners, 4 repeaters, and 3 strangers. The products consist of up to five BOM levels. An MPS of two years demand is prepared for these products and run through an MRP system resulting in POR schedule for some 50,000 batches (parts), with 60% for purchase and 40% for manufacture.

Table 2. Summary of header and footer data from ANOVA

Source	Sum of Square (SS)	Degree of Freedom (df)	Mean Square (MS)	F	p
Corrected Model	57225.029	92	622.011	98.463	.000*
Intercept	149609.592	1	149609.592	23682.779	.000*
Error	9103.130	1441	6.317		
Total	256965.068	1534			
Corrected Total	66328.159	1533			

* P < 0.05

The POR schedule is fed into the simulation model for the experiments. Simulation results are collected and analysed in ANOVA using SPSS statistical package. A summary header and footer ANOVA result is shown in Table 2. For all ANOVA results, p values of significant uncertainty at 95% confidence level are asterisked. Resolution VIII configuration ensures only up to three-way interactions are not confounded, therefore higher order interactions are excluded from the analysis.

Main Effect

Main effect analysis reveals the significant uncertainty on PDL. Table 3 shows the main effect results. Four significant uncertainty are identified, namely LDFS, BD, MA, and CDC.

When LDFS transpires, the purchase part affected directly will be recorded as PDL. However, within a multi-level dependent demand ERP-controlled manufacturing supply chain, delay at the lower level in the BOM chain will have a knock-on effect to the higher level. The propagation of the knock-on effect depends on the level at which the first part initially being affected to its subsequent and last parent parts. The greater is the where-used of an affected part, the larger is the knock-on effect and hence the higher is the PDL. Within any typical BOM, purchase parts tend to be at lower levels, resulting in maximum knock-on effect. Thus, LDFS is found to be significant.

BD results in machines stoppage. Although the direct effect is on the affected machine, parts from several different products that are in the queue when the event occurs will be delayed. As there is no way one could predict in advance parts that are going to be in the queue of a broken machine in the future, the consequence is

Table 3. Main effect results

Source	SS	df	MS	F	p
LDFS	3705.849	1	3705.849	586.626	.000*
INSC	19.618	1	19.618	3.105	.078
PSE	6.953	1	6.953	1.101	.294
BD	50881.286	1	50881.286	8054.365	.000*
WFL	.240	1	.240	.038	.846
WFT	.532	1	.532	.084	.772
MA	378.375	1	378.375	59.896	.000*
CDC	53.634	1	53.634	8.490	.004*

*$P < 0.05$

Figure 6. Knock-on and compound effects of uncertainty

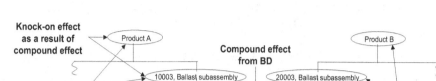

more immense than from a knock-on effect. To explain this volatile nature, compound effect is coined.

BD produces compound then knock-on effects on PDL. Those parts that are directly affected by BD, which are in-processed and/or in the queue of the broken machine will be recorded as PDL. In addition, their parent parts will also be delayed due to knock-on effect, causing multiple parts to be recorded as PDL. This persists until the backlog is cleared. These effects have significantly resulted in high PDL and therefore BD is found to be significant. Figure 6 illustrates how knock-on and compound effects result in PDL.

When MA affects an order, the increase in batch size causes an extended stay within all resources visited. This produces compound then knock-on effects to PDL. Queue will be built-up waiting for the resources while their delay will result in their parent parts to be released late and hence delivered late. The effects are identical with BD, but the level of significance is not as strong as with BD.

Additional operations of CDC have resulted in significant effect on PDL. As some resources capacity is unexpectedly consumed, resources unavailability has delayed scheduled order and therefore creating queue. Parts in the queue are unpredictable hence resulting in compound effect. Consequently, timeliness of parent parts of the delayed parts will also be affected. In short, CDC produces compound then knock-on effects on PDL.

To demonstrate how each level of the significant uncertainties affect PDL, a PDL plot for those found to be significant at both low and high levels is produced and shown in Figure 7. It can be concluded that levels of significant uncertainty must be minimised to reduce PDL.

Figure 7. PDL plot of significant uncertainties at low and high levels

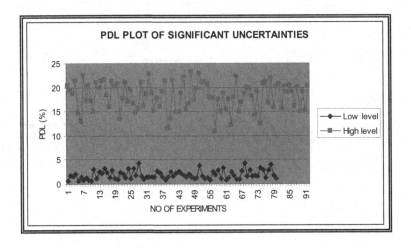

Two-Way Interaction

Two-way interaction analysis reveals uncertainty that results in additional effect on PDL when interacting with another uncertainty. It is important to understand not only PDL will be increased as a result of their interactive effects, but also to be aware of the condition when they could interact. Table 4 shows the two-way interaction results. Two significant two-way interactions are identified, namely LDFS* BD and BD*MA.

Significant additional PDL is resulted due to the effects from LDFS and BD. Although LDFS directly affects purchased part, changes in resources loading profile could result in its interaction with BD. When the affected part ultimately arrives, resources loading profile will be different to what is used to be. At this time, BD could occur in the new profile subsequently resulting in their parent parts to be delayed again. This condition has occurred frequently and hence is found to be significant on PDL.

Significant interactions between BD and MA occur when the same part is being affected at a different time frequently. Parts that are affected by MA would have been delayed. If they are routed to a machine, which will be broken down, then a second delay is applied. Therefore, additional PDL is recorded.

Table 4. Two-way interaction results

Source	SS	df	MS	F	p
LDFS * INSC	3.741	1	3.741	.592	.442
LDFS * PSE	3.500	1	3.500	.554	.457
LDFS * BD	238.565	1	238.565	37.764	.000*
LDFS * WFL	2.790	1	2.790	.442	.506
LDFS * WFT	7.019E-02	1	7.019E-02	.011	.916
LDFS * MA	18.429	1	18.429	2.917	.088
LDFS * CDC	.304	1	.304	.048	.826
INSC * PSE	6.159	1	6.159	.975	.324
INSC * BD	.441	1	.441	.070	.792
INSC * WFL	18.540	1	18.540	2.935	.087
INSC * WFT	8.060	1	8.060	1.276	.259
INSC * MA	7.424	1	7.424	1.175	.279
INSC * CDC	3.170	1	3.170	.502	.479
PSE * BD	.743	1	.743	.118	.732
PSE * WFL	8.382	1	8.382	1.327	.250
PSE * WFT	1.695	1	1.695	.268	.605
PSE * MA	7.012	1	7.012	1.110	.292
PSE * CDC	.857	1	.857	.136	.713
BD * WFL	2.185	1	2.185	.346	.557
BD * WFT	14.844	1	14.844	2.350	.126
BD * MA	38.791	1	38.791	6.140	.013*
BD * CDC	6.730	1	6.730	1.065	.302
WFL * WFT	5.890E-02	1	5.890E-02	.009	.923
WFL * MA	12.627	1	12.627	1.999	.158
WFL * CDC	12.763	1	12.763	2.020	.155
WFT * MA	5.120	1	5.120	.810	.368
WFT * CDC	3.107	1	3.107	.492	.483
MA * CDC	13.499	1	13.499	2.137	.144

* $P < 0.05$

Three-Way Interaction

Three-way interaction analysis reveals uncertainty that results in additional effect on PDL when interact with two other uncertainties. Table 5 shows the three-way interaction results. If an uncertainty is not identified to be significant from the main effect analysis, it does not imply that any interactions with other uncertainties are not significant. Thus it is possible to have significant interactions between uncertainties that are themselves not significant. Four significant three-way interactions are identified, namely LDFS*PSE*WFL, INSC*PSE*MA, INSC*BD*WFL, and WFL*WFT*MA.

Table 5. Three-way interaction results

Source	SS	df	MS	F	p
LDFS * INSC * PSE	3.746	1	3.746	.593	.441
LDFS * INSC * BD	2.905	1	2.905	.460	.498
LDFS * INSC * WFL	7.418	1	7.418	1.174	.279
LDFS * INSC * WFT	1.787	1	1.787	.283	.595
LDFS * INSC * MA	17.826	1	17.826	2.822	.093
LDFS * INSC * CDC	.504	1	.504	.080	.778
LDFS * PSE * BD	1.922	1	1.922	.304	.581
LDFS * PSE * WFL	25.076	1	25.076	3.970	.047*
LDFS * PSE * WFT	.120	1	.120	.019	.890
LDFS * PSE * MA	7.984	1	7.984	1.264	.261
LDFS * PSE * CDC	2.925	1	2.925	.463	.496
LDFS * BD * WFL	2.285	1	2.285	.362	.548
LDFS * BD * WFT	3.499E-02	1	3.499E-02	.006	.941
LDFS * BD * MA	5.894	1	5.894	.933	.334
LDFS * BD * CDC	4.889	1	4.889	.774	.379
LDFS * WFL * WFT	1.390	1	1.390	.220	.639
LDFS * WFL * MA	4.289	1	4.289	.679	.410
LDFS * WFL * CDC	4.337	1	4.337	.687	.407
LDFS * WFT * MA	1.072	1	1.072	.170	.680
LDFS * WFT * CDC	5.557	1	5.557	.880	.348
LDFS * MA * CDC	2.810	1	2.810	.445	.505
INSC * PSE * BD	1.149E-02	1	1.149E-02	.002	.966
INSC * PSE * WFL	5.699	1	5.699	.902	.342
INSC * PSE * WFT	6.791E-03	1	6.791E-03	.001	.974
INSC * PSE * MA	43.305	1	43.305	6.855	.009*
INSC * PSE * CDC	3.237	1	3.237	.512	.474
INSC * BD * WFL	29.125	1	29.125	4.610	.032*
INSC * BD * WFT	1.551	1	1.551	.245	.620
INSC * BD * MA	.309	1	.309	.049	.825
INSC * BD * CDC	4.253	1	4.253	.673	.412
INSC * WFL * WFT	8.392	1	8.392	1.328	.249
INSC * WFL * MA	14.411	1	14.411	2.281	.131
INSC * WFL * CDC	7.622E-02	1	7.622E-02	.012	.913
INSC * WFT * MA	16.836	1	16.836	2.665	.103
INSC * WFT * CDC	5.130	1	5.130	.812	.368
INSC * MA * CDC	7.289E-03	1	7.289E-03	.001	.973
PSE * BD * WFL	9.729	1	9.729	1.540	.215
PSE * BD * WFT	2.459	1	2.459	.389	.533
PSE * BD * MA	8.607	1	8.607	1.363	.243
PSE * BD * CDC	.474	1	.474	.075	.784
PSE * WFL * WFT	1.353	1	1.353	.214	.644
PSE * WFL * MA	17.624	1	17.624	2.790	.095
PSE * WFL * CDC	14.235	1	14.235	2.253	.134
PSE * WFT * MA	1.964	1	1.964	.311	.577
PSE * WFT * CDC	5.912	1	5.912	.936	.334
PSE * MA * CDC	7.584	1	7.584	1.201	.273
BD * WFL * WFT	1.766	1	1.766	.280	.597
BD * WFL * MA	.779	1	.779	.123	.726
BD * WFL * CDC	6.426	1	6.426	1.017	.313
BD * WFT * MA	2.190	1	2.190	.347	.556
BD * WFT * CDC	5.017	1	5.017	.794	.373
BD * MA * CDC	.179	1	.179	.028	.866
WFL * WFT * MA	30.846	1	30.846	4.883	.027*
WFL * WFT * CDC	9.779	1	9.779	1.548	.214
WFL * MA * CDC	8.887	1	8.887	1.407	.236
WFT * MA * CDC	2.675	1	2.675	.424	.515

* $P < 0.05$

Delay of parent parts of the purchase parts that are affected by LDFS could easily be delayed again by other uncertainties. As time zone changes, PSE is found to be interactive because set-up/change-over routine will be distorted and therefore resulting in further delay at the machine-oriented resources. This condition triggers WFL to occur because labour that was scheduled to work on the parts will now not be available, as they will be working on other parts that are on scheduled. Interaction between LDFS, PSE, and WFL is found frequently occurring and hence producing significant additional effect to PDL. Both PSE and WFL are examples of uncertainties that are themselves not significant but creating significant interactive effect.

INSC is found to be not significant in the main effects analysis. INSC has the same type of knock-on effect as LDFS, with the extension that it also affects manufacture parts. Delay resulting from INSC at parts affected or parent parts are found to be frequently being delayed again by PSE and MA. The same condition for the earlier discussion of interactive effect from LDFS and PSE can be applied here. It is found that if the delayed parts whether have been affected directly or indirectly, are affected also by MA, significant additional PDL is recorded. As MA is significant on its own and produces compound effect, the significant interaction found between INSC, PSE, and MA is not surprising.

Delay resulting from INSC at parts affected or parent parts are found to be frequently being delayed again, this time by BD and WFL. When the delayed parts are routed to a broken down machine or being processed by a yet broken down machine, then additional PDL will be recorded. These delays will result in labour that was scheduled to be consumed, now being located to others on-scheduled work, therefore producing WFL effect. The interaction between INSC, BD, and WFL is found to produce significant additional effect on PDL.

When WFL and WFT affect the same part twice at different time, additional PDL will be recorded. This can easily happen because completions of all manufacture orders require input from labour and tool. If MA also affects the parts, then further delay will be resulted due to resources unavailability. Since the frequency of this condition is found to be high, interaction between WFL, WFT, and MA has produced significant additional effect on PDL.

Conclusion

The literature review showed that knowledge of the performance of an ERP-controlled manufacturing supply chain when perturbed by several significant uncertainties simultaneously is not as widespread as it should have been. This chapter discussed the developmental and experimental work on modelling uncertainty within an ERP-controlled multi-product, multi-level dependent demand planning and scheduling system in a simulation model programmed using SIMAN within ARENA simulation software, and analysed the effects of uncertainty on late delivery.

Two important challenges faced during development of the simulation model were resolved. They were the problems of modelling the parent-child dependency logic and release timeliness in a finite manufacturing and scheduling environment. To overcome these problems, some additional attributes and conditional sub-routines were programmed.

Sensitivity study for the simulation model identified PDL to be more sensitive and provided an accurate performance measure of effect of uncertainty. Experimental design of eight uncertainties, each at two levels was modelled. The levels set were based on sensitivity of the response and with reflects to industrial reality. Data from a real case company was used to parameterise the model.

A total of 1,534 simulation run was made to ensure normal distributed responses were obtained. Simulations results were analysed in ANOVA. The main effects analysis identified four significant uncertainties to PDL, namely LDFS, BD, MA, and CDC. It was concluded that the levels of significant uncertainties should be minimised to reduce PDL. Some uncertainties were found significantly interactive in two and three-way. This finding suggested that it is extremely difficult to accurately enumerate the effect of combinations of uncertainties.

To provide a criterion for decision-making, knock-on, and compound effects were identified and introduced. Compound effect was found most unpredictable because it affects products indirectly due to its volatile nature. It can be concluded that the compound effects from BD, MA, and CDC should be tackled most urgently. Since the knock-on effect from LDFS is more predictable, its effect can be tackled much more easily.

References

Brennan, L., & Gupta, S. M. (1993). A structured analysis of material requirements planning systems under combined demand and supply uncertainty. *International Journal of Production Research, 31*, 1689-1707.

Duchessi, P., Schaninger, C. M., & Hobbs, D. R. (1989). Implementing a manufacturing planning and control information system. *California Management Review Journal, 31*(3).

Enns, S. T. (2001). MRP performance effects due to lot size and planned lead time settings. *International Journal of Production Research, 39*(3), 461-480.

Geary, S., Disney, S. M., & Towill, D. R. (2006). On bullwhip in supply chains-historical review, present practice and expected future impact. *International Journal of Production Economics, 101*(1), 2-18.

Grasso, E. T., & Taylor, B. W. (1984). A simulation based experimental investigation of supply/timing uncertainty in MRP systems. *International Journal of Production Research, 22*, 485-497.

Ho, C. J., & Carter, P. L. (1996). An investigation of alternative dampening procedures to cope with MRP system nervousness. *International Journal of Production Research, 34*(1), 137-156.

Ho, C. J., & Ireland, T. C. (1998). Correlating MRP system nervousness with forecast errors. *International Journal of Production Research, 36*, 2285-2299.

Ho, C. J., Law, W. K., & Rampal, R. (1995). Uncertainty dampening methods for reducing MRP system nervousness. *International Journal of Production Research, 33*, 483-496.

Homem-De-Mello, T., Shapiro, A., & Spearman, M. L. (1999). Finding optimal material release times using simulation-based optimisation. *International Journal of Management Science, 45*(1), 86-102.

Koh, S. C. L., & Gunasekaran, A. (2006). A knowledge management approach for managing uncertainty in manufacturing. *Industrial Management and Data Systems, 106*(4), 439-459.

Koh, S. C. L., & Saad, S. M. (2002). Development of a business model for diagnosing uncertainty in ERP environments. *International Journal of Production Research, 40*(13), 3015-3039.

Koh, S. C. L., & Saad, S. M. (2006). Managing uncertainty in ERP-controlled manufacturing environments in SMEs. *International Journal of Production Economics, 101*(1), 109-127.

Koh, S. C. L., Saad, S. M., & Jones, M. H. (2002). Uncertainty under MRP-planned manufacture: Review and categorisation. *International Journal of Production Research, 40*(10), 2399-2421.

Koh, S. C. L., & Tan, K. H. (2006). Translating knowledge of supply chain uncertainty into business strategy and actions. *Journal of Manufacturing Technology Management, 17*(4), 472-485.

Krupp, J. A. G. (1997). Safety stock management. *Production and Inventory Management Journal*, 3rd quarter, 11-18.

Mather, H. (1977). Reschedule the reschedules you just rescheduled—way of life for MRP? *Production and Inventory Management Journal, 18*, 60-79.

Moon, Y. B., & Phatak, D. (2005). Enhancing ERP system's functionality with discrete event simulation. *Industrial Management and Data Systems, 105*(9), 1206-1224.

Murthy, D. N. P., & Ma, L. (1996). Material planning with uncertain product quality. *International Journal of Production Planning and Control, 7*(6), 566-576.

New, C., & Mapes, J. (1984). MRP with high uncertainty yield losses. *Journal of Operations Management, 4,* 315-330.

Parnaby, J. (1988). A systems approach to the implementation of JIT methodologies in Lucas Industries. *International Journal of Production Research, 26*(3).

Pegden, D, Shannon, R. E., & Sadowski, R. P. (1995). *Introduction to simulation using SIMAN/C* (2nd ed.). McGraw-Hill.

Saad, S. M., & Gindy, N. N. (1998). Handling internal and external disturbances in responsive manufacturing environments. *International Journal of Production Planning and Control, 9*(8), 760-770.

Tinham, B. (1999). The MRP/ERP user satisfaction survey 1999. *Manufacturing Computer Solutions, 5*(7), 25-29.

Wight, O. (1981). *Manufacturing resource planning: MRPII.* Essex Junction: Oliver Wight Limited Publications, USA.

Yang, C. O., & Pei, H. N. (1999). Developing a STEP-based integration environment to evaluate the impact of an engineering change on MRP. *International Journal of Advanced Manufacturing Technology, 15*(11), 769-779.

Yusuf, Y. Y., & Little, D. (1998). An empirical investigation of enterprise-wide integration of MRPII. *International Journal of Operations and Production Management, 18*(1), 66-86.

Chapter IV

Software Architectures and Requirements for a Web-Based Survey System

Dirk Baldwin, University of Wisconsin-Parkside, USA

Suresh Chalasani, University of Wisconsin-Parkside, USA

Abstract

Many businesses obtain feedback by surveying customers and business partners. Increasingly, these surveys are conducted via the Web. This chapter reviews briefly literature regarding Web-based surveys and describes a software architecture for a Web-based survey system. The architecture for the survey system is based on three-tiers comprised of a Web server, Web application server, and database server. The Web application server hosts the application modules that display and process the surveys. The application software consists of packages for establishing connections to the database and for reading static and dynamic data from the database. The processed surveys are written to the database with the survey responses. This system allows for anonymous survey responses and maintains user confidentiality. At the University of Wisconsin-Parkside, we have implemented this Web-based survey system, and used it to conduct three different surveys. This survey system is easily extensible to new surveys, and is used for instructional purposes to teach server-side programming.

In this chapter, we discuss the key ideas behind the design and implementation of the extensible survey system, and provide results on its application.

Introduction

Maintaining a high-level of customer satisfaction is critical for any business to succeed. Especially in today's difficult economic environment where economic growth is limited by intense competition, businesses are seeking to improve customer satisfaction with their products. Traditionally, businesses have obtained feedback from their customers using surveys. These surveys used to be conducted via paper or telephone. However, with the advent of the Internet an increasing number of businesses are conducting surveys via the Web. Businesses prefer electronic commerce (or e-commerce) because of the inherent advantages such as increased efficiency and reduced costs associated with selling products. Consumers are attracted by the ease of shopping, the ability to search among different brands and products in less time, and the reduction in the overall costs. As businesses use the Internet to sell their products, many have concluded that it is cost effective and convenient to conduct surveys using the same medium.

In this chapter, we first review general advantages, disadvantages, and recommendations regarding Web surveys discussed in the literature. Next, we describe a Web-based survey system that we developed at the University of Wisconsin-Parkside. We discuss the software architecture for this survey system and the processes involved in constructing the system. One guiding principle of this system is that it should be easily extensible to conduct new surveys. We have used this system at UW-Parkside (UWP) to conduct three different surveys. The system uses server-side Java programs such as servlets and Java Server Pages (JSPs). We have also used this survey system for pedagogical purposes. That is, it is used to teach students how to model/construct survey databases and develop server-side Java programs.

The remainder of this book chapter is organized as follows. The next section gives an overview of the existing literature on Web-based survey systems. The third section describes a general architecture for Web-based survey systems. The fourth section briefly describes a few commercial survey applications, and provides a critical difference analysis of our approach versus the approach of the commercial software vendors. The fifth section describes the processes involved in conducting a Web-based survey. The sixth section discusses a high level software architecture for the Web-based survey system that we developed at the University of Wisconsin-Parkside (UWP). The seventh section discusses the database model for the Web-based survey system. The eighth section discusses the current state of the Web-based survey project at UWP. The ninth section discusses time estimates for extending this survey system to new surveys. The final section concludes this chapter with directions for future work.

Literature on Web-Based Survey Systems

Although research regarding the effectiveness of Web-based surveys is just beginning, the number of articles addressing the topic has increased significantly over the last few years. In addition to business use of Web surveys, academics increasingly turn to the Web to conduct research. It is therefore crucial to understand the advantages and limitations of the Web as a research tool.

Although little empirical evidence exists, many researchers believe Web-based surveys offer several benefits. The benefits include:

- **Lower costs:** Web-based surveys save costs related to mailing, phone calls, and transcribing data (Davison, Li, & Kam, 2006; Healey, Macpherson, & Kuijten, 2005; Kaplowitz, Hadlock, & Levine, 2004). However, the development of the system may result in higher start-up costs (Tinglining, Parent, & Wade, 2003). The empirical results regarding cost savings are mixed (Truell, 2003).

- **Time savings:** Data is electronically entered into a database. The research process is not subject to postal delays (Davison et al., 2006) In addition, data cleansing, transcription, and validation are performed electronically upon data entry (Davison et al., 2006; Tinglining et al., 2003).

- **Enriched survey experience:** The survey can be enhanced through pictures, video, different interaction opportunities (checkboxes, rank order, text boxes), multiple typefaces, and colors (Davison et al., 2006; Tinglining et al., 2003). In one empirical study, Couper, Tourangeau, and Kenyon (2004) found that pictures influenced survey answers, but did not necessarily influence motivation to complete the survey.

- **Reach to distant target groups:** The Internet has the ability to reach many subjects that may be more difficult to reach through mail or phone (Tinglining et al., 2003)

- **Better item completion rate:** Empirical research has shown that respondents to Web surveys are more likely to complete all the questions (Fricker, Galesic, Tourangeau, & Yan, 2005; Truell, 2003).

Similarly, several disadvantages have been mentioned. Some of the disadvantages include:

- **Response rates:** Historically, Web-based surveys suffer from low response rates compared to other forms of surveys (Bosnjak, Tuten, & Wittmann, 2005; Fricker et al., 2005; Healey et al., 2005; Morrel-Samuels, 2003; Tinglining et al., 2003; Truell, 2003). In a study of IT professionals in China, Davison et al. (2006) contacted 5,000 individuals, 37% visited the Web site, and only 5.8% submitted the survey. Kaplowitz et al. (2004) found that the response rate problem can be mitigated by sending a postal mail reminder to the surveyed population.

- **Bias due to sampling errors:** Web-based surveys target those who have access to the Internet and are computer literate (Bosnjak et al., 2005; Davison et al., 2006; Fricker et al., 2005; Morrel-Samuels, 2003). This target may bias the survey results.

- **Privacy concerns:** Some individuals will not respond to Web-based surveys because of the fear that they can be tracked (Davison et al., 2006; Truell, 2003). On the other hand, some respondents believe that the Internet is more private than paper or the phone (Davison et al., 2006).

- **Multiple submissions:** Depending upon the design of the survey, a respondent may be able to submit multiple survey responses, biasing the results (Davison et al., 2006; Truell, 2003).

- **Technical issues:** Several studies have sited technical problems, such as a down web server (Healey et al., 2005; Truell, 2003).

- **Sugarcoating and clipping:** Poorly designed surveys frequently produce implausibly favorable results or compress the range of scores (i.e., clipping). Sometimes favorable results are caused by confidentiality concerns (e.g., using a Web survey on a company Web server to provide feedback on management). Some believe that sugarcoating and clipping are common in Web-based surveys (Morrel-Samuels, 2003).

The disadvantage of Web-based surveys is a serious concern. Morrel-Samuels (2003, p. 16) warns, "Web surveys typically yield higher scores than print surveys, lower response rates, a more restricted range of responses (fewer very high or very low scores), and a host of other distortions. But in our experience designing, executing, and troubleshooting surveys for large companies like Disney, EDS, Xerox, Fallon Clinic, and GM, we've found that each of these problems can be corrected if they are properly understood."

One way to enhance the reliability of Web surveys is by carefully crafting the survey design. Several design features have been suggested:

- Keep the Web pages simple, easy to use, and efficient to load (Truell, 2003).

- Build the survey dynamically based upon the user's response (Tinglining et al., 2003).
- Build the system for a variety of browsers (Tinglining et al., 2003).
- Use instant error checking (Morrel-Samuels, 2003).
- Provide a progress bar that indicates how much longer the survey will take (Truell, 2003). A study by Healey et al. (2005) did not find that this feature influenced the response rate on the survey, however.
- Adjust the format so that scales are centered in order to reduce the sugarcoating and clipping effect (Morrel-Samuels, 2003).
- To augment fears about confidentiality, move the Web survey off the company Intranet to a secure third party server (Morrel-Samuels, 2003).

The advantages, disadvantages, and design suggestions suggest that generic Web-based survey systems be designed in an extensible fashion so that the best practices can be incorporated into newly-developed surveys.

General Architecture of E-Commerce Systems

Many Web-based survey systems can be thought of as business-to-consumer (B2C) Internet applications, since customers (consumers) use the Web-based survey system to provide data to the business. This data is processed by the business to analyze the strengths and weaknesses of their products, service and operations. The concept of B2C applications is simple on the surface, but building and deploying these systems presents serious technical challenges (Allamaraju et al., 2001a; Pyke et al., 2001). Computing systems for use in the Internet age must be designed carefully to meet the performance demands of the users while protecting the information privy to the business and the users with stringent security measures.

To develop applications with Internet technologies, we need to integrate processes with the Web to achieve the best return on the IT investments. To do this, it is important to consider the following elements:

- Robust software architectures for accessing data via the Internet; and
- Efficient database infrastructure for storing and retrieving data.

It is widely accepted that the thin-client model is the de facto standard when it comes to developing Web applications. Typically, a thin-client application is most readily associated with a browser-hosted user interface (UI), which is dynamically generated and sent to the client, in the form of HTML, by the server. It is considered thin because clients of Web applications are expected to have a browser pre-installed on their machine so the application need only focus on feeding the browser UI instructions it can understand and use to build a presentation to the end user. With this configuration, Web clients are essentially dummy terminals that send requests to the server, where all the business logic and data source integration occurs (Allamaraju et al., 2001b).

A typical information system model for a B2C system, based on thin-client architecture, is shown in Figure 1. User requests for information from the business may first pass through the firewall. User requests are intercepted by the Web server, which services simple requests (for example, requests for static HTML pages or images). More complex requests that involve execution of business logic and/or retrieval of information from the database are forwarded by the Web server to the Web application server. Such requests that require execution of business logic are executed by the application code running under the Web application server. The application code first may authenticate the user against the security database and may interact with multiple databases to execute a single user request. In this model, a user interacts with the business via a browser such as Internet Explorer and the user requests as well as business responses are transmitted back and forth using the Hypertext Transfer Protocol (HTTP).

In the rest of this chapter, we will use this information system model for developing and implementing a Web-based survey system. Typical hardware and software technology choices for implementing this information system model are indicated in Table 1.

Figure 1. General thin-client architecture for B2C applications

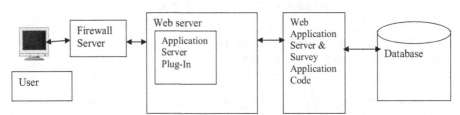

Table 1. Technology choices for a typical B2C information system

Component	Typical Technology Choices (Hardware)	Typical Technology Choices (Software)	Operating System Choices
Application Server	IBM RS/6000 or SUN or HP Servers or Windows 2000 Servers	For IBM/SUN/HP Servers IBM Websphere or BEA Systems Weblogic with Java application code For Windows 2000 Servers Microsoft .NET Platform with C# or VB .Net application code	IBM AIX or Sun Solaris or HP Unix or Windows 2000
Databases	IBM RS/6000 or SUN or HP Unix Servers	Oracle 9i or IBM DB2 or Sybase	IBM AIX, Sun Solaris, HP Unix
Firewall Servers	Windows 2000 Servers or SUN or HP Unix servers	N/A	Windows 2000 or Sun Solaris or HP Unix

Existing Web-Based Survey Systems

Several commercial systems for conducting Web-based surveys have been developed by different vendors. Examples of such Web-based survey systems include Survey Said Survey Software (2006), Perseus Corporation's Survey Solutions System (2006), and Net Reflector's Online Survey System (2006). All these survey systems can be easily implemented, allow quick dissemination of results and can be easily extended to conduct new surveys. However, the cost of the software including installation and license costs appear to be very expensive for small businesses. For example, Net Reflector's pricing is based on each survey that is received through the system. That is, if the system receives 10,000 responses, it will cost the business $10,000, which is about $1 per survey. In addition, project management services for conducting surveys cost a minimum of $2,000. Other companies offer fixed pricing. Even with fixed pricing, site licenses cost anywhere from $2,999 to $6,999 with the Internet survey machine system. Persues Corporation charges $2,985 per end user for commercial licenses with recurring annual license/maintenance costs.

Another option for conducting surveys is to partner with companies that host the surveys including the survey data. Two such examples are SurveyMonkey.com and Zoomerang.com. Hosting surveys at these sites is fairly inexpensive, and they offer customers a variety of options ranging from leasing the site for surveys to using the site for free. The "free" option does not give the survey customers too many choices.

Due to these costs, it is difficult to purchase a survey system for small businesses. The case in point is the survey systems needed in an academic environment. For example, at the University of Wisconsin-Parkside, we needed to conduct multiple surveys via the Internet. Due to the limited budget, purchasing, and maintaining a commercial survey software system was deemed prohibitively expensive. As a result, we decided to develop and implement our own Web-based survey system. This decision has the following advantages:

Table 2. Critical difference analysis between purchasing a commercial survey soft-ware system, hosting surveys at survey companies such as SurveyMonkey.com and developing an in-house survey software system

Criteria	Purchasing a Commercial Survey Software System	Hosting Surveys at survey companies such as SurveyMonkey.com	Developing In-House Survey Software System
Overall Cost	Con	Pro	Pro
Ability to teach students web development	Con	Con	Pro
Alignment with the current IBM Websphere-based web infrastructure at UWP	Con	Con	Pro
Ease of maintenance	Con	Pro	Pro
Ability to customize the survey system for UWP's needs	Con	Pro	Pro
Ability to conduct any general survey	Pro	Pro	Con

- Limited cost for developing, implementing, and maintaining the Web-based survey system. Costs are limited because student-time and effort can be utilized for constructing the survey system.

- Ability to customize the survey system to our specific needs.

- Ease of maintaining the in-house developed system versus maintaining an external system.

- Ability to teach students the techniques of web development.

Table 2 provides a critical difference analysis of the two approaches: purchasing and implementing a commercial survey system, hosting the surveys at survey companies such as SurveyMonkey.com versus developing a Web-based survey system in-house.

Based on this critical difference analysis, we decided to develop a Web-based survey system. The following section details the processes involved in conducting a survey using a Web-based survey system.

Processes Involved in Conducting Web-Based Surveys

There are several processes involved in conducting Web-based surveys. To discuss these processes, we first describe different personnel involved in conducting Web surveys.

1. **Survey administrator:**

   - Designs the survey questions, the type of response (free-text or multiple choice, etc.), and the possible responses for each question.

   - Works with the developer to ensure that the survey questions are presented correctly in the HTML pages.

   - Advertises the survey to its intended audience.

   - Obtains survey results electronically and processes them using a statistical package such as SAS (SAS Institute, 2006).

2. **Survey developer:**

   - Designs and develops the database to hold survey questions and survey responses.

   - Develops the HTML content for presenting survey questions and appropriate choices to the user.

   - Develops application code that processes survey responses when each user completes and submits the Web-based survey.

   - Extracts the survey results and communicates the survey results to the survey administrator in a pre-determined format.

   - Maintains the survey system and ensures its availability to the users as per a service-level agreement.

3. **Survey user:**

   - Completes and submits the Web-based survey.

For the sake of simplicity, we have indicated only three roles—survey administrator, survey developer and survey user—in the earlier discussion. Some of these roles can be expanded. For example, the survey developer role can be expanded into survey designer, survey developer and survey support roles. Based on this discussion, Figure 2 indicates the use cases involved in conducting Web-based surveys.

Arriving at survey questions and appropriate response choices is highly dependent on the survey and is done by the survey administrator. Similarly, advertising the survey to its intended audience is often accomplished using e-mail lists and advertising the survey on a related Web site. In this chapter, we mainly consider the activities related to the survey developer. That is, we discuss the database and application designs for the survey systems and the ease of extending this system to conduct new surveys. The next section describes a high-level software architecture for the Web-based survey system.

Figure 2. A use case model for processes involved in conducting Web-based surveys

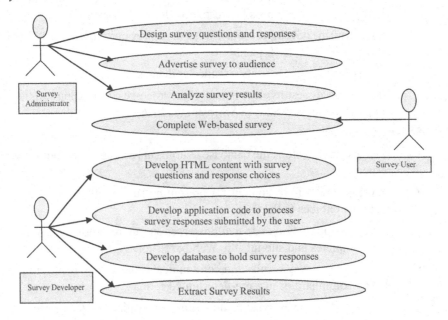

A Software Architecture for
Web-Based Survey System

Three principles influenced the software architecture of the Web-based survey system.

1. **Easy extensibility:** The software must be easily extended to conduct new surveys. This is a key principle since we anticipate a growing need for surveys at the University of Wisconsin-Parkside from different research groups. Ability to modify and extend the software to new surveys without spending too much time is important so that the faculty and staff can conduct new surveys.

2. **Easy understandability:** Design and code must be easily understood. This is important because of the turnover of students in the MIS program. Knowledge transfer to a new group of students becomes much simpler when the code is easy to understand. To achieve this goal, we followed standard design guidelines for documenting the design using class diagrams and sequence diagrams as proposed in the UML (Unified Modeling Language) methodology

(Arrington, 2001). In addition, the code developed in this project is thoroughly commented.

3.   **Ease of implementation:** We have two different platforms at UW-Parkside on which the survey software can run: an AS/400 as well as personal computers. To minimize the risk of incompatibility from one platform to another, we are using Java as the standard development language. In addition, we will be developing implementation plans for each platform so that installation of the software becomes much easier.

The Web-based survey system runs using the following software components:

*   **Web Application Server:** IBM Websphere 3.5.3 (to be upgraded to Websphere 4.0)
*   **Database:** Microsoft Access 2000 (to be migrated to IBM DB2)
*   **Application Code:**
    1.   HTML pages for presenting the survey
    2.   Java server pages (JSP) code for receiving survey responses and processing survey responses
    3.   Server-side Java code for formatting the survey responses and writing the survey responses to the database.

Different packages/modules in the application code and their interaction are depicted in Figure 3. These modules are discussed in detail next.

Figure 3. Software architecture for Web-based survey system

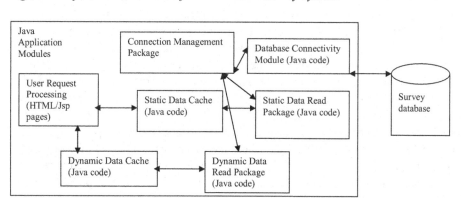

User Request Processing Module

This module receives requests from the user via the Web server and is responsible for parsing and obtaining the parameters of the user request. For example, if the user request is for the first page of the survey, the corresponding HTML page for the survey is returned to the user. On the other hand, if the user completes and submits the survey, the user's submit request is handled by a JSP page (named ProcessSurvey.jsp). Such user requests are HTTP requests and may contain parameters such as the following:

- **User ID:** The unique ID for the user. This could be the session ID for the user's browser session or the login ID for the user, if the survey system requires the user to login.

- **Question number and Response choice:** This contains the unique survey question number and the response choice filled by the user for this question.

- **User's details:** User's name and address (if the user wishes to provide those details)

User request processing module interacts with both the static data to obtain survey question related data, and the dynamic data to write user responses to the database.

Static Data vs. Dynamic Data

We label the data that changes frequently or the data that is specific to a single user's request as "dynamic" data. Examples of this data include responses entered by a single user to a survey questions. Similarly, we label data that changes infrequently as "static" data. Examples of this data include survey questions and possible choices of answers for each survey question. A significant amount of data in the Web-based survey system is static, since survey questions and possible choices for answering a survey question are known prior to the user completing the survey. We distinguish between static and dynamic data, since we design the software architecture differently for the two types of data. Static data is read and stored by the application in memory cache at the beginning of the application (before any user accesses the survey application). In other words, static data is brought into the cache before it is used or required; static data is pre-cached. This is *not* wasteful of memory space, especially since the memory costs are very low these days (with each 1MB of memory costing approximately $1). In our design, static data is read and pre-cached when the application server (see Figure 1) is started; starting of the application server will trigger the survey system's application code which in turn triggers reading of static data and pre-caching of data inside the application server.

Static Data Read Package and Static Data Cache Package

Static data cache module shown in Figure 3 refers to the packages and classes that hold different surveys, survey questions, and possible responses. In our architecture, data for different surveys is held in different packages. For example, all the static survey data related to the first survey is saved in classes that belong to the following package:

edu.uwp.survey.staticdata.survey1

Reading of the static data is facilitated by the package labeled "Static Data Read" in Figure 3. This package is named:

edu.uwp.survey.staticdata.read

It has classes such as SurveyReadAccessBean and SurveyReadAccessHome. This Java code is developed so that there is only one copy of these classes (objects) in memory, so different users reuse the same memory copy; this leads to increased efficiency of user request processing. Reading of static data and storing the information in the memory cache is facilitated by using the connection management and database connectivity modules.

Dynamic Data Read Package and Dynamic Data Cache Package

These are very similar to the static data packages discussed previously, except that they pertain to dynamic data such as individual user responses to survey questions.

Connection Management Package

Database connections are used to read from and update the survey database. To serve hundreds of simultaneous users, we maintain a pool of database connections in the application code. This pool is managed using a robust connection management algorithm whose principles are outlined in the following:

- **Step 1:** Check whether the connection pool is empty.
- **Step 2:** If the pool is not empty, retrieve a connection from the pool; otherwise, create a new connection to the database.
- **Step 3:** Check whether the connection obtained from the pool in step 2 is a valid connection by verifying that:
  - ○ The connection is still open, and
  - ○ The connection has not been timed out by the database.

For more details on this algorithm and performance results, the user is referred to Chalasani and Boppana (2005). The connection management package interacts with the database connectivity package (see Figure 3) to read data from or write data to the database.

Database Connectivity Module

These modules contain Java database connectivity (JDBC) drivers for different databases. For example, the following table indicates a few JDBC drivers for some of the existing vendors:

Vendor	JDBC Package
MySQL	org.gjt.mm.mysql.Driver
Oracle	oracle.jdbc.driver.OracleDriver
Sybase	intersolv.jdbc.driver
IBM DB2/UDB	com.ibm.db2.jdbc.app.db2driver

Figure 3 represents the Java software modules needed for Web-based processing of user requests. However, not all data processing in the survey system takes place via the Web. For example, extraction of survey results is done by the survey developer, and these results are used by the survey administrator. To extract survey results, we have designed a data-extraction Java module (see Figure 4). This data-extraction module can be invoked by an administrative user, and is used to import results from any survey database into a flat-file or a comma-separated-value (csv) file. The data-extraction module shown in Figure 4 also heavily uses the connection management package and the database connectivity packages discussed earlier and depicted in Figure 3. However, for the sake of clarity, they are not included in Figure 4.

Figure 4. Software modules for extracting data from the survey database

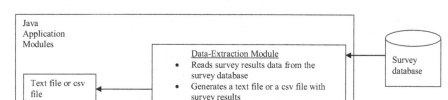

A Database Model for the
Web-Based Survey System

The key to designing databases for the Web-based survey system consists of separating the functionality between the survey data and the user data needed for security/authentication. In the following sub-sections, we provide a description of the sample database tables for each of these two areas.

Sample Database Tables for the Survey Data

The database model for the survey system is shown in Figure 5. This data model contains several tables. The Survey_Question table contains all possible questions in the survey. Each question receives a unique number and the question text (Question_Description). In addition, how a question should be displayed on the Web is indicated in this table. For example, some questions may be displayed with the responses in the form of radio buttons where a user is forced to select only one of the choices, while some others may be displayed as check boxes which allow the users to select more than one option. Question_Display table consists of all possible display choices such as check-boxes, text-boxes, drop-down lists, and radio buttons. The Survey_Question table also contains columns to indicate in which section a particular question should be displayed, and the relative position of a question within each section.

The Survey_Question_Possible_Responses table shows all possible valid responses for a question. For example, a question such as "How do you rate the service at the library?" may have five possible choices: (1) Poor, (2) Fair, (3) Good, (4) Very Good, (5) Excellent. All five choices are included as separate rows in the Survey_Question_Possible_Responses table. Depending on the Question_Display_Code, these

Figure 5. A database model for the extensible Web-based survey system

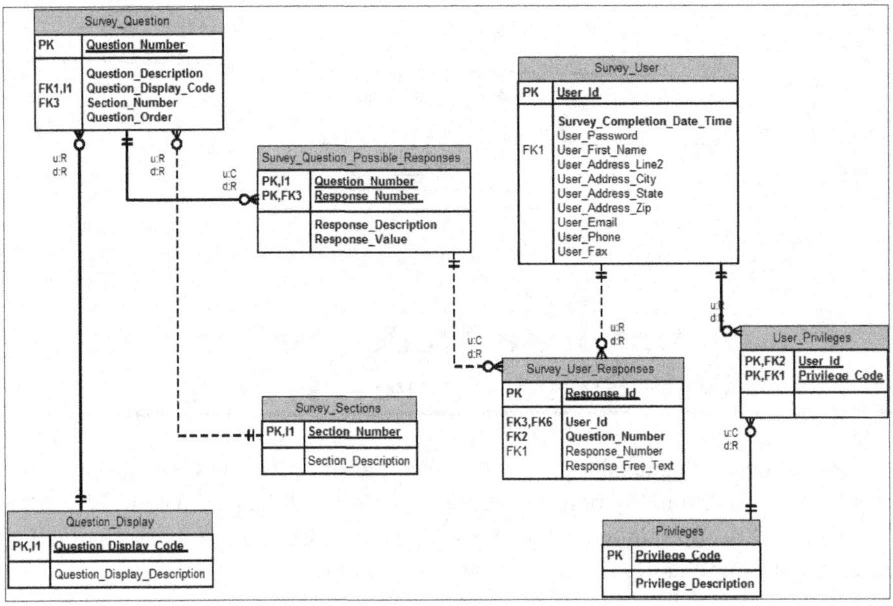

choices will be displayed as radio buttons, check-boxes, drop-down boxes, or some other format. For open-ended questions, where the user types free-form text as a response, the Survey_Question_Possible_Responses table may not contain any corresponding entries.

The Survey_User table consists of information on the users who took the survey. For some surveys, user information is not required, since they can be administered anonymously. Hence, almost all columns in the Survey_User table are non-required columns. The User_Id is generated by the software and assigned to each user who takes the survey. In addition, Survey_Completion_Date_Time is written when the user submits the survey results. The password field is used only when the users need to login to take the surveys.

Survey_user_responses table contains the response to each question by each individual user. The response_id is a unique, automatically-generated, number assigned to each response written to this table. It also contains the question number, and the unique anonymous id for each user. For free-text responses where the users can type text into text boxes, the response typed by the user is saved in the field response_free_text. Otherwise, the user response is captured in the response_number column. This response_number column refers to a possible response for the question (from among a list of choices) in the Survey_Question_Possible_Responses table.

The relationships between these tables are also shown in Figure 5. In Figure 5, relationships with solid lines indicate identifying relationships, which means that the foreign key from tables appears as part of the primary key in the related table. On the other hand, relationships with dashed lines indicate non-identifying relationships. In addition, each column (field) indicated in bold letters is a required field. The primary keys in the data model are indicated using PK, while the foreign keys are indicated using FKi. The relationships are one-to-many in nature between the master table and its dependent table. All relationships are built to enforce referential integrity, according to which updates in the master table are propagated (or cascaded) to the dependent tables and the deletion of records in the master table are prohibited as long as there are related records in the dependent tables. The cascaded updates are indicated in this data model using the notation u:C, while the restricted delete operations are indicated using d:R.

Database Tables for Authentication and Security

In our design, we assign security/authentication levels to each user of the survey system. Recall the users of the system can be any user who wishes to complete the survey or a survey administrator. The survey administrator has more privileges than an outside user. For example, the administrative user can modify the survey question data in the database and extract survey data (see Figure 4).

This privilege structure can be implemented completely in the application code. But implementing the privileges in the application may lead to frequent changes to the application code, if the rules on who needs to access which information changes frequently. Hence, we use a database table for saving the privilege information for each user. The Privileges table contains all possible privileges that users can be assigned. User_Privileges table contains information on privileges for individual users (see Figure 5).

Table 2. Privileges to complete surveys or to view/modify/extract survey data

User Type	View Only Privileges	Modify Privileges
Survey Administrator	Can view all survey data. Can extract survey data into a text-file or csv file.	Can modify only data related to survey questions.
Ordinary User via the World Wide Web.	Can view survey questions and appropriate response choices	No privileges to modify except completing and submitting survey data.

Application of the Survey System

We have used the Web-based survey system to conduct three distinct surveys at the University of Wisconsin-Parkside (UWP). These three surveys are discussed next.

Department of Business Student Survey System

This survey is intended to obtain anonymous feedback from students in the Department of Business at UWP. This survey is organized into approximately six sections, with each section containing anywhere between 20 and 40 questions. This survey has the following unique requirements:

- *(R1) Each student should be able to complete the survey only once.*

  This requirement has the following implications on the survey software.

  a. This required us to import the student data, including their unique student ID numbers, into our own database. Student data is obtained as a text file from a campus-wide master database on students, and was loaded into our survey database system into the users table. Loading the student data required additional Java code to be developed.

  b. Each student is required to indicate his unique student ID number before taking the survey. This did not pose technical challenges, but it did raise usability concerns. Since the survey was intended to be anonymous, asking the students to type their unique student ID number may have raised some concerns. However, this was addressed by placing a disclaimer that the student ID is only used to make sure that each student completes the survey only once and that it is used to identify the winners of the "26th respondents" (see requirement R2).

  c. After a student completed the survey, that student's record is flagged as having completed the survey. If the same student logs in again into the system, he is not allowed to submit the survey.

- *(R2) Every 26th respondent who completes the survey should receive gift-certificates for the University bookstore.*

  This function required the survey software to identify the 26th respondents of the survey. We accomplished this by generating a unique number (beginning at 1) for each respondent in sequential order, and identifying the student ID for the respondents whose unique numbers was divisible by 26.

AACSB Preparedness Survey System

This survey is intended to obtain anonymous feedback from the deans and other significant personnel at the schools (or departments) of business around the country concerning their school's preparedness for accreditation from AACSB (The Association to Advance Collegiate Schools of Business). This survey is also organized into approximately six sections, with each section containing about 10-20 questions. This survey did not require any special requirements, unlike the student survey system described previously. Users, if willing, were allowed to submit their e-mail addresses, for the dissemination of the survey results.

Ethics in Accounting Survey System

This survey is intended to obtain anonymous feedback from accounting instructors nationwide at different departments of business on how the ethics component is integrated into their accounting classes. This survey is organized into approximately four sections, with each section containing about 10-20 questions. This survey did not require any special requirements, unlike the student survey system described previously.

Table 3 provides a summary of the responses received for these surveys.

The survey administrators for the first two surveys (student survey system and AACSB preparedness survey system) feel that the number of responses for their surveys is adequate to interpret data and draw conclusions.

Table 3. Comparison of three surveys conducted using the Web-based survey system

Comparison Criteria	Department of Business Student Survey System	AACSB Preparedness Survey System	Ethics in Accounting Survey System
Intended Audience	Students in the department of business at UW-Parkside	Deans and other significant personnel of the schools of business nationwide	Accounting instructors at the departments of business nationwide
Maximum Number Who May Complete the Survey	665	Approximately 600	Approximately 500
Number of Respondents Who Completed the Survey	145	248	48
Special Requirements	Yes	No	No
Need Users to Login	Yes	No	No
Is this Survey Ongoing or Complete	Complete	Complete	Complete
# Students Involved	2	2	2

Effort Needed to Extend this Survey System to Conduct New Surveys

One of the key design principles for our Web-based survey system is that it should be easily extensible to conduct new surveys. To indicate how easily extensible this software architecture is, in Table 4, we indicate what changes are needed to each Java module and to the database for a new survey. The Java modules shown in Table 4 were discussed in the fourth section of this chapter.

From Table 4, it is clear that most of the Java modules in the software architecture for the Web-based survey system do not require any changes for constructing a new survey. Only the survey database requires major changes while the user request processing module requires minor changes.

Next, we give the list of tasks required for a new survey and approximate time-estimates for each of these tasks.

From Table 5, the Web-based survey system can be extended to new surveys in approximately one week. Note that this estimate only includes the time needed for

Table 4. Changes needed to each component of the survey software system for each new survey

Number	Software Component	Nature of Changes	Rating of Changes (None, Minor, Medium, Major)
1	User request processing module	Change the HTML content and JSP pages for survey presentation and survey response processing	Medium
2	Static data cache and static data read packages	No changes needed	None
3	Dynamic data cache and dynamic data read packages	No changes needed	None
4	Database connectivity module	No changes needed	None
5	Connection management package	Changes needed to obtain the new survey database location from a new initialization file	Minor
6	Data extraction module	No changes needed	None
7	Survey database	No changes needed to the database schema. However, data on the new survey questions and their possible responses needs to be entered into the database tables.	Major

Table 5. Tasks and approximate time estimates to extend the survey system to a new survey

Task Number	Task Description	Who Completes this task?	Approximate Time Estimate (in hours)
1	Construct HTML Pages and make database entries for survey questions and response choices	Survey Developer	10 hours
2	Construct server-side JSP to process responses for this survey	Survey Developer	5 hours
3	Extraction of survey data	Survey Developer	5 hours
4	Testing and implementation	Survey Developer	20 hours
		TOTAL	40 hours

the tasks related to the survey information system, and does not include the time for designing the survey by the survey administrator and other tasks not related to information systems. Time estimates for such tasks as designing the survey can vary widely from survey to survey.

Note that the estimates presented in Table 5 are for students who are beginning to gain experience with HTML and server-side programming. Students with considerable experience—for example, students who have already taken the Web programming courses—generally complete the tasks presented in Table 5 in approximately 20 hours, which is about half a week.

Our results compare well with the results presented by Tinglining et al. (2003) who built a Web-based survey system using Microsoft Active Server pages, server-side Java, and MS Access database. Their project required 200 hours of analysis and coding, 25 hours of database administration, 10 hours of graphic art work related to branding, and 20 hours of project management.

Concluding Remarks and Directions for Future Work

In this chapter, we discussed the design for a Web-based survey system. We described the software architecture for the survey system in significant detail, and indicated the hardware platforms on which this survey system can run. We also demonstrated that this survey system can be easily extended to new surveys within a time-frame of two weeks.

Three principles influenced the software architecture of the Web-based survey system: easy extensibility, easy understandability, and ease of implementation. The survey system software is organized into different modules such as connection management module, modules for static and dynamic data, and modules for survey results processing. We have presented a detailed data model for storing data on survey questions, possible responses, survey users, and their responses. In addition, the data model is capable of maintaining privileges for each user.

We have used the Web-based survey system to conduct three distinct surveys at UWP. These surveys include the Department of Business student surveys, AACSB preparedness survey, and the Ethics in Accounting survey. Out of these three, a sufficient number of responses were received for the first two surveys. For each survey, appropriate reports were generated with the survey results.

This work can be extended in different ways. One direction for future research is to make the presentation layer of the survey system more robust. Currently, the database table survey question holds how the survey questions should be displayed to the user. However, with the growing popularity of hand-held devices, it is required for the survey-system to handle different display targets. This can be accomplished by improving the data model so that it can allow different display types for different end-user devices. Such an extension will also cater to the needs of persons with disabilities by arranging the display preferences; for example, use of colors can be minimized for persons with color blindness. Another direction for future research is to study the reliability and availability of the survey system: One of the key drawbacks we faced in maintaining the survey system is the aspect of unplanned outages, when the system is down for any reason. The unplanned outages could be cause of any number of reasons ranging from network outage to application server failure. Such unplanned outages make it increasingly difficult to honor the service levels agreed upon in the service-level-agreement documents. We are currently designing plans to increase the system availability using redundant servers, and study the amount of redundancy required to achieve a given service levels. Such research was conducted in the context of supply chain management systems (Chalasani & Wafa, 2004). Extending this research to B2C systems such as the Web-based survey systems is a promising direction for future research.

Acknowledgments

This research work was supported by summer research grants to the authors from the University of Wisconsin-Parkside.

References

Allamaraju, S., et al. (2001a, February). *Professional Java e-commerce*. Birmingham, UK: WROX Press.

Allamaraju, S., et al. (2001b, September). *Professional Java server programming J2EE 1.3 Edition*. Birmingham, UK: WROX Press.

Arrington, C. T. (2001). *Enterprise Java with UML*. New York: OMG Press, John Wiley & Sons.

Bosnjak, M., Tuten, T. L., & Wittmann, W. W. (2005). Unit (Non) response in Web-based access panel surveys: An extended planned-behavior approach. *Psychology & Marketing, 22*(6), 489-505.

Chalasani, S., & Boppana, R. V. (2005). Software architectures for e-commerce computing systems with external hosting. *International Journal of Computers and Applications, 27*(3), 190-198.

Chalasani, S., & Wafa, M. (2004, March). Reliable technologies for SCM information systems. *International Journal of Operations and Quantitative Management, 10*(1), 1-17.

Couper, M. P., Tourangeau, R., & Kenyon, K. (2004). Picture this! Exploring visual effects in Web surveys. *Public Opinion Quarterly, 68*(2), 255-266.

Davison, R. M., Li, Y., & Kam C. S. P. (2006). Web-based data collection in China. *Journal of Global Information Management, 14*(3), 70-89.

Fricker, S., Galesic, M., Tourangeau, R., & Yan, T. (2005). An experimental comparison of Web and telephone surveys. *Public Opinion Quarterly, 69*(1), 370-392.

Healey, B., Macpherson, T., & Kuijten, B. (2005). An empirical evaluation of three Web survey design principles. *Marketing Bulletin, 16*(2), 9 pages.

Kaplowitz, M. D., Hadlock, T. D., & Levine, R. (2004). A comparison of Web and mail survey response rates. *Public Opinion Quarterly, 68*(1), 94-101.

Morrel-Samuels, P. (2003). Web surveys' hidden hazards. *Harvard Business Review, 81*(7), 16-17.

NetReflector Online Survey Software. (2006). Retrieved July 23, 2006, from http://www.netreflector.com/software/

Perseus Survey Solutions. (2006). Retrieved July 23, 2006, from http://www.perseus.com/survey/software/efm.html

Pyke, D., et al. (2001, January 1). E-fulfillment: It's harder than it looks. *Supply Chain Management Review*, (1).

SAS Institute. (2006). Retrieved July 23, 2006, from http://www.sas.com/

Survey Said Survey Software. (2006). Retrieved July 23, 2006, from http://www.internetsurveymachine.com/

Tinglining, P., Parent, M., & Wade, M. (2003). Extending the capabilities of Internet-based research: Lessons from the field. *Internet Research, 13*(3), 223-235.

Truell, A. D. (2003). Use of Internet tools for survey research. *Information Technology, Learning, and Performance Journal, 21*(1), 31-37.

Chapter V

Identity Theft and E-Fraud Driving CRM Information Exchanges

Alan D. Smith, Robert Morris University, USA

Allen R. Lias, Robert Morris University, USA

Abstract

Fraud and identity theft have been increasing with the use of e-commerce. In the U.S. alone, it has been estimated that victims may spend on average $1,500 in out-of-pocket expenses and an average of 175 hours in order to resolve the many problems caused by such identity thieves. Organizations that engage in e-commerce as a large part of their business need to protect their customers against these crimes. An empirical study of 75 managerial employees and/or knowledge workers in five large organizations in Pittsburgh, PA, revealed a number of interesting concepts of find out how much information they share with others, what the likelihood is that they will conduct business online, and whether or not they take steps to protect their personal identity and credit. Model construction and implications were generated concerning steps that employees and customers may take to avoid identity theft.

Introduction

Consumer Relationship Management (CRM) Basics

The Web has created a world of convenience for consumers who wish to purchase or gather information about a product, but online technology and e-businesses pose as many threats as opportunities. The concern by consumers about their private information is an ongoing headache, for example, a recent search on Google for the key words "identity theft" about 79,500,000 items. Many issues by consumers have been associated with the possibility that their information could be used or stolen by cyber-criminals and abused before the consumer could find out. Several studies have been produced that show the perceptions of consumer risk and how they may be the main complication in online e-commerce in the future (Culnan, 1999; Fernandez & Miyazaki, 2001). For this reason, it is important to provide security and privacy for online users in e-business and e-commerce (Smith, 2005a, 2005b, 2005c). With security and privacy also comes the question of how much is needed?

Organizations of every conceivable size and description are automating the way they do business in order to cut costs, speed service, and reach customers, suppliers and partners more easily and in a more efficient manner. As a result of these trends associated with e-commerce, more consumer and business data are online to meet the requirements of e-commerce. Throughout much of the academic and practitioner literature, trust, privacy of information, and systems security (Drake, 2003; Smith, 2002; Smith & Rupp, 2002a, 2002b) are important reoccurring themes factors in customer retention for a firm that engages in e-commerce. For example, research by Visa USA, which helped to develop the CyberSource fraud prevention software, credit card fraud on the Web is three times as likely as it is for all other forms of card use (Smith, 2002). In addition, Smith (2002) suggested, "Addressing customer service issues are extremely critical for the firm's continued survival and long-term success, but these services are merely academic if the firm ignores to enhance customer loyalty and retention through the development of trust" (p. 156). Hence, to promote trust and confidence, managers of Web sites should educate customers about the company, its products, its security and privacy policies, and prices. Failure of an e-commerce firm to instill a sense of security and have the appropriate technology and software to actually protect personal and proprietary information will most certainly lead to customer attrition and destruction of sound customer relationship management (CRM) principles.

Since several CRM-based studies have shown that it is more expensive to continually attract new customers than it is to satisfy existing, loyal customers, the cost of customer attrition can be financially draining on an e-commerce firm. In addition, the age of e-business decreases a customer's switching costs as a competitor's product or service is just a mouse-click away (Anton & Petouhoff, 2002). In consideration of these concepts, customers who do not feel that their personal and financial information will be protected need only to inspect the next Web site for a firm that is able to meet their needs. The exponential increase in the occurrence of identity theft makes this assurance more important than ever, for both e-commerce firms and their customers.

Sources of Identity Theft

A major type of identity theft occurs when another person uses the chosen victim's personal information to open fraudulent accounts. Personal information includes, but is not limited to, name, address, drivers' license, social security number (SSN), telephone number, mothers' maiden name, bank accounts, and credit card numbers. The resulting incurred expenses often remain unknown to the victim until he/she applies for some type of credit and are subsequently denied. The reason these unauthorized charges remain unknown is because thieves typically divert the statements to another billing address. The advantage of the Internet for thieves for leveraging tools for illegal activities is that it provides world-wide accessibility, allowing them to transmit and collect information globally. Thieves may do this by using e-mails to lure victims to freely give information (as in the recent sham concerning verifying credit card information for continued use of Paypal) and/or by obtaining information found by hacking into personal files.

Today's thieves have many avenues in which to steal individual identities. While the rise in the crime rate corresponds with the growth of the Internet, less than 1% of identity theft cases can be linked to Internet usage. This may be due to a lack of ability to track the source of theft back to the Internet. It is advisable to use the Identity Theft Data Clearinghouse (a national identity theft victim complaint database containing more than 815,000 complaints) (http://www.consumer.gov/idtheft/law_invest. htm) in order to search for identity theft victim and/or suspect information across the USA. Unfortunately, the Federal Trade Commission (FTC) does not have any criminal investigation authority with respect to identity theft.

Old-fashioned thievery is still the most prevalent means of stealing identities. For example, simple techniques such as "dumpster diving" and "shoulder surfing" are identity theft's number one partner in crime. Dumpster diving occurs when thieves sift through trash to find statements or solicitations that unsuspecting individuals failed to tear up. Shoulder surfing is the term used when a thief literally look over someone's shoulder to obtain information.

Another widely used method of obtaining information is "credit-card skimming". Through enlisting the help of restaurant personal, for example, a criminal can attach a skimmer to your credit card. Typically, a skimmer is about the size of a credit card, and it collects your credit card information. When a waiter takes a customer's credit card for processing, he/she runs it through the normal credit-processing machine; it is also easy to attach a skimmer, which allows the thief to collect your credit information.

Access to SSNs may also provide a means of thievery. Once a thief has access to an individual's SSN, they have the information they need to set up dummy bank accounts, which is one of the major reasons that universities refer not to post grades by SSN. The presence of having an account allows the thief to be issued credit cards, since most card companies are eager to grant credit accounts to new customers. From there, the theft has almost unlimited buying power under their newly assumed identity. Unfortunately, SSN are commonly listed on many of the items a person carries on a daily basis, such as health insurance identification and driver license cards. This makes this information easily accessible for others.

A new and fighting trend that is surfacing includes a new type of identity thief, namely parents (Pulliam-Weston, 2004). Many parents are fraudulently taking credit out in their children's name in order to extend their own credit. This practice may eventually place families in a precocious state, causing emotional and financial strain as well as increase the potential for identity theft. Children may be victimized in at least two ways: Occurs either by parents intercepting credit offers in the mail, sent to children who are old enough to establish credit in their own right; and/or by parents using the SSNs of minor children.

Overview of the Problem

Those guilty of identity theft, as defined by the language in the Identity Theft and Assumption Deterrence Act (ITADA), are "whoever knowingly transfer or uses, without lawful authority, a means of identification of another person with the intent to commit, or otherwise promote, carry on, or facilitate any unlawful activity" (Saunders & Zucker, 1999, p. 188). Unfortunately, this phenomenon is happening at an alarming rate, becoming one of the fastest growing white-collar crimes in the U.S. Often a victim is unaware that this information has been misappropriated, and once the crime is discovered, reclaiming one's identity is a lengthy and costly process. Typically victims in the U.S. may spend on average $1,500 in out-of-pocket expenses and an average of 175 hours in order to resolve the many problems caused by such identity thieves. Until 1998 when the ITADA, which sets a maximum penalty of 15 years in prison and $250,000 fine, was passed, the primary form of consumer protection was the Fair Credit Billing Act, which only holds a cardholder liable for the first $50 of unauthorized charges.

However, the rate of identity theft and the associated financial damage caused by fraudulent purchases is exploding at a rate of approximately 300% a year. The financial loss from identity theft was expected to reach nearly $74 billion a year in the U.S. alone, and approximately $221 billion world-wide by the end of 2003. These current figures, based on a 300% compounded annual growth rate, have the estimated losses associated with identity theft to be $2 trillion by the end of 2005 (Gaudin, 2003). For example, in 2002 the Federal Trade Commission (FTC) disclosed that 161,819 cases of identity theft were reported, and that identity theft fraud complaints comprised 43% of all FTC complaints in 2002, making it the most common type of fraud that affected American consumers (Gaudin, 2003).

A determination of the prevalence of identity theft on the Internet is a problematic issue as this crime is chronically underreported. A FTC spokesperson commented that, "If you drop your wallet on the street, and the next day someone is using your account at Saks Fifth Avenue, you make the connection. If someone's using your data online and your cards are still in your wallet, it's hard to know you've been robbed" (Ray, 2003, p. 2). Essential 84% of people reporting ID fraud have no idea how the perpetrator got hold of their information.

The incredible growth of the Internet, coupled with the universal acceptance of information technology (IT) for conducting e-commerce, has greatly enhanced a firm's ability to reach huge numbers of potential customers. In addition, application of such technologies has also resulted in enormous amounts of business and consumer data online in order to support automation (Smith & Offodile, 2002). A recent article in Consumer Reports included the following passage, which summarized the problem:

Identity theft is a problem largely because financial institutions, merchants, credit bureaus, and the government do not adequately safeguard vast databases and other records containing consumer's sensitive information, making it relatively easy for thieves—often insiders—to access these data. Many institutions use SSNs when other identifiers would suffice, fail to notify consumers when security breaches occur, and provide little help or recourse for consumers stuck cleaning up the mess. (Bass, 2003, p. 10)

The identity theft epidemic is compounded by the fact that most firms do not have the resources to fully address the privacy and security concerns in protecting customer's personal information. Firms take a reactionary approach to security breaches rather than a proactive approach to information security (Drake, 2003; Smith & Rupp, 2002a, 2002b). According to Groves (2002), most of the corporate focus is on perimeter protection, or preventing outside perpetrators from accessing proprietary and customer information, when the reality of the problem is that internal employees are just as likely to steal client financial information for fraudulent activity. These factors in turn directly impact the relationships with customers. Figure 1 illustrates the basic components in a conceptual model of CRM factors that directly affecting e-commerce-based fraud and identity theft. Clarification of the elements of this model forms the basis of the following discussion.

Figure 1. Model of CRM factors directly affecting e-commerce, fraud, and identity theft

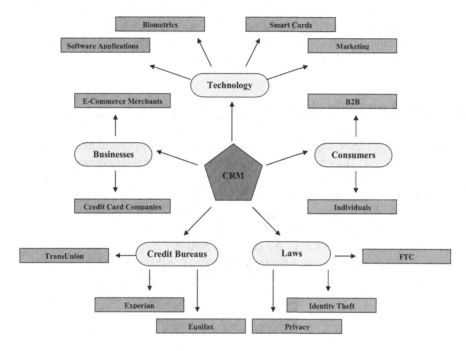

Demands of CRM in the Information Age

Achieving Success in E-Commerce

E-commerce is a booming segment of business today that affects organizations both large and small. It provides companies with the opportunity to reach an endless supply of consumers, but e-commerce also encourages fierce competition. Achieving success through this sales and information exchange channel requires a great deal of responsibility on the part of the business, which is based on earning the trust of possible customers, is critical. Such responsibility may include, but is not limited to, protecting customer databases from outsiders and those within the organization that do not require access, ensuring authentication of customers, and acting ethically in terms of marketing techniques that are used online and selling customer information to others for profits.

E-commerce forces customer relationship managers to constantly monitor how they consistently conduct business, identify current and potential competitors, and look for new ways to achieve a competitive advantage. Given the state of concerns over security, privacy, and protection, a major responsibility is also ensuring that firms should not only meet, but also exceed customer expectations in this arena. This may come with the necessity of large investments at the onset; however, a successful end result may be gaining new customers through the use of best practices (as discussed later in this chapter) and also avoiding customer attrition.

Relevant Laws and the FTC

The FTC and the U.S. Congress have played a significant role in addressing identity theft and fraud. The enactment of the ITADA was probably the most relevant piece of legislation in this area. Senator Jon Kyl of Arizona proposed this particular bill, and it was later passed by Congress and signed into law by President Clinton in October of 1998. It was constructed to achieve three main objectives: ensures private consumers who fall victim to an identity theft have standing as victims in federal criminal cases and forces the courts to consider damage to these consumers, provides for stiffer penalties for the perpetrators of this crime and implements certain procedures for investigation and enforcement, and directs the FTC to establish procedures for educating the public, receiving complaints, and coordinating enforcement efforts (Saunders & Zucker, 1999, p.189).

The FTC has become a major force in the evaluation of identity theft and other types of credit-related crimes with this legislation. They are the key agency responsible for the tracking and coordination of enforcement. They are a great resource for those who have experienced identity theft, or those looking to learn more about how to protect themselves. The FTC routinely produces very influential annual reports that outline the occurrences tracked each year, where they occurred, and what was done after the fact. Empowered consumers should consider visiting the FTC's Web site (www.ftc.gov) as they have many valuable resources that pertain to e-commerce. There are numerous articles and safeguards on identity theft, educational resources about spam e-mail, spyware, e-payments, and many other consumer alerts that are meant to protect.

Some of the other relevant legislation related to identity theft includes the Fair Credit Reporting Act (FCRA) (outlines actions to correct errors identified on your credit report), Fair Credit Billing Act (FCBA) (states how to handle incorrect credit card charges), Electronic Funds Transfer Act (EFTA) (protects consumers as it relates to electronic fund transfers), and Gramm-Leach-Bliley Act of 1999 (specifically deals with financial institutions and privacy). The latter is the primary reason that consumers today receive privacy notices in the mail from the financial companies they do business with such as banks, investment companies, and credit card companies. These types of institutions are required to allow the consumer the opportunity to opt out of having their information shared with unrelated third parties.

In December 2003, President Bush signed into law the Fair and Accurate Credit Transaction Act (FACTA). This most recent piece of legislation is another important step taken to try to help the victims of identity theft and the impact this crime has on their lives.

This legislation gives consumers unprecedented tools to fight identity theft and continued access to the most dynamic credit markets in the world. With a free credit report and powerful new tools to fight fraud, consumers have the ability to better protect themselves and their families. (The White House, 2003)

This bill was set forth to make certain that people are treated fairly when they apply for a home mortgage or any other line of credit. It is an extension of the 1996 National Standards on Credit Reporting (NSCR) that was set to expire, and will make such standards a permanent part of our laws. In addition to upholding the previous standards, it also gives the right to every consumer to obtain a free credit report once annually. The NSCR requires that all credit cards receipts may not provide more than the last five digits of an account number, enables a national fraud alert system that will be included on credit reports when enacted. NSCR further requires lenders and agencies to take a proactive approach in monitoring consumer accounts to identify problems before they are out of control (The White House, 2003).

Role of Credit Reporting Agencies

In the context of e-commerce, identity theft is the illegal access of personal and financial information in order to obtain credit fraudulently in a victim's name. This type of identity theft has two victims. The first victim is the firm that issues the credit, or creditor, that will actually lose the amount of credit extended. The second victim is the person whose name is stolen, and who will ultimately be accused of the fraud (LoPucki, 2001).

Once defrauded creditors realize that the victims will not pay the fraudulent charges, they may initiate collection actions that usually result in a negative entry on the victim's credit report. This practice often destroys the victim's ability to obtain credit from any source, may result in the victim being unemployable, or even result in a criminal prosecution and a jail sentence, even though the negative credit reporting is false. This situation may become even worse when the victim realizes that the U.S. currently has no legal remedy for the false reporting, provided that the credit-reporting agency followed reasonable procedures. Federal law exempts both creditors and credit-reporting agencies from liability for their false statements about the victim's identity theft.

Hence, victims of identity theft are forced to carry a huge burden in attempting to clear their names. It been estimated that victims spend an average of 175 hours of actively trying to resolve the credit and legal problems caused by identity theft, and spend an average of $808 in out-of-pocket expenses (LoPucki, 2001). In spite of the amount of time and money spent, victims still frequently report that credit-reporting agencies showed significant indifference to their claims of identity theft, and many victims reported not being even able to speak with a live representative at either Equifax (www.equifax.com) or Experian (www/esperian.com) (two of the three largest credit-reporting agencies). Since the individual consumer is not a customer of the credit-reporting agencies, no contact with the consumer is made when an adverse entry is made to their credit report. Upon discovery of fraudulent activity on a victim's credit accounts, the burden of investigation for false charges falls on the victim.

Among the three major credit-reporting agencies [TransUnion (www.transunion. com), Experian, and Equifax], only Experian provides information on its Web site that details what the company does to prevent fraud and to protect consumer credit information. Some specific actions include dropping several digits from each credit account on personal credit reports, apply sophisticated fraud products to assure the integrity of their credit database, continually monitor access to their database with sophisticated software in order to initiate an immediate investigation of unusual activity, and build extensive barriers to prevent computer hackers from access to consumer credit data (Experian, 2004).

Equifax offers varying levels of credit protection, but they are premium services that come with a monthly fee. Equifax Credit Watch™ programs provide electronic services that monitor an individual's credit accounts for possible fraudulent activity, provides credit protection insurance, sends monthly "no-alert" e-mails to subscribers and ensures peace of mind, provides access to dedicated customer service hotlines, and online dispute forms for consumers to report fraudulent charges more efficiently (Equifax, 2004). TransUnion provides a significant amount of fraud victim informa-tion, but it's important to note that the company is providing assistance once identity theft and fraud has already occurred (TransUnion, 2004).

Of course, all three credit-reporting agency Web sites provide tips that consumers can use to protect themselves from identity theft. Creditors are both customers and suppliers to the credit-reporting agencies in the fact that they not only provide in-formation regarding consumers repayment records for specific instances of credit repayment, they also pay to retrieve information from the credit-reporting agencies when an individual consumer applies for credit. In this regard, creditors have no real incentive to resolve a case of identity theft, as doing so will result in a write-off of the fraudulent charges. Unfortunately, according to LoPucki (2001), most credit-reporting agencies have no allegiance to individual consumers, and therefore, have no direct interest in correcting false records.

Technology and Identity-Related Issues

With identity theft being one of the fastest growing crimes of the new century, a strategic focus of many managers is how to prevent this crime from happening to their customers and employees. There are different types of pro-active approached leveraging technology that are geared toward security and privacy. In particular, there are two types of technology that are very promising in compacting identity theft, namely smart card and biometrics. These technologies can be applied to CRM to promote security and comfort among customers and employees.

Smart Card Technology

The smart card has a microprocessor and/or memory chip embedded in it. A microprocessor card can add, delete, and manipulate information on the card. A memory chip card can only undertake pre-defined operations. There are at least three categories of smart cards: the integrated circuit microprocessor card, the integrated circuit memory card, and the optical memory card. The integrated circuit microprocessor card offers better memory storage and more security than a traditional card such as a credit card. These cards have the ability to process data within an encrypted environment. The card has features such as an eight-bit processor and 16 KB read-only memory. These features give the card the virtual processing power of a computer. Although the card can be used for numerous applications, they are usually used to hold secure digital identity. Other examples of what these cards can be used for are to serve as money accounts, money equivalents, provide access to secure areas or networks, secure cellular phones from fraud, and allows television boxes to remain secure from piracy.

The integrated circuit memory cards are different than the previously-described type. These cards can only hold one to four KBs of data and they do not have a processor; therefore, they are unable to process the data they contain. This card needs a card reader to process the data and is used for fixed operations only. Examples of this kind of card are pre-paid phone card or a gift card. Optical memory cards can store up to four MBs of data. The data that are written onto the card cannot be changed or removed once it is placed on the card. These cards are ideal for record keeping functions, such as medical records, driving records, or travel histories.

Smart cards can be widely used when trying to protect customers and employees from identity theft. Managers can use this technology to provide customers with a secure card that they can put money so that they can purchase things in store and online. Instead of entering a bunch of unnecessary personal information on a Web site or onto some form of paperwork, the card can be simply swiped or card number entered, containing the information. This process significantly reduces the problems of customers having that fear of filling out paperwork or entering personal data onto a Web site because the encoded information will go right from the card to the database without any third-party participation. For employees, these cards can provide them with a secure card that gives them access to all personal computers and restricted areas that may pertain to their work. It would essential limit access to only those employees needing to access personal information.

Biometrics

Biometric technology has also been used to control identity theft for several years. Biometrics is a form of technology that can be used for personal identity verification. There are at least two types of biometric characteristics that can be captured for preventing identity theft: physiological and behavioral characteristics. Physiological characteristics include facial features, vein patterns in the retina, and fingerprints. Behavioral characteristics include voice analysis, signature dynamics, movement gaits, and keyboard typing rhythms.

There are certain requirements that a biometric characteristic must follow in order to be captured on individuals. It needs to be able to be measurable, such as finger length, distance between eyes, and/or the frequencies associated with voice patterns. The characteristic must be stable and not subject to significant change. It also must be easily measured without any inconvenience to the person. In addition, it must be immutable with no change in the measured feature according to the perspective of the image. Common characteristics that have been used are fingerprints, retinal scans, voice recognitions, and facial recognition. These characteristics have been used because they fit all the requirements. Other attributes, such as hair color and length, cannot be used due to the fact that they can be altered to change a person's appearance.

How can this type of technology be used in enhancing convenience and security in a knowledge-based CRM system? Biometrics, such as the voice recognition feature in place of entering pin number and retinal scans, can be used instead of a card to swipe in order to access a restricted area. Although relatively expensive, biometric technology is one of the newest technologies that offer the promise of increased security.

Confidence Online Software

Unfortunately, identity theft and security issues are putting a damper on many forms of e-commerce. Merchants have problems with getting customers to trust the online process. Software applications are being used to help with this problem, one example is Confidence Online software made by Whole Security. This software is designed to allow online merchants to protect their customers by providing a small downloadable browser add-on that monitors the users computer for spyware. Spyware is noted as a series of programs that collect user-related information and collects it for marketing companies. Confidence Online also looks for other software that tracks Web traffic, records keystrokes, and takes screen captures. This type of software can also be used to track and dismantle unwanted processes within a company. For example, applications can prevent employees from surfing the Internet or using instant messenger programs while on the job. Confidence Online is a 175-KB download, which installs itself without the help of the user, although it needs the user's permission to download. There is no need to restart the browser or reboot the computer, and it does not rely on e-signatures; unlike anti-virus programs, since it monitors behaviors, it frequently updates. Confidence software typically runs about $30 to 40 per user for the employee version, while other versions are still being negotiated. This is just one example of a software application, and how it can be used to prevent identity theft and help with CRM. Software applications can be very useful because they can detect and solve the problem at the source. Many online vendors can benefit from such programs, since they can reassure the customer that the sites are secure and their information is safe. Knowledge-based technology can be the means for merchants to provide their customers and employees with the confidence that their identities are relatively safe; hence, implanting the feeling of trust and security into the customer is a major goal of CRM.

Best Business Practices

Privacy Policies

Privacy policies are an important factor in e-commerce and promoting growth in this channel of business. Privacy concerns could be cited as one of the growing problems that come with new technologies. When asked to provide personal information over the Web, nearly 95% of users have avoided doing so, and at times simply choose to fabricate the answers to protect their real information. In a recent survey of the Fortune 500 companies' public Web sites, the results proved that just over half of these industry leaders had a privacy policy posted (Liu & Arnett, 2002). The FTC sets forth four privacy dimensions including access/participation, security/integrity, choice/consent, and notice/awareness. Surprisingly, 92.2% of the privacy policies in this survey addressed notice/awareness. However, they were seriously lagging in the additional three areas (ranging from 26.5 to 46.7% in the others). Privacy policies should consider addressing the following issues in order to attempt to curb some of the trust issues that clearly exist, as demonstrated in Table 1.

Table 1. Guidelines for developing privacy policies

Content	Why is this concept important for CRM and promoting e-commerce?
Use	Tell customers how their information may be used (both personal and non-personal). The customer's perception will be that your company is up front and honest.
Collection	Explaining what information is collected and through what methods will also help customers to build trust, further appreciates honesty, and possibly make them more willing to accept these practices.
Disclosure	Make customers aware of whom you may share their information with including third parties. Again, letting them know this at the onset will help them to know that you are not concealing anything.
Contact	In case the privacy statement overlooks any of their concerns, provide them with a means to contact someone with questions.
Opt Out	This item is probably the most important in CRM. Give customers the choice to protect their information. This can be broken down into two areas: internal and secondary (external) uses. If you gain their trust in the other steps, they may be more willing to share information with you that can aid your business in marketing and understanding customer wants. But, give them the option of not sharing with other companies.
Security	By explaining the steps you take and the amount of effort put into providing security and protection to your customers, you have gained more credibility and possibly more loyalty.
Cookie	By providing details on the way you use cookies, the customer might not view this as so deceitful and intrusive.
Link Warning	Lay out the knowledge that is often taken for granted such as the fact that when a customer uses a link to another site, they are no longer protected under your policies. Customers will appreciate the warning you provide.
Access/Correction	By enabling the customer to access their information and correct errors, they will feel more empowered and in control. This will help alleviate distrust and other relevant concerns.
Internal Protection	Further explain the steps you take internally to prevent unauthorized parties from accessing a customer's personal information.
Children Protection	By emphasizing a dedication to protecting the privacy of children online, you will additionally gain respect from the customer.

In a B2C-enabled e-commerce environment, customer information is collected explicitly and implicitly. Implicit methods of collection may include the use of cookies and other forms of tracking software online.

Typically, when managers discuss the value of customer relationships, for example, what they really mean is the proprietary information that they have about their customers and that their customers have about the company and its products. (Evans & Wurster, 1997, p. 72)

Essentially every business revolves around information and knowledge management in today's economy. Regardless of what is being collected and for what purposes, a company should consider having a privacy policy to address the issue of identity theft.

Seal Programs

Even when privacy policies are clearly posted, does this mean that those companies adhere to them? Maybe not, but it is a step in the right direction. Since many businesses would prefer to be self-regulated to regulation coming from the government, another method to establish higher trust from customers would be to participate in a seal program. The Better Business Bureau online seal program (BBBOnLine) is an example of such a pro-active solution, and it goes above and beyond simply having a privacy statement.

Privacy is a major concern voiced by online consumers. The fear of how their information may be used is often cited as a reason for not doing business with a company online. By participating in the BBBOnLine Privacy Seal Program and posting the Privacy Seal on your website you're letting visitors know that you treat their personal information in a way that meets BBBOnLine standards. It'll set your site apart from other sites, and boost the trust and confidence of potential customers. (BBBOnLine, 2004)

As suggested by Liu and Arnett (2002), the use of privacy seals represents an industry-wide effort to use self-enforcement mechanisms to make the Internet a safer forum for customers to exchange accurate information and conduct transactions. This is necessary in order for "Web commerce to reach its full potential" (p. 14). Privacy policies may contain technical language that may be difficult to understand or lengthy for the customer to bother reading. Seal programs not only allow a company to post the logo on their Web site, but also require that the company adheres to fair information practices and compliance monitoring. Hopefully, this means that such policies are not just declared, but instead they must follow through and do what they promise.

Cardholder Information Security Program and Verified by Visa USA

VisaUSA has incorporated a two-part system to help combat identify theft. The system is broken down into the business or merchant and consumer sectors. In April 2000, VisaUSA launched their Cardholder Information Security Program (CISP). This program defines a standard for securing cardholder data. Compliance is required for all entities storing, processing, or transmitting cardholder data. Members must be compliant with CISP and are responsible for ensuring compliance of their merchants and agents. Compliance is required regardless if they are support issuing or acquiring activity for all payment channels including brick and mortar, mail/telephone, and e-commerce. The VisaUSA board of directors to help mandated CISP members, merchants, and service providers protect their information assets and meet the obligations to the payment structure. CISP is governed by 12 basic requirements, and fines will be assessed to any entity that fails to comply with them (VisaUSA, 2004). The CISP requirements are as follows: install and maintain a working firewall to protect data, keep security patches up-to-date, protect stored data, encrypt data sent across public networks, use and regularly update anti-virus software, restrict access by a need to know basis, assign unique ID to each person with computer access, do not use vendor-supplied defaults for passwords and security parameters, track all access to data by unique ID, regularly test security systems and processes, implement and maintain an information security policy, and restrict physical access to data

This is a unique service that uses personal passwords or identity information to help protect Visa card numbers against unauthorized use. Once activated, no one can use the card number to make a purchase online at any participating stores, without your personal password. Activation is completed in three simple steps: entering card number over Visa's secured server, confirm identity by answering detailed account questions, and creating a password. Payment card information is transmitted using a high level of encryption, and is stored on a secure server behind a firewall to protect against unauthorized use.

Drivers of Identity Theft Prevention

An important concept is that the prevention of identity theft depends on the collective actions of consumers, business, and government.

The government has the ability to pass criminal and civil legislation to help directly deter theft and influence business policy by requiring better information handling practices and record security, and educate consumers to better protect their personal information. (Milne, 2003, p. 389)

Governmental agencies have the power and obligation to set better requirements and set more stringent standards for protecting consumers, but consumers also have a duty to take steps to protect themselves. Consumer carelessness concerning identity protection should not be taken lightly.

Technology can play a role in building trust, but only to the extent that it influences the assessment of risk and enhances customer loyalty. Individuals need to be able to trust the business they are transacting business with. Organizations have the duty to protect their consumers from harm, but first an organization must recognize the threats affecting consumer safety. When doing business online, it is important that knowledge-based organizations address the issues of authentication, security, authorization, reputation, privacy, logistics, dispute resolution, and CRM. These issues directly affect trust and consumer safety. In order to protect consumers from the perceived threats, while at the same time fostering trust, an organization must set guidelines and create a framework that incorporates detailed prevention strategies and/or polices concerning each one of the issues. Firms need to be able to make well-informed, intelligent decisions. Companies need better information and knowledge management systems, and they need to be held accountable for mismanagement. While technology and legislative efforts are helping to combat identify theft, business methodology, and procedures must pro-active against identity theft.

Empirical Exploration

Survey and Basic Results

A total of 75 managerial employees and/or knowledge workers were surveyed in five large organizations in Pittsburgh, PA, to find out how much information they share with others, what the likelihood is that they will conduct business online (from purchases to banking), and whether or not they take steps to protect their personal identity and credit (sample survey found in the Appendix). A response rate of 58% resulted in a number of revealing findings. Many professionals have embraced e-commerce, since 78.6% of respondents are participating in some form of e-commerce (shopping online and/or banking online). However, only 17.3% of those surveyed said that they would participate in all three activities (shopping online with credit cards, shopping with debit cards, and online banking). A basic correlation analysis illustrates that people who are likely to shop online with a credit card are probably likely to use a debit card interchangeably. Unfortunately, the same protection does not always exist to protect consumers from unauthorized charges when a debit card is used. Credit cards are probably the preferable method for online purchases because they can provide additional security. If fraud occurs with the use of a debit card, the perpetrator could gain access to your checking and savings account balances.

Table 2 illustrates the correlation matrix and the shows the commonality between using a credit card and a debit card to make online purchases. Figure 2 displays a breakdown by age categories of those respondents who will shop online, specifically using a credit card, displaying that the 26 to 45 age groups most apt to use credit cards for online shopping purchases.

Table 2. Correlation matrix of commonality between using a credit card and a debit card to make online purchases

		Had unauthorize charges	Do you online using credit	Do you online a debit
Had charges	Pearson	1	.090	-.061
	Sig. (2-	.	.440	.605
	N	75	75	75
Do you shop using a credit	Pearson	.090	1	.235*
	Sig. (2-	.440	.	.043
	N	75	75	75
Do you shop using a debit	Pearson	-.061	.235*	1
	Sig. (2-	.605	.043	.
	N	75	75	75

*. Correlation is significant at the 0.05 level (2-tailed).

Figure 2. Online shopping via a credit card vs. age

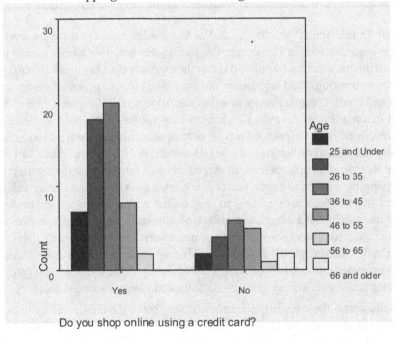

Interestingly, 6.6% of respondents have had their personal identity stolen. While this seems like a small percentage, this may have potentially equated to 875 hours of time spent collectively among the victims to try to clear their good names (based on 175 hour average for each occurrence stated earlier). Also, 32% had experienced unauthorized charges on their billing statements. Clearly the occurrence of fraud is much greater than the occurrence of identity theft; however, identity theft is a growing problem as discussed earlier in this paper.

From a review of the literature, it was also determined that it was relevant to determine if a relationship between the age of the respondent and the likelihood of using an online bill payment service. Based on the data, it appears that most of the respondents that currently use this service are under the age of 56, with the majority of users are between the ages of 26 and 45 (75%). It appears that as age increases of the current adopters (upwards to the 50s), there is an increase in the probability of use of this service (as shown in Table 3). Further investigation is needed on a larger scale to really determine if this is an accurate assessment.

To make determinations about how pro-active people tend to be to ensure their own security, questions were asked pertaining to ordering credit reports, sharing passwords, and finding out how their personal information will be used. Only nine respondents, or 12%, stated that they take all three precautions to protect themselves. The split was fairly even among those who create unique passwords and those who use easily identifiable information such as SSN, mother's maiden name, birth date, to name a few. Also, 65% of respondents have not ordered a credit report in the last year, which is a recommended procedure to ensure accurate reporting and to identify any unusual activity, as illustrated in Figure 3. The lack of attention to this

Table 3. Cross-tabulation of age and using an online bill payment service

Age * Do you use an online bill payment service?

		Do you use online bill payment service?		
		Yes	No	Total
Age	25 and Under	3	6	9
	26 to 35	11	11	22
	36 to 45	10	16	26
	46 to 55	4	9	13
	56 to 65		3	3
	66 +		2	2
Total		28	47	75

Figure 3. Ordered credit report as a function of age

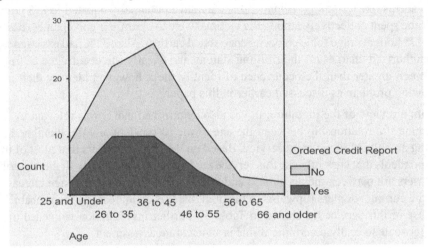

area is surprising given the number of respondents participating in some form of e-commerce and their professional standings.

General Applications and Recommendations

Knowledge-based firms must understand that CRM principles and e-commerce will likely be major factors that influence the success of their businesses. The need to better understand what drives customer behavior and the likelihood of a merchant choosing your company online to do business are essential drivers of these processes. Once firms have attracted a customer base, it becomes imperative to try to build customer loyalty and encourage repeat business in order to generate the highest attainable profits. This requires firms to develop policies, practices, and procedures that address privacy concerns. These include the use of privacy policies online, participating in seal programs that distinguish your Web site from the rest, understand your obligations to protect customers, make sure that you are meeting the requirements set forth by the FTC, invest in sound information technology security measures, and only partner with other businesses that will meet up to the same high standards.

Hence, organizations that engage in e-commerce must do everything possible to protect consumer's personal and financial information in B2C transactions as well as proprietary information of business partners in B2B applications. Unfortunately, an identity thief can assume an individual's identity in a matter of hours, but it may take years for unsuspecting individuals to restore their credit standing and good reputation. Throughout the chapter, a recurrent recommendation for a major security measure is for all businesses to cease the practice of using SSNs as a means of identity authentication. If a firm is not performing a credit or background check in order to process an application for credit, a person's SSN is simply not needed (Groves, 2002). In addition, access to customer's personal information should be limited to employees who absolutely need to have this information. It's been established that many occurrences of identity theft and fraud is perpetrated by internal employees, even temporary employees who have no valid purpose in having access to both customer and employee personal information.

E-commerce firms should perform a central risk inventory to determine where weaknesses exist within the current security systems in place. This includes identifying business units and partners, with which sensitive information is shared, to determine if this shared information is necessary throughout the normal course of business. Third-party firms with which customer information is shared should be asked to provide written commitments to provide timely notification if their information systems have been breached. Defense systems against security breaches should also be layered in order to combat vulnerability. Finally, e-commerce firms must realize that the pursuit of security for all customers and business partners is a continual process. Firms need to stay current with technology and security challenges and realize that protection from identity theft is an ongoing process (Bass, 2003).

Protecting an individual customer from identity theft is a very complex task. Even the most careful consumers fall prey to identity theft. In order for businesses to stay ahead of criminals and provide effective protection against identity theft, they need to provide consumers with prevention measures as well as prevention failure assurance. Technology is changing the way we do business. As fast as new technology is being implemented to stop thieves, thieves are finding ways to get around this new technology. Businesses need to be very dynamic in their approaches to solving these problems.

As a business implements new safeguards, they must also implement consequences for failure of these safeguards. Safeguards are of no use if they do not have safety nets. For instance, if you use some type of secure encryption technology to safeguard customer accounts, but you have a service failure, what are the consequences to consumers of that service failure? Consumers want to be able to know that you have adequate protection and policies in place, but they also want to know that you have some type of policy regarding the failure of these polices. They want to be assured that they will ultimately not be liable for a protective service failure. Businesses need to provide consumers with the security of knowing that they are protected in every aspect. It is much better from a CRM standpoint to take a pro-active approach rather than being reactive at the time a problem or dispute arises.

Finally, companies wishing to succeed in the dynamic e-commerce environment should try to be leaders instead of followers. Participate in seal programs and other types of technology that can help support building relationships with customers. Instead of approaching information security as an unwanted expense, begin viewing it as an inevitable requirement for success. Knowing that competition for online customers is fiercer because of the accessibility e-commerce has established across the markets, fundamentals of customer relationships are more important than ever before. Instead of spending endless amounts of time using technology to figure out what customers want, realize that privacy and security in the online environment is a major desire.

General Conclusions

The model of CRM factors effecting e-commerce, fraud, and identity theft, as first displayed in Figure 1, is a graphical illustration of the many demands and knowledge areas that are key to a customer relationship manager's success in the Information Age. Today's CRM manager must understand new technologies and how they can be used to benefit the company. They must recognize business relationships and consumer relationships and how these dealings affect the bottom line. CRM managers need to be able to work successfully with credit bureaus in terms of accurate reporting and obtaining customer information in good faith. Finally, they must also be aware of the laws that effect managing customer information, and work diligently to ensure that they are meeting high standards.

References

Anton, J., & Petouhoff, N. (2002). *Customer relations management: The bottom line to optimizing your ROI.* New Jersey: Prentice Hall.

Bass, G. (2003). Case study: One company's response to the California Identity Theft Law. SANS Security Essentials. *GSEC Practical Assignment*, Version 1.4b (p. 10-13).

BBBOnLine. (2004). *Seal programs.* Retrieved March 15, 2006, from http://www.bbbonline.org/privacy/answer.asp#2

Culnan, M. J. (Spring 1995). Consumer awareness of name removal procedures: Implications for direct marketing. *Journal of Direct Marketing, 9*, 10-19.

Drake, J. (2003, July 16). How to take the offense on identity theft. *Computer-World.* Retrieved April 3, 2006, from http://www.computerworld.com/print-this/2003/0,4814,82911,00.html

Equifax. (2004). *Equifax personal solutions.* Retrieved March 20, 2006, from https://www.econsumer.equifax.com/consumer/forward.ehtml?forward=default

Evans, P., & Wurster, T. (1997, September/October). Strategy and the new economics of information. *Harvard Business Review, 75*(5), 71-82.

Experian. (2004). *Experian personal services.* Retrieved March 20, 2006, from http://www.experian.com/identity_fraud/fraud_prevention.html

Fernandez, A., & Miyazaki, A. D. (2001 Summer). Consumer perceptions of privacy and security risks for online shopping. *The Journal of Consumer Affairs, 35*(1), 27-44.

Gaudin, S. (2003, May 22). Identity theft losses expected to hit $2 trillion by 2005. *IT Management: Security.* Retrieved March 15, 2006, from http://itmanage-ment.earthweb.com/secu/print.php/2211101

Groves, S. (2002). Protecting your identity. *Information Management Journal, 36*, 27-31.

Liu, C., & Arnett, K. (2002). An examination of privacy policies in Fortune 500 Websites. *Mid-American Journal of Business, 17*, 13-21.

LoPucki, L. (2001). Human identification theory and the identity theft problem. *Texas Law Review, 80*, 89-135.

Milne, G. (2003). How well do consumers protect themselves from identity theft? *The Journal Of Consumer Affairs, 37*, 388- 405.

Pulliam-Weston, L. (2004, April 7). The newest identity thieves: Parents. *MSN Money.* Retrieved March 15, 2006, from http://moneycentral.msn.com/con-tent/Banking/FnancialPrivacy/P77623.asp

Ray, T. (2003, June 20). New frontiers in the identity theft war. *CRM Buyer.* Retrieved December 8, 2005, from http://www.crmbuyer.com/perl/story/21718.html

Saunders, K., & Zucker, B. (1999). Counteracting identity fraud in the information age: The identity theft and assumption deterrence act. *International Review of Law, Computers and Technology, 13*,183-192.

Smith, A. D. (2002). Loyalty and e-marketing issues: Customer retention on the Web. *Quarterly Journal of Electronic Commerce, 3*, 141-161.

Smith, A. D. (2005a). Exploring the inherent benefits of RFID & automated self-serve checkouts in a B2C environment. *International Journal of Business Information Systems, 1*(1/2), 149-183.

Smith, A. D. (2005b). Exploring the acceptability of biometrics & fingerprint technologies. *International Journal of Services & Standards, 1*(4), 453-481.

Smith, A. D. (2005c). Identify theft as a threat to CRM and e-commerce. *Electronic Government: An International Journal, 2*(2), 219-246.

Smith, A. D., & Offodile, F. (2002). Information management of automated data capture: An overview of technical developments. *Information Management and Computer Society, 10*(3), 109-118.

Smith, A., & Rupp, W. T. (2002a). Application service providers (ASP): Moving downstream to enhance competitive advantage. *Information Management and Computer Security, 10*(2), 64-72.

Smith, A., & Rupp, W. T. (2002b). Issues in cybersecurity: Understanding the potential risks associated with hackers/crackers. *Information Management and Computer Security, 10*(4), 178-183.

TransUnion. (2004). *TransUnion personal solutions.* Retrieved March 15, 2006, from http://www.transunion.com/content/page.jsp?id=/personalsolutions/general/data/FraudInformation.xml

VisaUSA. (2004). *Cardholder information security program.* Retrieved April 3, 2006, from http://www.usa.visa.com/business/merchants/cisp_index.html

The White House. (2003, December 4). *Fact sheet: President Bush signs the Fair and Accurate Credit Transactions Act of 2003.* Retrieved April 3, 2006, from http://www.whitehouse.gov/news/releases/2003/12/20031204-3.html

Appendix:
Survey

Identity theft is becoming the fastest growing white-collar crime in the United States. Identity theft is defined as the appropriation of someone else's identity to commit fraud or theft. The prevention of identity theft depends on the collective efforts of government, businesses, and consumers. We are conducting a study to determine how well consumers protect themselves from identity theft. Please take a moment to fill out the following questionnaire.

1.   Gender _____

2.   Age _____

3.   I have ordered a copy of my credit report within the last year.

YES _____ NO _____

4. When asked to create a password, I have used either my mother's maiden name, or my pet's name, or my birth date, or the last four digest of my SSN.

YES _____ NO _____

5. Before I reveal any personal identifying information I always find out how marketers are going to use it.

YES _____ NO _____

6. I carry more credit cards than I need in my wallet.

YES _____ NO _____

7. I always check each item in my billing statements for mistakes an report these immediately.

YES _____ NO _____

8. If asked by a merchant, I provide my social security number (SSN) so they can write it on my check.

YES _____ NO _____

9. I sometimes leave my mail in my mailbox (at home) for a day or two before I pick it up.

YES _____ NO _____

10. I keep a copy of my pin number and passwords in my wallet or purse in case I forget them.

YES _____ NO _____

11. I carry my social security card with me in my wallet or purse.

YES _____ NO _____

12. Have you ever had the following happen?

A.	Stolen identity	YES _____	NO _____
B.	Stolen credit cards	YES _____	NO _____
C.	Stolen SSN card	YES _____	NO _____
D.	Unauthorized charges on statements	YES _____	NO _____

13. Do you do any of the following?

A.	I shop online using my credit card	YES _____	NO _____
B.	I shop online using my debit card	YES _____	NO _____
C.	I use online bill payment services	YES _____	NO _____

Chapter VI

Pricing Outcomes in Dual-Channel Monopoly and Partial Duopoly

Farooq M. Sheikh, SUNY, USA

M. Ruhul Amin, Bloomsburg University, USA

Nafeez Amin, Tigris Strategies, Inc., USA

Abstract

In this chapter, the authors first study the pricing strategies of a monopolist sell-ing a product through stores in two channels, but under single management (or coordinated management) and then propose a framework for a model for a partial duopoly market conditions. The authors find that the monopolist generally charges a higher price in the brick and mortar store than the price charged in the Internet store. If, however, there is a sufficiently large fraction of buyers who would strictly prefer to buy the product from the Internet store instead of the physical store at any given price, the monopolist might charge the same price in both the stores. The authors also find that physical store price of a dual-channel monopoly is higher than the physical store price of a single-channel monopoly; the price charged in the Internet store is generally lower than the single channel monopoly price. This chapter concludes with an identification of parameters for channel pricing strategies under partial duopoly market conditions.

Introduction

The initial outburst of optimism in the potential of the Internet to herald an era of perfectly competitive markets has been undoubtedly subdued by events that unfolded in the recent past amidst the plethora of dot-com failures. Even so, the Internet remains a channel of promise as evidenced by the increasing number of traditional *brick and mortar* firms that continue to open up Internet stores to function alongside their physical stores.

Indeed our understanding of the Internet as an alternate market channel continues to evolve to this date. An attractive feature of e-tailing that has received unequivocal recognition lies in the inherent capacity of Internet to support mass customization of products and buyers' shopping experiences; this touches on the notion of buyer discrimination in mutually acceptable ways. Under such circumstances, opportunities for higher surpluses for the buyers and higher aggregate profits for the supplier begin to appear feasible. As sellers experiment with different business models to exploit opportunities on the Internet, the Internet market environment undergoes rapid shifts that need to be coped with; scholars have proposed a good number of strategies (Urban, Sultan, & Qualls, 2000) to address the dynamic marketplace of e-tail. Researchers have sought to approach the issues from various perspectives (Calkins and Farello, 2000; Dewan, Jing, & Seidman, 2000; Lu, 2003; Lee, Lee, & Larson, 2003; Odekerken-Schroder & Wetzels, 2003; Ward, 2001; Cao & Gruca, 2003) leading them to describe and propose various dimensions of the emerging market conditions. The available literature reveals a number of new issues including the nature of customer profiles (Koyuncu & Lien, 2003; Schoenbachler & Gordon, 2002) and behavior (Chiang & Dholakia, 2003), the issue of trust (Urban et al., 2000), and the expense of technological innovations and updates rarely addressed in the traditional distribution theories and logistics. In addition, the issue of privacy and concerns with regard to the integrity of the e-tailer in the appropriate use of "secured" information has come under wide discussion (Forsythe & Shi, 2003; Yoon, 2002).

With the tremendous growth witnessed in e-tail business, the need for an empirically grounded, rational behavioral model that explains the consumer preferences and seller strategies in electronic commerce cannot be overemphasized. The increasing number of commercial banks and financial institutions extending their services onto the Internet attest to the volume of transaction that must take place on the Internet.

In a seminal article, Schoenbachler and Gordon (2002) offered 22 propositions pertaining to multi-channel shopping and drivers of shoppers' channel preferences. All the propositions are illustrations or descriptive of a conceptual causal model consisting of 17 independent variables affecting three mediating (perceived risk, direct marketing experience, motivation to buy from a channel) variables of channel selection. While the ideas proposed are interesting, no testable empirical model was provided in the article. Such a task was left to future researchers. As the Internet shopping mall appeals to global customers, the issues of cultural differences, terms of trade, tariffs, and legal barriers have need to be studied, an exercise that is likely to lead to the homogenization of a global retail culture. In the same way, the variables affecting pricing strategies should also be studied (Anderson & Wilson, 2003; Frazier, 1999; Schoenbachler & Gordon, 2002). It is in this context that this article was conceived.

A consumer by his/her very choice of deciding to shop on the Internet screens himself/herself out to a seller. Why would a consumer shop on the Internet when he/she could easily visit a local physical store and buy the product by actual examination? To put it more bluntly, why does a consumer prefer a depersonalized online channel which does not even have a guarantee of existence? There are perhaps several plausible explanations, but one commonly accepted explanation is *convenience* (Burke, 1998; Chiang & Dholakia, 2003). But indeed the level of perceived convenience might not be the same for all buyers, or at least there might be factors that erode convenience. For instance, in the same household, some members may prefer to shop in the physical store, while others might prefer the *e*-store. James (2000) suggests that unresolved issues pertaining to online buyers include customer loyalty, product variety, and product fit.[1] A recent study (Liu & Wei, 2003) indicates that the perception of risks associated with the fit between the *perceived* physical good and physical good *actually received*, and the perception of ease of use in service influence the adoption of e-commerce. This is the line of investigation pursued in this research. Our general approach is that the buyers' decision in regard to channel choice is based on the value of channel transaction net of risk costs and prices. In particular, we model buyers that are heterogeneous in (1) their willingness to pay for the product and (2) their assessment of risks and cost of Internet transaction. We consider a monopolist operating both Internet and brick and mortar stores. In this connection, two papers need special mention—Lal and Sarvary (1999) and Lu (2003). Lal et al. consider a model of competition between two e-tailers where buyers have asymmetric perceptions about the product each seller sells but incur search costs in price search and information search. The paper pursues a different modeling approach and addresses a competitive market. The model used in this article assumes that buyers do not incur any price search cost. Lu considers a model similar to the model proposed in this chapter, except that buyers are homogeneous in their assessment of risk associated with Internet transactions. This actually amounts to a model of two vertically differentiated products, and the results match those of quality differentiated products under similar conditions of competition. Our model is a generalization of the model used by Lu.

As is apparent from this, a number of studies have been published on consumer behavior in the sphere of e-commerce. The issue of pricing strategy is still not understood as evidenced by the anomalous price dispersion so widely observed on the Internet. The focus of this chapter is to understand pricing strategies of monopolistic firms that offer their products through both electronic stores and physical stores. It is well known that the cost of making products available through Internet stores is strictly less than making it available through physical stores, yet it is often observed that some manufacturers offer a uniform price in both channels while others offer different prices across the channels. In this chapter, we use a simple model to characterize the environment that may support one strategy or the other. Instead of studying how different the prices are or how the difference in prices may vary, this chapter deals with conditions leading to price differentiation.

Model

We assume a set of heterogeneous consumers independently characterized by utility parameter, θ, distributed between 0 and 1 with cumulative distribution $G(\theta)$ and density function $g(\theta)$, and an Internet shopping dis-utility parameter, ρ, also distributed between 0 and 1 with cumulative distribution $F(\rho)$ and density function $f(\rho)$. The dis-utility parameter, ρ, may include a variety of factors. It can for instance be supposed to comprise/include the variance of quality/characteristic of the product from what is seen on the Internet and what it actually proves to be. It could also include the variance of the time it takes to reach the customer versus what is promised, and so forth. We consider a single period model for a monopolistic firm offering a single product sold through both physical stores and Internet stores. We assume that a customer arrives at the store only after having previously decided that he/she will buy it from the physical store. The cost of making it available through Internet stores is normalized to zero while the cost of making it available through physical store is c.

The product when bought from the Internet store comes bundled with a dis-utility factor t. This dis-utility parameter t is inherent to Internet stores only. The dis-utility that Internet buyers experience is the product of two factors: (1) t and (2) ρ. While t is a characteristic of the store, ρ is a characteristic of the buyer. In our model $t \geq 1$. The buyer characteristic ρ measures the internal inhibition that a buyer might have for buying on the Internet. It can be a result of many factors. For instance, a buyer might have fears that she might not get exactly what she thought she was ordering;

in this case ρ would incorporate her sense of value loss or inconvenience associated with the transaction. Buyers privately know how they would feel about such discrepancies, and their buying decision is informed by this knowledge. Given its ρ, a buyer might also assess some inconvenience arising from the design of transaction and buying environment used by the seller. For instance, a seller offering perfect customer service[2] and seamless return policy will be of greater assurance to a buyer than a store that introduces hurdles like restocking charges and limited customer service. Sellers, of course, would make all attempts to eradicate this fear, but not all is in their control. When a firm achieves a customer service reputation or assurance corresponding to parameter value, $t = 1$, the dis-utility experienced by a buyer is entirely due to its own inconvenience characteristic, ρ, and the seller has no control over it. We will assume that the cost of shipping and handling is borne by the Internet buyer and has been internalized into the parameter ρ or that it has been normalized to zero in complete equivalence to the cost of visiting the physical store as borne by a physical store a buyer.

The net utility accruing to buyer type (θ, ρ) for the product bought on the Internet and the physical store is given by:

$$U_\theta = \theta - \rho \cdot t - P_e \qquad\qquad (1)$$

$$U_\theta = \theta - P_p \qquad\qquad (2)$$

where P_p and P_e are prices paid for the product in the physical store and Internet store, respectively. Equating the individual rationality constraints for the indifferent buyer, the consumer who is indifferent between buying from the Internet and the physical store is defined by the dis-utility parameter,

$$\rho^* = \frac{(P_p - P_e)}{t}.$$

The consumers problem is to maximize its utility given its type characterized by θ and ρ, and the prices that are offered on the Internet and the physical store. We assume consumers are fully informed about both the stores. The buyers will form two classes on the basis of their dis-utility parameter, ρ: all consumers who are characterized by $\rho < \rho^*$ will buy from the Internet store while those characterized with parameter $\rho > \rho^*$ will buy from the physical store. Anticipating buyers' behavior, the firm chooses the prices P_p (physical store price) and P_e (Internet store price) to maximize its overall profit:

$$Max \; \Pi = \int_{0}^{\rho^*} \int_{P_e + t\rho}^{1} P_e g(\theta) f(\rho) d\theta d\rho + \int_{\rho*}^{1} \int_{P_p}^{1} (P_p - c) g(\theta) f(\rho) d\theta d\rho \qquad (3)$$

The major result of this chapter is to argue that in the event of continuously distributed ρ and a cost c (> 0) per unit of physical-store product, a monopolist will charge differentiated prices in the two channels specifically, $P_p \geq P_e$. A necessary condition for optimally charging the same price in the two stores would require a probability mass on $\rho = 0$. For the rest of the chapter, we assume that θ and ρ are each uniformly distributed in the unit interval $[0,1]$.

Single Management and Non-Atomic Distribution

In this section, we assume that ρ is also uniformly distributed in the interval $[0,1]$. A graphical depiction of an equilibrium outcome would be as in Figure 1.

Assumption 1. *A monopolist with a physical store as well as an Internet store has $t = 1$ for its Internet store.*

Figure 1. A 2-D graph describing buyers distribution in a dual-channel market. The x-axis represents ρ, buyers' inconvenience factors, and the y-axis represents θ, buyers' valuation. Shaded regions identify buyers by the channel they use for shopping: □ *ABEF represents Internet store buyers,* □ *BCDE represents physical store buyers, line $\overline{AB}$ and its extension $\overline{BD}$ correspond to $\theta = \rho t + P_e$; $\overline{HE}$ corresponds to the line $\rho^* = \dfrac{P_p - P_e}{t}$; $\overline{GC}$ describes the straight line $\theta = P_p$, physical store price, and point A marks the Internet store price, P_e.*

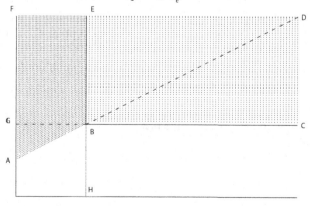

Basically $t = 1$ is the best that an Internet store can do in terms of facilitating transactions. This assumption is based on empirical observation. Almost all firms that have a physical as well as Internet stores offer the convenience of returning merchandize to their nearest physical store. This undoubtedly adds to the convenience of the buyers, and facilitates Internet transaction. Second, the existence of a physical store inspires consumer confidence and buyer trust in the quality they are paying for. Third, all such firms or sellers offer the same quality of buyer convenience as pure Internet sellers. In short, a firm having both physical stores and an Internet presence generally offers all the convenience that a pure Internet firm offers, but exceeds the latter by virtue of their physical stores, and, consequently, offers the best available buying convenience.

Consequently the profit function of the monopolist seller can be written as

$$\Pi = \left(\frac{1}{2}(P_p - P_e)^2 + (1 - P_p)(P_p - P_e) \right) P_e + (1 - P_p)(1 - P_p - P_e)(P_p - c) \qquad (4)$$

where the first component is the profit accruing from the Internet store, and the second component is the profit accruing from the physical store. For the purpose of bench-marking, we refer to equilibrium price of the monopolist under a single physical store as P_p^m.

Proposition 1. *In equilibrium (1) $P_p > P_p^m$, (2) $P_e < P_p$ and (3) $P_p^m - P_e < c$.*

Proof. First note that $P_e < P_p$, or else no one would buy from the *e*-store. Since without *e*-store the seller sells the product at P_p, with *e*-store the seller will not charge a $P_p < P_p^m$, charging less than P_p^m, in the presence of a cost efficient alternative would imply that P_p^m is sub-optimal; hence $P_p \geq P_p^m$. Let's say that $P_e < P_p = P_p^m$ and that $P_e = P_p^m - c$, that is the seller earns the same margin per unit of the product in the e-tail store as in the physical store.

Consider Figure 2 where the vertical axis represents θ and the horizontal axis represents ρ. Point L represents P_p^m, and point M, $P_p^m - \delta$, where $\overline{LM}$ is an infinitesimal decrease in price equal to δ. Note that the PS-monopolist price P_p^m implies that

$$(P_p^m - c) \square \, KLFP > (P_p^m - \delta - c) \square \, KMEP \qquad (5)$$

The relation will hold true for any positive factor multiplied throughout the inequality. In particular,

$(P_p^m - c) \,\square\, HBFP > (P_p^m - \delta - c) \,\square\, HCEP,$

since the rectangles $\square\, HBFP$ and $\square\, HCEP$ are the same fractions of rectangles $\square\, KLFP$ and $\square\, KMEP$, respectively. Now consider the gains to the DC-monopolist by decreasing the price from P_p^m to $P_p^m - \delta$. Note that by assumption monopolists' net earning from buyers in $\square\, HCAG$ is also $(P_p^m - c)$. By decreasing the price by δ the monopolist's net profit from the affected buyers' is,

$(\square\, GKFP + \square\, KCEF + \square\, HCAG)\ (P_p^m - \delta - c) \; = \square\, HCEP(P_p^m - \delta - c)$

On the other hand, the net profit from the affected buyers before the price decrease was $\square\, HBFP\ (P_p^m - c)$. Clearly, using inequality (5)

$$\square\, HBFP(P_p^m - c) > \square\, HCEP(P_p^m - \delta - c) \qquad\qquad (6)$$

Hence the DC-monopolist will charge $P_p > P_p^m$. Now to see the it will make a higher margin off its e-tail store product, consider Figure 3. The buyers affected by a decrease in price from $(P_p - c)$ to $(P_p - \delta - c)$ would be given by $\square\, HLAF$. The decrease would be sub-optimal if,

Figure 2. Monopolist with e-tail and retail stores: t = 1

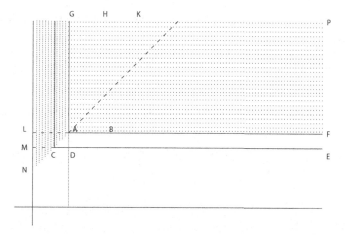

Figure 3. Monopolist with e-tail and retail stores: t = 1

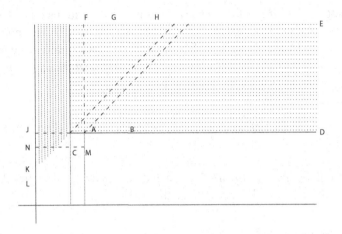

$$(P_p - c) \;\square\; HKBG > (P_p - \delta - c) \;\square\; HLAF \qquad\qquad (7)$$

Note that $\square\, HLAF = \square\, HJAF + \square\, JNCA$. If P_p is optimal then it is easy to see that inequality (7) will hold true. Hence $P_p^m - P_e < c$

Special Case: $P_p = P_e$

It is observed that many retailers with e-tail stores tend to charge the same price for their products in either stores. This is a little puzzling; since the cost of merchandising goods on the Internet is lower, one would expect a lower price to be charged on the Internet. In this section, we examine when such pricing might be optimal.

Lemma 1. *It is sub-optimal to charge $P_p = P_e$ when the probability distribution is non-atomic.*

Proof. Since the distribution is non-atomic, $P_p = P_e$ will result in zero sales in the e-store, hence would be sub-optimal.

Lemma 2. *A seller will optimally set $P_p = P_e$ if and only if there is a probability mass on $\rho = 0$.*

Proof. By Lemma 3, we know that it is sub-optimal to set $P_p = P_e$ if there is no probability mass on $\rho = 0$. This proves the *if* part. Similarly setting $P_p = P_e$ is optimal only if there are buyers in the e-tail store. But that will not be true unless there we a probability mass on $\rho = 0$.

Hence we can see that the seller will use the same price for both the stores only if there was a fraction of buyers that had absolutely *no qualms* about buying from Internet stores. Who are such buyers? One example of such a set of buyers would be those who live far away from physical stores; other possible buyers would be those that set high value on time and would prefer to buy on the Internet at a time of their choosing instead of visiting stores, and yet there are others that would buy from the Internet just as matter of utter preference. However, there needs to be a threshold market size comprising such buyers for the monopolist seller to charge the same price in the two stores. Let $F(\rho = 0) = \alpha$.

Proposition 2. *The monopolist seller will charge the same price for the two products if and only if*

$$\alpha \geq \frac{1}{4}(1-c^2)$$

Proof. The monopolist's profit function

$$\Pi = \left(\frac{1}{2}(P_p - P_e)((1-P_e)+(1-P_p)) + (1-P_e)\alpha P_e \right) + (1-P_p)\alpha(P_p - c)$$

The profit accruing to the monopolist seller from its e-tail store is $(1-P_e)\alpha P_e$, where $P_e = P_p = P_p{}^m$. A decrease in P_e to $P_p - \delta$ will result in an increase in sales volume and its profit now would be

$$(1-P_p - \delta)\alpha(P_p - \delta) + \frac{1}{2}((1-P_p - \delta)+(1-P_p))\delta(P_p - \delta).$$

The monopolist would find it sub-optimal to decrease price if

$$(1-P_e)\alpha P_e > (1-P_p - \delta)\alpha(P_p - \delta) + \frac{1}{2}((1-P_p - \delta)+(1-P_p))\delta(P_p - \delta),$$

or

$$(1-P_e)\alpha\delta + (P_p - \delta)\alpha\delta > \frac{1}{2}((1-P_p - \delta)+(1-P_p))\delta(P_p - \delta),$$

or

$$\alpha\,\delta(1-\delta) > \frac{1}{2}(2(1-P_p)-\delta)\delta(P_p-\delta),$$

or

$$\alpha(1-\delta) > \frac{1}{2}(2(1-P_p)-\delta)(P_p-\delta).$$

Setting the limit $\delta \to 0$, it reduces to the condition,

$$\alpha \geq (1-P_p)P_p,$$

or

$$\alpha \geq \frac{1}{4}(1-c^2).$$

In other words, if the market of Internet-biased buyers is nearly a quarter of the total market, the monopolist seller would charge the same price for its product on the Internet as well as the physical store. Indeed there are reports that sellers selling through distributors and retailers have opened up e-tail stores primarily meant for buyers for whom physical stores cannot serve.

Separate Management for E-Tail Store and Retail Store

In efforts to facilitate operations, a monopolist may assign two separate managers for the e-tail and retail outlets with minimal coordination between them. Although the option of separating the management appears inferior[3] to that of keeping the two units under the same management, the former may prove attractive from two points of view: (1) it might prove costly to implement integrated management, and (2) segregated management may be an interim stage necessitated by a strategic urgency of adopting the second channel (Internet channel) when it is believed that following the due process of re-designing the current operations to incorporate the new channel would lead to strategic failures. However, it is not rational for the monopolist to have both managers competing for buyers. To prevent competition between the channel stores the monopolist is likely to establish operational directives that inhibit competitive forces between the sister concerns.

Even though the two managers are independent, it is not quite obvious how the units will interact in the market. There could be central policy guidelines to coordinate the pricing activities of the two units. One such guideline would be for the two to charge the same price; another could be for the physical store to price as it would have priced the product disregarding the e-store, while the e-store is given to price its product assuming the price of the physical store. In the case of non-atomic distribution, the former is impossible. Hence, in this section we will assume the latter.

Assumption 2. *When the stores operate under independent managers, the monopolist will direct the physical store (with higher marginal cost) to act as a monopoly store—to disregard the existence of the e-tail store—while giving a price policy directive to the e-tail store to fix its price with reference to that of the physical store.*

Note that coordination between the two stores is ruled out as too costly. We reiterate that operationalizing two managers without a coordination mechanism is itself sub-optimal.

The choice of independent management can only be justified by some simplified coordination mechanism, and thus calls for the monopolist to set some ground rules for price determination in both stores. If the physical store is given to follow the policy of monopolistic pricing disregarding the e-tail store, while the latter is allowed to price its product competitively, the monopolist can end up earning profits lower than monopoly profits. It can be shown that with this mode of pricing the monopolist would always make less than its reservation incremental profit even when its aggregate profits from the two stores exceeds its monopoly profits. Note that the monopolist can make an incremental profit of $\frac{1}{2}c^2$ above its monopoly profits by simply pricing the Internet product so as to earn the same net margin per unit that it earn on the product sold in the physical store. Hence, whichever operational strategy the monopolist follows, its profits must at least be equal to the reservation level incremental profit of $\frac{1}{2}c^2$. Obviously, setting one store to the fixed strategy of acting monopolistically while letting the other act competitively is sub-optimal.

Proposition 3. *With regard to channels with independent management, the optimal policy would be such that $P_p = P_p^m$ and $P_e \geq P_p^m - c$; the profit increment from including the e-tail store.*

$$\Delta \Pi \geq \frac{1}{2}c^2.$$

Proof. We have seen that at, $P_e = P_p^m - c$, the monopolist will have the incentive to increase the price in the Internet store; at, $P_e = P_p$, no sale will take place in the

Internet store. Hence the monopolist will use a directive to set the price in the Internet store anywhere between P_p^m and $P_p - c$, with the condition that it is strictly less than P_p^m.

Partial Duopoly

Here we would like to consider the scenario when the dual channel monopoly is faced with a competitor in one channel, namely the Internet, but retains its monopoly in the other channel. This is an idealization of the competition in the book market between Amazon and Barnes and Noble. We can use our current model to forward a few conjectures or propositions about the qualitative aspects of the outcome prices without undertaking extensive analysis (which is the subject of a future paper).

Note that the dual channel monopoly has an advantage over the Internet-only firm in regard to the level of service it can offer a customer. The physical existence of the brick'n mortar store offers a greater degree of confidence of dealing to the buyers in the sense that they can refer any complaint to a physical location. This assurance of tangible existence lends credibility and offers insurance on the validity of a sale transaction. Second, the monopolist adds a dimension of quality to his product by facilitating returns of items bought through Internet stores to physical stores (as is commonly done); this dimension of quality is inaccessible to his Internet-only rival. Thus the monopolist by matching every other feature of the Internet-only firm can maintain a clear quality lead over its rival, and hence for the same cost commands a better quality!

Proposition 4. *The price of the Internet-only firm is lower than the dual-channel firm.* *Proof.* For proof we refer the reader to the preceding argument.

To facilitate competitive response to the Internet channel, the dual channel firm may decide to decouple the business operations of the two channels. If this policy is followed, the price in the physical or brick'n mortar store remains the same as monopoly price, while the price in Internet store is *lower* than it would be if coordination were maintained, and in consequence Internet prices in general are lower.

Remark 1. *Prices in channels of competition are lower when dual channel firms lets it stores to operate independently.*

Conclusion

The literature on e-tailing has considered various issues in buyers' behavior in regard to Internet shopping; such issues include convenience, price search costs, information search costs, customization, and so forth. In this chapter, the innovation was to consider buyers' behavior in light of the risk they assess with regard to Internet purchase; we consider the buyers to be *heterogeneous* in their assessment of risks. We consider a monopolist with stores in both channels, selling its product to buyers heterogeneous in this sense. We find that the buyers in brick and mortar stores pay a price premium for their insurance for the risk they perceive for Internet purchases; Internet buyers, on the other hand, enjoy relatively lower prices. The surpluses accruing to the industry through Internet transactions are shared by buyers and the seller. The seller, however, might charge the same price for the product on the Internet as well as in the physical store if there is a significant fraction of buyers with a clear preference for the Internet store. This implies that e-tailers will tend to charge the same price for their product if there exists a potential market of buyers outside of the geographical region covered by its chain of physical stores.

Using the model we predict that dual channel firms can maintain higher quality for their products for the same cost (fixed and variable). So an Internet-only firm offering the same product and Internet-specific qualities lags behind the brick'n mortar firm in the overall quality of the product. As a consequence, the dual channel firm is in a position to sell the same product at a higher price. We also argue that granting operational independence to its Internet store results in lower Internet prices in general and restore monopoly prices to the physical store products. The analytical presentation of this result is the subject of a future paper. It would be interesting to see how, in this framework, multiple sellers, differing in quality, would price their products in competitive markets—an approach that can address the price variability issue as witnessed in the Internet market. This is the subject of a follow-up.

References

Anderson, C. K., & Wilson, J. G. (2003). Wait or buy? The strategic consumer: pricing and profit implications. *Journal of the Operational Research Society, 54*(3), 299-307.

Burke, R. R. (1998). Do you see what I see? The future of virtual shopping. *Journal of the Academy of Marketing Science, 25*, 352-360.

Calkins, J., & Farello, M. (2000). Net profit from clicks and bricks. *BRW, 22*(8), 56-58.

Cao, Y., & Gruca, T. S. (2003). The effect of stock market dynamics on Internet price competition. *Journal of Service Research, 6*(1), 24-36.

Chiang, K.-P., & Dholakia, R. R. (2003). Factors driving consumer intention to shop online: An empirical investigation. *Journal of Consumer Psychology, 13*(1), 177-183

Dewan, R., Jing, B., & Seidmann, A. (2000). Adoption of Internet-based product customization and pricing strategies. *Journal of Management Information Systems, 17*(2).

Forsythe, S. M., & Shi, B. (2003). Consumer patronage and risk perceptions in Internet shopping. *Journal of Business Research, 56*(11), 867-875.

Frazier, G. L. (1999). Organizing and managing channels of distribution. *Academy of Marketing Science Journal, 27*(2), 226-240.

James, D. (2000). Online loyalty: Don't waste your bandwith. *Marketing News, 34*(18), 3.

Koyuncu, C., & Lien, D. (2003). E-commerce and consumer's purchasing behaviour. *Applied Economics, 35*(6), 721-725.

Lal, R., & Sarvary, M. (1999). When and how is the Internet likely to decrease price competition? *Marketing Science, 18*(4), 485-503.

Lee, Y., Lee, Z., & Larsen, K. R. T. (2003). Coping with Internet channel conflict. *Communications of the ACM, 46*(7), 137-142.

Liu, X., & Wei, K. K. (2003). An empirical study of product differences in consumers' e-commerce adoption behavior. *Electronic Commerce Research and Applications, 2*(3), 229-239.

Lu, D. (2003). Pricing behavior of a conventional retailer's online-branch. *Singapore Economic Review, 48*(2), 173-179.

Odekerken-Schroder, G., & Wetzels, M. (2003). Trade-offs in online purchase decisions: Two empirical studies in Europe. *European Management Journal, 21*(6), 731-739.

Schoenbachler, D., & Gordon, G. (2002). Multi-channel shopping: Understanding what drives channel choice. *The Journal of Consumer Marketing, 19*(1), 42-53.

Urban, G. L., Sultan, F., & Qualls, W. J. (2000). Placing trust at the center of your Internet strategy. *Sloan Management Review, 42*(1).

Ward, M. (2001). Will online shopping compete more with traditional retailing or catalog shopping. *Netnomics: Economic Research and Electronic Networking, 3*(2), 03-117.

Yoon, S. (2002). The antecedents and consequences of trust in online-purchase decisions. *Journal of Interactive Marketing, 16*(2), 47-63.

Endnotes

*   This is an extended and modified version of the authors' "Channel Prices of a Homogenous Product in a Dual Channel Monopoly", published in *IJEIS, vol. 1(2), 2005.*

[1]   By product fit we mean a measure of how close an actually available product is to the ideal product perceived by the buyer

[2]   The notion of *perfect customer service* is not specifically defined in the literature nor do we propose one; all we mean is a customer service that, by common agreement, is the best possible available at the given time.

[3]   From the optimization perspective, outcomes in separate management is subsumed by outcomes in integrated management.

Chapter VII

Enterprise Information Systems and B2B E-Commerce:
Enhancing Secure Transactions Using XML

C. Richard Baker, Adelphi University, USA

Abstract

While the overall investment in information technology (IT) decreased somewhat during the first several years of the 21st century, B2B e-commerce technologies have expanded at an increasing rate (Lim & Wen, 2002). The expansion of B2B e-commerce has been technologically based on enterprise-wide information systems (EISs) that allow electronic data transmission and execution of transactions in a secure and efficient manner. Since B2B e-commerce is Internet-based, the EISs used to support B2B e-commerce must be Internet capable. The primary language of the Internet, Hypertext Mark-up Language (HTML), is not well-suited for transmitting data and executing transactions. Consequently, Extensible Mark-up Language (XML) was developed to facilitate electronic information exchange applications, including many applications related to B2B e-commerce. As initially conceived, XML had a number of constraints, particularly in the area of data integrity and security, however, these constraints have gradually been overcome. This chapter reviews the objectives of using XML in B2B e-commerce, reviews the technical structure of XML, and discusses ways that security and privacy can be enhanced while engaging in B2B e-commerce.

Introduction

The rapid growth of B2B e-commerce has been facilitated by enterprise-wide information systems (EISs) that allow electronic data transmission and transaction execution in a secure and effective manner. Because B2B e-commerce is Internet-based, the EISs used to support B2B e-commerce must be Internet capable. Extensible Mark-up Language (XML) was developed in order to facilitate a variety of Internet-based data transmission applications, including various applications in B2B e-commerce. XML has some constraints, but these constraints are gradually being overcome. This chapter discusses the reasons for using XML in B2B e-commerce. It also reviews the technical structure of XML and discusses ways that data integrity can be maintained and security enhanced while engaging in B2B e-commerce.

Overview of B2B E-Commerce

B2B e-commerce is defined as the electronic transmission of data and the electronic execution of transactions between one or more business entities, or parts of business entities, using the Internet or privately-owned networks. B2B e-commerce requires an ability to transmit information between computer systems located in different places. Flanagen (1997) notes that B2B e-commerce includes various kinds of electronic communications between customers, suppliers, trading partners, and other parties. In many ways, B2B e-commerce is a bridge between the public Internet and privately-owned intranets. While the Internet belongs to everyone, intranets belong to specific organizations that construct secure networks using Internet protocols. The integration of private intranets within the more general Internet can be an important aspect of a business strategy, product delivery system, or customer support system. In effect, B2B e-commerce is a distributed processing environment that links various business entities. It is a virtual network within the Internet, one with security walls that prevent infiltration. The growth of B2B e-commerce has had important implications for how companies conduct their businesses, and it has dramatically reduced the cost structure in many industries (Lim & Wen, 2002).

B2B e-commerce improves business efficiency by increasing the speed of data transmission and reduction of errors. There is usually no need to re-enter data from paper documents, therefore clerical errors are reduced or eliminated. There is also a reduced need for human involvement in order-taking and accounts processing. At the same time, it must be recognized that if B2B e-commerce is to continue to expand there must be a common language to transmit information between different computer systems. HTML is not suited for that task because it can define only the format of data, not its meaning. XML was developed to address this problem. All of the major hardware and software vendors, including IBM, Microsoft, Sun, and Oracle support XML and have developed applications based upon it (Lim & Wen, 2002).

Background of XML

XML was introduced in 1996 by the World Wide Web Consortium (W3C) (Bos, 1999; Bray, Paoli, Sperberg-McQueen, & Maler, 2000). The creators of XML were: Jon Bosak, Chief Engineer of Sun Microsystem; Tim Bray of Textuality and Netscape; and C.M. Sperberg-McQueen of the University of Illinois at Champaign-Urbana. The purpose of creating XML was to establish an Internet version of the Standard Generalized Mark-up Language (SGML) (Markoff, 2000). The objective of XML is to allow organizations to create less expensive, more efficient, and more maintainable information systems which can interact with systems external to the primary entity (Webber & Dutton, 2001).

Mark-up Languages

Mark-up languages are widely used in Internet applications because they facilitate communication between differing computer systems. In a general sense, a mark-up language identifies the structure in a document (Walsh, 1998). There are three primary mark-up languages: SGML (Standard Generalized Mark-up Language); HTML (Hypertext Mark-up Language); and XML (Extensible Mark-up Language). In effect, SGML is the mother tongue of all mark-up languages (Flynn, 2003); but it is very complex and costly to use. The primary users of SGML are government agencies, such as the U.S. Department of Defense and the Internal Revenue Service, as well as large aerospace, automotive, and telecommunications companies (Johnson, 1999). As noted before, HTML is not suited to data transmission or transaction execution. Consequently, XML was created to facilitate the expansion of the Internet.

The Goals of Using XML in B2B E-Commerce

There is a number of goals associated with the use of XML in B2B e-commerce (see Webber & Dutton, 2000). These include:

1. Reducing the over all cost of doing business.
2. Reducing the cost of entry into e-business.
3. Providing an easy to use tool-set.
4. Improving data integrity and accessibility.
5. Providing security controls.
6. Providing extendable and controllable technology.
7. Integration with existing systems.
8. Utilizing open standards.
9. Providing interoperability.
10. Being globally deployable and maintainable.

These goals will be briefly discussed next, the first goal being to reduce the overall cost of doing business.

The human and process cost is where CFOs are going to expect reductions as part of initiatives to lower fixed costs and improve profitability. This will be done through deployment of enterprise applications, process re-engineering and automating inter-business processes such as procurement, supply chain, and distribution management. (Brockman, 2002)

Using XML, Web sites can exchange data easily and rapidly, thus facilitating the growth of e-commerce (Streitfield, 2000). XML can be used to link companies in various parts of a supply chain thereby allowing companies to automate the supply chain using the Internet (Markoff, 2000). XML also allows the creation of Internet based information tools that can be accessed in the office, at home, or while traveling (Markoff, 2000). These technologies can reduce the overall cost of doing business.

The second objective of using XML is to reduce the cost of entry into e-commerce. The ability to transmit and interpret data using XML can lower the cost of entry into e-commerce for small and medium-sized companies (Webber & Dutton, 2000). Essentially, XML simplifies the process of transition from traditional brick and mortar business to e-commerce. Providing an easy to use tool-set is the third goal of using XML in e-commerce. XML permits the implementation of automatic lookup features, such as those used for search engines (Webber & Dutton, 2000). Search engines have become essential tools for navigating the Internet. Using XML's automatic lookup interfaces, the Internet user can perform a search by typing a word or phrase. This has enhanced access to all types of information.

Goal four is to assure data integrity, while maintaining accessibility. The ability to transmit information and execute transactions in marketing, sales, customer service, and supply chain management permits integration between disparate entities and allows the creation of virtual entities (Brockman, 2002). The use of XML in combination with other technologies also permits multimedia transmission through the Internet. The ease with which data can be transmitted makes the use of XML essential to businesses that need reliable and fast data transmission.

The fifth goal is to provide appropriate levels of security and control. This is an issue that is crucial to the development of e-commerce. The fact that XML contains not just words and objects, but also logic and embedded programs, makes security easier to accomplish. Businesses rely on software developers to create XML application programs that can encrypt data and, at the same time, allow the data to be readable by the intended recipient.

Providing extendable and controllable technology is the sixth goal. As with any computer technology, further growth is predicted. XML is designed to be flexible so that it can adapt to changing environments. Goal seven addresses the issue of integration with existing, legacy systems. Various appliance programs have been designed to aid in the transition to XML. These applications can reuse software, thereby reducing integration time and expense (Brockman, 2002). In addition, because XML is text-based, it avoids some of the problems associated with binary coding (Streitfield, 2000).

The eighth goal is to utilize open standards. This goal is being achieved through the implementation of a registry system for companies using XML. The registry system categorizes companies by industry codes created by the U.S. government, by United Nations/SPSC codes, and by geographical location. The registry also allows companies to interact with other registered companies by indicating which XML formats they support (Webber & Dutton, 2003).

Providing interoperability is the ninth goal.

The plan is to create a new Internet operating system that will shift an array of applications from the hard disks of personal computers onto the Net. A range of software services, from word processing and spreadsheet programs to data storage and other peripherals, will be on powerful network computers accessible through the Internet. (Markoff, 2000)

Achieving this goal might eliminate the need to use a personal computer within a network to obtain data and information.

The tenth goal is to assure that XML is globally deployable and maintainable. The Internet is a world-wide phenomenon, therefore XML must permit global applicability of business processes. For example, using XML, a user might be able to input his or her name in Japanese characters (kanji) in a business transaction originating in Tokyo, or in the Cyrillic alphabet originating from Moscow, thereby minimizing the impact of a strictly "Anglophone Internet" (Streitfield, 2000). A single global electronic marketplace based upon a public XML-based infrastructure could permit global electronic business to be conducted in a secure and consistent manner (Webber & Dutton, 2003).

Technical Aspects of XML

Like SGML, XML is a meta-language. A meta-language is a language that can define or describe another language (Johnson, 1999). The advantage of a meta-language is that a user is able to create customized e-commerce applications. XML is also extensible because users can create their own elements and attributes and assign them any names they wish, instead of being restricted to a limited number of pre-defined elements. Examples of elements are: lists, tables, headings, paragraphs, images, and hyperlinks (Young, 2001). Although XML does not contain a set of pre-defined elements, it has a strictly defined syntax which is easy to understand. The XML syntax rules are simple but strict. These rules give XML documents a predictable format which makes it easier for users to write and read (Young, 2001).

XML Structure

An XML document has both a logical and a physical structure. The logical and physical structure of an XML document must be nested correctly so that the document can be processed. The logical structure of an XML document includes: *declarations*, *elements*, *comments*, and *processing instructions* (Bray et al., 2000). These are discussed in the following sub-sections, and in Exhibit 1. An example of a simple XML document relating to the purchase of a compact disk is shown in Exhibit 1.

Declarations

Various types of declarations can be used in a document. One type of declaration specifies the version of XML that is being used. This declaration appears in the first line entered in an XML document. For example, the following code indicates that the XML version is 1.0: *<?xml version="1.0"?>*. Another type of declaration, is a document type declaration (DTD), which specifies limitations on the logical structure of the document. DTDs will be discussed in a later section.

Exhibit 1.

```
<?xml version="1.0" encoding="iso-8859-1" ?>        Declaration

<?xml-stylesheet href="orders.xsl"?>       Processing Instruction

<order>
<order id="ord123456">
<customer id="cust0921">
<customer>                                  Element
        <first-name>Bill</first-name>
        <last-name>Gates</last-name>
<address>
        <street>One Microsoft Way</street>
        <city>Redmond</city>
        <state>WA</state>
        <zip>98052</zip>
</address>
</customer>

<item>                                      Sub-Element
    <compact-disc>
        <title>White Album</title>
        <artist>Beatles</artist>
        <price>16.95</price>
    </compact-disc>
    <compact-disc>
        <title>Trucking</title>
        <artist>Grateful Dead</artist>
        <price>17.55</price>
    </compact-disc>

</item>

<!-- Always go the extra mile for the customer -->    Comment

<special-instructions xmlns:html="http://www.w3.org/1999/xhtml/">
    <html:p>If customer is not available at the address then attempt to
       leave package at one of the following locations listed in order of
       which should be attempted first
    <html:ol>
       <html:li>Next Door</html:li>
       <html:li>On Doorstep</html:li>
    </html:ol>
    <html:b>Note</html:b> Remember to leave a note detailing where
       to pick up the package.
    </html:p>
</special-instructions>
</order>
```

Elements

An XML document also includes elements which are separate and distinct from each other. Elements can be names and attributes of data. For example, a <customer> element would indicate that some data follows which contains information about a customer. Elements can be nested under elements (e.g., customer, address, product). The sub-elements are placed under the "parent" element within the document.

Comments

Comments can appear anywhere in the document. Comments are not part of the data. They are only reminders.

Processing Instructions

Processing instructions allow XML documents to include instructions about an application. Processing instructions also include instructions regarding how the document should be displayed. For example, a processing instruction could specify how a document should be displayed by a Web browser.

Enhancing Data Integrity in XML

Document Type Definitions

An XML document must be readable by a "parser" which converts the document into machine code. While an XML document may be able to be processed by a parser, this does not necessarily mean that the document is valid. To be valid, an XML document must also be validated. This is done by comparing data in the document to a pre-determined structure using a document type definition (DTDs). A DTD establishes the structure of the elements in a document. Exhibit 2 provides an example of a DTD (called "address.dtd").

The DTD in Exhibit 2 indicates that every address must have one or more address lines, one city line, one state line, and one zip code line. The address must be written in text, and it must appear in the sequence specified. Using DTD to structure an XML document is one way to validate the data. However, using DTDs in this way has several shortcomings. First, the DTD is not an XML document in and of itself, and it cannot be processed or parsed. Second, a DTD does not recognize data as

Exhibit 2.

```
<?xml version="1.0" encoding="UTF-8"/>

<ELEMENT address (addressLine, city,
        state, zip)>
<ELEMENT addressLine (#PCDATA)>
<ELEMENT city (#PCDATA)>
<ELEMENT state (#PCDATA)>
<ELEMENT zip (#PCDATA)>
<!DOCTYPE address SYSTEM
        "address.dtd">

<address>
        <addressLine>One Microsoft Way</addressLine>
        <city>Redmond</city>
        <state>WA</state>
        <zip>98052</zip>
</address>
```

DTD

Element

being numerical. Instead a data sequence is treated as a string. This is a shortcoming because it requires users to invent ways to validate the data without using concepts like greater than, equal to, or less than. Finally, a DTD does not permit element names to be used a second time within the same document. This restricts the use of element names and forces developers to choose names that may not be intuitive or natural (Lin & Wen, 2002).

XML Schema

To address the shortcomings of DTDs, the W3C introduced "XML Schema" in 2001 (Lin & Wen, 2002). Unlike DTDs, an XML schema is an XML document. This permits processing of the information included in the XML schema. An XML schema also permits the treatment of data as numerical, and allows the data to be constrained within certain values. The types of constraints that can be used in an XML Schema include:

- Data type constraints (String, Boolean, floating point, and others).
- Cardinality constraints (The minOccurs and maxOccurs attributes specify that the number of occurrences of an element can be 0, 1, or unbounded).
- Range constraints (<xsd:minExclusive>, <xsd:minInclusive>, <xsd:maxExclusive>, and <xsd:maxInclusive> allow users to specify the range of values that are allowable for an element or an attribute).
- Length constraints (<xsd:length>, <xsd:minLength> and <xsd:maxLength> allow the programmer to constrain the length of an element).

- Precision constraints (The totalDigits and fractionDigits attributes specify the number of digits for a number).

- Enumeration constraints (A programmer can use <xsd:enumeration> to specify that an element must be chosen from a list).

- Pattern constraints (<xsd:pattern> allows a programmer to specify the pattern of a certain type of data; for example, <xsd:pattern value="[0-9]3[0-9]{7} "/> for a phone number).

- Primary key constraints (Through the use of <xsd:key>, a programmer can specify the primary key for an element in a manner similar to how a primary key can be defined in a relational database).

- Foreign key constraints (<xsd:keyref> permits the programmer to set up a foreign key in a manner similar to a relational database).

An example of an XML schema is shown in Exhibit 3, followed by an XML document which relates to the schema shown in Exhibit 4.

Exhibit 3.

```
<?xml version="1.0"?>
<xsd:schema xmlns:xsd="http://
    www.w3.org/2001/XML.Schema">          Schema
<xsd:element name="item"
      type="itemType"/>
      <xsd:complexType name="itemType">
      <xsd:sequence>
      <xsd:element name="compact-disc"
      type="music"
      minOccurs="0"
      maxOccurs="unbounded"/>
      </xsd:sequence>
      </xsd:complexType>

      <xsd:complexType name="compact-disc">
      <xsd:sequence>
      <xsd:element name="title"
      type="xsd:string"/>
      <xsd:element name="artist"
      type="xsd:string"/>
      <xsd:element name="price"
      type="xsd:float"/>
      </xsd:sequence>
      </xsd:complexType>
</xsd:schema>
```

Exhibit 4.

```
<?xml version="1.0"?>
<item>
    <compact-disc>
        <title>White Album</title>
        <artist>Beatles</artist>
        <price>16.95</price>
    </compact-disc>
    <compact-disc>
        <title>Trucking</title>
        <artist>Grateful Dead</artist>
        <price>17.55</price>
    </compact-disc>
</item>
```

XML Document

Enhancing Security in B2B E-Commerce

Beyond the use of DTDs and XML schemas, e-commerce enterprises can also establish security policies using XML tools created by developers and user groups such as W3C. Using these tools, XML documents can have sections that are encrypted, or the documents themselves can be digitally signed, distributed, and interpreted by the recipients (Hondo, Nagaratnam, & Nadalin, 2002).

There are various important business reasons for creating technologies that enhance security in B2B e-commerce. The ability to authenticate the identity of a person or an entity when they initiate a transaction allows businesses to offer different types of services to different customers, and prevents losses from identity theft and repudiation. Enhanced data integrity also helps to ensure that each party to a transaction has confidence in the transaction. It is important to create an audit trail and to maintain evidence in case of repudiation. In addition, it is necessary to protect against internal threats from employees or others with inside access to the company's systems. Many transactions require that confidentiality be maintained from the inception of the transaction (e.g., for credit card numbers and other sensitive data). Finally, businesses need to protect themselves from denial-of-service attacks which can disrupt operations (Hondo et al., 2002).

Various technologies have been developed to enhance the security of XML documents in B2B e-commerce. The following is a brief discussion of some of these technologies.

Digital Signature

An XML digital signature provides a way to verify the origin of a message. A digital signature allows XML documents to be signed using various algorithms. Digital signatures can be used for validation of messages and to protect against repudiation of transactions (see http://www.w3.org/Signature for more information)(Hondo et al., 2002).

Security Assertion Mark-up Language

Security Assertion Mark-up Language (SAML) was created to provide a common language for sharing security services between companies. SAML permits companies to exchange authentication, authorization, and profile information between customers, partners, or suppliers regardless of differences in their security systems or in the EISs that support their B2B e-commerce activities. SAML helps to promote interoperability between disparate security systems and allows security of e-business transactions across company boundaries (see http:www.oasisopen.org/committees/security/docs for more information; Hondo et al., 2002).

Encryption

XML encryption technologies permit encryption of digital content, including graphical interchange format (GIF) images. XML encryption also allows parts of an XML document to be encrypted while leaving other parts un-encrypted. There can be complete encryption of the XML document, or super-encryption (i.e., encrypting an XML document when some parts have already been encrypted; see http://www.w3c.org/Encription for more information; Hondo et al., 2002).

Simple Object Access Protocol

Simple object access protocol (SOAP) is a way to exchange data between different computer networks by superimposing an envelope around an XML document. SOAP consists of three parts: an envelope that defines the content of a message; a set of encoding rules for expressing application-defined data types; and a way to implement communication and responses between the sender and receiver. SOAP can be used in combination with a variety of network communication protocols such as file transfer protocol (FTP) (Hondo et al., 2002).

An Example of Enhanced Security in E-Commerce

The following is a basic scenario involving an Internet-based reservation system for a travel agency (e.g., Expedia.com or Travelocity)[1]. A customer of the travel agency accesses the agency's Web site to search for air travel from New York City to Seattle. After accessing the Web page, the customer is asked to input information about him or herself and to initiate a reservation request based on desired travel dates and times and preferred airlines. After receiving the information, the reservation system interacts with an airline reservation system to request a reservation. The travel agency reservation system and the airline reservation system both use XML tags to exchange information and payment details. This is done using a common specification established by the airline industry. The industry specification requires requests from the travel agency reservation system to be marked with a <makeReservation> tag. The travel agency's reservation system is designed to include a <makeReservation> tag when it receives a travel request from a customer.

Prior to completing the reservation and finalizing payment, the customer is able to search the reservation system for itineraries based on price, time of travel, airline, and so forth, and then decide whether to purchase the travel from that agency. The customer's request to the travel agency reservation system will ultimately include personal information, itinerary, and credit card details. This data is transmitted in a SOAP protected message, such as that described previously and in Exhibit 5. The SOAP contains all of the information necessary to complete the reservation in a secure and protected envelope. The travel agency reservation system interacts with the airline reservation system by sending the reservation request, which also includes

Exhibit 5.

```
<SOAP-ENV:Envelope                                              SOAP
   xmins:SOAP-ENV="http://schemas.xmlsoap.org/soap/envelope/">
<SOAP-ENV:Header>
<SOAP-ENV:Signature
    xmls:SOAP-SEC="http://schemas.xmlsoap.org/soap/security/2000-12">
    <ds:Signature xmins:ds="http://www.w3.org/2000/09/xmldsig#">
      ...
    <ds:Reference URI="#BODY"../>
      ...
    </SOAP-ENV:Signature>
    </SOAP-ENV:Header>

<SOAP-ENV:Body xmins:                                           Body
    SOAP-SEC="http://schemas.xmlsoap.org/soap/security/2000-12"
    SOAP-SEC:id="Body">

    <m:Issue Tickets xmins:m="some-URI">
    <m:company>Expedia.com</m:company>
    <m:ticket holder>Bill Gates</m:ticket holder>
    <m:customerCC>Visa</m:customerCC>
    <m:CC#>123-456-7890</m:CC#>
    </m:Issue Tickets>

</SOAP-ENV:Body>
</SOAP-ENV:Envelope>
```

the agency's details as well as the customer's details. When the airline reservation system receives the reservation request, the airline reservation system queries a database concerning the availability of seats for that particular itinerary. Using XML, the airline reservation system returns a response after noting the reservation in its own backend database. The response specifies the details of the reservation along with a record locator number such as: <recordLocator>ABCXYZ123</recordLocator>. When the travel agency reservation system receives the message from the airline reservation system, the travel agency system looks for the <recordLocator> tag, and when it finds the record locator it initiates an order to issue a ticket to the customer.

This is a simplified scenario which omits most of the technical details of the system and the security enhancement mechanisms employed. The scenario is intended to demonstrate that XML, and the security enhancement mechanisms which accompany it, make the process of making travel reservations much easier for customers and reduce the overall cost of making such reservations.

Recent Developments

In recent years, there has been an increased emphasis on security and privacy in B2B e-commerce. One particular aspect of this increased emphasis has been the development of what has been called the semantic Web. The semantic Web was created by members of the same team that developed XML (Berners-Lee, Hendler, & Lassila, 2001). The semantic Web combines XML coding with other technologies that permit the creation of machine understandable Web pages. One of the primary reasons for the creation of the semantic Web was to host e-business applications. Such applications utilize not only XML coding, but other knowledge management technologies such as ontologies and intelligent information integration (Singh, Iyer, & Salam, 2005). Security in B2B e-commerce necessitates the identification and authentication of participants in a transaction as well as tracing all of the elements of the transaction. One way to enhance security is to require participants to possess certain credentials when they execute transactions. Such credentials, for example, random numbers, may vary with each transaction. Identity theft and repudiation can be reduced through the use of such credentials. However, there may be a problem if the credentials are stolen. Various encryption techniques have also been proposed to enhance security in e-business transactions in combination with the use of credentials.

As an example, a hospital might decide to order surgical equipment from a hospital supply company. There may be certain negotiations and agreements made between the participants to the transaction. However, the hospital supply company may also want to order some of its sub-components from another company and may not want to divulge the fact it is selling equipment to a particular hospital. In this case, there must be access control and encryption techniques to protect sensitive information from being made available to other participants in the supply chain. Thus, security in B2B e-commerce involves the inclusion of security features in all aspects of the knowledge management cycle. In other words, an enterprise must protect its intellectual property and trade secrets using electronic technologies. Security measures must therefore be incorporated into all aspects of the knowledge management process (Thuraisingham, 2005). The semantic Web is therefore a logical extension of the use of XML in B2B e-commerce.

Conclusion

The rapid growth of B2B e-commerce has relied on accounting and enterprise-wide information systems (EISs) that permit data transmission and transaction execution in an more effective and efficient manner. Since B2B e-commerce is Internet-based, the EISs required to support e-commerce must be Internet capable. The primary language of the Internet, Hypertext Mark-up Language (HTML), was not well-suited for transmitting data and executing transactions; therefore, Extensible Mark-up Language (XML) was developed to facilitate a wide range of Internet-based information exchange applications, including B2B e-commerce. XML also allows legacy data to be accessed using the Internet. Initially XML had a number of constraints, particularly in the area of data integrity, however, these constraints are rapidly being overcome. This chapter has discussed the goals of using XML in B2B e-commerce. These goals are primarily related to reducing the cost of engaging in both traditional brick and mortar businesses and in e-commerce. The goals of XML in e-commerce are also directed toward developing technologies that can improve business processes. The chapter has also reviewed the technical structure of XML in order to demonstrate the relative ease with which XML documents can be created and the manner in which such documents can be understood even by persons who are not conversant with the language. Finally, the chapter has discussed ways that data integrity can be maintained and security enhanced while using XML in B2B e-commerce. These include the use of DTDs, XML Schema, and SOAPs.

References

Berners-Lee, T., Hendler, J., & Lassila, O. (2001, May). The semantic Web. *Scientific American, 284*(5), 34-43.

Bos, B. (1999, March 27). XML in 10 points. *W3C Communications Team.* Retrieved September 28, 2003, from http://www.w3.org/XML/1999/XML-in-10-points

Bray, T., Paoli, J., Sperberg-McQueen, C. M., & Maler, E. (2000, October 6). Extensible markup language (XML) 1.0 (2nd ed.). *W3C XML Working Group.* Retrieved September 28, 2003, from http://www.w3.org/TR/REC-xml

Brockman, P. (2002). *What's XML got to do with it?* Allen, TX: A4 Neworks.com. Retrieved February, http://www.thedacs.net/topics/xml/xml2dowithit.pdf

Flanagen, P. (1997, May). The 10 hottest technologies in telecom. *Telecommunications,* 25-32.

Flynn, P. (2003, January 14). *The XML FAQ.* Cork, Ireland: University College Cork. Retrieved September 23, 2003, from http://www.ucc.ie:8080/cocoon/xmlfaq

Hondo, M., Nagaratnam, N., & Nadalin, A. (2002). Securing Web services. *IBM Systems Journal, 41*(2), 228-242.

Johnson, M. (1999, April). XML for the absolute beginner: A guided tour from HTML to processing XML with Java. *Java World.* Retrieved September 23, 2003, from http:javaworld.com/javaworld/jw-04-1999/jw-04-xml_p.html

Lim, B. L., & Wen, H. J. (2002). The impact of next generation XML. *Information Management & Computer Security, 10*(1), 33-40.

Markoff, J. (2000, June 7). The next big leap? It's called XML. *The New York Times,* H4.

Singh, R., Iyer, L., & Salam, A. F. (2005). Semantic e-business. *International Journal on Semantic Web and Information Technology, 1*(1), 19-35.

Streitfield, D. (2000, September). Three little letters but one big leap? Internet experts enthusiastic about XML programming potential. *The Washington Post,* G25.

Thuraisingham, B. (2005, December). Directions for security and privacy for semantic e-business applications. *Communications of the ACM, 48*(12), 71-73.

Walsh, N. (1998, October). What is XML? *XML.com.* Retrieved September 27, 2003, from http://www.xml.com/lpt/a/98/10/guide1.html

Webber, D., & Dutton, A. (2001, January 4). Understanding ebXML, UDDI, XML/EDI. *Computer Business Review Online.* Retrieved September 23, 2003, from http://www.cbronline.com/cbr_archive/b7f9971eada4d46f80256d350047ceec

Young, M. J. (2001). *XML step by step: Second edition.* Redmond, WA: Microsoft Press.

Endnote

[1]   Adapted from Hondo et al. (2002).

Chapter VIII

Unleashing the Potential of SCM:
The Adoption of ERP in Large Danish Enterprises

Charles Møller, Aarhus School of Business, Denmark

Abstract

This chapter argues that with the present state of enterprise resource planning (ERP) adoption by the companies, the potential benefits of supply chain management (SCM) and integration is about to be unleashed. This chapter presents the results and the implications of a survey on ERP adoption in the 500 largest Danish enterprises. The study is based on telephone interviews with ERP managers in 88.4% of the "top 500" enterprises in Denmark. Based on the survey, the chapter suggests the following four propositions: (1) ERP has become the pervasive infrastructure; (2) ERP has become a contemporary technology; (3) ERP adoption has matured; and (4) ERP adoption is converging towards a dominant design. Finally, the chapter discusses the general implications of the surveyed state of practice on the SCM research challenges. Consequently, we argue that research needs to adjust its conceptions of the ERP concept towards ERP II in order to accommodate to the emerging practices.

Introduction

SCM (supply chain management) is perhaps the most critical logistics issue in the majority of today's businesses. The challenge of SCM is to integrate and to coordinate activities across organizational boundaries in order to manage the entire supply chain as a whole. Various enterprise systems (ES) and above all the most recent ERP systems from the major vendors include new technologies to integrate the supply chain. The ERP system provides a platform for SCM, and businesses can adopt the new functions offered by the new generation of enterprise systems thus taking advantage of the technological innovations.

ERP (enterprise resource planning) is a constantly changing and evolving concept (Klaus, Rosemann, & Gable, 2000). The ERP systems have gradually been designed, developed, and improved by the ERP vendors in response to new technologies and emerging business requirement (Mabert, Soni, & Venkataramanan, 2001). As a result, the contemporary ERP packages from the major vendors now include not only the basic ERP functionality but also e-business functions like CRM, EAI, and in particular SCM and other functions that previously were associated with other classes of systems (Callaway, 2000).

Research is less responsive to the emerging new business practices, and often we have seen ERP research using an outdated perspective. Most papers on ERP cite Davenport's (1998) paper as a baseline for their perception of the ERP phenomena or the more generic concept of enterprise systems (ES). Another large body of ERP papers quotes forecasts from analyst like Gartner, Forrester, or AMR to argue for the importance of ERP and the state of the ERP market. In general, these sources are reliable but the research companies themselves are actors in the ERP industry and their predictions are often rather optimistic.

In the aftermath of a Danish research project on the implementation of APS (advanced planning and scheduling) and ERP, the discrepancies between the conceptions based on theoretical studies and the practices experienced in the case studies (Hørlück et al., 2001) led to a study of the adoption of ERP based on practitioner perception. Consequently, a study of ERP practices in large Danish enterprises was initiated (Møller, Kræmmergaard, & Rotbøl, 2003). The aim of this chapter is to present an overview of the findings and to discuss the implications for SCM.

This chapter will first discuss the dynamics of enterprise systems concepts and the relation between the ERP systems and SCM. Based on this discussion, the survey focus is established. Then the survey is outlined along with the research method. The findings from the survey are then presented and discussed in the proceeding chapter. Finally the conclusions are summarized and further research on ERP and SCM is proposed.

Enterprise Resource Planning Systems

The concept of ERP has often been explained through the historical development of ERP (Chen, 2001; Klaus, Rosemann, & Gable, 2000; Markus & Tanis, 2000). The fundamental structure of ERP has its origin in the fifties and in sixties with the development of the early inventory control (IC) systems and bill of material (BOM) processors. The progress continued during the seventies and eighties with the development of the material requirement planning (MRP) systems and the manufacturing resource planning (MRP II) systems. The vendors gradually integrated more areas into the scope of the standardized information systems and the advances peaked in the early nineties with the advent of the enterprise resource planning (ERP) system—often embodied in the SAP R/3 system (Bancroft, 1998).

ERP is a standardized software package designed to integrate the internal value chain of an enterprise. According to Nah (2002), the American Production and Inventory Control Society (APICS) defines ERP as: "a method for the effective planning and controlling of all the resources needed to take, make, ship and account for customer orders in a manufacturing, distribution or service company". The APICS definition extends the concept of ERP from an IT system towards a technology to manage and organize the processes of an enterprise.

The research on ERP up until 2000 is reasonably well documented and analyzed through the works of Esteves and Pastor (2001). They review the ERP literature through an ERP life cycle model reflecting the phases of the adoption process. Adoption is the foundation of a large strand of ERP implementation research (e.g., Nah, Lau, & Kuang, 2001; Shanks, Seddon, & Willcocks, 2003). Adoption and phased life cycle thinking is also found in Markus and Tanis (2000) who provide an overview of the implementation issues.

Another strand of ERP research is the process-oriented research (e.g., Al-Mashari, 2001). This strand emphasizes the ERP technology as an enabler of BPR (business process re-engineering) and change (Siriginidi, 2000). The research deals with issues of process orientation, integration, and the organizational change—both internally and as a second phase in the supply chain (Willis & Willis-Brown, 2002).

A third strand of ERP research is concerned with ERP in a strategic business context (e.g., Kalling, 2003). Davenport's sequel on enterprise systems evolution (Davenport, 1998, 2000; Davenport & Brooks, 2004; Davenport, Harris, & Cantrell, 2004) is an excellent indicator of the evolution of business managers' perception of ERP. The discussions on ERP developed over the first enthusiastic expectations regarding business integration, via a growing number of horror stories about failed or out-of-control projects, toward a more profound understanding of the issues of integration. Today we see the same expectations being uttered on the impact of e-business and SCM (Davenport & Brooks, 2004).

Supply Chain Management

Supply chain management (SCM) has become one of the most important new business concepts and the source of competitive advantage (Christopher, 1998). In SCM, the role of the ES is to extend the internal business processes into the extended enterprises and thus to develop integrated supply chains (Fox, 1999). Theoretically SCM has emphasized the management of the entire supply chain as one entity, and one of the frequently quoted cases of successful SCM is Dell (e.g., Margretta, 1998). IT played a major role in the transformation of the Dell supply chain and IT has a tremendous influence on achieving effective SCM in general (Gunasekaran & Ngai, 2004).

European supply chain executives identified four important key SCM issues (Akkermans et al., 2002): (1) further integration of activities between suppliers and customers; (2) on-going changes in supply chain needs and required flexibility from IT; (3) more mass customization of products and services leading to increasing assortments while decreasing cycle times and inventories; (4) the locus of the drivers' seat of the entire supply chain; and (5) supply chain consisting of several independent enterprises. The same executives saw only a modest role for ERP improvements in future supply chain effectiveness and a clear risk of ERP actually limiting progress in SCM.

On the other hand, Davenport and Brooks (2004) argue that early ERP were not primarily focused on the supply chain, but the businesses that have been able to extend their enterprise systems into the supply chain with "bolt on" SCM systems have experienced substantial benefits. The key to this is the development of infrastructural and strategic capabilities embodied in ERP and SCM systems, also known as the next generation of ERP or ERP II.

The Next Generation ERP

The ERP market experienced a hype triggered by companies rushing to solve the Y2K problem, but after Y2K, the ERP market soured. Back in those days, the Internet boomed and Gartner Group which originally named ERP, redefined ERP into ERP II (Bond et al., 2000). ERP II includes six elements that touch on business, application, and technology strategy: (1) the role of ERP II; (2) its business domain; (3) the functions addressed within that domain; (4) the kinds of processes required by those functions; (5) the system architectures that can support those processes; and (6) the way in which data is handled within those architectures. These ERP II elements represent an expansion of traditional ERP and ERP II is essentially componentized ERP, e-business, and collaboration in the supply chain.

Figure 1. The conceptual framework of ERP II (Source: Møller, 2003)

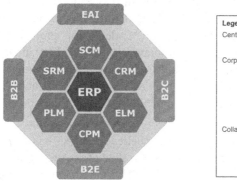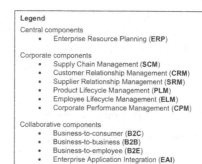

It was doubtful that traditional ERP would meet the e-business challenge (Mabert, Soni, & Venkataramanan, 2001). New vendors of "bolt-on" systems like, for example, i2 Technology with supply chain management (SCM) systems and Siebel with customer relationship management (CRM) systems emerged on the scene (Callaway, 2000). Application integration (EAI) became a serious issue (Thermistocleus, Irani, & Keefe, 2001) and a new ERP integration strategy called "Best of Breed" (BOB) opposed to the single-vendor strategy became a feasible strategy to integrate an enterprise (Light, Holland, & Wills, 2001) by using EAI and the BOB solutions. New delivery and pricing methods like ASP (application service provider) and ERP rentals were conceived (Harrell, Higgins, & Ludwig, 2001) and the traditional ERP vendors were challenged.

The single ERP vendor strategy competed with the "Best-of-Breed" strategy. Markus, Petrie, and Axline (2000) discuss two possible views on the future of ERP: a continuity view extending on the existing ERP systems and a discontinuity view where exchanges drive the supply chain integration and ERP is replaced by BOB.

Table 1. "Top 5" world-wide ERP software application new license revenue market share estimates for 2002 (Source: Gartner Dataquest, June, 2003)

Vendor	2002 Market Share	2001 Market Share
SAP AG	25.1%	24.7%
Oracle	7.0%	7.9%
PeopleSoft	6.5%	7.6%
SAGE	5.4%	4.6%
Microsoft Business Solutions	4.9%	4.6%
Others	51.1%	50.3%
Total Market Share	*100.0%*	*100.0%*

Throughout the ERP industry the new philosophy of ERP and e-business was gradually incorporated into the legacy system offering, systems architectures were redesigned and modularized, for example, like SAP did with the NetWeaver platform and like Microsoft intends to do with their "Code Green" project. This is why the contemporary standard systems incorporate ERP II. The ERP industry survived the challenge, and a recent market analysis does not render any signs of market fragmentation. Table 1 illustrates the "top 5" ERP vendors, 2001 and 2002 market shares, and we see one dominant actor, a handful of major vendors, and a large number of insignificant vendors.

To conclude the discussion on enterprise systems, we believe that ERP has evolved from being a state-of-the-art technology toward being a state of practice. The new package offered by the major vendors has been extended by adoption of the e-business technologies into the ERP systems and by extending the systems scope into the supply chain—they have in fact transformed into ERP II systems. Thus a company, which has adopted a recent ERP system from one of the major vendors, will now have an adequate platform for integrating its processes into the supply chain. The managerial implication of this development could be that most enterprises now have a huge potential for reaping the benefits that ERP has lead them to expect for years (Davenport & Brooks, 2004).

Survey Method and Focus

The purpose of the study is to explore the adoption of ERP in large Danish enterprises. Danish enterprises are relative small compared to the U.S. companies. However, we expect findings comparable to those of other European countries and maybe to North America. Experience has shown that a traditional survey using a detailed questionnaire yields a low response rate. Therefore, we chose telephone interviews as our survey instrument.

A recent study by Hunton, Lipincott, and Reck (2004) suggested better financial performance for ERP adopters, but the pattern of ERP adoption is not homogeneous. Different business sectors (Duplaga & Astani, 2003) and different company sizes (Mabert, Soni, & Venkataramann, 2003) have different practices. Therefore the survey has been focused on: (1) ERP installation, (2) business sector, (3) company size, and (4) financial performance.

This survey is based on telephone interviews with ERP managers in 500 Danish enterprises. The interviews were carried out from the beginning of March until the end of April 2003, that is, the period covers before, during, and after the war in Iraq. The uncertain business climate may have had an impact on the survey results.

Table 2. Overview of DK-500 enterprises (2002)

	N	Minimum	Maximum	Mean
Revenue (DKK m)	500	535	89,073	3,062
Profit (DDK m)	482	-9,176	5,819	76
Staff	485	5	259,813	2,422
Own capital (DDK m)	500	-7,274	13,679	125

The 500 companies originated from the Børsen list (DK-500) of the largest Danish companies. The Børsen 500 list (http://borsen.dk/videnresearch/dk500/) is the equivalent of the U.S. Fortune 500 list. Børsen 500 (DK-500) is published annually by the Danish magazine *Børsen*. The large Danish corporations are ranked according to revenue and other publicly available data. This survey is based on the 2002 list. The DK-500 data included revenue, profit, and the number of employees. In most cases, data is available for 2001 and 2002. The public and government sectors are not included in the list.

The Danish enterprises are small compared to U.S. companies. The U.S. Fortune 500 company ranking #500 alone pulls over 3 billion USD and that would qualify to a Danish rank of above #15. Table 2 presents the 500 surveyed Danish companies. Revenue and profit is shown in DKK (100 DKK approximate. 13.5 EUR or 17 USD). The average DK-500 company revenue is thus DKK 3 billion (USD 180m) with 2,500 employees.

The 500 enterprises are grouped into three groups based on size: (1) the large "top 10" companies with average revenue of DKK 40 billion; (2) the medium-sized "top 100" companies with average revenue of DKK 7 billion; and (3) the small "top 500" companies with average revenue of DKK 1 billion. The DK-500 list operates with one single line of business code per company. In this survey, we have aggregated these codes into four groups of almost equal-sized sectors: (1) general trade; (2) traditional industry; (3) new industry; and (4) service, and so forth.

The interview was conducted using a structured interview guide recording both quantitative and qualitative data. The ERP managers were asked about: (1) their position in the organization; (2) the company's ERP system(s); (3) the ERP supplier/consultants; (4) the number of users in Denmark; (5) the time of going-live with their present system/release; and (6) this year's ERP investments. The ERP managers' answers and assessments (e.g., their definition of ERP) were never discussed but they were presented with sample answers if they were in doubt. This article only presents partial results, but the entire survey is available in Møller, Kræmmergaard, and Rotbøl (2003) in Danish.

The survey is intended to render the Danish condition and was designed to optimize the response rate. The sample was not intended for generalization purposes and there are interpretation issues in the survey that may jeopardize reliability. For instance, the definition of primary ERP system, number of Danish users, and so forth, are statements made by the interviewed manager. Also the key figures calculated for the DK-500 list are based on estimates on the Danish share of business. Danish enterprises have previously been known as fast adopters of ERP but as the ERP market tend to be global the conclusions based on Danish conditions are believed to be valid for European and North American enterprises too.

Survey Results

In total we got interviews with 88.4% of the 500 companies. Seventy-three point four percent had their own ERP system and 2% had group or corporate ERP and these are included as adopters too. Five point two percent had no ERP and 7.8% specifically declined to participate in the survey, and finally 11.6% did not answer or were not identified. The non-responses were mainly from new industries, and all of the largest companies participated in this study and they were ERP adopters.

Of the 26 companies with no ERP, one company had an implementation date set, and five present group IT/ERP issues as the reason for not having ERP. One hundred percent of the companies in the "top 10" participated in the survey (vs. 87% of "top 100" and 89% of "top 500"). The responses are summarized in Table 3 and shown for each of the three different size groups: the "top 10" large companies, the "top 100" medium sized companies, and the "top 500" small companies.

The ERP managers were asked to name their ERP system and if they had more than one ERP system (13.6%) they were asked to identify their primary system. We found 55 different ERP systems (several variants) of which only 25 systems were found in more than one company. Almost two-thirds of the ERP systems were systems supplied by the "top 5" vendors. Table 4 shows the frequency of the "top 5" vendors' systems: Microsoft, SAP, EDB Gruppen, Intentia, and Oracle. Only

Table 3. Overview of the responses (N=500)

Response	Frequency	Large companies	Medium companies	Small companies	Percent	Cumulative Percent
Have their own ERP	367	10	61	296	73.4%	73.4%
Have corporate ERP	10	0	4	6	2.0%	75.4%
Have no ERP	26	0	5	21	5.2%	80.6%
Declined to participate	39	0	8	31	7.8%	88.4%
Did not answer	29	0	8	21	5.8%	94.2%
Were not identified	29	0	4	25	5.8%	100.0%
Total	*500*	*10*	*90*	*400*	*100.0%*	

Table 4. Overview of the identified ERP installations (N=392)

Installation	Total Percent	General Trade	Traditional Industry	New Industry	Service, Etc.	Total	Cumulative Percent
Microsoft	34.2%	25.4%	32.8%	23.9%	17.9%	100%	34.2%
SAP	19.9%	21.8%	39.7%	28.2%	10.3%	100%	54.1%
Other vendors	17.3%	29.4%	30.9%	16.2%	23.5%	100%	71.4%
In-house	9.4%	48.6%	27.0%	13.5%	10.8%	100%	80.9%
EDB Gruppen	5.1%	45.0%	25.0%	15.0%	15.0%	100%	92.6%
Intentia	4.1%	18.8%	75.0%	0%	6.3%	100%	96.7%
No ERP	6.6%	38.5%	34.6%	19.2%	7.7%	100%	87.5%
Oracle	3.3%	7.7%	30.8%	53.8%	7.7%	100%	100.0%
Total	*100%*	*28.6%*	*34.7%*	*21.7%*	*15.1%*	*100%*	

6.6% of the companies have no ERP and 9.4% have an in-house developed legacy ERP system as their primary ERP system.

As many other countries Denmark has several small and local vendors specializing in various sectors or dedicated to various aspects of the ERP domain. But above all, two successful vendors originate in Denmark, namely Navision and Damgaard Data, which now have been merged into Microsoft Business Solution, from now on just Microsoft. Microsoft (also offering Great Plain and Solomon) has an outstanding position on the Danish market based on a broad but also older range of platforms, primarily focused on the small and medium-sized enterprises (SME). Another Danish venture is the EDB Gruppen (EG), partly owned by IBM. EG grew out of an IBM AS/400 based system aimed at specific local industries and they have now emerged as a strong provider of vertical solutions in Scandinavia.

ERP adoption relies on company size. All the large companies have adopted ERP. SAP is the preferred vendor in large and medium-sized companies, whereas Microsoft is the preferred vendor in small companies. ERP adoption also relies on the business sector. The non-adopters of ERP are mainly found in general trade. Also the preferred vendor relies on business sector. This is mainly due to the stronghold of Intentia in traditional industry, Oracles stronghold in new industry, and due to the extent of in-house developed systems in general trade businesses.

Almost 70% of the large Danish enterprises have adopted ERP from the "top 5" vendors. Only 17.3% of businesses use ERP from vendors outside the "top 5" list and the vendors outside the "top 5" list have only insignificant shares of the installation in this sample. An overview of the ERP vendor' share of the installations is provided in Table 5. The combined SSA ranks #6 on the list if considering SSAs acquisition of Baan. PeopleSoft, ranking #3 on the global list (Table 1) is marginal

Table 5. Overview of the ERP vendors' share of installations (N=329)

Top 5 vendors	Percent	Top 10 vendors	Percent	Top 15 vendors	Percent	Top 20 vendors	Percent
Microsoft	40.7%	IBS	2.1%	IFS	0.9%	ADP	0.6%
SAP	23.7%	Baan	1.5%	Bording Data	0.9%	MarineProvider	0.6%
EDB Gruppen	6.1%	Mapics	1.2%	SSA	0.9%	QAD	0.6%
Intentia	4.9%	Astra	1.2%	Scala	0.9%	T-System	0.6%
Oracle	4.0%	IBM	1.2%	JD Edwards	0.6%	Datacon	0.6%
Rest (20 vendors)							*6.1%*

in Denmark, even when considering the acquisition of JD Edwards. The impact of Oracle's potential takeover of PeopleSoft will still leave Oracle ranking #5 in Denmark.

The companies were asked to name their ERP supplier if different from the vendor's sales organization. We found 71 different suppliers but only 33 mentioned by more than one company. The distribution channels are the source of major competitive advantage for Microsoft Business Solution in Denmark. We found that considering recent year's mergers and acquisitions amongst the distributors, the "top 3" Microsoft distributors supplied more than 50 % of the installations and the "top 5" distributors supplies almost two-thirds of the installations.

Figure 2. Most recent ERP going live years/system age (N=334)

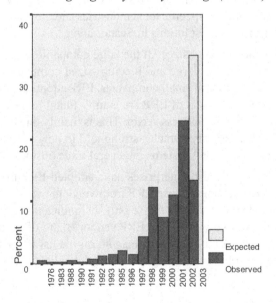

The companies in the survey were asked when they went live (year/quarter) with their most recent system/release and from that the age of the systems is deduced. The age of the ERP systems was 2.8 years on average ranging from 0 to 27 years. Figure 2 provides an overview of the distribution of the most recent going-live years. Only the first quarter of 2003 was observed during the survey. Almost 40% of the companies went live during the first quarter and 20% in each of the other quarters. Therefore, the total number of new installation in 2003 is estimated based on first quarter. Figure 2 also illustrates the impact of Y2K on the rate of ERP adoptions. An increasing number of enterprises went live with a new system towards year 2000, then a recession followed in 2001, and then again from 2002 we experience an increasing number of new installations.

The companies were asked to estimate their ERP-related investments in 2003. Almost one third of the companies answered that they have no plan for ERP investments, and 50% of the remaining two-thirds of the companies only had plans for maintenance. The rest invest in upgrades as well as maintenance. There are different practices among the vendors concerning new releases, but in general maintenance contracts include new releases. In average, the ERP investment was DDK 29 million or 0.9% of the average revenue, but the majority of companies had more modest projects. In Figure 3, the distribution of the ERP investments is illustrated.

The managers were asked the estimated number of users (in Denmark) giving an average of 397 users per installation. Given the average company size is 2,708, we have 15% ERP user per staff in average.

Figure 3. Estimated 2003 ERP investments (N=210)

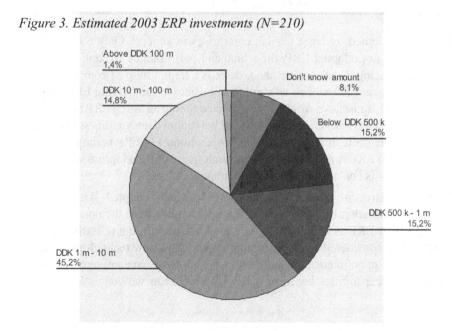

Table 6. Summary of the installation averages

Installation	# of ERP installations	Revenue (DDK m)	Revenue (%)	Staff	Staff (%)	ERP users	ERP users (%)	ERP age	Return on revenue (%)
Microsoft	34.2%	1,408	15.0%	793	10.1%	137	12.8%	2.4	4.2%
SAP	19.9%	6,975	43.2%	8,196	61.2%	779	41.0%	2.4	3.6%
EDB Gruppen	5.1%	2,421	3.8%	1,529	3.0%	401	5.6%	3.2	2.3%
Intentia	4.1%	1,268	1.6%	1,165	1.8%	267	3.0%	2.8	3.0%
Oracle	3.3%	5,855	6.0%	3,355	4.2%	372	3.4%	0.7	-3.8%
Other vendors	17.3%	2,580	13.9%	1,489	9.4%	265	12.5%	3.6	5.5%
In-house	9.4%	4,233	12.4%	2,324	7.9%	885	21.7%	4.8	1.2%
No ERP	6.6%	1,898	3.9%	1,083	2.5%	-	-	-	-19.8%
Total	100%	3,212	100%	2,708	100%	397	100%	2.8	2.3%

Table 6 compares averages of the ERP installations. The table compares different ERP vendors and non-adopter on the number of installations, average: revenue, staff, ERP users, ERP age, and return on revenue (ROR). Based on revenue, staff, and number of ERP users the dominance shifts between Microsoft and SAP. Also we see poor financial performance for the non-adopters and for companies with in-house developed systems. Companies with an Oracle installation also have poor financial performance, but those installations are the most recent in this study.

Discussion

ERP has been adopted by large Danish enterprises in general. Only 6.6% of the companies have not adopted ERP, their financial performance is poor, and their number is decreasing. On the other hand, there is a large group of companies not investing actively in ERP as well as a group of businesses with aging ERP. Based on the theoretical studies, we would have expected to find an aging ERP base and a flourishing e-business market, which, however we cannot detect in this study. Anyhow this study suggests the following four propositions: (1) ERP is the pervasive infrastructure; (2) ERP is a contemporary technology; (3) ERP adoption stable; and (4) ERP adoption is converging towards a dominant design.

ERP is the pervasive infrastructure because it is so widely adopted. Based on the high percentage of adopters and based on the explanations from the non-adopters, we conclude that ERP as a technology is a prerequisite to run any business, and that it should be considered an infrastructure rather than a new technology. Therefore, it will be of great interest to explore how the adopters have implemented and developed their capabilities based on ERP. However, can we conclude that the businesses have developed streamlined internal logistics processes just because they've adopted ERP?

ERP is a contemporary technology because the installed base is renewed. Based on the average age of the systems (2.8 years), we conclude that the ERP technology follows the normal IT life cycle. There are differences, and we can see that the in-house developed ERP systems are still to be considered a legacy technology. The overall implications are that the latest releases and technologies are available to be used by the industry. However, can we conclude that the advanced collaborative supply chain functions have been adopted and deployed?

The ERP adoption is stable, because the market is consolidated. Based on the adoption level, the vendors market shares and the systems age, we conclude that the ERP market is matured. Indications are that we end up with one (SAP) maybe two or three major vendors, a handful of global vendors, and a small number of vendors specializing in specific industries or countries. We find a similar pattern among the systems suppliers and implementation consultants. This is further reinforced by the fact that ERP investments are below 1% of the revenue in average. However, can we conclude that the ERP market is no longer innovative?

ERP adoption is converging toward a dominant design due to the facts mentioned previously. Only 14% of the companies use more than one ERP vendor. This indicates that the businesses are pursuing a "single-vendor" strategy rather than a "best-of-breed" strategy. Consequently, the ERP II functions are provided by the major vendors systems, and add-on modules or third-part bolt-on systems may only have a limited scope. This may have the implication that supply chain planning will be dominated by, for example, SAP APO (advanced planning and optimization) modules and hence that the reference models provided by the major vendors will be the future supply chain templates. This might imply that the variety in the applied logistics concepts is reduced to the standards defined by the major vendors. However, can we conclude that inter-organizational integration will be much easier with enterprises using the same platforms?

Conclusion

This study has provided some new insight into the ERP market and into the adoption of ERP by large Danish enterprises. We conclude that ERP is an institutionalized component of enterprise infrastructure. The implications to research are that the time is now ripe to rethink the concept of enterprise systems and to gain a deeper insight into the business impact of ERP, which ERP II may provide the conceptual framework for. This is especially critical to research into SCM. The potential benefit from supply chain integration is contingent on a large number of factors determined by *how* the ERP II technology is adopted by companies.

One of the potential directions could be to develop a generic taxonomy of processes and the SCM functions. Industry has been working on the SCOR model (Huan, Sheoran, & Wang, 2004) for analytical and benchmarking purposes. Inter-organizational logistic concepts and processes like CPFR or VMI are also developed by industry. Research needs to formulate general theories on the effective use of enterprise system functions to support SCM. A first step could be to develop detailed maturity models for ERP II adoption (Holland & Light, 2001) in tandem with the process taxonomy. These models would be instrumental in the management of second-wave ERP adoption. Theories for managing enterprise systems architecture is an emerging discipline of paramount interest to the practice of supply chain management to unleash the potential of SCM.

References

Akkermans, H. A., et al. (2003). The impact of ERP on supply chain management: Exploratory findings from a European Delphi study. *European Journal of Operational Research, 146*(2), 284.

Al-Mashari, M. (2001). Process orientation through enterprise resource planning (ERP): A review of critical issues. *Knowledge and Process Management, 8*(3), 175-185.

Bancroft, N. H., Seip, H., & Sprengel, A. (1998). *Implementing SAP R/3: How to introduce a large system into a large organization.* Greenwich: Manning.

Bond, B., et al. (2000). *ERP is dead—long live ERP II.* GartnerGroup.

Callaway, E. (2000). *ERP—the next generation: ERP is WEB enabled for e-business.* South Carolina: Computer Technology Research Corporation.

Chen, I. J. (2001). Planning for ERP systems: Analysis and future trend. *Business Process Management Journal, 7*(5), 374.

Christopher, M. (1998). *Logistics and supply chain management – Strategies for reducing costs and improving services* (2nd ed.). London: Pitman Publishing.

Davenport, T. H. (1998, July/August). Putting the enterprise into the enterprise system. *Harvard Business Review,* 121-131.

Davenport, T. H. (2000). The future of enterprise system-enabled organizations. *Information Systems Frontiers.*

Davenport, T. H., & Brooks, J. D. (2004). Enterprise systems and the supply chain. *Journal of Enterprise Information management, 17*(1), 8-19.

Davenport, T. H., Harris, J. G., & Cantrell, S. (2004). Enterprise systems and ongoing process change. *Business Process Management Journal, 10*(1), 16-26.

Duplaga, E. A., & Astani, M. (2003). Implementing ERP in manufacturing. *Information Systems Management*, (Summer), 68-75.

Esteves, J., & Pastor, J. (2001). Enterprise resource planning systems research: An annotated bibliography. *Communications of the AIS, 7*(8), 1-52.

Fox, M. L. (Ed.). (1999). *Charting the course to successful supply chain management. Achieving supply chain excellence through technology* (Vol. 1). Montgomery Research Inc. Retrieved from http://www.ascet.com

Gartner Group. (2003, June). Dataquest. Gartner Inc.

Gunasekaran, A., & Ngai, E. W. T. (2004). Information systems in supply chain integration and management. *European Journal of Operational Research, 159*(2), 269-295.

Harrell, H. W., Higgins, L., & Ludwig, S. E. (2001). Expanding ERP application software: Buy, lease, outsource, or write your own? *Journal of Corporate Accounting & Finance, 12*(5), 37-43.

Holland, C. P., & Light, B. (2001). A stage maturity model for enterprise resource planning systems use. *Database for Advances in Information Systems, 32*(2), 34.

Hørlück, J., et al. (Eds.). (2001). *Organizing for networked information technologies: Cases in process integration and transformation.* Aalborg: Aalborg University Press and PITNIT.

Huan, S. H., Sheoran, S. K., & Wang, G. (2004). A review and analysis of supply chain operations reference (SCOR) model. *Supply Chain Management, 9*(1), 23-29.

Hunton, J. E., Lippincott, B., & Reck, J. L. (2003). Enterprise resource planning systems: Comparing firm performance of adopters and nonadopters. *International Journal of Accounting Information Systems, 4,* 165-184.

Kalling, T. (2003). ERP systems and the strategic management processes that lead to competitive advantage. *Information Resources Management Journal, 16*(4), 46-67.

Klaus, H., Rosemann, M., & Gable, G. G. (2000). What is ERP? *Information Systems Frontiers, 2*(2), 141-162.

Light, B., Holland, C. P., & Wills, K. (2001). ERP and best of breed: A comparative analysis. *Business Process Management Journal, 7*(3), 216.

Mabert, V. A., Soni, A., & Venkataramanan, M. A. (2001). Enterprise resource planning: Common myths versus evolving reality. *Business Horizons, 44*(3), 69-76.

Mabert, V. A., Soni, A., & Venkataramanan, M. A. (2003). The impact of organization size on enterprise resource planning (ERP) implementations in the U.S. manufacturing sector. *Omega: The International Journal of Management Science,* (31), 235-246.

Margretta, J. (1998). The power of virtual integration: An interview with Dell Computer's Michael Dell. *Harvard Business Review, 1998*(March-April), 73-84.

Markus, M. L., Petrie, D., & Axline, S. (2000). Bucking the trends: What the future may hold for ERP packages. *Information Systems Frontier, Special issue of on The Future of Enterprise Resource Planning Systems, 2*(2), 181-193.

Markus, M. L., & Tanis, C. (2000). The enterprise systems experience – From adoption to success. In R. W. Zmud (Ed.), *Framing the domains of IT research: Glimpsing the future through the past* (pp. 173-207). Cincinnati, OH: Pinnaflex Educational Resources, Inc.

Møller, C. (2003). ERP II: A conceptual framework for next-generation enterprise systems? *Journal of Enterprise Information Management, 18*(4), 483-497.

Møller, C., Kræmmergaard, P., & Rotbøl, M. (2003). *Virksomhedssystemer i Danmark 2003—En analyse af de 500 største danske virksomheders ERP systemer.* Aarhus: Department of Information Science.

Nah, F.F.-H. (Ed.). (2002). Enterprise resource planning solutions and management. Hershey, PA: IRM Press.

Nah, F.F.-H., Lau, J.L.-S., & Kuang, J. (2001). Critical factors for successful implementation of enterprise systems. *Business Process Management Journal, 7*(3), 285.

Shanks, G., Seddon, P. B., & Willcocks, L. P. (Eds.). (2003). *Second-wave enterprise resource planning systems: Implementing for effectiveness.* Cambridge: Cambridge University Press.

Siriginidi, S. R. (2000). Enterprise resource planning in reengineering business. *Business Process Management Journal, 6*(5), 376-391.

Themistocleous, M., Irani, Z., & Keefe, R. M. O. (2001). ERP and application integration. *Business Process Management Journal, 7*(3), 195.

Willis, T. H., & Willis-Brown, A. H. (2002). Extending the value of ERP. *Industrial Management + Data Systems, 102*(1/2), 35.

Chapter IX

Using Simulation to Evaluate Electronic Data Interchange

Dothang Truong, Fayetteville State University, USA

Abstract

Reluctance of organizations to invest in electronic data interchange (EDI, Internet based EDI, and XML/EDI) is largely due to their inability to assess the return on these investments. We identify prescriptive and evaluative methodologies for analyzing investment in EDI: non-financial methods, purely financial methods, and financial and strategic consideration methods. We also show how computer simulation can be used as a tool for assessing EDI. Evaluating the benefits resulting from EDI implementation were illustrated through the well-known Beer Game. Our analysis and review also identifies difficulties involved in assessing the benefits of EDI in supply chains.

Introduction

Electronic data interchange (EDI) is a form of electronic communication that allows firms to exchange transaction data and documents in structured formats that can be processed by computer applications software. EDI is described (Monczka & Carter, 1998) as the direct electronic transmission, computer to computer, of standard business forms between organizations. The ability of companies to compete and survive in a global market will depend on their ability to be flexible and to adapt to changing market needs. EDI is a tool that can help companies meet this challenge (Lankford & Johnson, 2000). It has been widely demonstrated that EDI enables organizations to redesign their processes significantly because of its three main capabilities: high speed, reliability, and ease of data capture (Hoogeweegan, Streng, & Wagenaar, 1998; Leonard & Davis, 2006). However, the traditional conduct of EDI using value-added networks (VANs) has set up enormous barriers to its widespread usage and acceptance (Angeles, 2000). High costs and technical limitation of EDI make it appropriately only for large firms. These barriers can be overcome by using Internet-based EDI or EDI/XML that enables to reduce costs, reduce delay in transmission and improve global accessibility (Angeles, 2000; Lu, Tsai, & Chou, 2001).

Despite these arguments, organizations are still reluctant to implement EDI unless they are forced to do so (Webster, 1995). One main reason is that companies do not know whether, and to what extent, they should invest in EDI. They are also unable to assess the return on these investments (Hoogeweegan et al., 1998). Thus assessing EDI properly is a critical element that affects the organizations' decision in investing in EDI. As long as adequate assessment of the costs and benefits of EDI is not done, decision makers tend to give priority to other investment rather than EDI despite its benefits.

This chapter aims to categorize the benefits and barriers of EDI and alternative forms of EDI such as Internet-based EDI and XML/EDI, and provide the taxonomy of prescriptive and evaluative methods to assess the value of EDI. The evaluation criteria for adopting EDI are investigated based on theoretical and empirical reviews. We also show how the benefits of EDI can be quantified using simulation. This approach is illustrated with the well-known Beer Game Simulation. Suite of methodologies identified by us, along with the Beer Game as an illustrative simulation tool, provide decision makers powerful methods to assess EDI before making decision to invest in it.

Our chapter is organized as follows: in the next section, we provide an overview of EDI, Internet-based EDI, XML/EDI, and benefits and barriers to their implementation. In the third section, we classify and review various methodologies used for justifying investment in EDI. The fourth section shows how computer simulation can be used to quantify the benefits associated with using EDI. We use the well-known Beer Game as a vehicle for this purpose. Finally, we provide conclusions and future research directions.

Electronic Data Interchange

Definition

Defining EDI is somewhat difficult. Some definitions attempt to be highly specialized, while others convey a broad concept. According to Cannon (1996), EDI is defined as the electronic transmission of standard business documents in a pre-defined format from one company's business computer application to its trading partners' business computer application. In this definition there are five keyword phrases. First, *electronic transmission* is central to the EDI concept. Since one of the primary purposes of EDI is to speed the communication of information, it is more efficient to do this electronically than manually (i.e., the post office or a messenger service). Second, *standard business documents* include invoices, purchase orders, or shipping manifests, plus other documents that are specific to an industry. Third, standard documents must be converted into a *pre-defined format* so they can be processed by each computer. In EDI all data elements that should be contained in a standard business document are defined. Fourth, EDI should link *business computer application* to business computer applications. Finally, *trading partner* is another company or person outside a company with whom the company transacts business, including customers, suppliers, and government agencies.

Categories of EDI

VAN-Based EDI

Traditional EDI allows trading partners to, typically, connect to a value-added network (VAN) in order to exchange EDI documents on a store and forward basis. VANs provide mailbox service that sort EDI documents from a sender's to the receiver's mailbox, thus allowing the receiver to pick an EDI document when convenient. In addition VANs also provide other service such as translating flat files from the subscriber's application into EDI formatted documents, interfacing with other vans and supporting various telecommunications modes and data transfer protocols (Kalakota & Whinston, 1996; Ratnasingham, 1998b).

VAN-based EDI has some advantages. First, IT reduces need for manual processing, reduces administrative costs, and improves the timeliness and accuracy of data
(Cannon, 1996; Laage-Hellman & Gadde, 1996; Ratnasingham, 1998a). Second,
advanced EDI significantly reduces the probability of rework and delay, thus lowering the supplier's and customer's order-processing costs. The simplification of the
process by reducing the complexity of orders or increasing the fraction of standard
items sold also improves business performance (Mukhopadhyay & Kekre, 2002).
Finally, strategic benefits derive from the long-term gains a business makes by developing closer ties with customers and suppliers, and by using EDI to improve its
competitive position such as increased market share (Baker, 1991; Ratnasingham,
1998a).

VAN-based EDI also has some disadvantages which need to be addressed to facilitate
EDI acceptance and implementation. First, it is difficult to quantify the return on
investment for using EDI. This has made EDI difficult to justify using a cost/ben-
efit analysis (Ratnasingham, 1998a; Scala & McGrath, 1993). Second, the absence
of interconnection among suppliers was the most significant barrier to EDI usage
(Marcella & Chan, 1993; Ratnasingham, 1998a; Smith, 1995). Third, EDI personnel
must possess a combination of unique skills, including not only strong technical and
business process skills, but also strong communication and people skills (Jilovec,
1998). Fourth, implementing EDI is not simple because of the differences in standard
documents transmitted between industries (Ratnasingham, 1998a). Finally, lack of
experience and knowledge of security, control and audit ability when using EDI
have contributed to false impression of unreliability, enforceability of electronic
transaction records and legal uncertainty in the electronic area (Ratnasingham,
1998a; Weiss, 1993).

Internet-Based EDI

The traditional conduct of EDI using the VANs has set up enormous barriers to its
widespread usage and acceptance. Not only is it costly, but it is also technically
prohibitive. In the traditional e-commerce model, it was too expensive for firms
to be connected to a VAN in order to communicate with customers or suppliers.
That barrier is taken care of by the widespread interconnectivity and accessibility
of the Internet (Angeles, 2000; Jun & Cai, 2003). Internet-based EDI have been
developed to use either direct Internet connection or via a third-party site. The direct
connection type requires a front-end translation software (additional to or replacing
any existing EDI software) to transmit and display documents or interface within
the existing in-house application systems. Also a third-party Web site can act as an
Internet value-added network service (IVANS) to link business partners together
(Ratnasingham, 1998b). Conducting EDI transactions through the Internet consists
of two phases (Angeles, 2000; Wreden, 1997). *The first phase* involves the front end

where an Internet browser is used for simplified online ordering. *The second phase* involves the backend where received EDI transactions need to be integrated with order processing, procurement, and financial operations via automated, computer-to-computer data exchanges.

Basically, Internet-based EDI is perceived to have two primary advantages over traditional EDI: delay reduction in transmission (real-time transmission), and costs reduction. Theoretically, by using Internet EDI transaction would be much closer to real time. With traditional store-and-forward EDI, delivery time is 12 to 24 hours vs. minutes on the Internet (Lankford & Johnson, 2000). Internet transmission rates could be about 300 times as fast as the average speed of VANs (Dugdale, 1997). In addition, the cost of operating on the Internet is very low comparing to PCN (private communication network) or VAN. In the U.S., many Internet service providers (ISP) charge only flat fees for unlimited usage (Lee, 1998). Moreover, the reduction of delay in transmission also reduces the cost (Barber, 1997). Finally, the ISPs provide many of the service formerly purchased at a greater cost from traditional VANs (Ratnasingham, 1998b). As a result, medium-sized firms that cannot afford to develop their own network and software for EDI, can afford to piggyback on their Internet investments (Lankford & Johnson, 2000).

Although the Internet has been touted as a cheap, easy-to-use communications vehicle, most companies are still hesitant to use it for exchanging EDI transaction sets. Internet-based EDI has also its vulnerabilities that most companies have to cope with. Doing EDI over Internet requires a standard formatted document transfer, which implies that every trading partner produce material in a standardized manner (Lankford & Johnson, 2000). The current methods of standardization in the structure of data that are being interchanged between machines, via an interface, totally ignore the way in which applications and programs are designed and operated (Ratnasingham, 1998b). Unreliable Internet performance also could result in message loss—totally unacceptable to trading partners (Lankford & Johnson, 2000). There is insufficient trust in the reliability of Internet-based commerce to create rapid take-up. There is a need for a great deal of co-ordination to ensure that trading partners can interpret the data received correctly (Ratnasingham, 1998b).

XML/EDI

Another alternative of traditional EDI is XML/EDI that enables firms to overcome two primary barriers that constrain the acceptance of EDI: high entrance cost and complex EDI standards. Extensible Mark-up Language, or XML, has caught considerable attention in the marketplace due to the current demand for real time and more dynamic information exchanges among electronic trading partners (Angeles, 2000). XML is new technology to facilitate Internet-based EDI. It is a language used to define document structures and elements (Shim, Qureshi, Siegel, & Siegel, 2000). XML inherits extensibility, but removes unnecessary complexity, from the Standard Generalized Mark-up Language (SGML) developed by the International Organization for Standardization (Adam, Dogramaci, Gangopadhyay, & Yesha, 1999; Lu et al., 2001). An XML/EDI framework integrating XML with EDI was proposed by the XML/EDI group founded by David Webber and Bruce Peat in July 1997 (Webber, 1998; Lu & Hwang, 2001). The objective of XML/EDI framework is to provide businesses, regardless of their size, a smarter and cheaper system so that they can conduct transactions electronically with any trading partner world-wide (Lu et al., 2001).

With those characteristics, the XML/EDI model has several advantages. First, XML/EDI lowers costs which can be achieved by using Internet. Also since most users are familiar with Web browsers, the training cost will be reduced. It is estimated

Table 1. Advantages and disadvantages of VAN-based EDI, Internet-based EDI, and XML/EDI

	Advantages	Disadvantages	References
VAN-based EDI	• Reduced manual processing • Simplified information handling • Improved quality of information • More accurate data • Eliminated errors • Lower administrative costs • Lower material handling costs • Improved trading partnership	• Complex standards • High setup cost • High operating cost • High cost of communication transmission • High cost for security checks • High training cost • Limited global accessibility • Time delay	Cannon, 1996; Weiss, 1993; Scala & McGrath, 1993; Kalakota & Whinston, 1996; Ratnasingham, 1998a, 1998b; Laage-Hellman & Gadde, 1996; Mukhopadhyay & Kekre, 2002; Jimenez-Martinez & Polo-Redondo, 2004
Internet-based EDI	• Lower setup cost • Lower cost of communication transmission • Global network access • Wide range of applications • Interorganizational communication • Real time transmission	• Message loss possibility • Security concern • Lack of a standard formatted document transfer • Lack of organization	Baer, 1996; Dugdale, 1997; Barber, 1997; Lee, 1998; Angeles, 2000; Ratnasingham, 1998b; Lankford & Johnson, 2000; Jun & Cai, 2003
XML/EDI	• Lower setup cost • Lower cost of communication transmission • Lower training cost • Improved global accessibility • Interorganizational communication • Real time transmission • Removed standard complexity • Easy to define structured documents • Portable and widely used message • Easy to integrate with other systems	• Increased length and size of message • Security concern	Angeles, 2000; Shim et al., 2000; Adam et al., 1999; Lu et al., 2001; Webber, 1998; Walsh, 1999; Brooker, 1999; Lu & Hwang, 2001

that XML can help cut costs by up to 50% (Brooker, 1999). Since the exchanges of commercial documents using XML it is not longer required to define standards before communications. Therefore, XML/EDI is suitable for trading partners of short-term relationship. XML/EDI also improve global accessibility since the Internet reaches almost everywhere in the world and the fee to access the Internet is low. Finally, XML messages become portable and can be used by any system that can interpret the messages. Also by using modern distributed object techniques, it is easy to integrate XML/EDI with existing systems (Lu & Hwang, 2001).

Although XML/EDI overcomes most problems that restrain EDI adoption by small and medium-sized enterprises, it still faces some challenges. The length of EDI messages increases significantly (Lu et al., 2001). It is found that the size of the EDI messages increases by four to eight times (Ogbuji, 1999). Moreover, XML-related standards are not finalized yet. For example, since DTD (document type definition) is limited, XML schema has been proposed and is still under development (Lu et al., 2001). Finally, security issues are not considered. Since an XML message is not different from other text messages used in other areas of electronic commerce, the XML/EDI did not consider security issues. Advantages and disadvantages of those three categories of EDI are shown in Table 1.

Methodologies for Evaluating EDI

The proliferation of different forms of EDI from traditional EDI using VANs, through Internet-based EDI, to XML/EDI with substantive improvements indicates the benefits of EDI usage in strengthening business performance. However, firms, specially small and medium-sized enterprises, are still reluctant to adopt EDI. This fact questions the selecting an appropriate methodology for evaluating EDI. While tremendous studies have been done to examine methodologies for evaluating general IT investment, very few of them have focused on methods that can be used to evaluate EDI investments (Hoogeweegen et al., 1998; Mukhopadhyay & Kekre, 2002).

As discussed in the previous text, the usage of EDI confers on organizations both tangible and intangible benefits. EDI benefits can be categorized as direct, indirect and strategic benefits (Ratnasingham, 1998a), or operational and strategic benefits (Jimenez-Martinez & Polo-Redondo, 2004; Mukhopadhyay & Kekre, 2002). The availability or the level of those sets of benefits (whenever they were available) became the determining factors in influencing the investment in EDI. The benefits that an organization can drive depend upon the business environment and organization's capability to exploit the environment to its benefit. Such capability of the organization to exploit is called the strategy. So benefits of the same technology are different for different organizations and different situations. This makes the evaluation of technology somewhat difficult. In addition, EDI benefits are different for different three phases of technology deployment: adoption, implementation, and post-implementation. While operational benefits are mainly employed in the implementation phase, strategic benefits of EDI are employed primarily in both implementation and post-implementation phase (Mukhopadhyay & Kekre, 2002). Finally, strategic benefits are clearly different for customers and suppliers indicating the necessity to investigate the benefits of EDI from various entities' perspective (Mukhopadhyay & Kekre, 2002).

These complications in evaluation of EDI benefits point out the importance of selecting an appropriate methodology for evaluating EDI. Earlier evaluation methodologies that used financial criteria such as discounted cash flow were more suitable for the stable economic environment than in the current situation. There is widespread belief among practitioners and academicians that the financial evaluation methods such as discounted cash flow is inadequate for the evaluation of features such as flexibility or shorter lead-time etc. Figure 1 shows alternative methodologies of the evaluation that we have considered in this article.

Figure 1. Methodologies for evaluating EDI

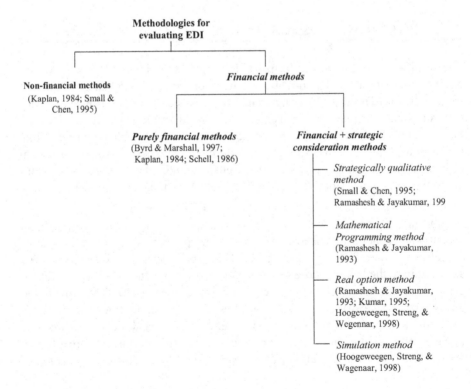

Non-Financial Methods

Because of the difficulty in computing value of intangible benefits deriving from EDI, some managers argue that EDI should be evaluated simply on the basis of non-financial qualitative criteria. Such criteria have been described as faith based (Kaplan, 1984), or strategic considerations (Small & Chen, 1995). Majority of the firms do not use the discounted cash flow or other acceptable financial criteria in the investment decisions for IT-related issues (Small & Chen, 1995). It is also argued that such practice is not correct on conceptual grounds (Kaplan, 1984), or from the purely practical consideration of making an investment that gives the desired performance (Small & Chen, 1995).

Financial Methods

There is broad agreement that the evaluation of the information technology related investments should include the financial criteria (Kaplan, 1984; Ramashesh & Jayakumar, 1993; Small & Chen, 1995). Discounted cash flow is mostly used as the financial criterion. There is a strong consensus that discounted cash flow is adequate, provided that all tangible and intangible benefits related to the introduction of the information system are properly accounted for (Kaplan, 1984; Schell, 1986). However, more detailed analysis of those benefits, and translation of the benefits in terms of cash flow are needed. Small and Chen (1995) found that although the evaluation criteria can be improved by the inclusion of strategic considerations in addition to the financial ones, resulting improvement is found to be minimal. Byrd and Marshall (1997) showed that the investment in information technology can improve the financial performance of the company.

Financial and Strategic Consideration Methods

The strategic benefits are taken into account in various ways. How one takes this into account is one of the main areas of argument. One approach is to let the managers decide how to account for the strategic factors based on their experience or intuition (Small & Chen, 1995). First, the evaluation is done on the conventional discounted cash flow basis. If the value of the investment, as determined using the discounted cash flow, is found adequate no further analysis is done. But if the value, thus calculated, is lower than the desired value, then the manager has to decide if the gain from the strategic considerations is high enough to account for the difference. Such methods are inadequate in the sense that investment is decided more by the prejudice or the bias of decision makers than any scientific or valid reasoning. For example, if the decision maker has a background in high technology, the investment in that area is more likely to be considered (Ramashesh & Jayakumar, 1993).

Second approach is to take a more quantitative approach to the evaluation. Many such methods are available. One is to use the mathematical modeling to take account benefits of flexibility and similar intangible benefits. Ramashesh and Jayakumar (1993) developed a mathematical programming model to take into account factors such as product mix, new product flexibility, resource flexibility (raw material, machine, labor flexibilities), and modification and expansion flexibilities. The mathematical model considers the probabilities of different scenarios, brought about by flexibilities, and includes the probable cash flows from each of the considered scenario into discounted cash flow analysis. The mathematical model is akin to the discounted cash flow analysis suggested by Kaplan (1984).

Third method that is commonly considered in evaluation of advanced manufacturing technology and information technologies is real options. A real option is developed as a tool to value the tangible and intangible benefits from the strategic considerations. A real option takes cue from the option-pricing model of Black and Scholes, which was developed to evaluate stock options. The word "real option" is used to distinguish it from options on financial instruments (or any other financial assets) (Hoogeweegen et al., 1998; Ramashesh & Jayakumar, 1993). Kumar (1995) also used the option pricing mechanism to value the flexibility in manufacturing systems. However, the stock option-pricing models developed with many underlying assumptions that are realistic for the stocks, would not necessarily be valid for other assets. For example, in the stock option evaluation model, changes in the value of underlying asset are supposed to be characterized by Brownian motions. This may be adequate for stocks, but not necessarily so for other assets (Ramashesh & Jayakumar, 1993).

Another method that is gaining popularity is the simulation. Properly modeled simulation should not be constrained by the weakness of the underlying assumptions in the mathematical models. Complexities associated with any specific EDI implementation can be captured in simulation models (Lee, Kim, & Lee, 2004). So depending on the benefit one is looking for, the value of the investment would be unique and different from the value the other firm may realize from the same investment (Hoogeweegen et al., 1998). That justifies the need for the individually tailored evaluation method. Simulation is the perfect tool for such evaluation. In short, simulation can take the strategic and financial factors into account and assess the evaluation of the specific strategic benefit the company can reap from its investment in the EDI.

Using Simulation to Evaluate EDI

The main difficulty in evaluation of any new technology such as EDI is in deciding exactly what benefit company can get from investing in such technologies. The issue of EDI is made further complicated by the fact that the benefit accruing to the firm depends upon the inter-organizational relationships. Managers do not agree on the type of benefit they are likely to get (Chircu & Kauffman, 2000; Scala & McGrath, 1993). If the benefit can be agreed upon with some adjustment, the cash flow for such benefit can be estimated (Kaplan, 1984). The significant and tangible benefit of EDI that many agree on is the reduction in the order lead-time. That will reduce the inventory carrying cost (through reduction in safety stocks), ordering costs, and improved customer service (Machuca & Barajas, 1997, 2004; Scala & McGrath, 1993). The savings from such reduction are gained by more than one participating entity in the supply chain.

As discussed in the earlier section, simulation is an individually tailored evaluation method that can capture specific benefits a company can gain from investing in EDI. Since the reduction on carrying and ordering cost is the focused benefit of EDI in this research, simulation is selected as an appropriate method. One of the main objectives of the simulation can be to find out the level of saving on the carrying and ordering costs of the inventory. The Beer Game, introduced first by MIT in 1960's, is perceived to be a good tool to evaluate those costs savings. It is a role-playing simulation developed to clarify the advantages of taking an integrated approach to supply chain management (Simchi-Levi, Kaminsky, & Simchi-Levi, 2003). Machuca and Barajas (1997) used the Beer Game to demonstrate the reduction in the total inventory carrying and ordering costs in the supply chain. They found such savings could be as high as 60%. Goodwin and Franklin (1994) used the Beer Game as a simulation tool to teach the supply chain systems. Van Ackere, Larsen, and Morecroft (1993) used the Beer Game to demonstrate the system and business process design.

We use the Beer Game simulation to illustrate the impact of EDI. In order to quantify the influence of EDI, we experimented on the Beer Game. A number of computerized versions of the Beer Game have been developed (Forrester, 2000; Kaminsky & Simchi-Levi, 2003; Machuca & Barajas, 1997). In this chapter, we use Beer Game 1.10, the computerized version of Beer Game developed by Kaminsky and Simchi-Levi (2003). This is a useful simulation model that can be used to study some configurative issues in supply chain management. The advantage of this version is that it enables players to select different options: players, policy, demand, centralization, lead times, and so forth. Thus, the players can configure the scenario of their own choice.

Description of the Game Scenario

We provide a brief overview of the game for the benefit of readers unfamiliar with the game. It refers to a simplified beer supply chain consisting of a retailer, a wholesaler that supplies the retailer, a distributor that supplies the wholesaler, and a factory with unlimited raw materials that brews the beer and supplies the distributor. Each entity in the supply chain has unlimited storage capacity, and there is a fixed supply lead time and order delay time between the entities (see Figure 2).

Every week, every entity in the supply chain tries to meet the demand of the downstream entity. Any orders that cannot be met are recorded as backorders, and met as soon as possible. No orders will be lost, and all orders must eventually be met. Backlogging cost is $1.00 per backordered item per week. Each entity owns the inventory at its facility. In addition, the wholesaler owns inventory in transit to the retailer, the distributor owns inventory in transit to the wholesaler, and the factory owns both items being manufactured and items in transit to the distributor. Each location is charged $0.50 inventory holding cost per inventory item per week that it owns. Supply chain members have no knowledge of the external demand, or the orders and inventory of other members. The goal of the retailer, wholesaler, distributor, and factory is to minimize total cost, either individually or for the entire system (Simchi-Levi et al., 2000).

Figure 2. Beer game schedule (Source: Kaminsky & Simchi-Levi, 2000).

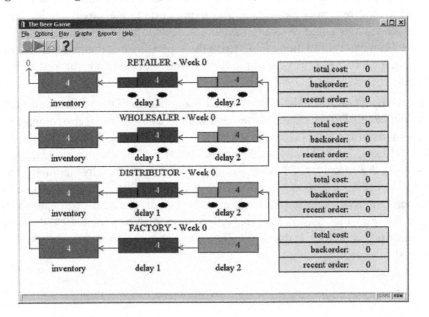

Evaluate EDI Investments Using Beer Game Scenario

We have four levels in the supply chain. The lead-time was reduced from two weeks to one week with the use of EDI. Experiments were done for 30 weeks in each of

Table 2. Results of the experiment

Trial#	Long leadtime (2 weeks)					Short leadtime (1 week)					Total cost saving
	Retailer	Whole saler	Distribu tor	Factory	Total cost	Retailer	Whole saler	Distrib utor	Factory	Total cost	
1	$272	$558	$904	$1,686	$3,420	$85	$216	$332	$651	$1,284	$2,136
2	$323	$574	$882	$1,724	$3,503	$172	$255	$343	$608	$1,378	$2,125
3	$268	$533	$852	$1,709	$3,362	$123	$193	$224	$487	$1,027	$2,335
4	$208	$529	$1,098	$1,843	$3,678	$131	$248	$416	$797	$1,592	$2,086
5	$336	$594	$1,059	$1,831	$3,820	$157	$281	$414	$754	$1,606	$2,214
6	$120	$443	$899	$1,610	$3,072	$95	$197	$234	$499	$1,025	$2,047
7	$199	$470	$855	$1,553	$3,077	$135	$245	$376	$719	$1,475	$1,602
8	$193	$493	$973	$1,760	$3,419	$143	$245	$321	$635	$1,344	$2,075
9	$289	$528	$753	$1,319	$2,889	$141	$240	$388	$663	$1,432	$1,457
10	$251	$548	$865	$1,654	$3,318	$79	$248	$686	$1,026	$2,039	$1,279
11	$248	$535	$670	$1,300	$2,753	$157	$283	$428	$801	$1,669	$1,084
12	$156	$425	$847	$1,659	$3,087	$112	$307	$604	$999	$2,022	$1,065
13	$168	$420	$699	$1,384	$2,671	$72	$195	$288	$547	$1,102	$1,569
14	$241	$543	$788	$1,528	$3,100	$110	$215	$295	$530	$1,150	$1,950
15	$268	$590	$870	$1,688	$3,416	$163	$285	$457	$846	$1,751	$1,665
16	$231	$552	$1,067	$1,822	$3,672	$71	$239	$616	$1,139	$2,065	$1,607
17	$273	$536	$932	$1,752	$3,493	$129	$292	$509	$932	$1,862	$1,631
18	$238	$558	$1,079	$1,707	$3,582	$56	$204	$465	$954	$1,679	$1,903
19	$204	$378	$738	$1,499	$2,819	$134	$263	$502	$799	$1,698	$1,121
20	$264	$511	$753	$1,504	$3,032	$139	$207	$244	$461	$1,051	$1,981
21	$191	$518	$958	$1,724	$3,391	$84	$208	$276	$573	$1,141	$2,250
22	$231	$505	$674	$1,509	$2,919	$101	$251	$398	$799	$1,549	$1,370
23	$209	$506	$1,140	$1,827	$3,682	$94	$253	$482	$862	$1,691	$1,991
24	$166	$481	$1,068	$1,803	$3,518	$93	$213	$305	$588	$1,199	$2,319
25	$169	$444	$918	$1,711	$3,242	$104	$275	$475	$923	$1,777	$1,465
26	$173	$492	$1,019	$1,801	$3,485	$116	$290	$594	$1,086	$2,086	$1,399
27	$180	$517	$1,061	$1,855	$3,613	$90	$226	$401	$798	$1,515	$2,098
28	$160	$519	$837	$1,629	$3,145	$106	$260	$556	$1,036	$1,958	$1,187
29	$207	$482	$1,028	$1,755	$3,472	$111	$267	$474	$932	$1,784	$1,688
30	$163	$415	$718	$1,468	$2,764	$121	$244	$356	$633	$1,354	$1,410

the 30 trials. The results are shown in the Table 2. Weekly data collected are: costs incurred by the retailer, wholesaler, distributor, and the factory. We analyzed the results using Excel Data Analysis Tool. We calculated the total supply chain costs incurred when we did not use EDI (long lead time), and when we used EDI (short lead time), while all other conditions remained the same. Then the total costs saving are computed. The total costs saving estimated to be $1736.97 ± 147.36 at the 95% confidence level. The average saving was 52%. This is a substantial saving for the one week reduction in lead-time. The problem from the standpoint of evaluation is what discount rate to use to capitalize the perceptual savings. The discount rate can be different for each of the companies in the supply chain. But once the decision on division of saving is decided, each can discount their portion of saving and find the present value of saving and compare it against the investment required.

Extending the example, the point estimate for total saving for all entities in the system is $1,736.97 for thirty-week period, that is, $3,010 per year. If all the entities have same discount rate (for example 12%) and the saving is expected to be earned in perpetuity, then the value of saving is $25,090 (i.e., $3,010/0.12). So the total value of EDI is $25,090 when the whole supply chain is considered. Suppose, retailer wants to know his own benefits from EDI. The average saving for 30 weeks is $220, and the annual saving is $381. The value for the retailer alone is $3,177. This value is contingent upon other entities also reducing their order lead times.

As our illustrative simulation shows, the benefits deriving from the implementation of EDI can be different for different entities in the system. Also, the evaluation is difficult because the hurdle rate for the firms will most likely be different. But once the use of EDI, and the division of resulting savings is agreed upon, the simulation helps to determine the amount of savings (cash flow), which can form the basis for evaluation using the traditional discounted cash flow.

Conclusion

We addressed the issues and complexities involved in identifying and evaluating the tangible and intangible benefits from implementing EDI. Our review of literature suggests that the difficulties involved in identifying and quantifying the intangible benefits derived from EDI make its assessment difficult. This tends to result in the decision makers favoring alternate investment opportunities. We identified various methodologies suggested by the researchers for evaluating EDI, and provided a taxonomy which should be useful to both practitioners and researchers. Simulation was selected as an appropriate evaluation method since it can capture all complexities associated with differences in EDI benefits perception. Evaluating the benefits resulting from EDI implementation were illustrated through the well-known Beer

Game. A simulation model was developed, and experimental data was collected from the Beer Game.

Our simulation study identifies some important findings involved in assessing the benefits of EDI in supply chains. First, as our simulation model has shown, the benefit derived from EDI implementation need not accrue proportionately to all firms in the chain. Hence firms which do not see significant benefit accruing to them may be reluctant to invest in EDI unless others are willing to share some of their gains to ease the EDI implementation. This raises the issue of how the benefits from EDI are to be shared by the entities in the system (through subsidies or cooperative arrangements). Second, evaluation of the benefits is also dependent on the cost of capital for various firms in the chain, which need not be the same. Third, our simulation study also points to an important issue related to implementing EDI- multi-functional approach needed to take full advantage of benefits from EDI. In our simulation study, same inventory policies were used both before and after implementing EDI. Clearly, irrespective of the class of inventory policies deployed in the supply chain, optimal inventory policies in the system would be distinctly different after EDI implementation from those used before lead-time reduction. Thus the savings reported in the study are an underestimate. Hence in order to take full advantage of the lead time reduction from EDI, firms need to re-assess their ordering policies after EDI implementation. This calls for multi-functional approach not only in implementing EDI, but also in assessing its benefits in supply chains at the evaluation stage.

The future research may focus on developing a comprehensive and customized simulation model which can capture all different benefits that a company can gain from investing in EDI, not only lead time and cost reduction. That will provide decision makers powerful methods to assess EDI before making decision to invest in it.

References

Adam, N., Dogramaci, O., Gangopadhyay, A., & Yesha, Y. (1999). *Electronic commerce: Technical, business, and legal issue.* Englewood Cliffs, NJ: Prentice Hall PTR.

Angeles, R. (2000). Revisiting the role of Internet-EDI in the current electronic commerce scene. *Logistics Information Management, 13*(1), 45-57.

Baer, T. (1996). Don't try this at home. *Computer World: Electronic Commerce Journal Supplement, 29,* 34-36.

Baker, C. (1991). EDI in business. *Accountancy, 107,* 121-124.

Barber, N. (1997, September). Will EDI survive? *Transportation and Distribution*, 3-4.

Brooker, E. (1999, April). XML applications stand up to EDI. *InternetWeek*, 2-3.

Byrd, T. A., & Marshall, T. E. (1997). Relating information technology investment to organizational performance: A causal model analysis. *Omega International Journal of Management Science, 25*(1), 43-56.

Cannon, E. (1996). *EDI guide: A step by step approach.* London: International Thomson Computer Press.

Chircu, A., & Kauffman, R. (2000). Limits to value in electronic commerce-related IT investments. Journal *of Management Information Systems, 17*(2), 59-80.

Dugdale D. (1997). VANs open access. *LAN Times*, June. Retrieved February 15, 2003, from www.lantimes.com

Forrester, N. (2000). *A.T. Kearney inventory distribution simulator.* Chicago: A.T. Kearney Inc.

Goodwin, J. S., & Franklin, S. G. (1994). The beer distribution game: Using simulation to teach system. *The Journal of Management Development, 13*(8), 7-15.

Hoogeweegen, M. R., Streng, R. J., & Wagenaar, R. W. (1998). A comprehensive approach to assess the value of EDI. *Information and Management, 34*, 117-127.

Jilovec, N. (1998). *The A to Z EDI and its role in e-commerce.* Loveland, CO: Duke Communications International.

Jimenez-Martinez, J., & Polo-Redondo, Y. (2004). The influence of EDI adoption over its perceived benefits. *Technovation, 24*(1), 73-79.

Jun, M., & Cai, S. (2003). Key obstacles to EDI success: From the U.S. small manufacturing companies' perspective. *Industrial Management & Data Systems, 103*(3), 192-203.

Kalakota, R., & Whinston, A. (1996). *Electronic commerce: A manager's guide.* Reading, MA: Addison-Wesley.

Kaminsky, P., & Simchi-Levi, D. (2003). *Computerized version distribution beer game.* New York: McGraw-Hill.

Kaplan, R. S. (1984). Must CIM be justified by faith alone? *Harvard Business Review, 64*(2), 87-95.

Kumar, R. L. (1995). An option view of investment in expansion-flexible manufacturing systems. *International Journal of Production Economics, 38*, 281-291.

Laage-Hellman, J., & Gadde, L. (1996). Information technology and the efficiency of materials supply: The implementation of EDI in the Swedish Construction Industry. *European Journal of Purchasing and Supply Management, 2*(4), 221-228.

Lankford, W., & Johnson, J. (2000). EDI via Internet. *Information Management and Computer Security, 8*(1), 27-30.

Lee M. (1998). Internet-based financial EDI: Towards a theory of its adoption. *Computer Networks and IDSN Systems, 30,* 1579-1588.

Lee, S., Kim, B. G., & Lee, K. (2004). Fuzzy cognitive map-based approach to evaluate EDI performance: A test of causal model. *Expert Systems with Applications, 27*(2), 287-299.

Leonard, L. N. K., & Davis, C. C. (2006). Supply chain replenishment: Before-and-after EDI implementation. *Supply Chain Management: An International Journal, 11*(3), 225-232.

Lu, E. J., & Hwang, R. (2001). A distributed EDI model. *Journal of Systems and Software, 56,* 1-7.

Lu, E. J., Tsai, R. H., & Chou, S. (2001). An empirical study of XML/EDI. *The Journal of Systems and Software, 58,* 271-279.

Machuca, J. A., & Barajas, R. D. (1997). A computerized network version of the beer game via the Internet. *System Dynamics Review, 13*(4), 323-340.

Machuca, J. A., & Barajas, R. P. (2004). The impact of electronic data interchange on reducing bullwhip effect and supply chain inventory costs. *Transportation Research Part E: Logistics and Transportation Review, 40*(3), 209-228.

Marcella, J., & Chan, S. (1993). *EDI security, control and audit.* Norwood, MA: Artech House Inc.

Monczka, R., & Carter, J. R. (1998). Implementing electronic data interchange. *Journal of Purchasing and Materials Management, 25*(1), 26-33.

Mukhopadhyay, T., & Kekre, S. (2002). Strategic and operational benefits of electronic integration in B2B procurement processes. *Management Science, 48*(10), 1301-1313.

Ogbuji, U. (1999, February). XML: The future of EDI? *SunWorld,* 2-3.

Ramashesh, R. V., & Jayakumar, M. D. (1993). Economic justification of advanced manufacturing technology. *Omega International Journal of Management Science, 21*(3), 289-306.

Ratnasingham, P. (1998a). EDI security: The influence of trust on EDI risks. *Computers and Security, 17,* 313-324.

Ratnasingham, P. (1998b). Internet-based EDI trust and security. *Information Management and Computer Security, 6*(1), 33-39.

Scala, S., & McGrath, R. (1993). Advantages and disadvantages of electronic data interchange: An industry perspective. *Information & Management, 25*(2), 85-91.

Schell, G. P. (1986). Establishing the value of information system. *Interfaces*, *16*(13), 82-89.

Shim, J., Qureshi, A., Siegel, J., & Siegel, R. (2000). *The international handbook of electronic commerce*. Chicago: The Glenlake Publishing Company Ltd.

Simchi-Levi, D., Kaminsky, P., & Simchi-Levi, E. (2003). *Designing and managing the supply chain* (2nd ed.). New York, NY: McGraw-Hill.

Small, M. H., & Chen, M. H. (1995). Investment justification of advanced manufacturing technology: An empirical analysis. *Journal of Engineering and Technology Management, 12*, 27-55.

Smith, B. (1995, September 26-29). *EDI: The opinion of Australian business.* Presented at the 6th Australian Conference on Information System, School of Information System, Curtin University.

Van Ackere, A., Larsen, E. R., & Morecroft, J. D. (1993). Systems thinking and business process redesign: An application to the beer game. *European Management Journal, 11*(4), 412-423.

Walsh, N. (1999). The extensible style language—styling XML documents. *Web Techniques, 4*(1), 4-6.

Webber, D. R. (1998). Introducing XML/EDI frameworks. *Electronic Markets, 8*(1), 38-41.

Webster, J. (1995). Networks of collaboration or conflict? Electronic data interchange and power in the supply chain. *Journal of Strategic Information Systems, 4*(1), 31-42.

Weiss, K. (1993). Data integrity and security: Who's in charge here anyway? *Information Management & Computer Security, 1*(4), 4-9.

Wreden, N. (1997, August). E-commerce goes from EDI to extranets—VAR 500 companies are wiring themselves and their customers together. *VAR Business*. Retrieved March 3, 2003, from http://www.techweb.com

Chapter X

Vertical Application Service Provision:
An SME Perspective

Nigel J. Lockett, Lancaster University, UK

David H. Brown, Lancaster University, UK

Abstract

Against a background of the low engagement of small to medium-sized enterprises (SMEs) in e-business, this chapter investigates the impact of e-aggregation applications, provided by emerging vertical application service providers (VSP), and defined as "an e-business application, promoted by a trusted third party, which engages a significant number of SMEs by addressing an important shared business concern within an aggregation". By conducting quantitative surveys of four aggregations of SMEs using these applications (users) and comparing these results with similar enterprises who are not (non-users) the research takes a deliberate SME perspective.

Introduction

This chapter seeks to contribute to the understanding of the engagement in e-business by small to medium-sized enterprises (SMEs) and in particular the impact of complex e-aggregation applications provided by the emerging vertical application service providers (VSP). Such e-aggregation applications, can be defined as "an e-business application, promoted by a trusted third party, which engages a significant number of SMEs by addressing an important shared business concern within an aggregation" (Brown & Lockett 2004; Lockett & Brown 2006; Lockett, Brown, & Kaewkitipong, 2006). SMEs are highly heterogeneous and typically represent over 98%, by number, of businesses in an economy. They contribute significant proportions of employment and turnover in the European and U.S. economies. For example in the U.S., there are over 25 million small businesses (less than 100 employees) provide 53% of employment and generate 47% of turnover (SBA, 2006). Unsurprisingly in the context of the "information society", governments see the adoption of information and communication technologies (ICT) by SMEs as crucial since the vast majority of new jobs, some 80% in Europe during the 1990s (CORDIS, 2006), are generated by this sector. As an example in the UK, the government has established policies to encourage the adoption of ICT by all enterprises and has set benchmarked targets to monitor progress. Recent studies suggest that this adoption is proving more difficult then anticipated.

The government target of having 1 million businesses trading online by 2002 was missed.... the study has found a slowdown in the uptake of ICTs, and for micro and small businesses there has been a clear reverse....for larger firms, this slowdown reflects the high proportion of businesses already using ICTs. For micro and small businesses the slowdown is less easy to explain. (DTI, 2003, p. 6)

To begin to understand the issues involved in e-business adoption, we need to classify e-business applications, as there are significant differences between e-mail and e-marketplace applications both in terms of complexity and added value. The EC (2005) E-Business Watch 4th synthesis report represents an important move toward tracking e-business engagement across 15 industry sectors and over a range of e-business throughout all EU member states. The report concluded that *access* to ICT was no longer a barrier to e-business uptake with connectivity at 84% for small businesses. It highlighted the digital divide between small and medium-sized enterprises, stating "for many e-business applications, medium firms (50-249) appear to have the 'critical size' for adoption. For instance, e-standards adoption by micro and small firms generally trails behind." (EC, 2005, p. 9). However this indicates an oversimplification evidenced by the tendency to equate e-business with e-mail and

Table 1. Classification of e-business application complexity (Adapted from Gillian et al., 1999)

Proposed classification	Examples	Complexity
Communication	E-Mail, Web access	Very Low
Marketing	Web site	Low
Productivity	Microsoft Office, intranet	Low
E-Commerce	Buying & selling online	Medium
Collaborative	Extranet	Medium
Enterprise	Financials, SFA, vertical applications	High
Marketplace	E-Marketplaces	High
Collaborative enterprise	SCM, CRM	Very High
Collaborative platform	Emerging platforms	Very High

Web access. A proposed classification for e-business adoption based on application complexity is shown in Table 1.

Importantly this proposed classification of application complexity stresses the roles of collaboration and interaction as key features of e-business applications and recognises the resultant increase in complexity. In the context of this research application complexity incorporates both technical and organisational factors, for example, both the security technologies underpinning virtual private networks used in higher complexity hosted applications and perceived commercial risk from storing sensitive client information in third-party data centres. Thus application complexity provides a meaningful framework in which to consider, compare, and analyse e-business engagement. Using this classification the most recently available

Figure 1. SMEs e-business engagement (Updated from Lockett & Brown, 2005)

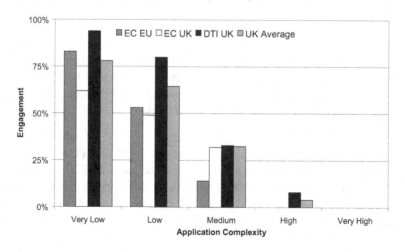

survey data (EC, 2002; DTI, 2002) was analysed to show the level of e-business engagement by SMEs in terms of application complexity (Figure 1).

In summary, Figure 1 suggests that most SMEs appear comfortable with e-mail and Web access (lower complexity, about 80%), are tentative with the use of the Internet for online buying and selling (medium complexity, about 30%), but have little or no engagement in the high or very high complexity applications, such as e-marketplaces, supply chains, or inter-organisational collaborative networks (less than 10%). This is despite the early promise of application service providers (ASP) facilitating such access to complex applications. Hence the trend in Figure 1 is not merely surprising in terms of the early expectations of engagement, but raises the important question of what this relative lack of engagement will mean not only for SMEs but also the larger organisations that have significant numbers of SMEs in their supplier networks.

It is against this background that this chapter explores the evidence of the adoption or non-adoption of the higher complexity applications by SMEs. The remainder of the chapter is structured into four further parts: the second part provides an overview of the literature framework; the third part describes the methodology; the fourth part presents the findings; and finally the fifth part draws some conclusions with a view to informing both the theory and practice of e-business adoption.

Literature Review

The recent and rapid emergence of e-business applications has been primarily as a result of the availability of a low cost, ubiquitous electronic communication network, the Internet. Telecommunication, technology, and service companies have emerged or evolved to provide a range of e-business services. Typically these are known as ASPs and defined as:

(providing) a contractual service offering to deploy, host, manage and rent access to an application from a centrally managed facility, responsible for either directly or indirectly providing all the specific activities and expertise aimed at managing a software application or set of applications. (Gillian et al., 1999)

However ASPs form part of the wider service provider (xSP) sector, which includes, storage service providers (SSP), content service providers (CSP), wireless ASPs (WASP) and others. ASPNews (2003) provided a directory of 1,720 companies involved in service provision and highlighted 235 vertical market ASPs, defined as providing support to a specific industry, which constituted 15% of the total number of companies involved in service provision. Desai and Currie's (2003) longitudinal research of 424 ASPs concludes similarly that 12% are vertical application service providers (VSP) with the remaining being classified as horizontal ASPs. This chapter focuses on these minority VSPs and their role in engaging SMEs in industry specific higher complexity e-business applications, rather than the more dominant horizontal ASPs capable of offering services across multiple industries.

Three principal theory domains are relevant to the interpretive framework, namely: (1) ICT adoption by SMEs, (2) inter-organisational networks, and (3) the emerging field of e-business models.

Inter-Organisational Networks (IONs)

Of particular interest in this chapter is how the concept of aggregations of enterprises, be they online or off-line groupings in a specific industry, use or might use e-business applications and how these applications are provided. Business groupings or aggregations is not a new concept with many businesses being fully aware of the importance of relationships within their industry, supply chain, or trade association. Particularly useful here is the perspective of networks to help understand firm behaviour, where networks are one of three institutional ways of organising in business markets including markets and firms. Key areas include the delineation of the network, trust and the benefits, and tensions of network collaboration and competition. This latter issue has been commented upon by Hamel and Prahalad (1994) and Jarillo (1993). Research has focused on network structure and embeddedness (Shaw & Conway, 2000) and the governance of networks (Johannisson, 1998) with more recent work considering SMEs and networks and their contribution to promoting enterprise (Blundel & Smith, 2001) and the role of ICT in SMEs networks. The concept of a business aggregations is well understood and can encompass many forms of relationship, from local retail traders campaigning for improvements to their local infrastructure to the highly-developed supplier-based networks of the motor manufacturing industry. Such aggregations are now characterised by IONs, which develop either to reduce costs (Zajac & Olsen, 1993) or to increase revenue (Contractor & Lorange 1988) directly or indirectly or to mitigate risk in response to economic factors (Ebers, 1997). These emerging, stable, non-equity based collaborative arrangements have become increasingly important and have generally been termed strategic networks (Ebers, 1997). At the core of Jarillo's rationale for these networks is increased competitiveness through specialization, focus, and size. This research takes strategic networks to be a type of ION. Other authors have in turn emphasised the change in market structures, the move to long-term focus and different firm behaviours as important factors in the formation of IONs (Ebers, 1997; Oliver, 1990; Powell, 1987).

Figure 2. Taxonomy of aggregations for SMEs (Source: Brown & Lockett, 2004)

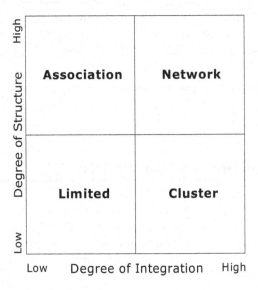

Classifying Networks

There are many possible manifestations of the network form and many ways of classifying them. Grandori and Soda (1995) differentiate networks by the extent to which the links between organisations are formalised and networks are termed bureaucratic, social, or proprietary. Aldrich and Glinow (1992) classify networks into personal and social networks and provide a basis for understanding the role of network as a broker within a set of relationships. In the context of SMEs, the proposed taxonomy of aggregations links the degree of structure (informal to formal) to the degree of integration (independent to integrated) (Figure 2).

Within the broad concept of aggregation, this taxonomy locates "networks" as one form of strong or complex aggregation which can be contrasted with other weaker or simpler aggregation forms—a distinction which can be useful when considering the nature of an SME's engagement in an aggregation and the role of any intermediaries. While online aggregation, at SME or industry level, was seen as a way of engaging the SMEs; consideration needs to be given to existing off-line aggregations or groupings. SMEs operate in business markets comprising relationships within their supply chain or industry sector, which can range from simple to complex in nature. The degree of structure (informal to formal) and degree of integration (independent to integrated) provides a taxonomy suitable for both online and offline aggregations and comprises four types:

- **Limited:** Any relationships are loose and participants are independent, characterised by little or no aggregation. Intermediaries range from local business groups to more sophisticated organisations

- **Association:** Including trade associations and professional bodies, where reputation is enhanced by membership and structure is high, but businesses remain largely independent.

- **Cluster:** Forming part of an identifiable business market, business cluster, or economic cluster (Porter, 1998) where SMEs are increasingly dependent on complex linkages within a sector, but structure is low.

- **Network:** Represents a more highly developed form of cooperation which exhibits both relatively high structure and integration. In the literature, these networks are often implicitly described from a large business perspective.

ICT Adoption by SMEs

Many authors have tried to develop an understanding of adoption in the specific context of IT and SMEs. Three strands of work can be identified, which although overlapping can usefully be separated, namely strategic, technological, and organisational. The first is that which emphasises the strategic logic in the decision to adopt information systems (IS) (Blili & Raymond, 1993; Kowtha & Choon, 2001; Sadowski, Maitland, & van Dongen, 2002). In this context, SMEs can be both victims and beneficiaries depending on their degree of proactivity. Blili and Raymond (1993) showed that IS planning by SMEs became more critical as technology became more central to their products and processes and concluded that IS planning needed to be integrated with business strategy. However, Hagmann and McCahon (1993) concluded that few SMEs plan their adoption of IS and that the limited planning that was evident was focused on operational improvements and was not concerned with competitiveness. The notion of strategic information systems planning in SMEs is further developed in Levy and Powell (2000) and Levy, Powell, and Yetton (2001). This strand of research has resulted in frameworks, such as Levy's "focus domination model", to help position and integrate IS investments—one of which could be e-business applications. A model of the strategic use of IS by SMEs was proposed by Levy and Powell (2000) consisting of three interdependent factors, namely strategic content, business context, and business process. Within the latter the analysis of business activities and their strategic use of IS was considered by using, in part, the McFarlan's (1984) "strategic impact grid", consisting of factory, support, strategic, and turnaround,where:

- **Factory:** Applications are essential for success. There is a heavy dependence on IS for smooth operations. Future IS may not be likely to give a competitive edge.

- **Support:** Applications are valuable for success. These may speed up administration or occasionally improve processing but may not be critical.

- **Strategic:** Applications are critical to sustaining future performance. Few IS have a strategic role in existing and future developments.

- **Turnaround:** Applications may be important in achieving the future. Existing IS not too important but future developments are likely to have a major impact.

Levy and Powell (2000, p. 259) found that IS were predominantly located in support (63%) and to a lesser extent in factory (28%) and strategic (11%) with no evidence of turnaround. They concluded that the use of strategic IS by SMEs "is firmly directed at improving the operation with limited appreciation of the value of strategic information".

A second technological strand, and arguably the most prolific, has seen adoption as an outcome of a complex process of evaluation, frequently informal, by SMEs of multiple factors both external and internal. These factors are frequently cast as enablers or barriers to adoption (Cragg & King, 1993; Lefebvre, Harvey, & Lefebre, 1991; Mehrtens, Cragg, & Mills, 2001; Stansfield & Grant, 2003; Thong & Yap, 1995; Walczuch, Van Braven, & Lundgren, 2000). Iacovou, Benbassat, and Dexter (1995) focused on the single technology of EDI and identified perceived benefits, organisational readiness (resources) and external pressures (competitive and non-competitive) as the critical factors in adoption. Since EDI is a complex application (but not necessarily Internet-based) these findings may be particularly relevant in the adoption of similar higher complexity e-business applications.

The third strand is that which takes an explicit organisational stance, and frequently that of the owner-manager and the social parameters within which the firm operates. As such the approach counters the strategic or technological emphasis of the first two strands (Barry & Milner, 2002; Blackburn & McClure, 1998; Dierckx & Stroken, 1999; Fuller & Southern, 1999; Hussin, King, & Cragg, 2002; Poon & Swatmann, 1999; Quayle, 2002; Southern & Tilley, 2000). An important observation of Southern and Tilley is that "when small firms use IT complex relations unfold. It is by no means a simple linear development whereby observers can expect an incremental build up of knowledge and expertise on ICT to be established within the firm" (1999, p. 152). In the context of the adoption of increasingly complex e-business applications, this view appears highly pertinent.

Throughout these strands of literature, three characteristics prevail: namely (1) the unit of analysis is the single firm; (2) the perspective adopted is that of the user; and (3) the dimension of application complexity as a key variable is often absent. In their original context these characteristics are reasonable, but they are also limiting.

For example the notion that once a firm has decided to adopt an IT application that obtaining the application is non-problematic. In the case of complex applications, such as integrated e-business, this assumption may be unwise. From a provider perspective the issue of user readiness (technical and financial) together with the ongoing support and maintenance issues may signal an uneconomic contract and mitigate against initial supply.

Much research on the adoption of ICT by SMEs has tended to assume progressive adoption (DTI, 1999; Willcocks, Sauer, & Associates, 2000; Clegg, 2001; Kendall, Tung, Chua, Ng, & Tan, 2001; Rao, Metts, & Mora-Morge, 2003). Although the DTI (2003, p. 1) acknowledges that "it is important not to assume that business needs to pass through all the steps of the ladder in sequence", it continued to emphasise the "e-adoption ladder" originating in previous studies (DTI, 1999, 2003). Interestingly non-linear ICT adoption models for SMEs have emerged, including Dixon, Thompson, and McAllister (2002) who concluded that "the typical linear model of ICT adoption may be inappropriate". This change was further supported by the "transporter model" proposed by Levy and Powell (2003, p. 125) which states SMEs are unlikely to follow a linear stages model but "rather, they will focus on what is best to meet the owners' strategy for business growth", Figure 3. The model identifies of four SME groupings, namely brochureware, business opportunity, business network, and business support, where:

- **Brochureware:** Internet value was low and firms did not plan business growth.
- **Business opportunity:** Internet to offered high value but are not planning growth.
- **Business network:** Internet is seen as key to business network development.
- **Business support:** Internet used for support and are planning growth.

Levy and Powell (2003, p. 125) conclude that their research "demonstrates that different types of business will view Internet adoption in very different lights" and "will focus on what is best to meet the owners' strategy for business growth."

Diffusion of Innovations

Studies on the adoption of e-commerce by SMEs are relatively recent but research antecedents are well established. Rogers' work (1962, 1983, 1995) on the diffusion of innovations, while initially neither IT nor SME-focused, has evolved to incorporate diffusion networks and critical mass in order to appreciate the adoption of interactive innovations, such as the Internet (1995, p. 313). The early work of Rogers took a provider (or supplier) perspective and identified the characteristics of innovation which would impact on its rate of diffusion including such factors as compatibility, complexity, observability, relative advantage, and trialability. In particular Rogers highlights the important roles of change agents (intermediaries) in influencing innovation decisions, including developing a need, establishing communication, diagnosing problems, creating an intent to change, and then action. Theoretically the role of the intermediary as a means of facilitating the diffusion of complex ICT has been observed by a number of authors, most notably Swan and Newell (1995), Swan, Newell, and Robertson (1998), and Newell, Swan, and Galliers (2000). In these particular instances it was the professional associations that assisted in this way. Recent studies investigating the adoption of ICT by SMEs utilised Rogers' model of innovation (Kendall et al., 2001; Mehrtens et al., 2001). Kendall et al. highlighted three significant factors for the adoption of e-commerce, namely relative advantage, compatibility, and trialability. Relative advantage is the perceived benefits such as lower costs and increased business opportunities, compatibility is how well the innovation will fit into existing processes and trialability is the use of innovation without incurring high start-up costs. Mehrtens et al. also considered Internet adoption by SMEs in the context of diffusion of innovation concluding perceived benefits, organisational readiness, and external pressures were the key factors. These two recent studies show some correlation between firstly relative advantage and perceived benefits, and secondly compatibility and organisational readiness, providing strong support for these being two important factors from Rogers' model of diffusion when related to e-business engagement by SMEs.

E-Business Models

The final strand of theory is the emergent e-business model literature, which includes insights into how Internet-based technologies led to new business models. This was particularly important as it informed the understanding of this rapidly evolving area of business, provided the context for application service provision, and helped to conceptualise the role of intermediaries. The engagement of SMEs in e-business, through aggregations, could constitute a new model for doing business and is informed by the e-business model literature, albeit from a predominantly large company perspective. Two main themes have emerged from this body of work: first, attempts to define and identify the components that constitute the e-business models and, second, taxonomies which help to categorise existing business models and identify the trends (Afuah & Tucci, 2001; Amit & Zott, 2001; Earle & Keen, 2000; Hamel, 2000; Kalakota & Robinson, 2000; Margretta, 2002; Tapscott, Ticoll, & Lowe, 2000; Timmers, 2000; Weill & Vitale, 2001). First, attempts to define e-business models and identify the components resulted in several different but related contributions, namely:

Timmers (2000, p. 32) has been widely cited and defined e-business models as:

An architecture for the product, service and information flows, including a description of the various business actors and their roles; and a description of the potential benefits for the various business actors; and description of the sources of revenues.

Tapscott et al. (2000, p. 19) define business Webs as:

A distinct system of suppliers, distributors, commerce services providers, and customers that use the Internet for their primary business communications and transactions. The business web consists of nine characteristics, namely Internet infrastructure, value proposition, multi-enterprise capability, five classes of participants, co-operation, customer centric, context, rules and standards, and knowledge intensity.

Other authors have highlighted the various elements that constitute a business model, including the components, linkages, and associated dynamics, which take commercial advantage of the Internet (Afuah & Tucci, 2001) and major components, bridge links, and underpinning factors (Hamel, 2000). While Timmers and Tapscott produced useful overall taxonomies other authors have developed models specific to particular applications, including business-to-business (B2B) vertical supply chains (Kalakota & Robinson, 2000) and value-adding intermediaries facilitating collaborative and community-based enterprises (Earle & Keen, 2000). In the particular context of SMEs, the scope for application service providers to serve "natural" marketplaces of SMEs with SME-orientated applications has been noted (Mazzi, 2001). While large business may have the resources to take risks in order to identify and adapt to these trends, small businesses may find this challenging both from a resource and knowledge perspective.

When examining the uptake of e-business approaches among SMEs the concepts of collaboration, interdependence, power, and trust also provide important contributions. The need to encourage SME engagement in e-business has been readily acknowledged by industry and government but just how this was to be achieved, particularly with the more complex e-business application areas, remained unspecified. However the concept of aggregation addressed through new intermediaries is increasingly being recognised by many authors, including aggregations (Mazzi, 2001), B2B e-marketmaker (Kalakota & Robinson, 2000), and value-adding intermediaries (Earle & Keen, 2000). The Internet has spawned many new business models. Of special relevance to this research, however, has been the potential of Internet technologies to facilitate the development of new and economic inter-organisational systems (IOS), which has led in turn to new aggregation or network-based business models. The concept of aggregation and the addressing of online aggregations through new intermediaries, typically by ASPs, is increasingly being recognised as an important development. However, only recently have researchers published more critical, reflective, and impartial evidence of ASP business models and adoption by SMEs (Desai & Currie, 2003; Dewire, 2001; Kern, Kreijer, & Willcocks, 2002; Patnayakuni & Seth, 2001; Susarla, Barua, & Whinston, 2003; Yao, 2003). This lack of academic literature is noted by Heart and Pliskin (2001) and Desai and Currie (2003).

Ward and Peppard (2002) place application service provision within the context of outsourcing strategies and in particular its role in selective outsourcing. They note that "ASPs primarily target SMEs that cannot afford their own IS functions" (2002, p. 574) but conclude that customers remain to be convinced. Kern et al. (2002) explored the strategic outsourcing nature of ASPs arguing that there were many similarities with more traditional IT outsourcing through the use of a contingency model, which incorporated resource dependency, resource-based transaction cost and agency theory. Currie and Seltsikas (2001) also noted the similarity between IT outsourcing and applications service provision but also that SMEs had little experience of outsourcing. Interestingly their study stated that of the 424 ASPs reviewed over 45% failed, over the four years of the investigation, and that only 42% had survived in their original form with the remainder being the subject of mergers and acquisitions. Patnayakuni and Seth (2001) similarly described ASPs as a new model of IT outsourcing and proposed an adoption model which incorporated social exchange theory, particularly concerning power and trust. More elaborate and ambitious models have recently been proposed by Yao (2003) with an "integrative adoption" model, which included economic, strategic, and social factors and by Jayatilaka, Schwarz, and Hirschheim (2003) with an "interpretative perspective" model, which attempts to select appropriate elements from transaction cost, re-source-based, resource dependence, and knowledge-based theory. The comparison of the traditional IT outsourcing and ASP models highlighted the differences in the target clients, namely large organisations with their own IT departments and initially SMEs with low IT expertise respectively. Clearly there are differences between IT outsourcing and the ASP model both in terms of user, provider, delivery, and functionality but the extensive research on IT outsourcing has much to contribute to this emerging field, not least in the strategic nature of this decision regardless of the company size (Kern et al., 2002; Willcocks & Lacity, 1998; Willcocks et al., 2000). The impact of companies' decisions to adopt the ASP business model was beginning to emerge from published research and indicated the complex nature of measuring customer satisfaction and the strong relevance of the IT outsourcing literature (Susarla et al., 2003).

Methodology

The research required access to adopters and non-adopters of the higher complexity e-aggregation applications—hereafter termed users and non-users, respectively. For the former, five VSPs were approached resulting in permission being obtained in four cases. Having established this cooperation quantitative questionnaire-based survey research was undertaken in four specific industry sectors. Non-user samples from within the same four industry sectors were identified and a survey was conducted using a modified questionnaire. In order to support comparison, it was important that the user and non-user samples were independent of each other. Details of the survey sample are summarised in Table 2. For the user survey because the absolute number of users is small, populating the sample frame was governed by what was available, rather than some empirical ideal. Comparative analysis between the two sample groups, namely users of e-aggregation applications and non-users within the wider aggregation, was undertaken at a combined level, that is, all four specific industry sectors together. This was a deliberate part of the empirical research design necessitated by the low number of e-aggregation application users available. The quantitative survey sought data of two kinds. First, data on the factors which enabled or inhibited the adoption of high complexity e-business applications and second, data on the complexity of their current e-business applications. Although the quantitative survey detailed in this chapter was the main empirical research in-

Table 2. Selection and data collection for survey research

Aggregation	Users (*application*)	Non-users
Construction (Network)	Details of 15 SME users of a *project management* application were provided by an account manager. A jointly agreed letter of introduction was sent to each contractor. These contractors were then telephoned. 10 valid responses were received.	125 building contractors were alphabetically selected from an online directory for NW England. A letter of introduction was sent to each. Eighteen valid responses were received.
Dairy (Cluster)	Details of 15 SME users of a *herd management* application were provided by an ASP account manager. A jointly agreed letter of introduction was sent to each dairy farmer together with a questionnaire. Eight valid responses were received.	125 dairy farmers were alphabetically selected from an online directory for NW England. A letter of introduction was sent to each. Twenty-seven valid responses were received.
Knowledge worker (Association)	Access users of a *community management* application was negotiated with the chief executive and marketing manager. A jointly agreed request was e-mailed to members requesting completion of an online questionnaire. Nineteen valid responses were received.	125 accountants; solicitors; financial advisors; and surveyors were alphabetically selected from an online directory for NW England. A letter of introduction was sent to each. Twenty-one valid responses were received.
Organic (Cluster)	The manager of the *organic field management* ASP was interviewed and subsequently provided details of 6 SME users in the UK. These producers were e-mailed a jointly agreed statement and questionnaire requesting a telephone interview. Five valid responses were received.	125 organic producers were selected alphabetically from an online directory for England. A letter of introduction was sent to each producer. Thirty-eight valid responses were received.
Total	43 valid responses	104 valid responses

strument qualitative interviews with representatives of the four sectors was carried out to provide further context and interpretation.

The sum of the four surveys for each sample group were combined in order to enable statistically significant differences to be highlighted. In both independent samples, the number of responses was greater than 30 (being 43 for users and 104 for non-users) and the independent parametric t-test could be applied.

The following hypotheses were developed:

The null hypothesis H_0: *The values for the user and non-user groups are equal.*

The alternative hypothesis H_1: *The values for user and non-user groups are not equal.*

Findings and Discussion

Comparison between the two sample groups in terms of the factors facilitating or inhibiting adoption was undertaken at a combined level and the statistical differences are shown in Table 3. In order to accept or reject the null hypothesis the significance level, degrees of freedom (df), and one-tail tests were calculated. For there to be a significant difference, the null hypothesis was rejected if the critical value is less than 0.05 or 5% and therefore the alternative hypothesis is accepted (Table 3). The individual results for the enablers and barriers are presented (*in italics*) before listing the four main groups for both, that is first enablers: (1) sales and marketing, (2) operational, (3) innovation, and (4) external; and second barriers: (1) security, (2) cost & benefits, (3) infrastructure and services, and (4) information & education. This grouping of the enablers and barriers to e-business engagement by SMEs assisted in comparison with secondary data.

It can be concluded that users are significantly more positive and more knowledgeable and experienced than non-users regarding e-business. Users are significantly more likely to agree that e-business allows the same activities to be done more efficiently and allows new ways of doing business to develop. Users have an arithmetic mean greater than three (the neutral point) for all characteristics and greater than four regarding attitude, new ways of doing business, and knowledge and experience than non-users. Regarding enablers or drivers for e-business engagement, users are significantly more influenced by "sales and marketing" factors and "innovation" opportunities than non-users. There is no significant difference between users and non-users regarding "operational" and "external" drivers to e-business engagement. Interestingly users are neutral regarding external drivers but with an arithmetic mean greater than four identified "innovation" as a key driver, a very significant difference between the samples.

Table 3. Statistically significant differences between users and non-users

* indicates a significant difference (greater that 0.05 or 5%)		df	Critical Value % 5.0%, 2.5%, 1.0%	t-test
1. Characteristics of SMEs	*	100	1.660, 1.984, 2.364	4.260
Knowledge & experience of e-business	*	85	1.663, 1.988, 2.371	3.403
E-Business allows you to do same activities more efficiently?	*	100	1.660, 1.984, 2.364	4.855
E-Business allows you to develop new ways of doing business?	*	95	1.661, 1.985, 2.366	2.285
2. Enablers: What has helped or encouraged you to use e-business applications? (*category*)				
Improving company image (sales & marketing)	*	85	1.663, 1.988, 2.371	2.311
Opportunity for increased sales (sales & marketing)		80	1.664, 1.990, 2.374	0.453
Reducing operating costs (operational)		85	1.663, 1.988, 2.371	0.888
Improving customer services (operational)		75	1.665, 1.994, 2.381	0.537
Improving collaboration with partners (innovation)	*	90	1.662, 1.987, 2.368	4.046
Provides new ways of doing business (innovation)	*	90	1.662, 1.987, 2.368	2.516
Customer demands (external)		80	1.664, 1.990, 2.374	0.394
Supplier demands (external)		45	1.679, 2.014, 2.412	0.248
Category of enabler				
i) Sales & Marketing	*	100	1.660, 1.984, 2.364	1.864
ii) Operational		100	1.660, 1.984, 2.364	0.466
iii) Innovation	*	100	1.660, 1.984, 2.364	4.642
iv) External		100	1.660, 1.984, 2.364	0.564
3. Barriers: What is discouraging you from further use of e-business applications? (*category*)				
Concerned about confidentiality (security)		90	1.662, 1.987, 2.364	0.878
Concerned about security (security)		75	1.665, 1.992, 2.377	1.265
Concerned about risk of fraud (security)	*	75	1.665, 1.992, 2.377	1.882
ICT costs too high (cost & benefits)		85	1.663, 1.988, 2.371	0.969
No benefits to company (cost & benefits)	*	80	1.664, 1.990, 2.374	2.956
No suitable e-business applications available (infra/st & services)	*	80	1.664, 1.990, 2.374	1.733
Shortage of ICT skilled (internal) staff (infra/st & services)		50	1.676, 2.009, 2.403	0.580
Lack of knowledge of e-business (information & education)	*	80	1.664, 1.990, 2.374	2.372
Lack of information, support or training (information & education)	*	85	1.663, 1.988, 2.371	2.385
Category of barrier				
i) Security		100	1.660, 1.984, 2.364	1.193
ii) Cost & Benefits	*	100	1.660, 1.984, 2.364	5.130
iii) Infrastructure & Services		100	1.660, 1.984, 2.364	0.711
iv) Information & Education	*	100	1.660, 1.984, 2.364	3.870

Users are significantly less concerned regarding "cost and benefits" and "information and education" barriers than non-users. There are no significant differences between users and non-users regarding "security" and "infrastructure and services" barriers to e-business engagement. With arithmetic means of less than three for "cost and benefits" and "information and education", these factors are not identified as barriers by users. Interesting both users and non-user identified "security" as the main barrier to further e-business engagement.

There were significant differences in the levels of engagement in e-business between non-users and users levels of engagement in e-business both on a simple (very low to very high) scale of application complexity (Figure 3).

Self evidently all users had Internet connectivity and were engaged in high complexity aggregation-specific applications compared to non-users being 75% and 17%, respectively. Importantly however users had significantly higher levels of engagement in low (63%), medium (56%), and very high (14%) complexity applications

Figure 3. E-business engagement by SMEs

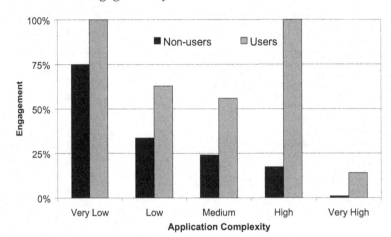

compared to non-users being 34%, 24%, and 1%, respectively. In particular, the difference at medium application complexity was over two-fold (24% to 56%) compared with non-users. It could be concluded that users of aggregation-specific applications have significantly higher levels of engagement in e-business applications, regardless of application complexity, than non-users in comparable aggregations. There may of course be a predisposition amongst users to have higher levels of engagement, however there is no reason to suppose this as the e-aggregation applications sought to reduce costs or increase sales.

Furthermore comparison to a European benchmarking study conducted at a similar time, which investigated SMEs, generally indicated some important differences. Significantly users had higher levels of engagement in e-business applications regardless of application complexity. In particular the difference at medium application complexity was nearly two-fold (32% to 56%) compared with UK SMEs, and nearly fourfold compared to EU SMEs (14% to 56%). It could be concluded that users of aggregation-specific applications have significantly higher levels of engagement in e-business applications, regardless of application complexity, than SMEs in the UK and EU.

There was no significant difference between users and non-users regarding the descriptive category of the current ICT use. Both non-users and users ranked *support* first (58% & 62%, respectively) and *turnaround* second (26% & 25%, respectively). This is similar to other studies conducted on the strategic use of information systems by SMEs. Users are more likely to consider themselves part of a business network (66%) than non-users (35%).

In summary, the survey of users of e-aggregation applications and non-users in the wider aggregation highlighted the many significant differences between users and non-users. Users were more positive and more knowledgeable and experienced regarding e-business generally and more likely to agree that e-business allowed the same activities to be done more efficiently and new ways of doing business. This may because users were predisposed to this position or that it was a consequence of using the e-aggregation application or a combination of both. More specifically users were more influenced by "sales and marketing" and "innovation" drivers of using e-business applications and less concerned with "cost and benefits" and "information and knowledge" barriers than non-users. The main driver for increased e-business engagement was "innovation" and the main barrier was "security", this latter characteristic was the same for non-users.

Understandably all users had Internet connectivity (very low complexity) and used an e-aggregation application (high complexity) as these were a prerequisite of the sample. However users were significantly more engaged in e-business regardless of application complexity. Again this may be because users were predisposed to this position or that it was a consequence of using the e-aggregation application or a combination of both. Importantly users were convinced that the e-aggregation application speeded up deployment of the application, reduced costs, and improved quality of service to customers and suppliers. These were clearly perceived business benefits from using these specialised hosted applications and tends to indicate that using the e-aggregation application either reinforced or created more positive views of e-business.

Interesting users are more likely to consider themselves part of a business network (66%) than non-users (35%). Clearly aggregation has an important part to play in the engagement of SMEs in e-business either by reinforcing existing relationships and creating new ones or simply as a mechanism for facilitating economic service provision of higher complex e-business applications. However the appreciation of these finding must be set in the context of the qualitative data in order to better understand why users of e-aggregation applications are acting in a significantly different way to non-users. More specifically what roles to trusted third parties and service providers play.

Conclusion

In conclusion both the secondary studies and the non-user survey indicate high levels of connectivity and usage of very low complexity applications, such as e-mail and Web browsers, among SMEs in the UK and Europe. One recent study concluded that SME connectivity was static or declining (Ofcom, 2005) and another that connectivity was no longer a barrier to e-business engagement (EC, 2005). This suggests that most SMEs appeared comfortable with e-mail and Web access (lower complexity). However as application complexity increased levels of engagement declined significantly indicating that SMEs are tentative with the use of the Internet for online buying and selling (medium complexity), but had little or no engagement in the high or very high complexity applications, such as e-marketplaces, supply chains, or inter-organisational collaborative networks. In direct contrast to these studies and the non-user survey there was evidence of SMEs engaged in complex e-business applications, most noticeably in e-aggregation applications, and that these users had significantly higher levels of engagement in other e-business applications. It was not possible to conclude either way if this difference was due to the use of the e-aggregation application or that users had a higher usage of ICT previously. However in our qualitative discussions both behaviours were confirmed in all aggregation types (Figure 2). One conclusion that can be drawn is that engagement in an e-aggregation arrangement, which provides access to an aggregation specific complex application, has been a positive experience—users do not withdraw from, or lessen, their commitment to e-business applications of all complexities. This research challenges the prevalent linear adoption model so evident with the policy-maker and provider communities. Clearly, there are messages from this research for VSPs both in terms of the factors that most interest SMEs and the positive impact of industry specific applications. However the absolute numbers of SMEs engaging in complex e-business applications remains very small and much more work is required to better understand the motivations of SMEs and the factor conditions that would accelerate adoption. This early work has highlighted the potential of e-aggregation applications in facilitating SMEs engagement in higher complexity e-business applications and makes an important contribution to our understanding of adoption behaviour of small firms in the context of inter-organisational networks.

References

Afuah, A., & Tucci, C. (2001). *Internet business models and strategies*. New York: McGraw-Hill.

Aldrich, H., & Glinow, M. (1992). Personal networks and infrastructure development. In D. Gibbon, G. Kozmetsky, & R. Smilor (Eds.), *The technopolis phenomenon: Smart cities, fast systems, global networks* (pp. 125-145). New York: Rowman and Littlefield.

Amit, R., & Zott, C. (2001). Value creation in eBusiness. *Strategic Management Journal, 22*, 493-520.

ASP News. (2003). Retrieved September 6, 2003, from www.aspnews.com

Barry, H., & Milner, B. (2002). SMEs and electronic commerce: A departure from the traditional prioritisation of training? *Journal of European Industrial Training, 26*(7), 316-326.

Blackburn, R., & McClure, R. (1998). *The use of information and communication technologies (ICTs) in small business service firms.* London: Small Business Research Centre, Kingston Business School.

Blili, S., & Raymond, L. (1993). Information technology: Threats and opportunities for small and medium-sized enterprises. *International Journal of Information Management, 13*(6), 439-448.

Blundel, R., & Smith, D. (2001). *Business networks report.* UK: Small Business Service.

Brown, D. H., & Lockett, N. (2004). The potential of critical e-applications for engaging SMEs in e-business: A provider perspective. *European Journal of Information Systems, 13*(1), 21-34.

Clegg, C. (2001). *E-commerce impacts: A review of 14 sector studies.* UK:Small Business Service.

Contractor, F., & Lorange, P. (1988). *Cooperative strategies in international business.* Lexington, MA: Lexington Books.

CORDIS. (2006). Retrieved July 28, 2006, from http://cordis.europa.eu/euroabstracts/en/home.html

Cragg, P., & King, M. (1993). Small firm computing: Motivators and inhibitors. *MIS Quarterly*, March, 47-60.

Currie, W., & Seltsikas, P. (2001). Exploring the supply-side of IT outsourcing: The emerging role of application service providers. *European Journal of Information Systems, 10*(3), 123-134.

Desai, B., & Currie, W. (2003, August 4-6). The application service providers business model: Issues and challenges. In *Proceedings of the Americas Conference on Information Systems*, Tampa, FL (pp. 131-138). Atlanta, GA: AIS.

Dewire, D. (2001, August 3-5). ASPs: Applications to rent. In *Proceedings of the Americas Conference on Information Systems*, Boston (pp. 2275-2282). Atlanta, GA: AIS.

Dierckx, M., & Stroken, J. (1999). Information technology and innovation in small and medium enterprise. *Technological Forecasting and Social Change, 60*(2), 149-166.

Dixon, T., Thompson, B., & McAllister. (2002). *The value of ICT for SMEs in the UK: A critical literature review.* UK: Small Business Service, UK.

DTI. (1999). *Business into the information age: International benchmarking study 1999.* UK: Department of Trade and Industry.

DTI. (2003). *Business into the information age: International benchmarking study 2003.* UK: Department of Trade and Industry.

Earle, N., & Keen, P. (2000). *From .com to .profit: Inventing business models that deliver value and profit.* San Francisco: Jossey-Bass.

Ebers, M. (1997). *The formation of inter-organisational networks*. Oxford, UK: Oxford University Press.

EC. (2002). *Benchmarking national and regional e-business policies for SMEs: Final benchmarking report*. European Commission. www.ec.europa.eu/

EC. (2005). *The European e-Business Report 2005: 4ᵗʰ synthesis report of the e-business W@tch*. European Commission. www.ec.europa.eu/

Fuller, T., & Southern, A. (1999). Small firms and information and communication technologies: Policy issues and some words of caution. *Environment and Planning: Government and Policy, 17*, 287-302.

Gillian, C., Graham, S., Levitt, M., McArthur, J., Murray, S., Turner, V., Villars, R., & McCathy, M. (1999). *The ASPs' impact on the IT industry*. Framingham, MA: IDC Corporation.

Grandori, A., & Soda, G. (1995). Interfirm networks: Antecedents, mechanisms and forms. *Organisation Studies, 16*(2), 183-214.

Hagmann, C., & McCahon, C. (1993). Strategic information systems and competitiveness. *Information & Management, 25*(2), 183-192.

Hamel, G. (2000). *Leading the revolution*. Boston, MA: Harvard Business School Press.

Hamel, G., & Prahalad, C. K. (1994). *Competing for the future*. MA: Harvard Business School Press.

Heart, T., & Pliskin, N. (2001). Is IT application services (ASP) alive and well? *Journal of Information Technology Theory and Application, 3*(4), 33-41.

Hussin, H., King, M., & Cragg, P. (2002). IT alignment in small firms. *European Journal of Information Systems, 11*(2), 108-127.

Iacovou, C., Benbassat, I., & Dexter, A. (1995). EDI and small organisations: Adoption and impact of technology. *MIS Quarterly, 19*(4), 465-85.

Jarillo, J. (1993). *Strategic networks: Creating the boundless organisation*. Oxford, UK: Butterworth-Heinemann.

Jayatilaka, B., Schwarz, A., & Hirschheim, R. (2003). Determinants of ASP choice: An integrated perspective. *European Journal of Information Systems, 13*(3), 196-210.

Johannisson, B. (1998). Personal networks in emerging knowledge-based firms: Spatial and functional patterns. *Entrepreneurship and Regional Development, 10*(4), 297-312.

Kalakota, R., & Robinson, M. (2000). *e-Business 2.0: Roadmap for success*. Upper Saddle River, NJ: Addison Wesley.

Kendall, J., Tung, L., Chua, K., Ng, C., & Tan, S. (2001). Receptivity of Singapore's SMEs to electronic commerce adoption. *Journal of Strategic Information Systems, 10*(3), 223-242.

Kern, T, Kreijer, J., & Willcocks, L. (2002). Exploring ASP as sourcing strategy: Theoretical perspectives, propositions for practice. *Journal of Strategic Information Systems, 11*(2), 153-177.

Kowtha, N., & Choon, T. (2001). Determinants of Website development: A study of electronic commerce in Singapore. *Information and Management, 39*, 227-242.

Lefebvre, L., Harvey, J., & Lefebre, E. (1991). Technological experience and technology adoption decisions in small manufacturing firms. *R & D Management, 21*(3), 241-249.

Levy, M., & Powell, P. (2000). Information systems strategy for SMEs: An organisational perspective. *Journal of Strategic Information Systems, 9*(1), 63-84.

Levy, M., & Powell, P. (2003). Exploring SME Internet adoption: Towards a contingent model. *Electronic Markets: The International Journal, 13*(2), 173-181.

Levy, M., Powell, P., & Yetton, P. (2001). SMEs: Aligning IS and the strategic context. *Journal of Information Technology, 16*(1), 133-144.

Lockett, N., & Brown, D. H. (2005). An SME perspective of vertical application service providers. *International Journal of Enterprise Information Systems, 1*(2), 37-55.

Lockett, N., & Brown, D. H. (2006). Aggregation and the role of trusted third parties in SME e-business engagement: A regional policy issue. *International Small Business Journal, 24*(2), 379-404.

Lockett, N., Brown, D. H., & Kaewkitipong, L. (2006). The use of hosted enterprise applications by SMEs: A dual market and user perspective. *Electronic Markets: The International Journal, 16*(1), 85-96.

Margretta, J. (2002). Why business models matter. *Harvard Business Review*, May, 86-92.

Mazzi, P. (2001, February 26-27). *Small business ebusiness: Bringing SMEs online.* The IDC European eCommerce Forum 2001, Rome, Italy. Framingham, MA: International Data Corporation.

McFarlan, F. (1984). Information technology changes the way you compete. *Harvard Business Review, 62*(3), 93-108.

Mehrtens, J., Cragg, P., & Mills, A. (2001). A model of Internet adoption by SMEs. *Journal of Information & Management, 39*(3), 165-176.

Newell, S., Swan, J., & Galliers, R. (2000). A knowledge-focused perspective on the diffusion and adoption of complex information technologies: The BPR example. *Information Systems Journal*, (10), 239-259.

Ofcom. (2005). Retrieved July 28, 2006, from http://www.ofcom.org.uk/research/

Oliver, C. (1990). Determinants of inter-organisational relationships: Integration and future directions. *Academy of Management Review, 15*(2), 241-265.

Patnayakuni, R., & Seth, N. (2001, August 3-5). Incorporating a social perspective to the adoption of application service provider model. In *Proceedings of the Americas Conference on Information Systems*, Boston (pp. 1848-1850). Atlanta, GA: AIS.

Poon, S., & Swatmann, P. (1999). An exploratory study of small business Internet commerce issues. *Journal of Information and Management, 35*(1), 9-18.

Porter, M. (1998). Clusters and the new economics of competition. *Harvard Business Review, 96*(6), 77-91.

Powell, W. (1987). Hybrid organizational arrangements: New form of transitional development? *California Management Review, 30*(1), 67-87.

Quayle, M. (2002). E-commerce: The challenge for UK SMEs in the twenty-first century. *Journal of Operations & Production Management, 22*(10), 11-48.

Rao, S., Metts, G., & Mora-Morge, A. (2003). Electronic commerce development in SMEs: A stage model and its implications. *Business Process Management Journal, 9*(1), 11-32.

Rogers, E. (1962, 1983, 1995). *Diffusion of innovations* (1st, 2nd, & 4th eds.). New York: Free Press.

Sadowski, B., Maitland, C., & van Dongen, J. (2002). Strategic use of the Internet by small to medium-sized companies: An exploratory study. *Information Economics & Policy, 14*(1), 192-203.

SBA. (2006). Retrieved July 20, 2006, from www.sba.gov

Shaw, E., & Conway, S. (2000). Networking and the small firm. In S. Carter, & D. Jones-Evans (Eds.), *Enterprise and small business: Principles, practice and policy* (pp. 367-383). UK: Pearson Education.

Southern, A., & Tilley, F. (2000). Small firms and information & communication technologies: (ICTs): Toward a typology of ICT usage. *New Technology Work & Employment, 15*(2).

Stanfield, M., & Grant, K. (2003). An investigation into issues influencing the use of the Internet and electronic commerce among small-medium-sized enterprises. *Journal of Electronic Commerce Research, 4*(1), 15-33.

Susarla, A., Barua, A., & Whinston, A. (2003). Understanding the service component of application service provision: An empirical analysis of satisfaction with ASP services. *MIS Quarterly, 27*(1), 91-123.

Swan, J., & Newell, S. (1995). The role of professional associations in technology diffusion. *Organization Studies, 16*(5), 847-874.

Swan, J., Newell, S., & Robertson, M. (1998). Inter-organizational networks and diffusion of information technology: Developing a framework. In T. Larsen, & E. McGuire (Eds.), *Information systems innovation and diffusion: Issues and directions* (pp. 167-186). Hershey, PA: Idea Group Publishing.

Tapscott, D., Ticoll, D., & Lowe, A. (2000). *Digital capital: Harnessing the power of the business Web*. London, UK: Nicholas Brealey.

Thong, J., & Yap, C. (1995). CEO characteristics, organisational characteristics and IT adoption in small businesses. *Omega International Journal of Management Science, 23*(4), 429-442.

Timmers, P. (2000). *Electronic commerce: Strategies and models for business to business trading.* Chichester, UK: John Wiley & Sons.

Walczuch, R., Van Braven, G., & Lundgren, H. (2000). Internet adoption barriers for small firms in the Netherlands. *European Management Journal, 18*(5), 565-571.

Ward, J., & Peppard, J. (2002). *Strategic planning for information systems* (3rd ed.). Chichester, UK: Wiley and Sons.

Weill, P., & Vitale, M. (2001). *Place to space: Migrating to ebusiness models.* MA: Harvard Business School Press.

Willcocks, L., & Lacity, M. (1998). *Strategic sourcing of information systems: Perspective and practices.* London: John Wiley and Sons.

Willcocks, L., Sauer, C., and Associates. (2000). *Moving to e-business.* London, UK: Random House.

Yao, Y. (2003, August 4-6). An integrative model of clients' decision to adopt an application service provider. In *Proceedings of the Americas Conference on Information Systems*, Tampa, FL (pp. 3438-3444). Atlanta, GA: AIS.

Zajac, E., & Olsen, C. (1993). From transaction cost to transaction value analysis: Implications for the study of interorganizational strategies. *Journal of Management Studies, 30*, 131-45.

Chapter XI

Planning and Designing an Enterprise-Wide Database System for E-Business

Alexander Y. Yap, Elon University, USA

Abstract

The planning and development of an enterprise-wide electronic database system for e-business usually calls for the re-engineering of information processes coupled with a push toward data content standardization across the entire organization. In this chapter, the case study involves a multi-national conglomerate that is in the process of integrating and Web-enabling their enterprise database systems. The objective of the system was to help engineers sift through millions of components offered by various suppliers and component manufacturers, where the end-result was to improved the integration and efficiency of the product development, engineering design, e-sourcing, and e-procurement processes. This research is a qualitative action research study on how different organizational, social, political, and technical forces influenced the social construction of an enterprise-wide information system. Understanding the dynamics and power of these socio-technical forces in shaping the development environment and change process of enterprise systems is the focal point of this chapter's discussion.

Introduction

In mid-2001, Invensys, a multi-billion dollar multi-national corporation initiated a project to implement an enterprise-wide electronic database system accessible via the Web. The envisioned database was to form part of the corporation's growing e-business system. This database was geared toward helping engineers sift through millions of electrical and mechanical components offered by various suppliers and component vendors. The database system was envisioned to be integrated with their e-procurement system, product data management systems (PDM), enterprise resource planning (ERP) systems, and computer-aided design and manufacturing (CAD/CAM) systems.

The objectives of initiating this enterprise-wide system were: (1) to significantly improve the product development process by providing Invensys engineers a better and faster means of identifying/choosing product components and cutting product development cost (by lowering product development errors caused by sub-standard components); (2) to improve e-sourcing (or the online search process for the right suppliers) by having access to a much wider range of supplier catalogs internationally and locally and be able to compare/analyze them; and (3) to improve the e-procurement process and lower procurement cost.

The contribution and significance of this research is to provide meaningful insights into different socio-technical milieus and their pivotal influence in the shaping of a new enterprise-wide system. Although systems requirements and functionality are delineated and envisioned at the onset of system planning, the resulting system is often implemented and developed differently from what was initially planned due to the underlying socio-technical realities that surface and influence the systems planning as more stakeholders and systems users become involve in it. Mitigating socio-technical factors ultimately determine the path of systems development and adoption. Therefore, it is important that more studies and research are conducted to shed light on how these underlying forces come into play when shaping enterprise systems.

Invensys is a diversified conglomerate that manufactures and provides various products and services. In the United States, Invensys is a leading global provider of heating systems, air conditioning, building systems, and commercial refrigeration. In Europe, Invensys acquired the AVP group of companies which specializes in engineering processes (such as brewery and dairy systems). Due to the conglomerate's diversified global business, it was of great interest to pursue this study to see how various Invensys subsidiaries world-wide could benefit from or change with a new enterprise-wide system. What was also interesting from a socio-technical research point of view was that at the time of this project's implementation (2001-2002), Invensys Corporation just acquired Baan, a leading ERP solutions provider (Baan was re-acquired by another company in 2003). This created an underlying situation that Baan, being an enterprise solutions provider, would have considerable influence in the direction of this enterprise-wide project.

Research Interest and Approach

The objective of this research is to determine the key factors that affect the planning and development of enterprise-wide systems. We were hired as information systems consultants tasked to plan and design the implementation of this project from 2001-2002. When hired, we realized it was a great research opportunity, because it would allow us to experience how an enterprise-wide systems development goes through the intricacies of a conglomerate environment. The retrospective value of this research was discussed and agreed upon with Invensys Technology vice president, Tim Matt. This research is a result of our documented analyses and insights as to how we strategically planned and tactically developed the system on a day-to-day basis considering the organizational, social, political, and environmental forces that ultimately shaped the systems design. We want to continue the discourse of Kim, Lee, and Gosain (2005) and Gosain (2004) who claimed that enterprise information systems are subjected to institutional forces and processes, and Soh and Kien (2000) who discussed the need to fit culture with enterprise systems solutions or there will be gaps that could lead to mismatch between the solution and the enterprise's needs.

Since the researchers were involved in the project, this chapter is clearly categorized as "action research". While quantitative methods are good for some type of research, we argue that qualitative research is the more appropriate approach to determining the casual effects of socio-technical and organizational factors in shaping the development of enterprise-wide systems.

Numerous studies in the field of information systems have acknowledged that "action research" is a well-suited method for dissecting the complex social dimensions of IS planning and development. Previous action research methodology studies by Baskerville (1999), Wood-Harper (1985), and Hult and Lennung (1980) discussed action research as appropriate for understanding the social setting of the information systems environment. To quote Baskerville on his adoption of Hull and Lennung's definition of action research, he cited four major characteristics of the action research methodology:

1. Action research aims at an increased understanding of an immediate social situation, with emphasis on the complex and multi-variate nature of this social setting in the IS domain.

2. Action research simultaneously assists in practical problem solving and expands scientific knowledge. This goal extends into two important process characteristics: First, there are highly interpretive assumptions being made about observation; second, the researcher intervenes in the problem setting.

3. Action research is performed collaboratively and enhances the competencies of the respective actors. A process of participatory observation is implied by this goal. Enhanced competencies (an inevitable result of collaboration) is relative to the previous competencies of the researchers and subjects, and the degree to which this is a goal, and its balance between the actors, will depend upon the setting.

4. Action research is primarily applicable for the understanding of change processes in social systems.

Although action research can be viewed as subjective, the intention of this research is to learn from experience, so we will not attempt to cloud it with our biases as we, too, want to fully learn from facts and events that transpired. We accepted the consulting role based on the opportunity to learn more about enterprise-wide systems planning and development. Baskerville (1997) stated that, "consultants are usually paid to dictate experienced, reliable solutions based on their independent review. Action researchers act out scientific interest to help the organization itself to learn by formulating a series of experimental solutions based on an evolving, untested theory." As academic researchers taking on the consultant's role, we fully concur with this statement.

Theoretical Framework: Socio-Technical Factors Shaping Enterprise-Wide Systems

There are *internal* and *external* factors affecting the way enterprise-wide information systems (EIS) are planned and developed. Figure 1 maps these influencing factors. Although socio-cultural forces (Bijker, Hughes, & Pinch, 1987), political forces (Robey, 1995), and business process (Hammer & Champy, 1993) are familiar factors that we occasionally come across as shaping information systems, it is also abstract as to how these factors help shape enterprise-wide systems. Our objective is to instantiate its influence in more concrete terms with qualitative data.

Figure 1. Socio-technical factors affecting EIS implementation

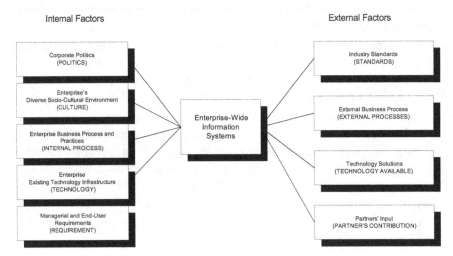

Internal Factors

Managerial and End User Requirements

The development of an enterprise wide system essentially starts with management and end-user inputs. The management team of an enterprise has a set of objectives for initiating an enterprise-wide system project. To avoid failure, management essentially needs to gather information about what end-users need (Cale, 1994) and dovetail those needs to the larger or broader objectives of the management team. This has to be clearly determined at the very start of the project.

Existing Technology Infrastructure

For an enterprise to implement a high-level application such as Web-based database application, there has to be some basic technology infrastructure in place. So, one question is whether the corporation has the right network infrastructure and servers for running the envisioned system? A Web application is a "high level" application because it needs several basic technologies on lower levels for it to work. Succinctly put, if an enterprise is running its database application online, the data content as well as the database system are running elsewhere, in a remote server. Without network technology infrastructure in place, it is impossible for such an application to be deployed. In addition, there has to be enough bandwidth to run the application.

Business Process and Practices

The way the entire business process of a conglomerate or corporation is structured affects the manner in which enterprise-wide systems are planned, developed, and implemented. While there are existing enterprise-wide processes, localized business processed are also affected during a major systems overhaul and implementation. Very localize business processes can hamper enterprise-wide systems implementation due to the fact that these processes were not designed with enterprise-wide systems in mind. At some point, companies need to re-design, standardize, or integrate localized processes across the enterprise-wide systems platform.

Socio-Cultural Environment

When conglomerates implement enterprise-wide systems, one of the challenges is how to deal with the different sub-cultures characterized by the nature of different departments and subsidiaries. The cultural differences are attributed to the different mind-sets of workers in their particular departments or subsidiaries. For example, a department dominated by engineers can have a different mind-set from workers in the procurement department.

Political Dimensions

Based on the agency theory (Jensen & Meckling, 1976), an enterprise has different agents (managers, systems users, workers) with certain decision-making power, and may have a different agenda from the owners or stockholders. In the implementation of an enterprise-wide system, we need to ascertain the different goals of agents. Such agenda, although beneficial to an individual, a department, or even a singular business unit, may be detrimental to the aggregate well-being of the entire enterprise or conglomerate. Varying agenda cause political maneuvering. Success or failure of a system can also be due to political reasons (Robey, 1995). We will, therefore, try and identify political factors that cause friction in enterprise-wide systems implementation.

External Factors

Partner's Input

Business and outsourcing partners contribute to the development of a system by either providing solutions to improve the system or adding content to the system.

Business partners collaborate with each other, and therefore expect to share knowledge and information for a collaborative work.

Technology Solutions

Systems developed for enterprise-wide deployments are not cheap and usually cost corporations millions of dollars. While large conglomerates may have their own internal software solution providers, it is sometimes cheaper or more effective to outsource systems development somewhere else.

External Processes

Enterprise-wide systems are created with the assumption that at some point it will be used to interface with inter-organizational business processes. With the growth of e-business platform and collaboration, corporations need to plan ahead on how such system will be utilized for external collaboration.

Standards

Foresight of a new system's integration into the broader e-business platform means that it is a necessity to adopt current industry-accepted standards for e-commerce transactions or e-business collaboration. This could result in information re-engineering and/or business process re-engineering across a conglomerate.

The Invensys Case

Assessing the pre-existing situation before the onset of the database project, it was gathered by the consulting team that Invensys was an expanding conglomerate acquiring several subsidiaries at a very rapid pace. Invensys was involved in the business of electronics and industrial manufacturing as well as providing expertise in industrial engineering. Invensys' purchase of the APV group of companies, a predominantly Scandinavian/British engineering group, and Baan ERP systems were some examples of its acquisitions after 1999. Because of several new acquisitions, Invensys found itself with new subsidiaries or strategic business units that had the same engineering needs and information systems requirements, but were not systemically integrated across the Invensys conglomerate. Invensys saw the need to put order into this systemic chaos by implementing a series of enterprise-wide systems that would allow various systems of different subsidiaries to work with each other. The enterprise-wide database system, which is discussed in this section, is a vital component of the broad enterprise systems integration initiative. Invensys needed to start integrating the newly-acquired subsidiaries and realizing synergies that could improve productivity and lower cost.

Preliminary Meeting

Invensys' management team, led by Tim Matt (Vice President of Technology) and Joe Rowlands (Supply Chain Manager), and the consultant group initially discussed a set of criteria on how the proposed online database should be designed. The criteria was the result of consultations with groups involved in the areas of engineering, procurement, and information systems. The database criteria that was finalized with Invensys had the following features and capabilities (Table 1).

The criteria was formulated to provide Invensys product design engineers the capability to "speed search" for the right components in terms of component quality, cost, and life cycle. When engineers are developing a new product, they search for possible components to use in their design and the appropriate manufacturers to source such components. The database should address engineers' needs by providing good information to make intelligent decisions about components.

Invensys agreed to hire the consulting group after finalizing the initial systems criteria with them. The consulting group was assigned to: (1) determine the right systems design after studying the Invensys needs and organizational structure; (2) find the appropriate solutions provider for the online database system and data content; (3) help implement and evaluate the pilot project; and (4) start implementing the

Table 1. Systems criteria

Systems Features	Systems Capability
Web Access	Database system should be searchable using the Web
Content	View Negotiated Price; Life cycle of component; manufacturer's list
Database	Database should have analytical functions
Content Updating	Content should be modifiable by Invensys
Search Engine	Search Engine should have a certain degree of filtering accuracy
Reference system	Should allow Invensys to use its product numbering system and link such system with the supplier's numbering system
Automatic Notification	It should be able to notify users of any component changes; thus, requiring it to be connected to an email server for automated notification
Cross Referencing	It should be able to cross-reference several parts related to each other.
Bill of Materials	It should be able to generate a bill of material and include estimate costs for components.
Cost Projection	It should have the capability to view the cost trend of components.

project on an enterprise-wide scale. The planning and implementation was divided into several phases.

First Phase of the Project

The main objective of this phase was to gather a long list of systems solutions providers and data content providers. The consulting group began to study the criteria and then searched for solutions providers. The first concern was to look for a software vendor that could provide the systems functionality and interface that were specified in the criteria. The second concern was to look for content providers that could actually provide the content for the component database needed for Invensys products (such as climate control systems, sensor systems, metering systems, and home control systems). For electronic components alone, there exist millions of components in the electronics industry that could be sourced from suppliers in the U.S., Europe, and Taiwan.

In the process, the consulting group started to initiate contacts with these solutions providers and communicate with them the initial criteria required. The most ideal situation was to look for a total solutions provider, if any existed, that could provide both the online database systems application and database content. While the search process for the systems and content solutions were ongoing, consultants began interviewing the users (Invensys engineers) and gathering more information to flesh out the details of the systems criteria; get a feel of user expectations and find potential problems.

The systems provider that the consultants were looking for needed to have expertise in deploying a Web-enabled database system, as well as expertise in creating an intranet system so that they could easily set up the system across the enterprise and behind a firewall. Within the first two weeks, the consulting group came up with 16 solutions providers that comprised the long list.

Second Phase

At this point, Invensys VP Tim Matt asked a Baan representative to join the weekly meetings. It was clear that Baan, Invensys' own software solutions provider, wanted to influence the outcome of the project. After all, Baan's expertise was enterprise-wide software applications.

The second phase focused on how the consulting team could manage to shorten the long list of possible solutions providers to a short list. More discussions on the requirements were laid out on the table as the consultants, coming from the outside and looking inward (having a different perspective), were concerned that there were more issues to clarify.

It was a logical decision for the consulting team to start sketching the systems process flow, because everyone had a fuzzy understanding of the systems criteria and how such criteria would actually translate to a real system design with long-term viability. After all, the project team had not fully scrutinized the tactical functions of the envisioned system.

Preliminary Steps Before Designing the System (Second Phase Continued)

First, to provide coherence across the cross-functional team involved in shaping the project, the project team decided to name the project as Invensys' Electronic Component Database (ECD). Fortifying the project's identity was a great way to market its acceptability within Invensys.

Second, the consulting team began to interview engineers who were the target end users for the proposed system. The consultants conducted a comprehensive interview with Engineers Mike Melton and Jim Triplett, and discussed their ideal possible solutions, the functionality they want with the database system, and the technology situation at Invensys (at the time of the interview).

Both engineers knew that the database application was going to run off the Internet, so the first concern they voiced out was "bandwidth". They have had previous experiences with slow bandwidth to the point that Internet connection would be down for a few days. They said that "we only get a fast connection from 6 a.m. to 10 a.m.". The local Invensys IT manager confirmed that this bandwidth bottleneck existed at the engineers' office, since they did not have a fast T3 connection. This posed as a dilemma because what good are web applications with a slow bandwidth and a faltering Internet connection?

If Invensys outsourced this system to a solutions provider and the server was running remotely, the consulting team noted that a short-term solution to circumvent the lack of bandwidth and intermittent disruption of Internet connection was to have a mirror database server inside Invensys' Intranet system which would automatically download some of the preferred database content periodically, preferably during early morning time when bandwidth was least problematic. In such case, even if the Internet connection went off-line, the engineers would still be able to access their preferred database content from a local area network. This was taken into consideration in designing the system.

The engineers also complained that it took them hours to sift through component databases in order to find the specific components they needed. There were several reasons for this—difficult and inaccurate database search engines; huge volume of components/parts (millions of components); poor content quality (inadequate information on several components); lack of content standards; and confusing reference numbers. On top of these, Invensys was using different component/part reference numbers that added confusion on how components were classified.

In terms of content quality and standards, the engineers clearly conveyed that they preferred to access component parts specifications via PDF format and, if possible, via a universal CAD formats so that they can immediately view the component schematics in their CAD software package, and see if the component fits with the rest of their design schematics. They wanted to have the most complete technical information available in order for them to make a better decision on which components to use.

After identifying these problems, the consulting team and engineers agreed on "key points" to approach the *systems design* and the *database content*. Key points were: (1) effectiveness of search engine; (2) a uniform parts numbering system; (3) a filtering process for "preferred content" (or content that can be accessed offline); (4) standard data access format and viewing; and (5) data manipulation capabilities (or the capability to download and manipulate CAD data).

Content Management: Establishing Database Standards for Enterprise-Wide Usage

Before proceeding to design the system, the consultants considered a more important issue that must be resolved first—"content standards". No matter how good the system is, the way content is represented and managed is key to the long term viability of this project. So, the team agreed to re-engineer the information process and management (or how component information was managed within Invensys) by adopting the following:

1. **Create a uniform Invensys parts numbering system:** One of the current problems within Invensys is the use of multiple numbering schemes for a single component part. Adding to this confusing numbering schemes is component suppliers also having different numbers for the very same components. Engineers agreed that it would be nice to have one uniform component number to which they can refer to; otherwise, it will be very confusing to have one Invensys subsidiary refer to an electronic transistor as Product No. 29323, while another subsidiary referring to exactly the same transistor as Product No. AC34553. This new uniform parts number scheme needs to be created and linked to all other legacy numbers (the old part numbers) and suppliers' part numbers. Tim Matt acknowledged that this would be very helpful considering that different Invensys subsidiaries in Germany alone use several parts numbering systems. Invensys subsidiaries in the UK and the U.S. also use different numbering sys-

tems. In order for Invensys to have one enterprise-wide electronic component database, it was best to adopt only one uniform parts numbering system.

2. **Create a standardized component parts catalog structure:** There are hundreds of millions of electronic and mechanical components being used in various industries today. Electronic component parts include integrated circuits, transistors, and circuit boards, among others. Cataloging millions of components is not an easy task, nor is it simple to search through such an enormous number of items. To help businesses create efficiency in this task, the United Nations created a standard for cataloging component parts—the UNSPSC (United Nations Standard Products and Services Code). UNSPSC (see www.UNSPSC.org; 2006) is a hierarchical coding system being used to classify goods/services into categories and sub-categories. Invensys design engineers face the same task as other engineers in the industry searching through volumes of component information. There was a need to create a uniform catalog structure for navigating through the suppliers' component catalogs in the ECD system. The UNSPSC was unanimously agreed upon as the preferred cataloging standard. Other standards set by the Rosettanet.org, such as DUNS and eClass, were also considered to allow easier identification of suppliers and products.

3. **Establish a filtering process for preferred data content:** Each Invensys site has a different set of data content needs. The project team anticipated that each site would prefer a more localized data set (or "preferred data content"). If the end users could anticipate what the data content they would be accessing most, such content could be uploaded to a local server within their local area network. The other reason for having a preferred content is to save engineers search time. The search engine will be faster if the localized database only contains the preferred content. So even if the Internet connection is off-line, engineers can still access the content they need. The team decided that there has to be a filtering process to identify the preferred content.

4. **Standardize data access format:** Invensys engineers have expressed the need to standardize the data access format. Adobe PDF was the preferred format for viewing component technical specifications. However, they have also stated that if the component data could be accessed as CAD schematics, that would greatly help them.

5. **Data manipulation capabilities:** If a content provider could include two-dimensional or 3D schematics of components/parts (using CAD file formats), then engineers could easily try to test such component schematics first by seeing if such component indeed "fits" with their new product design schematics. This would considerably lessen potential design errors. The capability of a database to provide CAD data files means that it is providing engineers data editing or manipulating capabilities—a high quality content.

Figure 2 shows the process of standardizing data content. First, a uniform Invensys parts numbering system (UIPN) is created for all components that Invensys use for its products. Second, the UIPN is then mapped to the different legacy (old) numbering systems being used by the different Invensys subsidiaries (in Germany, UK, and the U.S.) that reside in their respective local database or PDM systems. Third, the various numbering systems that different suppliers use will also be mapped to the UIPN. This will come from either a content provider or from suppliers. With the existence of an enterprise-wide numbering system, Invensys will be able to create its own standard catalog structure that will greatly diminish any miscommunication between Invensys subsidiaries regarding which parts they are using and which parts they have in their inventories. The UIPN will also allow subsidiaries to use only a single number when filtering the content they need for their preferred database content; thus simplifying the content filtering process.

The standard specs that Invensys engineers expected from the initial standardization of content was included in what we referred to as "primary data". For catalog navigation, UNSPSC was the standard agreed upon. To authenticate supplier identity correctly (international or local) during the online search process, the use of Rosettanet.org standard DUNS was also agreed upon. To access product component technical specs (product datasheet), PDF was the preferred format, but viewing it in HTML was acceptable. For viewing bill of materials, Excel spreadsheet and HTML were acceptable file standards. The engineers hoped that they could also standardize component schematics data. We refer to this as secondary data because we anticipated that content providers will have difficulty obtaining this type of data file. The ISO standard "STEP" (Weidemann, 1996) was chosen for 3D object-oriented modeling, while proprietary software file standards that Invensys was already using based on off-the-shelf CAD and PDM software (such as AutoCAD, Solidworks, Baan, and Ingenuuf) were incorporated as secondary data.

The consulting group was responsible for introducing the ISO STEP standard as it was widely used across several industries; while the Invensys end users influenced the adoption of proprietary standards that they were already using. Invensys had invested a lot into these CAD and PDM software that it was logical to retrofit the database formats with these software.

During the discussion for content standardization, Terry Wilson, a top engineer from the Invensys Rockwell office in Illinois somewhat objected to the UIPN. His reason was that they had been using a numbering system efficiently. It took the project team about 4-5 days to make him change his perception that while his local component numbering system worked for his group, it would not help the entire enterprise. He came back later and said that he had developed a narrow tunnel view of this issue as he never quite saw the big picture. Creating a uniform number system would actually save Invensys a lot of money if they knew that one subsidiary had an over-supply of a particular component, while another subsidiary actually needed such component. It would be easy to transfer the excess inventory of such component between subsidiaries, and the subsidiary in need of such component does not have to place a new procurement order for an overstock component. If there were two different numbering systems used separately by these two subsidiaries, they would never know that the other subsidiary had those components in stock because the database would only register two differently numbered components.

The importance of interoperable content standards and management has been strengthened by the creation of the iECM (interoperable enterprise content management)

Figure 2. Content standardization for EIS development in Invensys

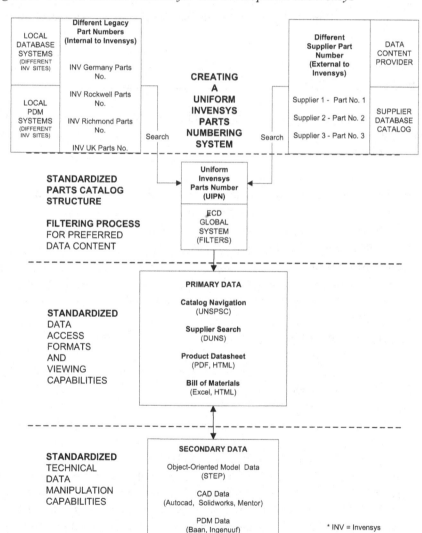

Consortium (Preimesberger, 2006). The tremendous need for interoperable content in enterprise content management in the last few years has encouraged industries to create such consortium hoping that data content can be seamlessly exchanged and accessed between different types of enterprise-wide systems. This recent development highlights the initiative behind the Invensys project, in its effort to managing content across an international enterprise setting.

Systems Design

This section describes the steps and processes of designing the system from the system feature to finding the appropriate software, hardware, and systems process flow.

Deciding on the Systems Feature

After the consulting team interviewed key end users, the group agreed on how to standardize content for the ECD, and proceeded to delineate the functions of the system as follows:

1. **Intelligent search engine:** The ability to do accurate multiple Boolean search based on the attributes of the components rather than a single field search entry is important in finding components accurately. A UPSPSC catalog structure should help in the progression of the search process.

2. **Automatic notification:** Users want to be notified of changes regarding components that are important to them. This needs personalized filtering and customization so that only relevant (user-specified) information is pushed back to the end users.

3. **Preferred content filtering (manual):** It was decided that some of the data content filtering has to be done manually. This involves hiring a "content master" or "content manager". The Rockwell group (the group targeted for the pilot site of the database) expressed that they wanted to focus only on three types of component parts—integrated circuits, capacitors, and transistors.

4. **Established vs. upcoming components (partial automation of preferred content filtering):** When components are frequently used by an Invensys subsidiary, such component will be branded as "established components", and the content provider could automatically push any information updates on these components to the Invensys ECD. However, there are also new "upcoming components" that Invensys engineers may want to search for. If these components are not in the database, they could request for new information

about these components using their local content server to electronically file such request.

5. **Dynamic data:** The Rockwell group expressed their need for a more "dynamic data content", which meant that they wanted to see the technical specs updated as frequently and accurately as possible. However, they would rather have the data content updated and maintained by a content provider rather than ask the manufacturers for a new catalog all the time.

Hardware, Software Application, and Information Flow

Figure 3 shows how the system and data flow was designed by the consulting team. It has the following features:

1. **The database application provides users the capability to personalize the database interface:** The users readily said yes when asked if interface customization was something they would like to have. Customizing the interface allows users to access information they frequently use more quickly. A lot of productivity time is wasted if data accessing tasks are not efficient.

2. **Two central database servers will be used:** (1) a universal database server—a database server that is maintained by an independent content provider (outsourced) containing different suppliers' catalogs, located outside of Invensys' Intranet, and has all the component data; and (2) Invensys ECD—a centralized Invensys database server which partially mirrors the universal database but is already filtered for Invensys preferred data content needs. The ECD is inside Invensys' intranet system and protected by a firewall. The Invensys ECD server runs the database application including the interface, search engine, and other user-defined functions. A Web Master and a DBA (Database Administrator) need to be hired to run the Invensys ECD.

3. **Local content management servers:** Ideally, each Invensys subsidiary will have its on content management server that handles the unique database content (the localized database) that a local subsidiary needs. Each Invensys subsidiary group should have its own content master to determine the content it requires. If the user cannot find the data content he/she is looking for in the central Invensys ECD, then he/she can use their local content management server to pull data from the universal database server and transfer such data to the central Invensys ECD. New data should first be mirrored in the central ECD system before they are again mirrored in the local content server. In that way, all local contents will have a back-up copy in the central ECD server.

4. **Flow of new data:** In case a supplier/manufacturer of components has a "new" component, this new information is usually pushed to a content provider who

keeps a database file of all product catalogs. In instances where the component data is not found in the universal database server of the content provider, then the content provider's system should pull such data directly from the supplier's system. Figure 3 shows how the system pulls and pushes data into the system.

Figure 3. Data and systems flow diagram

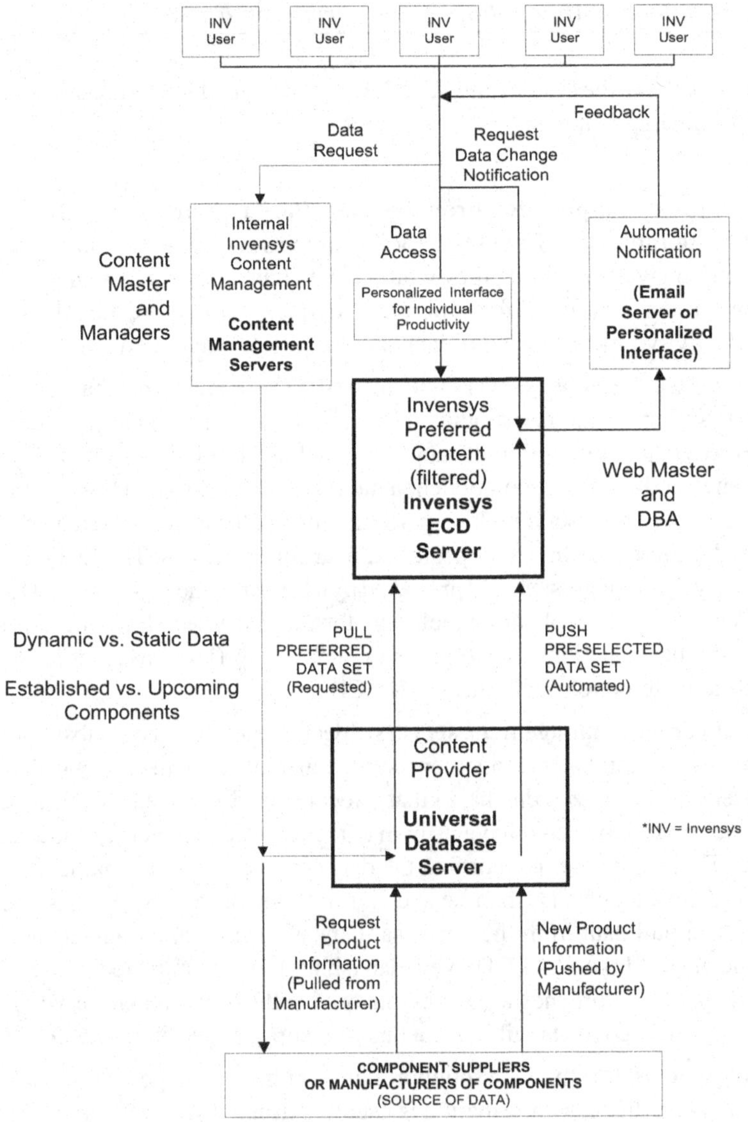

Table 2. The short list

Vendor	Strengths	Weaknesses
Requisite Technology (Systems provider with some data content)	- Impressive off-the-shelf solution - Effective component search engine - Software package had built-in data catalog structure mapping standards (e.g. UNSPCS) - Software could provide 2D or 3D CAD file formats (no other vendors had this function) - Their system could interface with Oracle, Baan, SAP, and other enterprise software	- Only about 140 suppliers provided their content, which was sparse compared to other content providers - New company and have not serviced large corporations before
I2 Technologies (Total solutions provider)	- Total solutions provider (provided both systems and data content) - 5 million components in their database - Top notch advance supply chain planning system (component search, identification, sourcing, and procurement) - Big on content factory – a content quality control process	- Expensive, considering their position as market leader in advance supply chain planning software - A direct competitor to Baan
IHS (systems provider) & **Partminer** (content provider)	- IHS and Partminer are partner subsidiaries - IHS has a good history in cataloging and structuring huge electronic component database for the US military - Partminer has the largest database content among all content providers	- IHS has no ready to use off-the-shelf solution and has to customize the system - Partminer's data quality suffers

Choice of Systems and Content Providers (Narrowing the List)

After the project team agreed with how content should be standardized and how the system is to be designed, the team started interviewing potential systems providers, content providers, or total solutions providers (providing both the system and content solutions). The list (Table 2) was narrowed down to three providers that could meet the demands and criteria of the ECD project.

Case Analysis: The Influence of Socio-Technical Factors in Vendor Choice

The analyses next focus on how the three solutions providers on the short list show potential compatibilities or non-compatibilities with the socio-technical environment of Invensys. The providers were assessed and selected depending on how they were perceived to fit into the socio-technical fabric of the Invensys organization. See Table 3.

Table 3.

Vendor	Assessing the Socio-Technical Influences
Requisite Technologies	**Political:** Requisite was not considered a political threat to Invensys' subsidiary Baan. It did overlap with Baan's supply chain planning systems (iBaan SCS and iBaan Collaboration), but Baan was not really worried about that. Baan representatives were supportive of Requisite.
	Cultural: Since Requisite's software was made for engineers, its appeal was readily accepted by the engineering team's sub-culture. The software used the engineer's "lingo" and understood their needs. Its ability to display components in a three-dimensional CAD format and provide technical specs in PDF immediately won the engineers' support. Requisite made an impressive demo of their software that pleased the engineers.
	Internal enterprise processes: Requisite made it clear that their software was easily compatible with Invensys' existing enterprise systems and processes (used for engineering and procurement processes).
	Internal technology infrastructure: Requisite was very open to setting up their system to work with the existing technologies of Invensys and even making sure that it will be compatible from the web application to the back-end application interface. Invensys software was compatible with Baan, Oracle, SAP, Ariba and other software being used in enterprise wide systems.
	End-user requirement: The interface of the off-the-shelf package was very user friendly based on the software demo. There were twelve different ways to search for components. The users could customize the software interface to their preference and the content they preferred to see. Requisite's content requirement for component suppliers was also based on Adobe's PDF format, which was part of the criteria laid out by Invensys, so such criteria were met.
	Industry standards: Requisite created their software with the industry standards in mind. They were using the UNSPCS cataloging standards and were also filing data standards such as PDF and CAD. They also brought in standards that were set by Industry consortium such as Rosettanet.org. Invensys was impressed with Requisite's long term vision to incorporate several standards into Invensys' own software.
	External business process: Requisite's system for content management was based on the formation of a supplier's hub. The electronic hub aggregates the suppliers' catalogs contents into Requisite's main database repository. The push for a better content quality and reliable data format was a strong focus of Requisite system's ability to make sure that the external procurement and component selection process would be handled smoothly across the supply chain.
	External technology: The integration between Requisite's search engine, engineering data standards and requirements, and its ongoing aggregation of supply chain data from different suppliers was a strong feature that met the Invensys criteria for being able to merge contents from different supplier's system (external systems) with Invensys' own internal enterprise information system.
	Partner's contribution: Requisite was very open to working with Invensys' major suppliers as well as other suppliers that provide data catalogs of product components that are useful to Invensys.

Table 3. continued

Vendor	Assessing the Socio-Technical Influences
I2 Technologies	**Political:** I2 was considered a high threat to Baan, since they were offering similar software packages for enterprise systems integration and supply chain management. It was very obvious that the Baan members of the team, assessing the vendors, did not feel comfortable with a large player like I2.
	Cultural: the I2 group was able to project that they were very flexible in dealing with different sub-cultures of a large enterprise. They wanted to meet the needs of top IT managers, the local engineers, the procurement and sourcing group, and other players involve in a supply chain management. Their ability to relate to the needs of agents/stakeholders in different hierarchies of a large enterprise reflected that I2 was a seasoned player in providing supply chains systems solutions.
	Internal Enterprise Process: I2 presented that they had turn-key solutions that could easily fit into the global supply chain process of Invensys. There was not really much resistance to such claim when I2 presented their systems solutions before the Invensys team, because I2 knew what they were talking about and their reputation preceded them. They have shown that other larger enterprises, like Dell, use their system successfully.
	Internal Technology: I2 was willing to provide the proper infrastructure to run their system within Invensys and see to it that their systems are compatible with that of Invensys. This was not seen as a problem from the project's standpoint. However, Baan was not too keen on the potential scenario that they may need to interface their own enterprise systems with that of I2. It also appeared that the more I2 needed to customize its existing software solutions and database content to fit the internal Invensys environment and existing technologies, the more expensive it will be.
	End-User Requirement: I2 did not provide very detailed information on how their software benefits specific end user functions. However, they claimed, based on their track record that their software and solutions can be very flexible and will meet all of the criteria set forth by Invensys for the ECD project.
	Industry Standards: I2 has established industry supply chain solutions for consumer electronics, semi-conductor industry, original equipment manufacturers, and other high-tech industries. It was obvious that their solution incorporates many of the industry standards that Invenys needed. There was no question about their capability in this respect.
	External Business Process: Like SAP, I2 has focused on vertical industry integration. One of the first industries that I2 focused on was the electronics and semi-conductor industry, which Invensys was part of. I2, not only had the experience, but also the expertise to link external supply chain process of electronic and semi-conductor component suppliers with that of Invensys internal processes. I2 was the ideal candidate in this respect.
	External Technology: I2 already had established its advance supply chain planning system in accordance with industry standards in the electronics and semiconductor industries. Invensys would stand to gain from I2's technology infrastructure in facilitating e-Sourcing and e-Procurement processes within such industries.
	Partner's Contribution: I2 had a huge content of component catalogs due to its partnership with thousands of suppliers. I2's acquisition of Aspect Development Inc. (a large data content provider) proved that I2 was serious about leadership in the supply chain content management area. Requisite had only140 suppliers during the assessment period and their supplier's catalog content volume could not match I2's.

Table 3. continued

Vendor	Assessing the Socio-Technical Influences
IHS/ Partminer	**Political:** Since IHS systems worked mostly with the military and government institutions, they focused on a different clientele. Baan did not feel politically threatened by their presence. **Cultural:** IHS did not appeal to the engineers and the team. This was because IHS did not have an off-the-shelf solution which could be evaluated or demoed. The engineering team did not like the uncertainty of trusting a vendor with nothing to show but reputation. The team included this vendor on the short list because Invensys wanted to consider a systems provider that could customize a system from scratch and cater to the unique needs of Invensys if no off-the-shelf application is compatible with Invensys needs. But it seemed that the corporate culture of Invensys did not like the idea of uncertainty and demanded that a provider already had a ready solution. **Internal Enterprise Process:** There was no indication of how IHS solutions can be integrated properly with Invensys. **Internal Technology:** No particulars were offered. IHS just simply stated that they can customize software to fit with Invensys internal technologies. **End-User Requirement:** They said they can customize software to fit end user's needs but no details were offered. **Industry Standards:** Although Partminer's data content quantity was impressive, a substantive portion of the data did not meet the quality needed for e-Commerce or e-Procurement purposes. Several of Partminer's data were old electric components and their specifications and data formatting needed updating. Several of Partminer's data still need to be converted to a PDF format. **External Business Process:** IHS did not seem to have an existing systems infrastructure to link Invensys internal process to external supply chain processes of different suppliers. **External Technology** was not explained in their presentations. **Partner's Contribution:** Partminer had the largest database/ content among the solutions provider in the short list. They had over 10 million components listed as the result of their extensive contacts with so many electronics and semi-conductor suppliers on an international scale. Their ability to gather contents from a magnitude of suppliers impressed Invensys.

Invensys finally chose Requisite to be its systems provider for the ECD project. However, Invensys was not satisfied with Requisite's sparse supplier's catalog content and supplier network. So, Invensys asked Partminer to be its content provider.

Conclusion

In retrospect, assessing the socio-technical fit between the three providers on the short list showed that it was really a toss up between Requisite and I2. IHS was not prepared to show a demo of any software and this was immediately seen as a negative point for them. Invensys had to separate its assessment of Partminer from its partner subsidiary, IHS.

I2 was particularly very strong on all four external socio-technical factors: (1) providing solutions that meet industry standards; (2) integrating external business processes (supply chain); (3) providing new innovative technologies for supply chain planning, e-sourcing and e-procurement; and (4) networking with supplier partners for collaboration. On the other hand, Requisite was particularly weak with the external factors. It did not have the same experience as I2 had on providing a good solid link with suppliers for external processes (supply chain). Requisite did not also have enough supplier catalog contents and supplier contacts as I2 had on both electronics and semi-conductor industries.

Requisite appeared to be strong in addressing the internal factors—politically they were not a threat; they provided a detailed demo that greatly appealed to the engineering group; their software was clearly flexible to end-user needs; and their software package was open to connection with Invensys' existing technology infrastructure.

Table 4 shows the impression of the team when they evaluated the providers.

Both I2 and Requisite fit in very well into the socio-technical environment of Invensys. However, the political factor was the strongest factor in deciding which one to choose. The threat that I2 had over Baan was the major factor that tipped the advantage towards adopting Requisite. To remedy Requisite's weakness (its weak content and low external ties to suppliers), Invensys asked Partminer to be its content provider. As seen in Table 4, Partminer balanced out the weakness of Requisite by providing the content for the ECD system. And since Partminer was not a solutions or systems provider, it was not a threat at all to Baan. Invensys believed that the synergy between Partminer's strong content base and Requisite system's ability to update Partminer's content quality was key to the solution.

The political fit was the strongest factor in choosing the systems provider, while the volume of data reflected the ability of the content provider to provide links to external suppliers. Because Partminer made up for the weakness of Requisite, Invensys preferred to deal with two separate providers than risk political tension in dealing with only one total solutions provider (I2).

In retrospect, the most critical factors internally were the political fit and the end-user requirements. The team made sure that the end users would love to use the system when it was deployed for adoption. The ability to provide external supplier

Table 4. Socio-technical influence from vendor assessment

SOCIO-TECHNICAL FACTORS	Requisite	I2	HIS	Partminer (Content)
Political Fit	Very Strong	Weakest	Moderate	Very Strong
Address the Cultural Diversity	Strong	Strong	Weak	NA
Compatibility with Internal Enterprise Process	Strong	Strong	Weak	NA
Internal Technologies (Compatibility)	Strong	Strong	Weak	NA
End-User Requirement	Very Strong	Moderate	Moderate	Strong
Industry Standards	Strong	Strong	Moderate	Moderate
External Business Process	Moderate	Very Strong	Weak	Strong
External Technologies	Moderate	Very Strong	Weak	Very Strong (data content management)
Partnership (Providing Solutions and Infrastructure for Collaboration)	Weakest	Very Strong		Very Strong (providing content for collaboration)

partnership and collaboration was also very critical. Invensys' goal was to save money on e-sourcing and e-procurement, and it was understandable why reaching as many suppliers as possible was a key element in choosing Partminer, who had extensive connection with suppliers and had the database to aggregate thousands of supplier catalogs. Industries are moving towards integrated supply chain using the e-business platform, so it was not hard to understand why the collaboration factor across the supply chain was a critical external component.

The limitation of this chapter is that it covered only the planning and development stage of an enterprise-wide application which took place within a four-month period. Full implementation of this system across the entire Invensys conglomerate will take at least three years to complete and this includes implementation at the global level. Three months after the pilot project was adopted in Invensys' Illinois site, the implementation team was already starting to create a French version of the online software application, and preparing a package training program for Invensys' engineers in France. It is only a matter of time when Invensys will be preparing for the systems diffusion and adoption in its offices in Germany and Italy. The long-term implementation phase will be an interesting subject for another future study. But in spite of the fact that the long-term success of the project will still depend on several factors and events, we believe that Invensys has set a good foundation for this project's long-term success. The move toward industry-standard data content and integrating Invensys' system with an external suppliers' hub for e-sourcing and e-procurement clearly indicated that Invensys provided the appropriate environment for their enterprise system to grow and adapt with ongoing changes in the external e-business environment.

References

Baldo, S. (2001). *Interview transcripts*. Partminer.

Baskerville, R. (1997). Distinguishing action research from participative case studies. *Journal of Systems and Information Technology, 1*(1), 25-45.

Baskerville, R. (1999). Investigating information systems with action research. *Communications of the Association of Information Systems, 2*(19), 1-30.

Bijker, W., Hughes, T., & Pinch, T. (1987). *The social construction of technological systems*. Boston: MIT Press.

Burk, D. (2001). Interview Transcripts. Partminer.

Cale, E. G. (1994). Quality issues for end-users developed software. *Journal of Management Information Systems, 45*(1), 36.

Duns Numbering Standard. (2006). Retrieved 2002-2006, from http://www.dnb.com/us/

Gosain, S. (2004). Enterprise information systems as objects and carriers of institutional forces: The new iron cage. *Journal of the Association for Information Systems, 5*(4), 151-182.

Hammer, M., & Champy, J. (1993). *Reengineering the corporation*. New York: Harper Business.

Hult, M., & Lennung, S. (1980). Towards a definition of action research: A note and bibliography. *Journal of Management Studies*, (17), 241-250.

Interoperable ECM. (2006). Retrieved 2006, from http://www.aiim.org/standards.asp?ID=29284

I2 Technologies. (2006). Retrieved 2002-2006, from http://www.i2.com/

Jensen, M. C., & Meckling, W. H. (1976, October). Theory of the firm: Managerial behaviour, agency cost and ownership structure. *Journal of Financial Economy, 3*, 305-360.

Kim, Y., Lee, Z., & Gosain, S. (2005). Impediments to successful ERP implementation process. *Business Process Management Journal, 11*(2), 158-170.

Matt, T. (2001-2002). *Dialogues with Tim Matt*. Invensys, Richmond Group.

Melton, M. (2001). *Interview transcripts*. Invensys, Richmond Group.

Miller-Herholtz, B. (2001). *Interview transcripts*. HSI Engineering.

Partminer. (2006). Retrieved 2002-2006, from http://www.partminer.com/

Preimesberger, C. (2006). *New content-management standards group begins opera-tion*. Retrieved 2006, from http://www.eweek.com/article2/0,1759,1963098,00. asp?kc=EWNKT0209KTX1K0100440

Requisite Technologies. (2006). Retrieved 2002-2006, from http://www.requisite. com

Robey, D. (1995). Theories that explain contradiction: Accounting for the contra-dictory organizational consequences of information technology. In J. I. De Gross, G. Ariav, C. Beath, R. Hoyer, & C. Kemerer (Eds.), *Proceedings of the Sixteenth International Conference on Information Systems,* Amsterdam, December (pp. 59-60). Atlanta, GA: ICIS Organization.

Rosettanet.org. (2006). Retrieved 2002-2006, from http://www.rosettanet.org

Rowlands, J. (2001-2002). *Dialogues with Joe Rowlands*. Invensys, Richmond Group.

Soh, C., & Kien, S. (2000). Cultural fits and misfits: Is ERP a universal solution? *Communications of the ACM, 43*(4), 47-51.

Slavich, F. (2001). *Interview transcripts*. Technology Consultant, Requisite Tech-nologies.

United Nations Standard Products and Services Code. (2006). Retrieved 2002-2006, from http://www.UNSPSC.org

Wales, J. (2001). *Interview transcripts*. Engineer, HSI Engineering.

Weidemann, C. (1996, November). Testing of STEP AP 203 processors. *ProduktMod-eller Conference Proceedings*, Linkoping, Sweden (pp. 371-386). Linkoping, Sweden: Linkoping University.

Wilcox, M. (2001). *Interview transcripts*. Regional Sales Manager, Requisite Technologies.

Wilson, T. (2001). Interview Transcripts. Invensys, Illinois Group.

Wood-Harper, T. (1985). Research methods in information systems: Using action research. In E. Mumford et al. (Eds.), *Research methods in information systems* (pp. 169-191). Amsterdam: North-Holland.

Chapter XII

Toward Always-On Enterprise Information Systems

Nijaz Bajgoric, Sarajevo University, Bosnia-Herzegovina

Abstract

Significant changes in information technology (IT), the Internet, and e-business technology have increased the need for continuous and agile data access, in particular for mission-critical applications. Modern business computing has evolved into an organizational engine that drives business and provides a powerful source for competitive advantage. IT has been integrated into organizational operations and activities in a way that application downtime is not an option since each hour, even minute of downtime may generate negative financial effects. In order to achieve higher levels of competitiveness, business has to be continuous from data availability perspective and agile with regard to data access. An enterprise information system (EIS) can be qualified as "high-quality" in terms of its architecture, application platform, and information it can provide to users but if that information is unavail-

able when it is needed by customer, manager, or any other end user, the value of that EIS simply becomes "zeroed" from end-users' point of view. The chapter presents a framework for implementation of continuous computing technologies for improving business continuity. The framework is presented within a systemic view of developing an "always-on" enterprise information system.

Introduction

Over the past decade, information has become an organizational resource that has to be managed in an efficient and effective way just like any other resource. In practice, however, many organizations still keep information management activities within computer centers even though information has become a corporate asset. Organizational management can not be effective if it does not integrate organization-wide information management as well. This is in particular important for contemporary businesses which require a continuous computing platform as a main prerequisite for business continuance. Therefore, modern business needs an efficient integration of business continuity management into organizational management, the process which is done by integration of continuous computing technologies into an enterprise information system.

In today's information age, information management comprises numerous activities with data processing/data management being the core component. In addition to data management, information management includes the following components as well: system management, network management, security management, and so forth. Recently, with advances in Internet technologies and e-business, the need for achieving "a near 100%" level of business computing availability was brought up yet again. Consequently, the term of "business continuity management" was coined up and became a significant part of organizational information management.

Business continuity management (BCM) involves several measures (activities) that have to be planned in order to achieve higher levels of the system/application availability ratios.

This chapter aims at developing a framework for designing an "always-on" enterprise information system which should provide higher availability ratios of continuous computing and business continuity. High availability is a term which describes the ability of a system (operating system, application, network) to continue with its operation in cases of hardware/software failures, even some natural disasters. It is all about keeping business-critical applications running all the times.

Downtime, Costs of Downtime, Business Continuity

In the past, information technologies (IT) were used within traditional computer centers organized as "behind-the-scenes" organizational units for performing transaction processing operations. However, in today's e-business world, in many cases the whole business is IT-dependent and data-driven. Contemporary business computing supported by the concepts and technologies of enterprise information systems (EIS) such as enterprise resource planning (ERP), supply chain management (SCM), customer relationship management (CRM), electronic commerce (EC), and business intelligence (BI), has evolved into an organizational engine that drives business and provides a powerful source for competitive advantage. To be truly competitive, contemporary business must be continuous and agile (adaptive, responsive). It needs an information system that enables both continuous computing and agile data access. The term of "business continuance" (business continuity—BC) has been introduced in order to emphasize the ability of a business to continue with its operations even if some sort of disaster on its computing resources occurs. At the same time, business has to be agile in order to cope with increasing complexity in its environment.

In contemporary business, even a few minutes of system downtime may cause thousands or even millions in lost revenues. In addition, such situations may result in bad decisions, unsatisfied customers, broken image of the company, and so forth. Simply put, when mission-critical applications are considered, system downtime (both planned and unplanned) should be avoided or minimized. This fact emphasizes the need for system's reliability, availability, and scalability. IDC (2006c) underscores the fact that a true high availability model expands the concept of availability beyond an infrastructure perspective in terms of system or servers.

In short, contemporary business has to be continuous from data availability perspective and agile with regard to data access. Therefore, system downtime is not an option in modern business since each hour, even minute of downtime may gen-

Table 1. Major causes of system downtime

Major Causes of System Downtime (in order of frequency)
1, Software defects/failures
2. Planned administrative downtime
3. Operator error
4. Hardware outage/maintenance
5. Building/site disaster (fire)
6. Metropolitan disaster (storm, flood, etc.)

erate negative financial effects. As stated by Barraza (2002), " ... with worldwide buyers and sellers operating on a 24/7/365 basis, the need for building information systems that approach 100 percent uptime and data availability is more acute that ever. Simply put, the global economy runs on information. More importantly, it runs on available information". Major causes of system downtime are given in a Table 1 (Szelong, 2002).

According to a survey provided by Gartner Dataquest (2005), the top three business risks from downtime continue to be lost revenue, increased customer dissatisfaction, and decreased employee productivity. This report unveiled that companies with more that 2,500 employees experience approximately 135 minutes of downtime per month, while the acceptable amount of downtime for companies of this size is less than 5 minutes per month.

Research results unveiled by META Group (Manning, 2004) indicate that IT system downtime costs American businesses $1 million an hour. MetaGroup estimated the average hourly revenue loss caused by downtime as follows (Vanston, 2004a, 2004b):

According to a recent survey made by AT&T/Economist Intelligence Unit (Ernest-Jones, 2005) the principal risks of a breakdown in business continuity are given below:

1. Loss of revenue
2. Loss of data
3. Deterioration of brand
4. Defection of customers
5. Loss of shareholder value
6. Higher insurance costs

In the same research (Manning, 2004), META Group estimates that by 2008, 45% of Global 2000 users will utilize two data centers to deliver continuous availability;

Table 2. Revenue loss caused by downtime

Industry	Hourly revenue loss
Energy	$2,817,846
Telecommunications	$2,066,245
Utilities	$643,250
Manufacturing	$1,610,645
Financial	$1,495,134
Retails	$1,107,274

of these, 25% will support real-time recovery. Through 2008, more than 50% of G2000 users will utilize a single "hardened" data center augmented by third-party services to deliver traditional, cost-effective disaster recovery services (48 to 72-hour recovery).

However, not every business must have high availability ratios such as 99,999% or even 99,99% for its mission-critical applications, it depends on the type of business. Therefore, an appropriate cost-benefits or return-on-investment analysis should be used before making decisions on increasing the levels of availability just because of the fact that the applications are mission-critical. Hill (2006) suggests not to equate high availability with high value when mission-critical applications are considered. Infonetics Research (2005) has revealed results of their study of five large organizations in different vertical markets: finance, transportation and logistics, health care, manufacturing and retail (North American Companies). They proposed a metrics for revenues loss calculation and productivity loss calculation. With regard to specific enterprise applications, Aberdeen Group (2006) reported that "... while 82% of companies are concerned about supply chain resiliency, just 11% are actively managing this risk. This action gap is one of the greatest weaknesses of current corporate global supply chain strategies; it threatens the continuity of a company's business and sets the stage for gross margin erosion due to under-managed supply chain uncertainty and risk."

Recent IDC report (2006c) indicates that priorities and spending intentions are aligned around the central theme of improving application availability and recovery from different failure types on increasing numbers of applications and services. According to this report it's not uncommon for availability and business continuity requirements to be published in a company's corporate goals. An emphasis is given also on a continued user productivity and connectivity, a platform in which the users remain seamlessly connected to critical applications and services. As stated by Michael Croy (Ybarra, 2006), "After Katrina, companies need a different paradigm. The heart of American business is now IT. Business continuity needs to be part of daily operations. It's not an IT issue, it's a business issue, it's a corporate governance issue."

Another research provided by the National Archives and Records Administration in Washington, D.C., identified that "Ninety-three percent of companies that lost their data center for 10 days or more due to a disaster filed for bankruptcy within one year of the disaster (Schraeder, 2004). Fifty percent of businesses that found themselves without data management for this same time period filed for bankruptcy immediately."

In short, an IT-infrastructure of a contemporary business in the form of an enterprise information system must be able to meet the requirements for continuous or "24×7×365" computing—an operating platform that represents the main prerequisite for business continuance. Such an infrastructure must be ready for any kind of possible downtime causes, both planned and unplanned, such as: daily glitches of hardware and software, systems/application software updates and/or upgrades, hardware upgrades, partial or full-scale disasters, business mergers or acquisitions, and so forth. It should employ several information technologies that help ensure business critical operations be continuously available, in order to meet customers' needs. These technologies provide a basis to ensure cost-effective business availability, reliability, and stability in all kinds of events of disruption. They are planned and implemented in organizations within so-called "business continuity planning" projects.

The term of "business continuance" (business continuity—BC) emphasizes the ability of a business to continue with its operations even if some sort of failure or disaster occurs. Several factors affect the level of BC such as: (1) data availability, (2) application availability, (3) network reliability, (4) operating system reliability, (5) availability and scalability, (6) server hardware reliability, and so forth. All these components can be affected by several types of failures and/or disasters (e.g., hardware/software glitches and failures, thefts, malicious acts, mistakes, floods, fires, earthquakes, hurricanes, terrorist attacks).

Business continuity has been treated as both an IT and managerial issue in the last 10 years particularly after the e-business boom and the "9/11" event. According to a survey done by the Security Services practice of Deloitte & Touche/TPM (2006), the number of companies that have developed formal business continuity management programs within the last six years has nearly tripled. According to this report, whereas just 30% of organizations had corporate business continuity plans in place six years ago, more than 83% of 273 survey respondents representing a cross-section of industries say they now have formal business continuity plans. Within the last year alone, 70% of respondents reported having business continuity management (BCM) programs for most, if not all, of their critical business functions, up from 41% a year ago.

Research papers on BCM focus either on frameworks or separate technologies that are used in order to improve the availability levels. Botha and Von Solms (2004) proposed a cyclic approach to business continuity planning. Gibb and Buchanan (2006) defined a framework for the design, implementation, and monitoring of a business continuity management program within the context of an information strategy. Pitt and Goyal (2004) see BCM as a tool for facilities management. Walker (2006) considers outsourcing options for business continuity. King (2003) introduced a term of "business continuity culture" and underscored the fact that "If you fail to plan, you will be planning to fail". Bertrand (2005) researches the relationships between business continuity and mission-critical applications. He emphasizes the role of replication point objective (RPO) and replication time objective (RTO) in recovering from disasters. He stresses the role of replication technologies in providing better RPO and RTO values. Yeh (2005) tried to identify the factors affecting continuity of cooperative electronic supply chain relationships with empirical case of the Taiwanese motor industry. Gerber and Solms (2005) emphasize the need for a holistic approach that should include a carefully planned security policy, the use of technology, and well-trained staff. Finch (2004) revealed that large companies' exposure to risk increased by inter-organizational networking and that having SMEs as partners in the SCM further increased the risk exposure. Wu, Chiag, Wu, and Tu (2004) identify continuity as a behavioral factor No. 1 on business process integration in SCM. Bartel and Rutkowski (2006) proposed a fuzzy decision support system for IT service continuity management. They argue that IT service continuity management (ITSC) is typically part of a larger BCM program, which expands beyond IT to include all business services within an organization. ITSC management allows an organization to identify, assess, and take responsibility for managing its risks or threats to IT. In their article, Herbane, Elliott, and Swartz (2004) examined the organizational antecedents of BCM and developed a conceptual approach to posit that BCM, in actively ensuring operational continuity, has a role in preserving competitive advantage.

All these works deal with BCM either from managerial or organizational perspective. However, they lack some guidelines for implementing numerous information technologies that can provide a platform for business continuity. It is an integrated operating environment which consists of several continuous computing technologies that plays a crucial role in achieving high availability ratios and represents a main building block of an "always-on" enterprise information system.

Framework for Developing an "Always-On" Enterprise Information System

The methodological framework used here is based on a MS/OR-based definition of a system given by C.W. Churchman[1] (1968). An attempt is made to apply his concept of systems approach in developing a framework for implementation of continuous computing technologies for improving performances of enterprise information systems with regard to business continuity. In addition, this framework is used to define a systemic view of an "always-on" enterprise information system.

The fundamental concept of systems approach as defined by Churchman is that all systems can be defined by a common set of elements. These elements (dimensions or attributes) are as follows:

1.   System is teleological and has a **measure of performance**. The **objective** of the system represents its intended impact on its environment.

2.   The **environment** of a system is the set of entities that exist outside of the system boundary. The entities affect the system or are affected by it.

3.   System **resources** are the elements that are used in building and operating the system. Resources may include people, row materials, capital, technologies, and so forth.

4.   The system has teleological **components** which co-produce the measure of performance of the system. These are the elements of the system that exist within its boundary.

5.   **Management** of the system as a set of activities intended for effective management.

Churchman (1971) continues his examination of this issue in a subsequent book, *The Design of Inquiring Systems*. He gives the necessary conditions that something *S* be conceived as a system as follows:

1.   S is **teleological.**

2.   S has **a measure of performance.**

3.   There exists **a client** whose interests (values) are served by S in such a manner that the higher the measure of performance, the better the interests are served, and more generally, the client is the standard of the measure of performance.

4.   S has teleological **components** which co-produce the measure of performance of S.

5.   S has **an environment** (defined either teleologically or ateleologically), which also co-produces the measure of performance of S.

6.   There exists **a decision maker** who—via his resources—can produce changes in the measures of performance of S's components and hence changes in the measure of performance of S.

7.   There exists **a designer**, who conceptualizes the nature of S in such a manner that the designer's concepts potentially produce actions in the decision maker, and hence changes in the measures of performance of S's components, and hence changes in the measure of performance of S.

8.   The designer's intention is to **change S so as to maximize S's value to the client.**

9.   S is "stable" with respect to the designer, in the sense that there is a built-in guarantee that the **designer's intention is ultimately realizable**.

The first Churchman's definition will be used as a framework for developing a systemic view of an "always-on" enterprise information system. Additional dimensions from the second definition (client, decision maker, designer) will be elaborated as well.

Objectives and Measure of Performance: Continuous Computing, Agile Data Access, and High-Availability Ratio

In this section, the first dimension of the system as defined by Churchman (system objectives and measures of performances) will be defined with respect to the implementation of continuous computing technologies in enterprise information systems.

As said before, implications of downtime can be expressed in financial terms and easily bound to company's economic results. Therefore, the terms such as "economics of availability", "economics of uptime/downtime" have become topics of interests in the field of the economics of enterprise information systems. Today, it is possible to measure or estimate losses in financial terms of each hour, even minute of downtime. These losses vary depending on the type of business (e.g., online banking systems, call centers, airline reservation systems, point-of-sale systems, dispatching systems, online shops, e-mail servers, etc.). According to Graham and Sherman (2003), each hour of downtime is estimated to cost an average company $44,000. Using that estimate, the cost to move from a level of 99.9% availability to 99.999% availability is far less than the estimated $435,600 reduction in downtime-related costs over a five-year life cycle. In a survey of 450 Fortune 1000 companies, Find/SVP found that the average hourly downtime cost is $82,500 (Barraza, 2002). As stated by Stanton (2005), "It can take less than 60 seconds for a company's reputation to be ruined and its business to be crippled. In just one minute a server failure or hacker can knock out vital applications and lead to a catastrophic series of events". According to the report unveiled by Adam Associates (Stanton, 2005), in the UK alone the annual cost of business interruption is estimated to be £3.9 billion. The average outage time following a fire is 28 days, 26 days for a theft, and 10 for flood damage. IT failures take an average of 10 days to recover from, and even a power failure can take up to 24 hours. A 2002 Standish Group study of downtime numbers (Graham & Sherman, 2003) found that the average mission-critical application had the following availability experience:

- 9%: greater than 99.99% (less than one hour down per month)
- 24%: 99.91% to 99.99% (one hour to less than nine hours)
- 67%: 99.9% or less (nine hours or greater).

Importance of available data varies by application with business-critical applications having higher levels of "data criticality". Therefore, these applications require recovery time expressed in minutes or even seconds, while some other applications may experience downtime in hours and recovery times in days.

A conceptual model based on Churchman's systems approach to illustrate the concepts of business continuity, continuous computing, and continuous computing technologies in the context of an enterprise information system is given in Figure 1.

Business continuance, fault-tolerance, disaster tolerance and recovery, and fast and reliable data access are just a few of the objectives of contemporary business. Business continuity strategy has become the No. 1 item for both CEO's and CIO's

Figure 1. A systemic model of business continuity, continuous computing, and continuous computing technologies

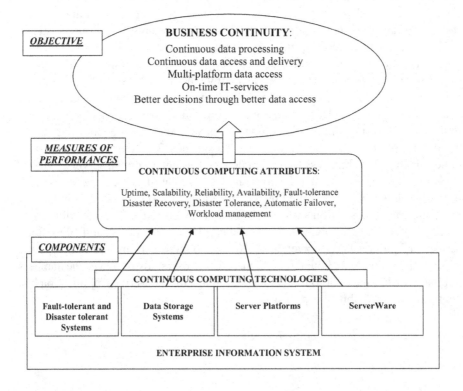

priority list. Business continuity today relies on continuous computing technologies that provide an efficient operating environment for continuous computing. Implementation of continuous computing technologies provides a platform for "keeping business in business" since business-critical applications are installed on enterprise servers, run by server operating systems that include serverware components, backed-up by data storage systems, and supported by several fault-tolerant and disaster-tolerant technologies.

Fault-tolerant and disaster-tolerant systems include the following technologies: redundant units, data replication, hot sites, data vaulting, disaster recovery sites. Some of these technologies overlap with data storage systems which comprise: standard tape backup technology, storage area networks (SAN), network attached storage (NAS), off-site data protection, Fibre Channel, iSCSI, Serial ATA, and so forth.

Server-based technologies include several types of hardware and software features that support so-called "high-availability" technologies: SMP/clustering, support for 64-bit computing, storage scalability, RAID technology, fault tolerance, online reconfiguration, N1 grid containers, dynamic system domains, virtual machine managers, and so forth. In addition, server platforms-based ServerWare suites include: bundled servers, reloadable kernel and online upgrade features, crash-handling technologies, workload management, Windows/UNIX integration, and so forth. Further details on these continuous computing technologies are presented in the sections that follow.

Environment: Application Infrastructure, Operating Environment, and Enterprise-Wide Agile Data Access

Contemporary business continuity and business agility rely on the following three sets of information technologies (Figure 2):

*   Operating environment infrastructure
*   Integrated application infrastructure
*   Information access technologies

As can be seen from Figure 2, information access technologies and integrated application infrastructure are important in boosting enterprise-wide agility while IT-solutions consisting of technologies that provide operating environment are critical for continuous computing and business continuity. Information access technologies

Figure 2. Technologies for business continuity and business agility

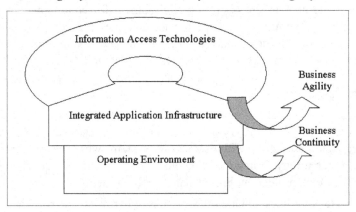

and integrated application infrastructure are implemented today in the form of enterprise information systems. The newest versions of ERP suites integrate core business applications and Web-based or portal-based access to data.

Information access technologies include several solutions such as: GUI technologies, data access, data transfer, data conversion, indexing-retrieving-searching capabilities, portal-based solutions, mobile computing technologies, content transformation, and so forth. They aim at easing information access no matter where data is stored, in

Figure 3. Manager's computing devices and agile management support system

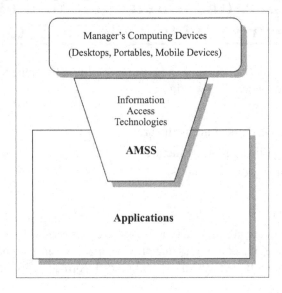

which format, how that data is accessed, and so forth. In that sense, an agile management support system (AMSS) can be defined as a sub-system of user interface that provides managers with an efficient and effective access to the information they need (Figure 3).

The primary goal of an AMSS is that the information it contains be easily accessible and retrievable by managers at the time they need it. AMSS does not have to contain all that information, rather it should provide a way of accessing it, no matter where that information is stored, and which device user connects from. Early efforts to develop such systems were limited to the implementation of terminal emulation access tools and PC/X Windows emulation programs. An extended scope of AMSS began with the advent of Internet and Web technologies. The structure of AMSS is very dynamic since it is based on the available data access technology. The lowest level of AMSS is based on using PC-terminal emulation tools, whereas the most sophisticated solutions include enterprise portal solutions and content transformation technologies.

Agility-enhancing integrated application infrastructure is based on information technologies that emerged over the last decade that helped in enterprise-wide data access and application-data integration such as: enterprise information systems for business-critical applications (ERP-SCM-CRM suites, business intelligence/reporting systems), groupware and videoconferencing technologies, middleware tools, Web services and intelligent agents, Web-to-host access technologies, portable computing technologies, content transformation technologies, and so forth. All these technologies enable agility in a sense that they enhance information access from data integration standpoint.

In general, enterprise-wide agility depends on so-called agility-enabling technologies in two main sets of business processes: manufacturing/services and management. Unlike agile manufacturing paradigm where several IT-related and manufacturing-oriented technologies are utilized to improve the level of manufacturing agility, the techniques and tools that can be applied in order to improve manager's agility are dominantly oriented to application-data access technologies. More than ever, today's managers need a seamless access to corporate information. In an information driven economy, every kind of information should be a "mouse-click-away".

According to HP White Paper (2002), Gartner, Giga and META Groups emphasize agility as contemporary business strategy. Gartner points out that "Progressive companies have adopted workplace agility as a competitive imperative." Giga calls agility a "critical element to deal with continuing innovation. Agility must characterize the business itself as well as the IT infrastructure and applications on which it depends".

Recent IDC Report (2006b) states that architecting for agility can be a whole new mindset regarding how to think about designing and maintaining systems. Some practices that contribute to agility include establishing enterprise-wide standards, centralizing control and accountability of IT investments and services, utilizing automated change and configuration technologies at all levels of the environment, and establishing repeatable (and collaborative) processes.

In short, an agile business is characterized by:

- Continuous data processing and data access operations
- Easy, continuous, reliable, secure, and company-wide (local and remote) data access from decision makers' and other knowledge workers' computing devices
- Continuous, reliable, and secure data access from customers within CRM platforms
- Multi-platform data access, including support for all commonly used computing devices (desktops, portable computing devices, mobile phones)
- Better decisions through better access to business-critical information wherever and whenever required

Resources and Components: Business Continuity Drivers, Agility Drivers, Servers, and Serverware

Business Continuity Drivers

Contemporary business computing is mainly based on client/server architecture and its several modifications (thin/thick, two-tier/three tier). Server's side of such architecture is called "operating environment infrastructure". It consists of standard server-based and additional continuous computing technologies that are used to enhance key server platform features such as reliability, availability, and scalability.

Both business continuance and business agility today rely on high-levels of application/data availability, reliability, and scalability. Operating environment for continuous computing is a dimension which encompasses several technologies that are necessary for an efficient business-critical application platform. High availability is the ability of a system (server, operating system, application, network) to continue with its operation even in cases of hardware/software failures and/or disasters. A said before, the three sets of technologies that can be used to provide high availability levels include:

Table 3. IT-based business continuity drivers, attributes, and technologies

Business Continuity Drivers	Continuous Computing/ Business Continuity Attributes	Continuous Computing/Business Continuity Enhancing Technologies
BCD1 - Fault-tolerant Technologies	Uptime Fault-tolerance Disaster tolerance Disaster recovery	Hot sites Data vaulting Disaster recovery sites Redundant units
BCD2 - Data Storage Technologies	Uptime Scalability Backup Disaster recovery Recovery Time Objective (RTO) Recovery Point Objective (RPO)	Standard tape backup RAID iSCSI Serial ATA Direct Attached Storage (DAS) Network Attached Storage (NAS) Storage Area Network (SAN) Storage Virtualization Online Backup Electronic Vaulting and Journaling Mirroring, Shadowing, Snapshot Hot Standby, Replication
BCD3 – a) Server Platforms	Uptime Scalability Reliability and availability Very high processing speed Support for 64-bit computing VLM and VLDB support Fault-tolerance support SMP/Clustering options Workload management Resilency functions Security solutions	SMP-clusters 64-bit computing Multi-core computing Storage scalability Scalability clustering options Low-level performance optimizations Fault tolerance Components' integratibility CPU and memory reconfiguration Online I/O reconfiguration Alternate root installation Dynamic kernel patching
BCD3 – b) SOS/ServerWare solutions	Uptime Reliability and availability Automatic failover Disaster recovery Fault-tolerance VLM and VLDB TCP/IP connections failover HTML/XML support Dynamic page caching Bandwidth allocation	Internet bundled servers Server Virtualization Reloadable kernel and online upgrade Crash-handling techniques Workload management solutions Server consolidation High-availability clustering functions Support for Windows/Unix integration Transaction prioritization Encryption accelerator support

- Fault-tolerant capabilities
- Data storage technologies
- Server platform-based technologies enhanced by ServerWare solutions

Fault-tolerant capabilities include three main technologies:

- Fault-tolerance technologies
- Disaster recovery technologies
- Disaster tolerance technologies

Fault tolerance is a term describing the ability of a computer system to resume operations in case of hardware failure. Fault-tolerant technologies consists of redundant units-based features (e.g., power supply, fan, disks-RAID, network cards, routers and other communication devices, UPS, etc.). Disaster recovery refers to the ability of computer system/operating system to resume operations after some sort of disaster that occurred in data processing unit. In most cases, disaster recovery operation takes some time and almost always there is a delay before data processing can continue. Disaster recovery methods include: standard tape backups and advanced methods such as: hot sites, data vaulting, disaster recovery sites, etc. Disaster tolerance is the ability to continue with performing operations despite a disaster. In addition to fault-tolerant technologies, contemporary business is forced to cope with demands for more efficient and effective storage solutions as part of its efforts to recover from any type of failure and/or disaster. Three mainly used storage technologies are: (1) standard tape backup solutions; (2) storage area network (SAN); and (3) network attached storage (NAS). SAN and NAS technologies are mainly based either on Fibre Channel as a mature storage backbone technology and/or newly developed Internet SCSI (iSCSI) and Serial ATA technologies.

All these technologies are presented here in the form of business continuity drivers—BCD (Table 3).

Agility Drivers

Information access is determined by several factors such as: (1) computing device that is used; (2) operating system interface; (3) application interface; (4) data/application availability; (5) server's availability; and so forth. Consequently, several IT-related factors can be identified in order to focus on those technologies that can enhance the level of manager's agility, as well as the agility of all knowledge workers. Here, they are identified as "agility drivers—AD" and presented in Table 4.

Server Operating Platform

Server platforms or enterprise servers play crucial role in modern computing environments especially from business continuity and business agility perspectives. Servers include several components such as server hardware, server operating system (SOS), application servers, and server-based applications called ServerWare. They

Table 4. IT-based agility drivers, attributes, and technologies

Agility Drivers	Agility Attributes	Agility Enhancing Technologies
AD1: **Computing** **Devices**	Portable computing Mobile computing Integration of communication and computing devices Pervasive computing Contextual Computing	Notebooks Hand-held PCs PDAs GSM devices Smart phones Embedded Computing technologies GPS devices RFID
AD2: **Information** **Access** **Technology**	User-friendly interface Integrated information access Remote/mobile access	GUI-based OS-app interface Browser-based interface Portals and Mobile Portals WAP technology
AD3: Fast and **Reliable Access** **Technologies**	Faster LAN/WAN communications Wireless LAN-WAN-Internet Data/voice/video integration Remote access Groupwork Real-time collaboration Virtual meetings Telecommuting Networked enterprise Virtual enterprise/Virtual Reaility	High-speed LAN/WAN technologies Remote access technologies Wireless technology/Wi-Fi Video conferencing/Web Conferencing Groupware technology GSM devices Smart phones IP telephony HTML/XML/WML/VRML protocols
AD4:Integrated **Application** **Platform**	Web-based access Thin client/server platforms Application/data integration SaaS (Software as a Service)	Internet technology Object-oriented paradigm Distributed computing Web-enabled applications ERP suites Business Intelligence Data/Text/Web Mining Middleware ASP app platform Web services - intelligent agents Information and Knowledge Discovery Data Visualization Visual Interactive Modelling
AD5: Server **Operating** **Platform**	Reliability Availability Scalability Serviceability Integratibility Manageability	SMP-clusters 64-bit computing Blade servers RAID technology VLM/VLDB support Fault tolerance ServerWare Internet bundled servers

are expected to provide such an operating environment that must meet much more rigorous requirements than a standard desktop operating system can provide (e.g., Windows XP). Such platforms are of special interest for businesses that require "always-on" or "online-all-the-time" computing environments. Therefore, server operating systems that provide zero-downtime or 100% uptime or some solution which is near it are of extreme importance for such businesses.

Server platforms must be reliable, available, and scalable such that server-based applications (application servers, data servers, e-mail servers, Web servers, etc.) run with high reliability/availability/scalability ratios. In addition, they are expected to provide several types of services: Internet-Web technology services, directory services, security services, and remote access capabilities including support for mobile computing.

An enterprise server, by definition, is a computer system within a client-server platform that supports core IT operations of the whole enterprise or its sub-system, providing processing capabilities for business-critical applications. Most widely used enterprise servers in contemporary computing are: mainframe servers, Unix/Linux-based servers, proprietary servers, Intel/AMD processors-based Windows servers, Apple Macintosh servers.

From the robustness standpoint, servers can be classified into several categories, but three of them are most widely used: entry-level, midrange, and high-end servers. High-end servers (mainframe servers, some proprietary systems, and Unix-based servers) are characterized by: very high processing speed, very high levels of the reliability, scalability and availability, support for several thousands concurrent users, VLM and VLDB support (Very Large Memory, Very Large Data Base), multi-processor and multi-node support, powerful "fault-tolerance" capabilities, and so forth.

A conceptual model to illustrate the role of server operating platforms in the design of an enterprise information system for continuous computing infrastructure is given in Figure 4.

Server and ServerWare Features for Business Continuity

The rapid advances in Internet technologies have resulted with changes in traditional SOS structures. Therefore, in addition to core SOS capabilities that are necessary to run a typical server configuration, an increasing number of both application and networking-oriented features, so-called "ServerWare" applications, are required on server systems to fully support contemporary Internet-based computing. Some of these applications come in the form of pre-installed or pre-integrated software "bundles" while some others are SOS-independent but very closed to a SOS.

Figure 4. Server operating environment for business continuance

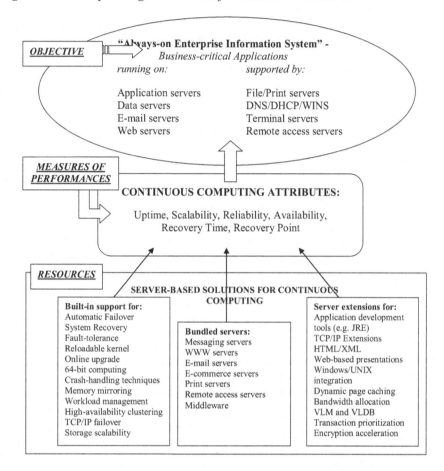

Modern server operating systems are expected to provide a set of features and functions that are crucial in achieving business continuance. These features and functions usually come bundled (pre-installed) together with core operating system. This "built-in support" include the following major functions/drivers (Figures 5 and 6).

Guidelines for Selection of SOS Platform for EIS

Enterprise information system applications are installed on enterprise servers and run by server operating systems. Therefore, availability of such systems is of extreme importance for organizations that implement them. When commercial hardware/OS

Figure 5. Server operating platform: Built-in functions

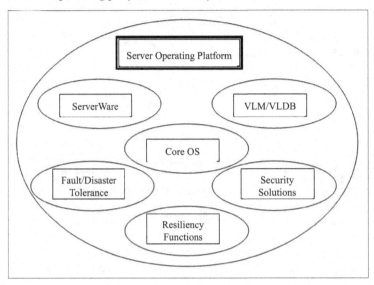

Figure 6. Server operating platform: Continuous computing drivers

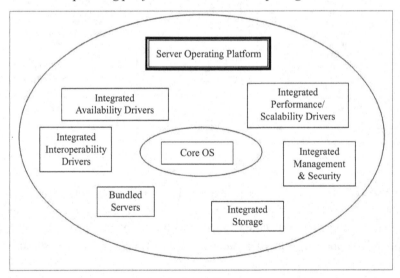

platforms are considered, server operating systems' availability is today expressed in terms of "nines" which determine the system's uptime. In this approach, the "five nines" is referred to as a system with 99.999 % uptime—the availability ratio which is regarded as the highest number achievable today[2]. The availability of mainframes, some proprietary platforms (e.g., OpenVMS) and some Unix systems

Table 5. Availability classification

Availability Classification	Level of Availability	Annual Downtime
Continuous Processing	100%	0 minutes
Fault Tolerant	99.999%	5 minutes
Fault Resilient	99.99%	53 minutes
High Availability	99.9%	8.8 hours
Normal Commercial Availability	99-99.5%	87.6-43.8 hours

can be as high as 99.999%, which corresponds to a downtime of five minutes per year. "Four-nines" availability (99.99%) corresponds to a downtime of 53 minutes per year, while 99.9% ("three-nines") means 8.8 hours of downtime per year.

Availability classification, levels of availability and corresponding annual downtime are given in Table 5 (Marchi & Watson, 2002).

The ability of a specific SOS platform to provide high levels of uptime depends on several factors (capabilities), such as:

- Reliability and availability of the server platform's components (processor, memory, server operating system)
- Components' integratibility
- Multi-processor and multi-node support
- Fault-tolerant capabilities
- Clustering options
- Workload management support
- Security solutions

D.H. Brown Associates[3] (2000) introduced a comprehensive model—a set of SOS-related attributes that can be used in evaluating performances of server operating systems. This model has been expanded to include 167 functional items across five areas: scalability, RAS (reliability, availability, scalability), system management, Internet and Web application services, and directory and security services. According to this model, the scalability of a system is determined by the following functional areas: 64-bit support, SMP support/SMP range, storage scalability, memory range, scalability clustering options, and low-level performance optimisations. Reliability, availability, and serviceability (RAS) basically include the following functions:

- **Resiliency functions** which allow SOS to adapt to outages by hardware components (online failure recovery functions)

- **Solutions that minimize planned downtime such as:** online CPU and memory reconfiguration, online I/O reconfiguration, alternate root installation, dynamic kernel patching

- **Crash-handling techniques** (kernel dump facilities, dump analysis tools, dynamic core file generation, multimode boots, automatic hang detection, etc.)

- **Workload management solutions such as:** partition fault isolation, dynamic partition reconfiguration, and so forth

- **High-availability clustering functions including:** fault tolerance, failover capabilities, disaster recovery/disaster tolerance, cluster file system, work with partitions, TCP connection failover, high-availability storage support

RAS model refers to a set of features which contemporary business is expecting from IT vendors having in mind business requirements toward a higher level of applications availability, in other words, in achieving "continuous", "always-on", or "24×7×365 uptime" computing. In that sense, businesses seek for solutions such as "automatic failover" and/or "disaster recovery" in case of the failure of a device or the whole system. RAS means that end users can use data and applications and system continues running even when system or application software is being upgraded or backed-up.

When commercial server operating systems are considered from the previously defined standpoint, it is well known that mainframes, Unix systems and some proprietary systems (e.g., OpenVMS) have exceptional systems availability and reliability. With respect to the overall standings of Unix server platforms, according to D.H. Brown's report (2002) HP's HP-UX 11i achieved the highest rates in almost every studied category. HP-UX, Sun Solaris and HP Tru64Unix shared the lead in the scalability category. When Internet and Web-applications services are considered, the same report named IBM AIX as leader. Report also revealed that AIX and Solaris are the only studied systems to build HTTP acceleration functions into their kernels, facility which helps to boost Web-server performance.

As for Linux and its performances compared to commercial Unix platforms, D.H. Brown (2003a) unveiled a study in which several Linux versions were compared with commercial Unix versions. According to that study, almost all studied Linux versions were behind the strongest Unix, but some of them like SuSE and RedHat were better that the weakest Unix in terms of overall functionality. However, newly developed Linux 2.6 kernel brought some new features such as: support for 64-bit processors, improved scalability (up to 16 processors or even more), asynchronous I/O for performance improvements, improved file-system performance, enhanced high-bandwidth networking support, and so forth. Increasing level of maturity of the existing 2.4 Linux kernel and planned new features of Linux 2.6 kernel position

Linux as an OS platform not only for so-called "edge-of-network" applications (mail servers, Web servers), but for mission-critical applications as well.

Another operating environment—Windows Server platform, which is using Microsoft Windows NT/Server technology on either Intel or AMD processors, includes the following versions: Windows NT Server 4.0, Windows 2000 Server, Windows 2003 Server. All these versions are still in use, but with different levels of availability. Main advantages of this platform over Unix are indicated as follows: ease of use and administration, price, support and integration with API/Windows application development environments. Most major application vendors have Windows NT versions of their packages, for example, five years ago more that 45% of the implementations of SAP's R/3 ERP package were on Windows NT.

Giga Group's report (Newman, 2001) revealed that Windows 2000 has been improved in terms of performance and reliability, for example, unnecessary reboots declined by 64% compared to Windows NT 4.0. They reported that "... even though Windows 2000 Server closed the reliability gap with all versions of Novell NetWare, Windows 2000 Server is still not as reliable as Unix. According to the respondents, Windows 2000 still requires 300 percent more unnecessary reboots than Unix." Current version of Microsoft Windows NT platform—Windows Server 2003 includes a number of functions that are particularly important for scalability, such as: 64-bit support for Itanium 2 processors; improved shared-memory multi-processing (SMP) scalability, ability to support up to 64 processors, support for NUMA systems, with several improvements to the IIS 6.0 Web server. Business continuity levels provided by Windows Server 2003 platform are additionally improved by separate server product—Windows Storage Server 2003. D.H. Brown (2003b) pointed out that Windows Server 2003 has made "considerable progress in addressing vertical scalability and reliability needs of enterprise datacenters".

According to Harvard Research Group (Marathon White Paper, 2005), Windows servers will continue to be the fastest growing server market segment in foreseeable future. HRG estimates the current Windows market at more than $10 billion. Gartner (2005) reported that, for midsize business, Linux presents many challenges, including not fully understanding the OS's benefits, resource constraints and the perceived high switching costs to move from Windows.

Microsoft's new version of this platform Longhorn Server/Vista is expected to bring a number of advancements such as: server core (server roles), Vista Group Policy, read-only domain controller, restartable active directory, BitLocker drive encryption, network access protection (NAP), terminal services gateway, secure anywhere access, new TCP/IP stack that supports IPv4 and IPv6 natively and enhanced set Unix interoperability features (SFU—Service for Unix).

According to the Yankee Group's (2006) annual server reliability survey (Keizer, 2006), only Unix-based operating systems such as HP-UX and Sun Solaris 10 beat Windows on uptime. Windows 2003 Server led the popular Red Hat Enterprise

Linux with nearly 20% more annual uptime. On average, individual enterprise Windows, Linux, and Unix servers experienced 3 to 5 failures per server per year in 2005, generating 10 to 19.5 hours of annual downtime for each server. Windows Server 2003 offers 20% to 35% better reliability on file/print, e-mail/messaging, and database servers when compared with the leading commercial Linux distributions in comparable workload scenarios. Windows Server 2003 trounced the Linux market leader, Red Hat Enterprise Linux, achieving nearly 20% more annual uptime in similar deployment scenarios. Microsoft's Windows Server 2003 recorded an average annual server downtime rate of about 770 minutes or 12.8 hours.

In a report published by Peerstone Research Inc. (Loftus, 2004), it has been stated that "… Linux is making 'undeniable inroads' into the core enterprise applications stack, of which the biggest component is the worldwide installed base of 800,000 servers running SAP, Oracle and PeopleSoft applications". This report examined 400 companies running SAP, Oracle or Peoplesoft ERP suites, showed roughly two-thirds were using Unix, 28% Windows Server or a version of NT, and only 2% were running on Linux.

Many businesses considered migration from commercial Unix platforms and proprietary systems to either Windows or Linux platform. META Group (2005) reported more than a 20% reduction in the number of servers **as** a result of the migration. Moreover, in an ERP environment in particular, upgrading major ERP versions often requires about one-third more processing power to provide the same functionality, in addition to the processing power needed to support the new modules or functional components themselves. However, IDC (2006a) predicts that UNIX servers will retain business-critical and mission-critical workloads for years to come. This research found real potential for Unix migration both to other Unix environments and to alternative platforms including Linux and Windows. On a unit basis, Windows was the leading platform for Unix migration with 45% of the volume. Other flavors of Unix generate the most server migration spending, capturing 48% of the Unix revenue opportunity.

Gartner (2005) reported that "… with more than 90 percent of mid-size businesses running predominantly on a Windows environment, Microsoft is the server operating system leader among small and mid-size businesses (SMBs). Microsoft will remain the dominant server operating-system provider for midsize businesses through 2010". According to this Gartner research, Linux presents many challenges for midsize businesses, including not fully understanding the OS's benefits, resource constraints and the perceived high switching costs to move from Windows.

As a conclusion, while assessing operating platforms for enterprise information systems, in addition to high levels of system uptime, both TCO (total costs of ownerships) and ROI (return on investments) approaches for a specific platform should be considered as well. Also, there may be businesses that need business continuity on a "8 hours × 5 days" basis only.

Management of the System: Integrating Business Continuity Management

Business continuity management consists of strategies, policies, activities, and measures that business undertakes in order to survive when some sort of catastrophic event occurs. Even though it represents a managerial activity, at the end, business continuity in information age relies on high-ratios of application/data availability, reliability, and scalability that should be provided by server operating environment. Therefore, business continuity management, being a part of the fifth dimension of Churchman's definition of the system, as defined in introduction, should be based on continuous efforts of integrating business continuity drivers into contemporary enterprise information systems.

In that sense, an enterprise information system should be managed from business continuity perspective in a way that it includes managerial and system administration activities related to managing the integration of the following business continuity drivers.

Integrating Availability and Reliability Drivers

Creating a highly available and resilient system represents a major effort when trying to improve the levels of availability and reliability of server operating platforms. Resiliency of the systems means their ability to return to their original state sooner or later after encountering some sort of problem which causes system shutdown. In that sense, a highly resilient system is a system which returns back to its function as soon as possible, if possible in a matter of seconds. Making a system resilient requires a lot of planning activities having in mind numerous possibilities that may occur and cause system shutdown (hardware and software crashes, cutting power for several hours, exhausting UPSs, etc.).

Reliability, availability, and serviceability (RAS) basically include the following drivers:

- **Resiliency drivers:** technologies that allow SOS to adapt to outages by hardware components (online failure recovery functions)
- **Solutions that minimize planned downtime such as:** online CPU and memory reconfiguration, online I/O reconfiguration, alternate root installation, dynamic kernel patching.
- **Crash-handling techniques** (kernel dump facilities, dump analysis tools, dynamic core file generation, multimode boots, automatic hang detection, etc.)

- **Workload management solutions such as:** partition fault isolation, dynamic partition reconfiguration, and so forth.
- **High-availability clustering features including:** fault tolerance, failover capabilities, disaster recovery/disaster tolerance, cluster file system, work with partitions, TCP connection failover, high-availability storage support

Integrating High-Performance and High-Scalability Drivers

This set of built-in drivers includes the following features: support for memory and processor-scaling, dynamic memory page sizing, support for large file and file systems, support for very large memory (VLM), and very large databases (VLDB), support for high-availability clustering. It includes support for 64-bit computing as well which means support of several "large" options such as: large files, large file systems, large-very large memory, large-very large databases, and so forth. VLM concept gives the ability to address large amounts of RAM on the order of several dozens gigabytes, while VLDB represents the possibility of addressing multi-giga-byte databases stored in RAM. In this context, for instance, SAP AG recommends migrating to 64-bit platforms for running SAP enterprise suites (Fritz, 2006). According to SAP, 64-bit servers are currently prerequisite for running SAP on HP-UX, AIX, Solaris, IBM OS/400, and z/Linux operating platforms. In addition, starting from 2007 on, new releases of SAP NetWeaver and applications based on this platform will no longer be supported on servers running 32-bit Windows and Linux operating systems.

SMP (symmetric multi-processing) support is intended for higher levels of avail-ability and scalability. Symmetric multi-processing system gives an ability to make use of multiple processors in a single machine. These technologies include: SMP range, storage scalability (maximum memory supported, maximum supported file system size), clustering capabilities. Support for workload management consists of partition fault isolation, dynamic partition reconfiguration, and so forth.

Integrating Compatibility, Connectivity, and Interoperability Drivers

This set of drivers consists of several protocols, extensions, bundles and supports that are intended to be used for resolving compatibility, connectivity, and interoper-ability problems. The integrated operating environment has to provide availability, reliability, compatibility, manageability, and interoperability required to control today's distributed, heterogeneous IT environments. In addition, it must be based on an infrastructure that enables systems integrators to manage every IT resource, from desktops to mainframes and Unix machines, from LANs to WANs, from standard data to knowledge, from databases to applications. To achieve true integration, it must contain integrated functions, built upon common objects and services which are open and available to all applications.

The integrated operating environment should provide support of the following drivers:

- **Extensions for application development tools and DBMS such as:** Windows/Unix/Linux-GNU compatibility, application binary interface (ABI), support for Microsoft .NET platform, HTML/XML protocol, SOAP and WSDL protocols, data and source code compatibility, binary compatibility

- **Support for HTML/VRML/XML development tools and Web services:** This kind of bundled software enhances capabilities of the server in order to support Web-based applications, such as: cgi-bin, Java, ActiveX, Perl and PHP support, FrontPage extensions, e-mail services, Active Server Pages, software for stabilizing Web server performances under heavy loads, bots or intelligent agents: Data Mining Bots, shopping bots, e-mail bots, search bots, news bots, and so forth. This support should also include integration languages such as: industry-specific XML vocabularies (FinXML-data interchange format for financial management, eBIS-XML for procurement management, HR-XML for HRM, etc).

- **Support for TCP/IP Extensions and/or protocols such as:** Mobile/Wireless TCP/IP, IntServ, DiffServ, SLP, BGP and RIP, including support for TCP connection failover, TCP/IP, IPv.4, IPv.6, Mobile IPv.4., DHCP, DNS, BIND, WINS protocols

- **Support for Windows/Unix/Linux integration, NFS/NIS, CIFS, SAMBA protocols:** Solutions such as SMB/CIFS which represent a middleware for Unix-to-Windows integration, PC-NFS, WebNFS, are extremely important from data integration point of view.

Integrating Management and Security Drivers

Integrated management and security comprises several server-based drivers that are aimed at enhancing manageability and security of the server operating platforms. Solutions that should be integrated include the following features:

- Centralized, online and GUI-based systems administration
- Online and GUI-based dynamic kernel configuration
- Reloadable kernel

- Online upgrade
- Crash-handling techniques
- Memory mirroring
- Centralized management of remote computers
- Automatic OS-related and application software updates
- Partitioning and virtualization
- Workload management
- Centralized cluster management
- TCP/IP failover
- Integrated authentication services, Active Directory, NIS, PKI, IPsec
- Host intrusion detection system
- Built-in encryption-decryption
- Secure socket layers
- Transaction prioritization
- Encryption acceleration

Integrating ServerWare Solutions (Bundled Servers)

Contemporary server operating systems usually come pre-installed and accompanied with a set of server-based applications which is aimed at enhancing its core capabilities. Mail server and Web server are just two examples of such server software. Among other server-based applications that may come bundled (integrated) with an SOS, the most important are: proxy servers and/or firewalls, e-commerce servers, chat server, news server, list server. Moreover, SOS vendors include parts or even the whole application servers to their SOS platforms. For instance, Sun's decision to bundle Java 2 Enterprise Edition application server and Sun ONE directory server with its Solaris 9 server operating system transforms the operating system environment into a fully-integrated platform for implementing Web services and Java-based applications. Vendors of commercial operating systems such as HP, Sun, IBM, Microsoft, in addition to standard messaging servers, Web servers, file and print servers, remote access servers, security servers, and so forth, provide in bundled form solutions that support and enhance e-commerce applications such as:

- **Dynamic page caching:** Utility which allows the system to dynamically cache frequently accessed pages in memory.
- **Bandwidth allocation:** Allows I/O bandwidth to be reserved or prioritized according to the type of Internet protocol, or location of the page.

- **Transaction prioritization:** A feature which gives priority to transactions or high volume customers.
- **Encryption accelerator support:** Aimed at improving performance and scalability of e-commerce sites.

Integrating Storage Solutions

Contemporary business is forced to cope with demands for more efficient and effective storage solutions as part of its efforts to recover from any type of failure and/or disaster. Three mainly used storage technologies are: (a) standard tape backup solution, (b) storage area network (SAN), and (c) network attached storage (NAS). SAN and NAS technologies are mainly based on (a) Fibre Channel as a mature storage backbone technology and/or (b) newly developed Internet SCSI (iSCSI) and Serial ATA technologies. SANs that use iSCSI protocol are gaining acceptance as a supplement or even complete replacement for Fibre Channel-based SANs. Today, these storage solutions and services are being integrated into server operating platforms. For instance, HP recently announced (Singer, 2005) integrating Smart Array serial controllers, storage enclosures, Hot-Plug Serial Attached SCSI, and Serial ATA hard drivers with HP ProLiant servers. Such an operating environment doesn't require separate connection devices/protocols for interconnecting servers, storage, networking devices. Support for storage scalability includes support for RAID systems and scalability clustering options.

Additional EIS Dimensions (Extended Churchman's Definition)

In order to give more comprehensive definition of an enterprise information system from business continuity perspective, additional dimensions of the second Churchman's system definition will be used as well.

Churchman says that "... *there exists **a client** whose interests (values) are served by S in such a manner that the higher the measure of performance, the better the interests are served, and more generally, the client is the standard of the measure of performance.*" In our case, business system represents the client of the EIS. The higher the measure of performance (availability ratio) provided by the EIS, the better the interests of an organization are served.

Churchman continues with the following dimension: "... *there exists **a decision maker** who—via his resources—can produce changes in the measures of performance of S's components and hence changes in the measure of performance of S.*"

Decision maker in our case can be one or more IT specialists including system administrator, network administrator, IT manager, business continuity manager, including CIO as well. All of them, via their resources that they manage, can make decisions and produce changes in the measure of performance of S's components and S as a whole (EIS).

Churchman's **designer**, *who conceptualizes the nature of S in such a manner that the designer's concepts potentially produce actions in the decision maker, and hence changes in the measures of performance of S's components, and hence changes in the measure of performance of S* in our case can be an EIS designer, EIS system developer, CIO or even CEO, who may create such solutions or define such business objectives that can be later implemented by IT specialists. The designer's intention is to change S (EIS) so as to maximize EIS' value to the client (business system, organization).

Conclusion

In modern business, system uptime and agile data access are two critical points in evaluating performances of enterprise information systems. If a system is down for any reason, be it application error, server component failure, or server operating system crash, the whole enterprise information system becomes "zero-value" from end-users' perspective. Therefore, information technologies that provide high-availability ratios and agile data access are crucial in enhancing performances of enterprise information systems.

The issue of the "economics of downtime" in contemporary business computing has been discussed as a starting point of the chapter. The main focus of the chapter has been put on so-called "continuous computing technologies" (drivers, enablers) for enhancing business continuity. Information technologies have been recognized as business continuity and enterprise-wide agility drivers. From systems performances perspective, especially in e-business world, information technologies can be used to reduce downtime (increase uptime) and consequently contribute in achieving better financial results as each minute of the downtime has its price. Therefore, continuous computing solutions are a main prerequisite for business continuity in modern business. In the same time, they are prerequisite for a continuous, reliable and available enterprise-wide data access such that they drive business agility as well.

The chapter aimed at developing a framework for an "always-on" enterprise information system as a new generation of business computing model for contemporary business. The framework has been developed by using two definitions of a system as defined by C.W. Churchman (objectives, environment, resources, components, management, client, decision maker, designer). This systemic model has been used to identify the framework for developing an "always-on" enterprise information system which is based on a holistic view. The development process of such an EIS starts with defining the main objectives of the system, continues with a comprehensive study of its environment (business system and its requirements), followed by implementing business continuity drivers as main resources, designing appropriate components of EIS, and integrating managerial activities related to business continuity management. Several information technologies in the form of business continuity drivers have been identified as major technologies in boosting business continuity and enterprise-wide agility. Particularly, server platforms are discussed in more detail with regard to their role in achieving an "always-on" computing environment.

The following are some future research directions for practitioners and researchers interested in this field:

a.   EIS-performance measurement with regard to the levels of downtime and uptime.

b.   A more precise model for implementation of continuous computing technologies for several types of businesses (small businesses, large companies, companies that operate on 5-days a week model, virtual enterprises, "dot-coms", etc.).

c.   Different models for implementation of continuous computing technologies within EIS implementations for different server operating system platforms such as: proprietary systems, commercial Unix platforms, different Linux versions, Windows Server-based environments, and so forth.

d.   Benchmarking with regard to system uptime between host-based legacy systems and modern client/server based EIS implementations which include ERP suites.

e.   Non-technology factors affecting the availability of enterprise information systems such as: migration from legacy system to ERP system, issues in ERP upgrades, problems related to so-called ERP-implementation gap, and so forth.

References

Aberdeen Report. (2006, June). *Global Supply Chain Benchmark Report*. Retrieved July 29, 2006, from http://www.aberdeen.com/summary/report/benchmark/RA_GlobalTrade_BE_3172.asp

Barraza, O. (2002). *Achieving 99,9998% + Storage uptime and availability.* DotHill Systems. Retrieved August 7, 2006, from http://www.dothill.com/products/whitepapers/5-9s_wp.pdf

Bartel, V. W., & Rutkowski, A. F. (2006). A fuzzy decision support system for IT service continuity threat assessment. *Decision Support Systems, 42*(December), 1931-1943. Retrieved July 18, 2006, (while in press) from http://www.sciencedirect.com

Bertrand, C. (2005, August). Business continuity and mission critical applications. *Network Security, 20*(8), 9-11.

Botha, J., & Von Solms, R. (2004). A cyclic approach to business continuity planning. *Information Management & Computer Security, 12*(4), 328-337.

Churchman, C. W. (1968). *The systems approach.* New York: Delacorte Press.

Churchman, C. W. (1971). *The design of inquiring systems: Basic concepts of systems and organisations.* New York: Basic Books.

Deloitte & Touche/TPM Report. (2006). *Emphasis on business continuity management programs increases dramatically.* Retrieved July 31, 2006, from http://www.deloitte.com/dtt/press_release/0,1014,sid%253D2283%2526 cid%253D109458,00.html

D.H. Brown Report. (2000). *Operating system function review.*

D.H. Brown Report. (2002). *UNIX Function Review 2002.* Retrieved August 7, 2006, from http://www.hp.ru/data/offline/category/0086/2002unix_report.pdf

D.H. Brown Report. (2003a). *Linux function review.* Retrieved August 8, 2006, from http://searchopensource.techtarget.com/originalContent/0,289142,sid39_gci901797,00.html?Offer=ik2

D.H. Brown Report. (2003b). *Windows Server reaches maturity.* Retrieved August 8, 2006, from http://www.microsoft.com/presspass/features/2003/apr03/04-16dhbrown.mspx

Ernest-Jones, T. (2005, August). Business continuity strategy—the life line. *Network Security, 2005*(8), 5-9. Retrieved July 18, 2006.

Finch, P. (2004). Supply chain risk management. *Supply Chain Management: An International Journal, 9*(2), 183-196.

Fritz, F.-J. (2006, July-August). 64-bit servers—no longer just an option, but a necessity, for enterprises running SAP. *SAP Insider*, 75-77.

Gartner Dataquest. (2003). *North America customers reveal preferred services for mission critical systems, users wants and needs.* Retrieved August 4, 2006, from http://ftp.hp.com/pub/services/continuity/info/continuity_availabilitywp.pdf

Gartner Report. (2005). *Costs and benefits still favor Windows over Linux among midsize businesses.* Retrieved July 21, 2006, from http://www.microsoft.com/windowsserver/facts/analyses/gartner_Midsize.mspx

Gerber, M., & Solms, R. (2005). Management of risk in the information age. *Computers & Security*, 24, 16-30. Retrieved July 18, 2006, from http://www.sciencedirect.com

Gibb, F., & Buchanan, S. (2006). A framework for business continuity management. *International Journal of Information Management*, 26, 128-141.

Graham, S., & Sherman, L. (2003). *Opinion: Windows can mean dependable uptime.* Retrieved July 5, 2006, from http://www.computerworld.com/softwaretopics/os/story/0,10801,80574,00.html

Herbane, B., Elliott, D., & Swartz, E. M. (2004). Business continuity management: Time for a strategic role? *Long Range Planning,* 37, 435-457.

Hill, D. (2006). *Storage tip: Don't equate high availability with high value.* Retrieved July 25, 2006, from http://storage.itworld.com/5002/nls_storage_hill060724/pfindex.html

HP White Paper. (2002). *Meeting the agility challenge, increasing business agility through adaptive IT infrastructure.* Retrieved July 22, 2006, from ftp://ftp.hp.com/pub/services/strategy/info/meeting_the_agility_challenge.pdf

IDC Report. (2006a). *Understanding Unix migration: A demand-side view.* Retrieved August 5, 2006, from http://www.microsoft.com/windowsserver/facts/analyses/idcdemand.mspx

IDC Report. (2006b). *Thinking outside of the box: Architecting for agility.* Retrieved July 29, 2006, from http://www.theitevolution.com/content/IDC_473.pdf

IDC Report. (2006c). *True high availability: Business advantage through continuous user productivity.* Retrieved July 30, 2006, from http://extranet.neverfailgroup.com/upload/PR%20%20True%20High%20Availability%20-%202006-05-18.pdf

Infonetics Research Report. (2005). *The costs of enterprise downtime: North American vertical markets 2005.* Infonetics Research. Retrieved July 28, 2006, from http://www.optrics.com/emprisa_networks/2005_UPNA05_DWN_ToC_Excerpts.pdf

Keizer, G. (2006). *Reliability survey: Windows servers beat Linux servers.* Retrieved July 5, 2006, from http://www.enterpriseserver.techweb.com/windows/showArticle.jhtml?articleID=189600508

King, D. L. (2003). Moving towards a business continuity culture. *Network Security*, 12-17.

Loftus, J. (2004). *Survey: Linux gets hot, Unix gets cold, and Microsoft stalls.* Retrieved August 7, 2006, from http://searchenterpriselinux.techtarget.com/originalContent/0,289142,sid39_gci1029190,00.html

Manning, R. (2004). *Managing the costs of system downtime.* Retrieved July 21, 2006, from http://www.cioupdate.com/budgets/article.php/3404651

Marathon White Paper. (2005). *At your own risk: A risk-based approach to Windows business continuity.* Marathon Technologies Corporation, Inc. Retrieved July 5, 2006, from http://www.repton.co.uk/library/Enterprise%20Systems/marathon_business_continuity_for_windows.pdf

Marchi, M. J., & Watson, A. (2002). *The network appliance enterprise storage architecture: System and data availability.* Retrieved August 7, 2006, from http://www.netapp.com/library/tr/3065.pdf

META Group Report. (2005). *Migrating UNIX ERP installations to a Windows server environment: A qualitative assessment of business impact.* Retrieved July 5, 2006, from http://unix.ittoolbox.com/white-papers/migrating-unix-erp-installations-to-a-windows-server-environment-a-qualitative-assessment-of-business-impact-3293

Newman, A. (2001). *Giga study reveals slow Windows 2000 server adoption.* Retrieved August 7, 2006, from http://www.serverwatch.com/news/article.php/1400201

Pitt, M., & Goyal, S. (2004). Business continuity planning as a facilities management tool. *Facilities, 22*(3-4), 87-99

Schraeder, J. (2004). *Served-based computing—old concept meets new technology.* Retrieved August 6, 2006, from http://209.116.252.254/7_2004_focus/f_14.shtml

Singer, M. (2005). *HP vows server, storage marriage.* Retrieved August 7, 2006, from http://itmanagement.earthweb.com/erp/article.php/3489651

Stanton, R. (2005). Beyond disaster recovery: The benefits of business continuity. *Computer Fraud & Security*, July, 18-19.

Szelong, M. (2002). *Assuring reliable enterprise data availability.* Retrieved August 7, 2006, from http://www.netapp.com/library/tr/3170.pdf

Vanston, M. (2004a). MetaGroup: Disaster recovery: Reaction, not reality. *ZDNET*, March 8.

Vanston, M. (2004b). Disaster recovery: Reaction, not reality. *ZDNET.* Retrieved July 28, 2006, from http://techupdate.zdnet.com/techupdate/stories/main/Disaster_Recovery_Reaction_Not_Reality.html

Walker, A. (2006). Business continuity and outsourcing—moves to take out the risk. *Network Security*, May, 15-17.

Wu, W. Y., Chiag, C. Y., Wu, Y. J., & Tu, H. J. (2004). The influencing factors of commitment and business integration on supply chain management. *Industrial Management & Data Systems, 104*(4), 322-333.

YankeeGroup/Sunbelt 2006 Server Reliability Survey. (2006). Retrieved July 24, 2006, from http://download.microsoft.com/download/8/3/8/838E0ACF-6B1B-4C97-9858-AF1B9B82AE93/Unix_Windows_and_Custom.pdf

Ybarra, M. (2006, January). The long road back. *CIO Decisions Magazine.* Retrieved July 31, 2006, from http://searchcio.techtarget.com/magItem/0,291266,sid19_gci1154418_idx3,00.html

Yeh, Y. P. (2005). Identification of factors affecting continuity of cooperative electronic supply chain relationships: Empirical case of the Taiwanese motor industry. *Supply Chain Management: An International Journal, 10*(4), 327-335.

Endnotes

[1]   C. West Churchman is one of the founders of operational research/management science and the systems approach. He died on March 21, 2004.

[2]   HP claims that its Integrity NonStop servers can provide 99.99999% availability ("seven nines"), uptime level which translates to less than 3 seconds of unplanned downtime a year (http://itmanagement.earthweb.com/erp/article.php/3508861).

[3]   Today part of Ideas International (www.ideasinternational.com).

Chapter XIII

The Financial Appraisal Profile (FAP) Model for Evaluation of Enterprise-Wide Information Technology:
A Case Example

Frank Lefley, University of London, UK

Joseph Sarkis, Clark University, USA

Abstract

Enterprise-wide information systems adoption by organizations has become common place. Even with the benefits offered by such systems, there have also been many failures. One of the important reasons for these failures is inappropriate project evaluation and selection. In order to reduce the level of project failures, we introduce an innovative methodology, the financial appraisal profile (FAP) model, which seeks to address some of the issues and limitations posed by standard appraisal and evaluation approaches for strategic technologies and programs. By making the right decision in the first place and involving senior managers in the appraisal process, the organization will be better placed to achieve project success. The adoption of a management team approach to investment appraisals will not only enhance the information base but will also result in greater managerial commitment to a project. We believe by adopting the FAP model greater awareness to strategic issues and goals will also be achieved, which should lead to a more focused top management team—with all members pulling in the same direction.

Introduction

Over the last two decades, we have seen growth and adoption of enterprise-wide information systems. The benefits of these enterprise integrative systems are likely to be felt by companies with a global outreach and with many business units, causing Fortune 100 firms to invest heavily in these systems with the goal of gaining or maintaining strategic advantage. The market for these systems has started to shift to medium and small-sized organizations. Even though there has been a stabilization of the enterprise information technology market since the bursting of the Internet Bubble, the market within the manufacturing sector is forecasted to rebound through the next few years and grow from $8.9 billion in 2002 to $11.9 billion by 2007 (ARC, 2003). The market for non-manufacturing, service, and government agencies, for these types of systems also represents significant opportunities for growth and investment.

These systems are expensive, with prices ranging from tens of thousands to millions of dollars per implementation. A survey of 63 companies with annual revenues ranging from $12 million to $63 billion indicated that the average implementation cost $10.6 million and took 23 months to complete (Umble & Umble, 2002). Thus, the budgetary pressures on organizations are great when seeking to invest in these technologies. With the many benefits of enterprise information technology, there have also been significant failures (Barker & Frolick, 2003; Brown, 2001; Stedman, 1999). Reasons for failure are manifold, with one of the more important reasons including poor planning and inappropriate selection of vendor and system (Umble & Umble, 2002). Thus, an appropriate approach to appraisal of these systems overall and specific selection should be a strategic exercise involving multiple levels and functions within the organization. Thus, the strategic justification problem is very much relevant, considering the short and long-term sustainability of the organization may be put at jeopardy with inappropriate and detailed evaluation of these systems.

Thus, in this chapter, we expand upon an innovative methodology that seeks to address some of the issues and limitations posed by standard appraisal and evaluation approaches for strategic technologies and programs. The procedure and models are meant to help integrate the organizations disperse decision vectors and influences such that an appropriate (if not an optimum) solution is determined. We begin this chapter by first providing some additional background on enterprise-wide systems, what they are and their influences, and the various factors that need to be considered in their evaluation. We then provide a brief review of various appraisal techniques, traditional and more advanced, that can prove useful in their evaluation. The following section provides an overview of a technique, which we call the financial appraisal profile (FAP) approach (Lefley, 1997, 2006a, 2006b; Lefley & Ryan, 2005). Although the FAP model was designed as a general application model for the appraisal of capital investments, the approach is equally applicable to specific type projects such as enterprise resource planning (ERP) and strategic information technology, where the risk and strategic and new dimensions of the FAP model can be focused on those issues specific to such systems and technologies. A case example provides some managerial insights into the application. We then summarize the chapter identifying various issues that may arise with the technique with managerial implications clearly defined.

Enterprise Resource Planning (ERP) Systems

The definition of ERP systems may vary depending on the source and description. One characteristic that defines these systems is their cross-functionality across the organization. Typically, these systems have modular characteristics, where various components may be implemented together or separately depending on the organizational requirements, size, and functionality sought. A modular listing of ERP-based sub-systems, and their definitions/characteristics are shown in Table 1. These modules range from functional-based systems such as marketing and accounting sub-systems to modules that aid in organizational monitoring and planning such as the business planning and performance management modules.

Figure 1 graphically shows the inter-relationships of these various modules. Internally, the information system function integrates the various modules. These internal modules are basically focusing on the major functions and the linkage of the internal organizational operations with external entities. The planning and monitoring modules help to make decisions and guide organizational development. These external systems are typically designed to help the organization optimize its resources. The linkage of the internal supply chain focuses on the relationships among the internal customers where internal functions are dependent on other functional activities to aid in delivering services or products. The external supply chains focus on linkage of internal systems to external supplier and customer systems. Within this external linkage may be systems that aid in (customer or vendor) relationship management.

Table 1. Examples of ERP modules

Business Planning includes the vision and the mission of the organization, and the strategies needed to accomplish them.

Enterprise Performance Measurement Systems help the organization to determine how well they are doing, to continuously improve, and manage the organizational processes. These systems include performance information on the internal and external supply chain.

Decision Support helps in the management of the internal and external supply chain, which may include optimization, simulation, heuristic, quantitative, and qualitative modelling approaches.

Marketing and Sales includes sales analysis and forecast of the demand of products in the business plan, sales order management, customer maintenance, and billing information systems.

Manufacturing includes the functions of a traditional manufacturing resource planning (MRP II) system (capacity planning, material requirements planning, inventory management, bills of material, etc.)

Finance and Accounting includes payroll, product costing, accounts payable and receivable, general ledger, and asset management information systems.

Engineering includes changes made by the engineering department with respect to routings, bills of material, quality control, machining programs, product designs, maintenance information, etc.

Human resources includes listing of employees, their status within the organization and benefits owed to them by the company.

Purchasing includes supplier, performance, product sourcing, in-bound logistics tracking, materials management information systems. These systems can provide direct linkage to the upstream external supply chain.

DRP/Logistics helps the outbound logistics management of the organization with control and linkage to external customers or other divisions of the same organization such as warehouses. These systems provide significant linkage to the downstream external supply chain.

After Sales Service is meant to aid the customers after sales of a product. Information concerning service parts inventory, such as locations and sources, product reliability, and other performance measures would be need in this system. Its inclusion is important because it is one of the more forgotten factors.

Information Systems is a function core to the management of the EIT. Data accuracy, maintenance, user and performance information are all important to this function. They assure the value chain operates efficiently and effectively with respect to information sharing, acquisition and delivery.

Figure 1. A conceptual model of ERP system modules and linkages

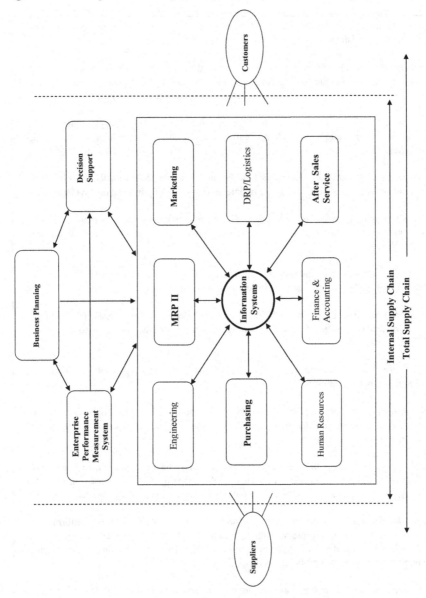

These systems have been defined as "middleware" and their ownership may be by the organization, its customers/suppliers, or a third party such as value-added networks for electronic data interchanges. The organization and/or its partners must make a financial and strategic evaluation whatever the ownership characteristic of the system or its elements.

Comprehensive Appraisal and Evaluation of ERP Systems and Enterprise-Wide Strategic Technology

There are numerous methods and factors that have been recommended for evaluation of strategic technology and projects. The strategic evaluation and justification of systems requires them to go beyond standard return on investment (ROI) and other short-term financial evaluations. The more complete evaluation of these systems requires the incorporation and consideration of strategic, operational, and economic factors. Elements of risk also need to be considered. In particular a new investment appraisal model has been developed which has been called the *financial appraisal profile* (FAP) model. This model looks at a capital investment project from a financial, risk, and strategic viewpoint. While the FAP model includes some of the more traditional approaches to investment appraisal, it also includes some new techniques and modifies others to create a model that embraces a wider profile of an investment opportunity. The FAP model adopts its own structured *process*, for, as some academics would argue, many management scholars believe that the process used to make strategic decisions affects the quality of those decisions (see for example, Fredrickson, 1985). Most models that have been used for appraisal and evaluation of strategic projects lack this overall structure to aid organizations in the process of evaluation, not just the application of models. A brief review of this area is presented to help identify the context within which the FAP model exists.

Evaluation Models

A number of approaches have been recommended to complete appraisals of strategic technology. Lefley (1996) and Raafat (2002) provide bibliographic overviews of the numerous chapters related to justification of strategic technologies, primarily from a manufacturing perspective. Clearly, most of the models and recommendations focus on the evaluation of a number of factors simultaneously. There are numerous multiple criteria evaluation approaches that are available for this simultaneous consideration of factors. Table 2 (adapted and updated from Sarkis & Sundarraj, 2000) provides a summary and overview of these techniques with specific emphasis on appraisal and justification of strategic technology including information and/or manufacturing systems. Many of these models are current, but some have existed for almost two decades. The practical adoption of more advanced models (beyond basic financial models such as ROI and discounted cash flow approaches) for technology investments is still lagging (see Lefley & Sarkis, 2005; Lin, Pervan, &

Table 2. Summary of multiple criteria evaluation technique characteristics and exemplary references. H = High, M = Medium, L = Low (Adapted from Sarkis & Sundarraj, 2000)

Evaluation Technique	Cost of Implementation	Data Requirements	Ease of Sensitivity	Economic Rigor	Management Understanding	Mathematical Complexity	Parameter Mixing - Flexibility	References*
AHP/ANP	M	M	L	L	M	L	H	A, B, C
DEA	M	M	L	M	L	H	M	D, E
Expert Systems	H	H	L	H	M	H	H	F, G
Goal Program	M	M	M	H	L	H	L	H, I
MAUT	H	H	M	M	M	M	H	J,K
Outranking	M	M	L	M	L	M	M	L
Simulation	H	H	H	H	H	H	M	M,N
Scoring Models	L	L	L	L	H	L	H	O,P

*A=Albayrakoglu (1996), B=Sarkis & Sundarraj (2006), C=Chan, Chan, & Chan (2003), D=Talluri & Yoon (2000), E=Sarkis (1997), F=Ordoobadi & Mulvaney, (2001), G=Stamelos, Vlahavas, Refanidis, & Tsoukiàs (2000), H= Schniederjans & Hamaker (2003), I=Suresh (1991), J=Kulak, Kahraman, Oztaysi, & Tanyas (2005), K=Pandey & Kengpol (1995), L=Hsieh, Chin, & Wu (2006), M=Suresh & Meredith (1985), N=O'Kane, Spenceley, & Taylor (2000), O=Lefley & Sarkis (2005), P=Semich(1994).

McDermid, 2000). Part of the reason for the lack of adoption is the complexity of many of these stand-alone models that have limited process structures on how the model fits within a broader scope of managerial decision making. Models should be developed such that they are useful to management and are capable of simplifying a relatively complex decision process. The FAP model fits this goal.

These models have been used to evaluate a variety of characteristics and factors. Included among these characteristics are standard financial and economic factors, but have also included a variety of other factors that include both tangible and intangible characteristics. They range from strategic and risk measures (such as flexibility, quality, and time measures) to operational considerations (such as specific software characteristics and material management capabilities).

Information Technology Specific Factors for Evaluation

In the literature there are many factors within software and hardware information technology (IT), strategic or otherwise, that should be considered at some level. These unique factors include the following:

- **Platform neutrality and interoperability:** The architecture of the systems must be such that it must be able to operate on different platforms and interact with other systems built for a different platform.

- **Scalability:** The performance of a system must scale well with business size.

- **Adaptability:** Adaptability is a factor to measure how well the EIT can interact with other systems.

- **Security:** Security of the databases and of the EIT processes must be inviolable.

- **Reliability:** Reliability consists of the time for which the system is running as well as the correctness of the system's outputs.

- **Customer support:** Customer support is important to managing user's expectations of a system during maintenance and upgrading activities.

- **Ease of use (EOU):** EOU is defined as the degree to which a prospective user expects the system to be free of effort.

These and other factors are also incorporated into the FAP model and are now described.

The FAP Model Overview

It is important that any capital investment appraisal model should include the assessment of two fundamental financial issues; it should identify those projects that are beneficial to the long-term interests of the shareholders/owners, and it should measure both a project's time-risk and its liquidity, which are interrelated. Regarding some projects, however, a third issue of "the abandonment option" may also be relevant, making it necessary to calculate abandonment values.

The Importance of Risk

Project specific risk must be identified and evaluated for all major projects. Knowing where this risk is coming from is important, together with its relevance to the overall success or otherwise of the project. It is only the "acceptable" project specific risk—the risk that will eventually have to be managed—that needs to be evaluated in greater detail. It is only by the identification of such risks that management is given the opportunity to take steps to reduce them. A "value" needs to be placed on each type of risk to highlight the level of its "importance". The highest level of importance will show the greatest risk exposure for any particular managerial area of responsibility.

To aid in risk minimization, managers need to be knowledgeable of the corporate and business strategy of their organization, and the organization's willingness to take risks. They also need to know: (1) the strategic benefits looked for in each project, (2) the importance placed on these benefits by corporate management, (3) the actual benefits and their level of importance within each project, and (4) the overall strategic value of the project.

Development of the Financial Appraisal Model

The FAP model is aimed at solving, in a practical and transparent way, some of the problems now facing organizations that are considering the investment in major capital projects, such as ERP. The FAP model considers three important aspects of an investment decision: financial, risk, and strategic. We shall also extend this appraisal with specific technology considerations for IT, which will be an extension of the strategic dimension analysis. The FAP model process is graphically described in Figure 2.

The financial part of the appraisal is conducted by using the *net present value profile* model. The risk and strategic issues are analyzed with the aid of the *project risk profile* model and *strategic index* model, respectively. The strategic index will also incorporate an IT factors index. These three models are sub-models of the FAP model.

An essential part of the FAP model is the establishment of an investment appraisal team. This team is "administered" by a *team facilitator* whose function is to guide the team members through the investment appraisal process. The whole investment appraisal process is overviewed by corporate management, who need to be directly involved at both the beginning and end of the appraisal process. Corporate management have the responsibility for formulating investment policy, which includes both corporate and business strategy, approving the discount rate used in the discounted cash flow calculations, and determining the level of project specific risk the organization is prepared to accept.

Once a proposal has passed the initial evaluation stage the investment appraisal team will consider, in greater detail, each proposed project's specific risk, financial, and strategic/IT attributes.

Project Specific Risk

The risk identification and evaluation portion of the FAP model uses the *project risk profile*. It is during this process that a project can be rejected outright. If a project is initially deemed to be too risky then there is no point in progressing with

Figure 2. Graphical flow description of FAP process

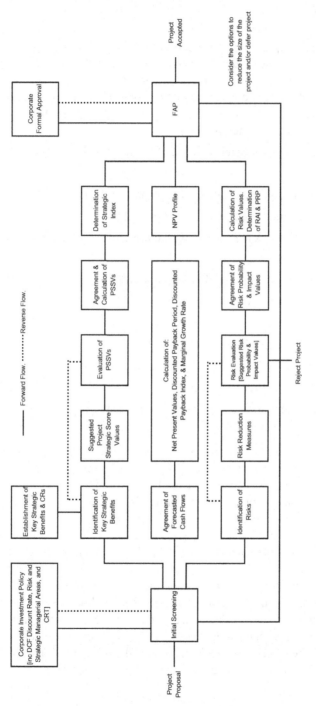

the financial and strategic issues if this risk cannot, in someway, be reduced to an acceptable level.

The *project risk profile* produces a "risk area index" on a negative scale of zero to -10, with minus10 representing the largest risk the organization is prepared to accept from a single risk area. A *corporate risk threshold* is introduced into the calculations so that the *risk area index* refers only to the "degrees of acceptable risk". It also highlights the extreme risk impact by "risk area" and "value" and the highest degrees of variance in team members risk "impact" and "probability" values, to produce a risk profile for each project.

There are three stages for determination of the project risk profile:

- **Stage One** (corporate management responsibility)
  - ○ Determine the corporate risk threshold.
  - ○ Establish risk areas (managerial areas of responsibility).
- **Stage Two** (appraisal team)
  - ○ Identify project specific risks (key risk elements).
  - ○ Determine risk values (probability and impact).
- **Stage Three**
  - ○ Calculate risk importance (R = P x DIV).
  - ○ Determine "risk area index" on a negative scale of zero to -10.
  - ○ Identify "extreme" risk events.
  - ○ Establish variances in risk values (measure of uncertainty in values).

The final stage in the risk analysis process is the calculation of the *risk values* for each *key risk element* and determination of the *risk area index*. The "importance" of a key risk element (R) can be measured as the product of the *probability of risk occurrence* (P) and its *impact* (I) on a project's outcome. Impact is defined as the perceived magnitude of the consequences in relation to project failure that the particular risk will have on the project as a whole. A *risk value* for a *specific risk area* is calculated as the sum of the total levels of risk "importance" for that area, expressed in relation to the company's *corporate risk threshold,* multiplied by -10. For example, if the total level of "importance" for all the key risk elements for a particular risk area is three and the corporate risk threshold is six, the risk value for that risk area would then be calculated as 3/6 x -10 = -5. From the profile of the risk values for each risk area, the highest value is determined and this represents the *risk area index* for the project. The *risk area index* identifies the weakest link, the most vulnerable risk area—the managerial area with the highest risk.

The *project risk profile* also highlights the area in which the highest risk impact is present and measures the size of the variances (*co-efficient of variation*) in the managerial values for specific risk "probability" and "impact". This gives a full risk profile of a proposed project. It is also important to keep sight of both the probability of a risk occurring and its impact (and not just the "expected value" of R = P x I). The *project risk profile* allows for this difference by applying a *disutility weighting* to the impact values to produce a *disutility impact value* (DIV), so that R = P x (DIV).[1] Managers need to have a greater knowledge and understanding of the "extreme" events. It is for these reasons that the model adopts a profile approach—presenting a risk profile of each project.

Project Financial Attributes

A *net present value profile* is produced at this stage. To arrive at the *net present value profile,* it is important that the discount rate used in its calculation has not been inflated to cover a project's specific risk or an organization's infrastructure costs. For, as Booth (1999) argues, "*for DCF calculations, 'risk' is intended only to refer to 'systematic' risk ... it does not include 'project specific' risk, no matter how great*". Having established this important assumption, it is then possible to extend the *net present value* to include the *discounted payback* model, the *discounted payback index*, and finally to arrive at a "*marginal growth rate*".

The *net present value* of a project is the sum of all the net discounted cash flows during the life of the project less the present value of the capital cost of the project. The *discounted payback* model calculates what may be described as the break-even point at which the discounted returns from a project are equal to the capital cost of the project. A natural progression from the *discounted payback* is the calculation of the *discounted payback index*, which is similar to the profitability index. The *discounted payback index* is calculated by dividing a project's initial capital cost into its accumulated discounted net cash inflows. This index shows how many times the initial cost of an investment will be recovered during a project's useful life and is therefore a further measure of a project's profitability.

The next stage in the development of the *net present value profile* is the calculation of the *marginal growth rate* (MGR) which is reached through the *discounted payback index* (DPBI) over n time periods, where MGR = $[(DPBI)^{1/n} - 1]$ x 100. The *marginal growth rate* is the marginal return on a project after discounting the cash inflows at the cost of capital, and can be viewed as a "net" variant of the modified internal rate of return. Unlike the *discounted payback index*, the *marginal growth rate* reflects the economic life of a project. It is observed that there is a mathematical "relationship" between the MGR and the most commonly used modified internal rate of return (MIRR) where (1 + MIRR) = (1 + MGR) x (1 + cost of capital).

The *net present value profile* also highlights the abandonment values for the first three years of a project's life, with a graded "classification" of such values with a high, medium or low rating depending on the percentage ranges as specified by management policy.

Project Strategic Benefits

In the FAP model, evaluating the strategic benefits from a project is made by applying the *strategic index*. Projects become strategic because they offer some form of competitive advantage or the potential to extend the corporate life of an organization. Strategic benefits, from the point of view of the *strategic index*, are therefore those benefits that create a competitive advantage or contribute to corporate survival, and which cannot be expressed adequately in financial terms.

By applying a *corporate ranking* to the *project strategic score values* a unique *strategic index* is achieved. This ranking is required, as not all strategic benefits will have the same level of importance to the organization. The corporate rankings are represented by a value between 1 and 10 and may be calculated by using a pairwise approach to check for consistency in ranking. The *strategic index* is measured on a positive scale of 0 to 10.

There are three primary stages to the determination of the strategic index:

- **Stage One** (corporate management responsibility)
  - o   Establish strategic benefits to be considered in all projects.
  - o   Give each strategic benefit a "corporate ranking" (CR) on a scale of 1 to 10.
  - o   Establish "key strategic benefit areas" (managerial areas of responsibility).
- **Stage Two** (appraisal team responsibility)
  - o   Identify key strategic benefits offered by the project.
  - o   Arrive at a "project strategic score value" (PSSV), on a scale of 0 to 10, for each strategic benefit.
- **Stage Three**
  - o   Calculate the strategic index (weighted average of the CRs and PSSVs) on a positive scale of 0 to 10.

The *strategic index* is the weighted average of the *corporate rankings* and *project strategic score values* of all the key strategic benefits and is measured on a positive scale of 0 to 10, with 0 representing no strategic benefits, and 10 representing the highest strategic level.

In this specific strategic IT project circumstance, we extend the strategic index to specifically measure the level of the "IT specific factors" within each project. This extension will enable us to refine the evaluation for mutually exclusive IT projects. Seven factors have been identified in a previous section with various levels of "importance" with respect to IT projects. An IT sub-team (having the specific IT technical knowledge) will be needed to determine the "score" values for each factor with respect to the project under review, in much the same way as the SI. This sub-index, which we will call the IT score, then becomes part of the overall profile of the project. By applying a weight to the "scores", we are able to produce a total IT score value for each project.

The Final Stage in the FAP Process

When the *net present value profile*, *project risk profile*, and *strategic index* (with an IT score included) have been determined, the FAP is compiled, which highlights the financial, risk, and strategic characteristic of a proposed project. It is then left to the investment appraisal team to make their recommendations to corporate management. The FAP model is now illustrated through a recent case study.

Case Study

The Organization

The case study was undertaken at the Association of International Accountants (AIA) which is one of six statutorily Recognized Qualifying Bodies (RQB) in the United Kingdom for company auditors under the Companies Act 1989.

Based in the UK, the Association was founded in 1928 and incorporated in London in 1932. The Association promotes and supports the advancement of the accountancy profession both in the UK and internationally. While supporting international accounting and auditing standards, the Association seeks to ensure that its examinations and membership requirements support the development of the accountancy profession in the countries in which it examines.

The Association has students and members in over 80 countries world-wide, including the UK, Ireland, Europe, Hong Kong, Malaysia, Singapore, Canada, Africa, Cyprus, and the Caribbean. An international network of branches provides a framework for support and guidance to students and members and to promote awareness of developments in accountancy.

Challenges and Concerns Facing the Association

The Association needs to build on its current success by satisfying the high expectations of both existing and prospective students and members, and providing a service second to none within the accountancy profession. To provide continued and sustained growth, the Association also needs to maximize revenues from current and new membership. The Association currently faces competition from other accountancy bodies in the area of Web site and IT functionality, especially in the areas of:

1.   Payment of subscriptions
2.   Student registration
3.   Registration for examinations
4.   Access to examination results

In order to provide additional services while maintaining current staffing levels, the Association must increase efficiency in its office procedures. In order to release more funds for promotional activities, and so forth, it also needs to curtail rising administration costs.

There are growing expectations from Association members that exceed the current IT systems capability. In particular, the current IT infrastructure raises the following concerns:

1.   The current database is not capable of Web-enablement. As a result, it cannot be used to provide online subscription payments, student registration, or registration for examinations.

2.   The existing database is obsolete making it difficult to be updated to introduce new services.

3.   The IT hardware and supporting software, used by the Association, no longer provide the advantages that they did five years ago.

4.   Expansion possibilities within the current IT structure are limited.

The Project

In order to address these concerns, it was proposed that the Association improve its IT systems by purchasing new enterprise-wide computer hardware and software together with new database facilities. Two suppliers will be required: (1) hardware and software, and (2) database.

Based on the recommendations, the basic details of the: (1) hardware/software include: Windows XP operating system, IBM A30 (Pentium 4) workstations, use current Cisco Pix 506 firewall, Trend NeatSuite anti-virus protection, MS Exchange E-mail server, additional network hardware requirement—16 port 10/100 Swith, 24 port patch panel, and Zeta Fax; and (2) database are: server to be provided by ST to include system study, project management and consultancy, implementation and installation, training, data conversion from Omnis 7, initial licence fee, additional tailoring of system to meet Association needs, integration to Sage Accounting, marketing/query tool, additional hardware, bar-coding facility, sort code and credit card validation, credit card and direct debit facility, BACS processing, Post Office addressing tool, Database/Oracle, front end application software—Delphi, Web integration, online—subscriptions, payments, view, update of records, examination entry, purchase of merchandise, and CPD registration. Altogether these systems and accessories support the full enterprise and represent a strategic project.

We now show the calculations in arriving at the financial appraisal profile of the project. The data used in the tables have been arrived at through the FAP process outlined earlier in the chapter. Although the IT is for a relatively small installation, it still has strategic implications for the organization and gives an excellent example of the workings of the FAP model.

Table 3 shows the calculation of the net present value profile. The other basic required data is shown in Table 3 with cash flows over a 10-year period and discount factor of 4%. A discount rate of 4% was used by the organization to reflect their opportunity cost of capital—the AIA is a non-profit-making organization with a very healthy cash position, it had no borrowings. As we can see the abandonment value has a low classification. The calculations of each of the major elements of the NPV profile are shown at the bottom of Table 3 and summarized in Table 4.

With respect to the assessment of a project's specific risk (Table 5), the company has established five risk management areas of responsibility (Departments A-E) and has determined a corporate risk threshold (CRT) rating of 9.5. The company also accepts the notion of applying a weighting to the risk "impact" values, to take into account the greater "importance" of higher impact values. With the aid of an external consultant, it arrived at a weighting formula to calculate the appropriate disutility impact values (DIVs). It is assumed that there are a total of five risk elements (project specific risks). The shaded boxes in the table highlight the values

Table 3. Calculation of the NPVP

Capital cost of project $337,550 (historic cost) $333,633 (discounted cost)						
	Net cash inflows from the project				Abandonment Values	
Year	Net cash inflow $	Discount factor 4%	PV of net cash inflows $	Cumulative PV $	Abandonment Value $	Discounted AV $
0	*235,816*	1.0000	*235,816*	*235,816*		
1	26,267	0.9615	25,256	*210,560*	15,310	14,721
2	52,456	0.9246	48,501	*162,059*	5,104	4,719
3	59,911	0.8890	53,261	*108,798*	0	0
4	67,604	0.8548	57,788	*51,010*	Abandonment option: The company has determined to highlight each project's AVs for the first three years of its life, and that if the average of the discounted AVs over this period is greater than 30% of the project's original capital cost, it will classify the AVs as "**high**", between 30% and 10% "**medium**", and below 10% **low**.	
5	75,043	0.8219	61,678	10,668		
6	87,461	0.7903	69,120	79,788		
7	95,498	0.7599	72,569	152,357		
8	103,780	0.7307	75,832	228,189		
9	112,335	0.7026	78,927	307,116		
10	121,160	0.6756	81,856	388,972		
Totals			388,972			

Calculations:
NPV: $388,972
$DPB = [4 + (51,010/61,678)]$ = **4 years and 10 months**
DPBI = (Present value of net cash inflows / capital cost of project) = (722,605/333,633) = **2.1658**
$MGR = [(DPBI)^{1/n} - 1] \times 100 = [(2.1658)^{1/10} - 1] \times 100 = \textbf{8.02\%}$
AVs = [(20,414)/3]/334,130x 100 = 2.04%. Classification = **Low**

Table 4. Summary of NPV profile

NPV	**$388,972**
DPB	**4 years 10 months**
DPBI	**2.1658**
MGR	**8.02%**
AVs	**Low**

suggested by the manager responsible for the risk area. The *degree of variance* is the *co-efficient of variation* in the suggested values. The co-efficient of variation is a relative measure of dispersion from the mean and is equal to the ratio of the standard deviation to the mean.

The disutility impact value (DIV) is arrived at after applying a disutility factor to the suggested impact value.

After determining the agreed values for risk probability and likely occurrence (see Table 5) the departmental risk values are calculated as shown in Table 6 after applying a corporate risk threshold factor of 9.5. Within the project risk profile (PRP),

Table 5. Calculation of the "agreed" risk probability and impact values for key risk elements

	Management areas of responsibility – suggested values					Agreed values	Degree of variance
	Department A	Department B	Department C	Department D	Department E		
Risk element (1) Risk Area [Dept. B].							
Probability	.05	.02	.03	.03	.05	**.033**	33.3
Impact	10	10	10	10	10	10.00	0
DIV	10.15	10.15	10.15	10.15	10.15	**10.15**	
Risk element (2) Risk Area [Dept. C].							
Probability	.03	.025	.01	.03	.05	**.026**	44.16
Impact	10	10	10	10	15	10.83	18.18
DIV	10.15	10.15	10.15	10.15	15.34	**11.01**	
Risk element (3) Risk Area [Dept. C].							
Probability	.05	.1	.025	.05	.05	**.05**	44.54
Impact	15	15	15	10	20	15	21.08
DIV	15.34	15.34	15.34	10.15	20.62	**15.36**	
Risk element (4) Risk Area [Dept. C].							
Probability	.05	.02	.02	.05	.05	**.035**	38.68
Impact	10	15	10	10	15	11.67	20.41
DIV	10.15	15.34	10.15	10.5	15.34	**11.88**	
Risk element (5) Risk Area [Dept. E].							
Probability	.05	.02	.05	.02	.05	**.04**	38.68
Impact	30	20	10	25	30	24.17	32.54
DIV	31.43	20.62	10.15	25.99	31.43	**25.18**	
Risk element (6) Risk Area [Dept. E].							
Probability	.1	.02	.05	.06	.1	**.072**	46.55
Impact	15	10	15	10	30	18.33	45.93
DIV	15.34	10.15	15.34	10.15	31.43	**18.97**	
Risk element (7) Risk Area [Dept. A].							
Probability	.03	.02	03	.03	.1	**.04**	69.66
Impact	35	30	25	20	30	29.17	18.21
DIV	36.97	31.43	25.99	20.62	31.43	30.57	
Risk element (8) Risk Area [Dept. B].							
Probability	.05	.05	.03	.02	.05	.042	31.62
Impact	10	10	10	10	20	11.67	33.33
DIV	10.15	10.15	10.15	10.15	20.62	11.89	

The disutility impact value (DIV) is arrived at after applying a disutility factor to the suggested impact value. The *variance* is the *coefficient of variation* in the suggested values. The shaded boxes highlight the values suggested by the manager responsible for the particular risk area and whose values have been given a weighting of 2.

it is only the "acceptable" level of risk that is of interest, if the final level of risk is unacceptable to the company, the project should be rejected. It is therefore necessary to introduce a corporate risk threshold (CRT) into the calculations, so that the scale of 0 to -10 refers only to the "degrees of acceptable risk", with -10 representing the greatest risk the company is prepared to accept from *any one risk area*. The CRT represents the cut-off point for risk acceptance.

Table 6. PRP: Calculation of departmental risk values (RV)

Details of key risk elements	Probability of risk occurrence [0 - 1]	DIV of risk on project [0 - 100]	'Importance' rating : RV
DEPARTMENT A			
risk element (7)	.04	30.57	1.22
risk element (8)	.042	11.89	.50
Total "importance" rating.			1.72
Agreed department A risk area RV [1.72 / 9.5 x -10]			**– 1.81**
DEPARTMENT B			
risk element (1)	.033	10.15	.34
Total "importance" rating.			.34
Agreed department B risk area RV [.34 / 9.5 x -10]			**– 0.36**
DEPARTMENT C			
risk element (2)	.026	11.01	.28
risk element (3)	.05	15.36	.77
risk element (4)	.035	11.88	.42
Total "importance" rating.			1.47
Agreed department C risk area RV [1.47 / 9.5 x -10]			**– 1.55**
DEPARTMENT D			
No specific risks allocated to this area			n/a
Total "importance" rating.			n/a
Agreed department D risk area RV			**0**
DEPARTMENT E			
risk element (5)	.04	25.18	1.01
risk element (6)	.072	18.97	1.37
Total "importance" rating.			2.38
Agreed department E risk area RV [2.38 / 9.5 x -10]			**– 2.51**
Note: Within the PRP, it is only the "acceptable" level of risk that is of interest. It is therefore necessary to introduce a "corporate risk threshold" (CRT) into the calculations, so that the scale of zero to -10 refers only to the "degrees of acceptable risk", with -10 representing the greatest risk the company is prepared to accept from *any one risk area*. The CRT represents the cut-off point for risk acceptance. The CRT in this instance is 9.5			

Table 7. PRP: Determination of the project risk profile (PRP)

Risk areas (Departments/areas of responsibility)	Risk value/profile
Department A	- 1.81
Department B	- 0.36
Department C	- 1.55
Department D	0
Department E	- 2.51
Project Risk Area Index [Department E]	**RAI – 2.51**
The project RAI is based on the highest risk value shown by the risk profile, which for this project is in department E risk area (RAI = -2.51).	
Extreme "risk impact" area and value:	**Department B: 29.17 (Variance 18.21%)** **Risk element 7.**
Highest Variance:	**Probability: Risk element 7. department B.** **69.66%**

The final risk profile for the project is given in Table 7, from which it can be seen that the level of risk in Department E needs to be specifically monitored together with that in Department B which shows an extreme risk impact factor.

Table 8. Calculation of the project strategic score values (PSSV)

Key Strategic Benefits:	PSSV's for each team member's managerial areas of responsibility					
	Department A	Department B	Department C	Department D	Department E	PSSV
Strategic benefit 1.	3	3	6	5	2	**3.8**
Strategic benefit 2.	6	5	9	5	4	**5.8**
Strategic benefit 3.	8	8.5	9.5	8	8	**8.4**
Strategic benefit 4.	5	7	7	6.5	7	**6.5**
Strategic benefit 5.	7	9	8.5	8.5	8	**8.2**
The 'agreed' PSSV for each strategic benefit is the weighted average of all the 'suggested' PSSVs for that benefit.						

The strategic importance of the project is measured by the strategic index. The figures in Table 8, are the consensus values for each departmental manager with respect to the strategic importance of five strategic benefits (these are the key strategic benefits looked for in all capital projects) determined by corporate management. An important strategic benefit/goal (which would have a high corporate ranking) looked for in all capital projects is "organizational growth"—in other words, will the acceptance of this project stimulate growth (membership recruitment). Other strategic goals and benefits include issues such as flexibility, recognition and status, and quality of service. We can see that in this example, strategic benefit 3 is viewed as the largest benefit that is accrued by the system. The data for the project strategic score values (see Table 8) are used in Table 9, when the corporate ranking (CR) is applied to arrive at a total strategic index.

In Table 9, key strategic benefits looked for in all capital projects are identified and a CR of "10" is given to the most important benefit(s). All other key strategic benefits

Table 9. Determination of the strategic index (SI)

Strategic benefits:	Corporate Ranking (a)	Project strategic score value (b)	(a) x (b)
Strategic benefit 1.	0.20	3.8	**0.76**
Strategic benefit 2.	0.22	5.8	**1.28**
Strategic benefit 3.	0.20	8.4	**1.68**
Strategic benefit 4.	0.20	6.5	**1.30**
Strategic benefit 5.	0.18	8.2	**1.48**
Totals	1.0		**6.50**
The strategic index			**SI 6.5**
The "corporate ranking" is the weight placed on a particular strategic benefit by senior corporate management to reflect its corporate importance in relation to other strategic benefits. Each individual benefit is also given a "project strategic score value", representing the benefit level within a given project [see Table 8]. Both the ranking and the strategic score values are on a scale of 0 to 10. The SI is the weighted average of the CRs and PSSVs.			

are than assessed against the CR of the "first" key strategic benefit by determining how *less* important they are to the organization in relation to that benefit. The benefits are then assessed against each other, in order to determine a consistency of ranking to make sure that the *laws of transitivity* have not been violated. The strategic index for this system is set at 6.5.

The project is finally appraised on its IT specific factors in a similar manner to the SI procedure, only in this case an IT sub-team is used to determine the "values" due to the technical issues involved. A weighting is applied to the average score values (see Table 10) to arrive at an IT score for the project. This weighting is required to reflect the level of "importance" of the individual specific IT factors—not all factors will have the same level of importance to the organization.

The weighting in column (a) of Table 10 is agreed to by senior corporate management to reflect its corporate importance in relation to each IT specific factor. The agreed upon score values in column (b) are specific to the project under review and are determined by a senior IT team. The IT score represents the total of the weighted score values with a maximum possibility (based on the agreed weights in this example) of 63. The final IT evaluation score for this system is at 53.86 (85.5%).

Table 11 provides a summary profile of four main investment criteria: (1) financial, (2) project-specific risk, (3) strategic importance, and, for this particular type of project, (4) IT specific factors.

The financial benefits from the project show a positive net present value of $388,972 with a reasonable payback period for this type of project of just less than five years. The project repays (in discounted terms) just over twice its original cost and has a high marginal growth rate of 8.02%, giving a modified internal rate of return of 12.34%, but has a *low* classification for the abandonment value—which is not uncommon for IT projects.

Table 10. The IT score

Key IT Specific Factors:	Weighting (a)	Average Agreed Scores 0 to 10 (b)	(a) x (b)
1. Platform Neutrality and Interoperability	0.7	5.5	3.85
2. Scalability	0.95	9.5	9.03
3. Adaptability	0.85	8.5	7.23
4. Security	1.0	9	9.00
5. Reliability	1.0	9	9.00
6. Customer Support	0.9	8.5	7.65
7. Ease of use	0.9	9	8.10
		The IT Score [(53.86 / 63) x 100] =	53.86 (85.5%)
The weighting in column (a) reflects the level of importance of each IT specific factor as determined by the senior IT specialist(s) within the Association. The agreed score values in column (b) were determined by an IT team and are specific to the project under review. The IT Score represents the total of the weighted score values with a maximum possibility of 63.			

Table 11. The financial appraisal profile (FAP)

Project: IT – Information communication technology including computer hardware and software		
Basic data	Capital cost of the project (Discounted $333,633)	$337,550
	Cost of capital	4%
	Estimated Life of Project	10
Financial:	**NPV**	**$388,972**
NPV Profile	**DPB**	**4 years and 10 Months**
	DPBI	**2.1628**
	MGR	**8.02%**
	AVs - Classification	**Low**
Project-specific risk:	**Risk Area Index [Department E]**	**-2.51**
Project Risk Profile	**Extreme "risk impact": Department A Risk element 7**	**29.17 (D. of V.18.21%)**
	Variance. Probability: Risk element 7. Department A	**69.66%**
Strategic Index		**6.5**
IT Specific Factors: **IT Score (maximum possible score 63)**		**53.86 (85.5%)**

The PRP shows that the highest risk is in Department E at -2.51, which on a scale of 0 to -10 is relatively low. The extreme risk impact is shown as being in Department A with respect to risk element 7 at 29.17 (on a scale of 1 to 100) with a degree of variance in the appraisal team members' individual values of 18.21%. The profile also identifies that the highest degree of variance in the values put forward by the appraisal team members was again with respect to risk element 7 in Department A at 69.66%—this result indicates a degree of uncertainty with respect to the probability of this particular risk occurring. The overall project-specific risk, as show by this profile, may be regarded as low.

The strategic importance of the project is highlighted by this average strategic index of 6.5 (on a scale of 0 to 10).

An overall IT score of 53.86 gives a high rating of 85.5%, which shows that of the seven important IT specific factors assessed, a relatively high overall score factor is offered by this project.

Given these summary results, and the supporting FAP model's comprehensive overview of the project's desirability, the project was recommended by the management team for corporate management approval.

Managerial Opinions on the FAP Model

Practical validation for the FAP model from the management team may be best summarized by the following three comments made by team members:

Having spoken to all the team members, it has been an enjoyable experience—one that people were unsure of in the beginning, because of the unknown, that grew into a kind of reassurance in some ways of the decisions and assumptions made along the selection process.

I have looked at the draft (report) with interest and found the work of first class.

I have found the process interesting, seeing that the model actually works. As far as I am concerned the whole process has gone very well.

When asked if they would use the model again to evaluate future capital projects, the Director of Administration said:

Yes, definitely, as it opens up many more questions that need to be answered.

One of the advantages of FAP is that it provides an outline for the logic and supporting documents necessary to convince decision makers of the ultimate decision. Evidence of this characteristic was from the corporate management of the Association with the following comments made by council members with respect to the final report:

It gave a better understanding of the project, much clearer, not only from the viewpoint of the objectives, but how those objectives were to be achieved.

It was quite clear in highlighting the financial benefits to be derived from the project.

It clearly linked the project with the Association's strategic objectives.

I thought the risk issues were very well defined and thought through—well done to all concerned.

Conclusion

This chapter has introduced the special characteristics of strategic IT projects and applied the financial appraisal profile (FAP) model approach to their evaluation, and is supported by an actual case application. We have described and shown how the integration of these factors can be completed into a comprehensive evaluation of a strategic information system for an organization. This method helps fill a gap in the IT investment literature where there is a paucity of comprehensive, structured and transparent methodologies that can prove acceptable to management decision makers from a variety of functions and viewpoints.

But, we need to reiterate at this point that the FAP model is an aid to management decision-making and not a substitute. It is important that investment decision tools should be flexible and guide management in making the most appropriate decisions. However, it must be remembered that it is management that will make the decision and who will be responsible for the consequences of that decision. No decision tool can take that responsibility away. One important characteristic of the FAP model is its ability to allow management the creativity of decision-making, the flexibility to demonstrate their judgmental skills. It also provides an outline of providing an argument for or against a particular investment.

Through the FAP approach, managers will have a broader and more flexible financial, risk, and strategic base to help make such important investment decisions. It also forces management to take a consistent approach to the appraisal of investments in new capital assets, irrespective of whether the project is a traditional cost reduction or machine replacement project, or an investment in new technology.

References

Albayrakoglu, M. M. (1996). Justification of new manufacturing technology: A strategic approach using the analytical hierarchy process. *Production and Inventory Management Journal, 37*(1), 71-76.

ARC. (2003). *ERP market opportunities change while remaining strong overall at $8.9 billion.* Retrieved February 2004, from http://www.arcweb.com/Community/arcnews/arcnews.asp?ID=328

Barker, T., & Frolick, M. N. (2003). ERP implementation failure: A case study. *Information Systems Management, 20*(4), 43-49.

Booth, R. (1999). Avoiding pitfalls in investment appraisal. *Management Accounting, 77*(10), 22-23.

Brown, J. (2001). Sobeys fires SAP over ERP debacle: Grocer says database failure will cost millions. *Computing Canada, 27*(3), 1.

Chan, F. T. S., Chan, H. K., & Chan, M. H. (2003). An integrated fuzzy decision support system for multicriterion decision-making problems. *Journal of Engineering Manufacture, 217*(1), 11-27.

Fredrickson, J. W. (1985). Effects of decision motive and organizational performance level on strategic decision processes. *Academy of Management Journal, 28*(4), 821-843.

Hsieh, L.-F., Chin, J.-B., & Wu, M.-C. (2006). Performance evaluation for university electronic libraries in Taiwan. *The Electronic Library*, 24(2), 212-224.

Kulak, O., Kahraman, C., Oztaysi, B., & Tanyas, M. (2005). Multi-attribute information technology project selection using fuzzy axiomatic design. *Journal of Enterprise Information Management, 18*(3), 275-288.

Lefley, F. (1996). Strategic methodologies of investment appraisal of AMT projects: A review and synthesis. *Engineering Economist, 41*(4), 345-353.

Lefley, F. (1997, June). Capital investments: The financial appraisal profile. *Certified Accountant, 89*(6), 26-29.

Lefley, F. (2006a). Can a project champion bias project selection and, if so, how can we avoid it? *Management Research News, 29*(4), 174-183.

Lefley, F. (2006b). A pragmatic approach to management accounting research: A research path. *Management Research News, 29*(6), 358-371.

Lefley, F., & Ryan, R. (2005). *The financial appraisal profile (FAP) model.* London: Palgrave Macmillan. (Also published in the USA in September 2005.)

Lefley, F., & Sarkis, J. (2005, April-June). Applying the financial appraisal profile (FAP) model to the evaluation of strategic information technology projects. *International Journal of Enterprise Information Systems, 1*(2), 68-87.

Lin, C., Pervan, G., & McDermid, G. (2000). Research on IS/IT investment evaluation and benefits realization in Australia. In the *Proceedings of the 2000 Information Resources Management Association International Conference on Challenges of Information Technology management in the 21st century*, Anchorage, Alaska, United States (pp. 359-362). Hershey, PA: Idea Group Publishing.

Nelson, C. A. (1986). A scoring model for flexible manufacturing systems project selection. *European Journal of Operational Research*, 24, 346-359.

O'Kane, J. F., Spenceley, J. R., & Taylor, R. (2000). Simulation as an essential tool for advanced manufacturing technology problems. *Journal of Materials Processing Technology, 107*(1), 412-424.

Ordoobadi, S. M., & Mulvaney, N. J. (2001). Development of a justification tool for advanced manufacturing technologies: System-wide benefits value analysis. *Journal of Engineering and Technology Management, 18*(2), 157-184.

Pandey, P. C., & Kengpol, A. (1995). Selection of an automated inspection system using multiattribute decision analysis. *International Journal of Production Economics, 39*(3), 289-298.

Raafat, F. (2002). A comprehensive bibliography on justification of advanced manufacturing systems. *International Journal of Production Economics, 79*(3), 197-208.

Sarkis, J. (1997). Evaluating flexible manufacturing systems alternatives using data envelopment analysis. *The Engineering Economist, 43*(1), 25-48.

Sarkis, J., & Sundarraj, R. P. (2000). Factors for strategic evaluation of enterprise information technologies. *International Journal of Physical Distribution and Logistics Management, 30*(3/4), 196-220.

Sarkis, J., & Sundarraj, R. P. (2006). Evaluation of enterprise information technologies: a decision model for high-level consideration of strategic and operational issues. *IEEE Transactions on Systems, Man and Cybernetics, Part C, 36*(2), 260-273.

Schniederjans, M. J., & Hamaker, J. L. (2003). A new strategic information technology investment model. *Management Decision, 41*(1), 8-17.

Semich, J. W. (1994). Here's how to quantify IT investment benefits. *Datamation, 40*(1), 45-47.

Stamelos, I., Vlahavas, I., Refanidis, I., & Tsoukiàs, A. (2000). Knowledge based evaluation of software systems: A case study. *Information and Software Technology*, 42, 333-345.

Stedman, C. (1999, November 1). Failed ERP gamble haunts Hershey: Candy maker bites off more than it can chew and "kisses" big Halloween sales goodbye. (Company Operations). *Computerworld, 1*(1).

Suresh, N. C. (1991). An extended multi-objective replacement model for flexible automation investments. *International Journal of Production Research, 29*(9), 1823-1844.

Suresh, N. C., & Meredith, J. R. (1985). Justifying multimachine systems: An integrated strategic approach. *Journal of Manufacturing Systems, 4*(2), 117-134.

Talluri, S., & Yoon, P. K. (2000). A cone-ratio DEA approach for AMT justification. *International Journal of Production Economics, 66*(2), 119-129.

Umble, E. J., & Umble, M. M. (2002). Avoiding ERP implementation failure. (enterprise resource planning). *Industrial Management, 44*(1), 25(10).

Endnote

[1]   In theory, the importance of risk is the product of its *impact* multiplied by its *probability of occurrence* (R = I x P). This therefore assumes that managers will treat, as having the same value (importance) and have no preference for either, a specific risk with an *impact of 60 (on a scale of zero to 100) and a probability of 10%,* and a risk with an *impact of 10 and a probability of 60%* (both having a value of 6.0). Tests, however, from a small sample of managers, suggested that they treated as "equal" a risk with an *impact of 55 and a probability of 10%* (5.5), and an *impact of 10 with a probability of 60%* (6.0). Managers were clearly placing a greater level of significance to higher levels of risk impact, by subconsciously applying a *disutility value* to the impact values—in this example the disutility value is 1.0909 so that 55 x 0.1 x 1.0909 = 6.0 which equates to 10 x 0.6 (= 6.0). So, by applying a *disutility value* to the perceived risk *impact* value, a *disutility impact value* (DIV) is achieved. This is an area of continuing research.

Chapter XIV

An Investigation of the Existence of Levels of Enterprise Integration

Delvin Grant, DePaul University, USA

Qiang Tu, Rochester Institute of Technology, USA

Abstract

A primary objective of ERP is to integrate the various parts of a company. The chapter discusses six levels of enterprise integration and the ability of ERP to satisfy each of them. We analyzed six case studies that included IBM, Cisco, Tecktronic, Vandelay, China Holdings, and APD Manufacturing. We found evidence to support the existence of the six levels of integration. APD and China Holding did not exhibit evidence of global integration while the others did. System-User (Level–II) integration was missing from all except APD. Islands-of-Technology integration is no longer the dominant integration issue it was in the 80's. The dominant integration issues are functional integration, customer relationship management, and supply chain management.

Introduction

Companies are subjected to many business forces including globalization, an increasingly volatile environment, fast changing customer demand, shorter product life cycle, increasing market diversity, higher knowledge intensity, operational transparency, up-to-the-minute on-line transactions, improved coordination, and rapid advances in information technology (IT) (Madnick, 1991; Scott-Morton, 1991). Companies mitigate these forces by resorting to enterprise integration (Mathew, 2006; Mendoza, Perez, & Griman, 2006) using ERP, which is still the most sought after enterprise integration solution. ERP provides an integrated, comprehensive, updated, and realistic view of a company's operation (Scalle & Cotteler, 1999; Sheu, Yen, & Krumwiede, 2003). Evidence suggests that ERP improves company performance (Chalmeta, Campos, & Grangel, 2001; Laframboise, 2005; Mabert, Soni, & Venkataramanan, 2000; Ward, 2006). This is why 70% of the Fortune 1000 companies have installed or experimented with ERP (Bingi, Sharma, & Godla, 1999) and the market may grow to $60 billion or more by 2004 (Callaway, 2000; Mabert et al., 2000).

ERP implementations are costly (Jones & Young, 2006; Mabert et al., 2000; Sanchez, 2006), involve considerable technical and financial risks, and the expected financial and business returns are very high. This is why CEOs, CIOs, and CFOs find it difficult to justify ERP expenditures when financial benefits are uncertain (Davenport, 1998; Deutsch, 1998; Sheu et al., 2003; Wailgum, 2005). Therefore, understand the risks of using ERP as an enabler of integration are important because it has not always lived up to its expectation (Mabert et al., 2000; Wailgum, 2005). Two reasons are that it disrupts the business processes (Kremers & Van Dissel, 2000; Scheer & Habermann, 2000; Soh & Kien, 2000) and threatens corporate culture (Hasselbring, 2000; Ward, 2006). Disappointing ERP results (Gattiker, 2002; Markus & Tanis, 2000a; Saccomano, 1999; Scheer et al., 2000; Schulz, 2000; Songini, 2005; Wailgum 2005) and intractable implementations are well known (Davenport, 1998; Deutsch, 1998; Sheu et al., 2003; Wailgum, 2005). Consequently, we decided to investigate if various levels of enterprise integration exist in organizations and how effective is ERP in achieving them.

To satisfy our research objectives, we define six levels of enterprise integration and discuss the role of ERP. We then analyze six industry case studies for exploratory evidence of the six levels of integration. The published case studies used in this research serve as a reality substitute for industry practice, which is a widely accepted research method (Grant, 2002; Grant & Ngwenyama, 2003; Sheu et al., 2003). The evidence gleaned from the cases provides impetus for a larger, scientific study.

The rest of the chapter is organized as follows. The next section is a literature review of integration. The third section defines ERP and integration. A model of enterprise integration is proposed in the fourth section. The fifth section is an analysis of six case studies. The sixth section is a summary, including the limitations of the chapter. The chapter concludes with implications for future research.

Literature Review of Integration

According to Mathew (1988), the primary components to be integrated in a manufacturing system are management information systems (MIS), computer-aided design (CAD), and computer-aided manufacturing (CAM). The components of MIS are master scheduling and control, distribution management, accounting, and finance. CAM consists of process planning and control, process automation, and shop floor management. CAD consists of conceptualization, analysis, visualization, and detailing. The primary vehicle for integrating the three components of integration is an integrated database. The article provides a starting point for discussing integration, but it has some limitations. First, major and necessary components of information systems such as decision support systems (DSS), office information systems (OIS), and expert systems (ES) that are required for management decision-making are missing. These components are now known as business intelligence (BI) in ERP packages. Second, there is no discussion of integration at the organizational level: that is, how well integrated islands of technologies support the stated organizational goals and objectives. Third, integration is confined to the internal organization and ignores the external environment that includes integration between geographically dispersed sites, and alliances between different companies. It also ignores the ability of multi-national companies to effectively conduct business across diverse cultures, time, and geography. Finally, it does not consider integrating the user with the existing technology.

Bullers and Reid (1990) discuss the need for integrating the four major types of information systems (IS) that include electronic data processing (EDP), MIS, DSS, and ES with computerized manufacturing systems (CMS). They discuss four types of integration: (1) horizontal integration, (2) vertical integration, (3) temporal integration, and (4) physical integration. Horizontal integration involves coordination among the manufacturing functions. Vertical integration allows for the access of information to aid decision-making at the various levels of management. Temporal integration allows for the use of historical information to be used in future planning efforts. Physical integration promotes cooperation between geographically dispersed production facilities. While the framework provides a good foundation for a theory of integration, it has certain limitations. First, their discussion of physical integration is primarily to link geographically dispersed production facilities. However, a growing trend in today's environment is the forming of business alliances between competitors, suppliers, and vendors. Second, there is no discussion on whether or not the various integrated systems support the organization's goals and objectives. Integration is not an end in itself but a means for achieving the corporation's goals and objectives.

Burbidge, Falster, Riis, and Svendsen (1987) talk about the need for integration inside business functions, and across business functions. Integration across functional boundaries emphasizes the linking of major business functions such as marketing, production, and manufacturing. The basis for this integration originates from the need to share common goals and information, the need to communicate, and the need for consultation. The chapter has several limitations: (1) The idea of integration put forth in the framework is very limited and does not extend beyond the integration of functions; (2) It is possible for the functions of a company to be integrated while at the same time the company's goals and objectives are not met; (3) There is no discussion of integration that considers integration of geographically dispersed organizations, business alliances, or the external environment at large; (4) The basis for integration in and across functions is unclear. Will it be technology, procedures, rules, or some combination?

Meredith and Hill (1990) present a four-level taxonomy of integration for cost justification of various types of manufacturing machinery. Level-I integration consists of stand-alone hardware, commonly controlled by programmable controllers such as numerically controlled machines. They consider this the most common form of manufacturing automation. Level-II integration, a higher level of integration and communication, consists of multiple pieces of level-I equipment connected in a cellular configuration to perform multiple tasks on a family of parts. Examples of level-II technology are group technology (GT) lines and FMS. Level-III integration consists of linking cells or islands of automation from level-II integration into computerized information networks. This level of integration affects multiple departments and functions due to the changes brought about by the introduction of technology. Examples of level-III technology are CAD, CAM, and manufacturing requirements planning (MRP) II. They consider level-IV to be full integration that links the manufacturing function and all its interfaces through extensive networks. This taxonomy is limited for several reasons. First, integration is confined within the boundaries of the firm and does not consider integration between business partners, vendors, or geographically dispersed divisions. It also does not discuss whether integration supports the attainment of organizational goals and objectives.

Truman (2000) in a recent study investigated the integration issues in electronic exchange environments, especially the business-to-business electronic data interchange (EDI) system environment. This study is a great improvement from earlier works on integration because it applies to any industry that uses EDI. While all four studies quoted earlier are limited to the manufacturing function. Truman (2000) discussed two types of integration: interface integration and internal integration. Interface integration refers to the level of integration between an EDI system and internal systems of the organization. Internal integration is the level of integration among the organization's internal systems. This study is one-step further toward a theory of ERP integration. However, it is still limited to only the EDI system. Although EDI is a system that interconnects businesses, the study does not specify the roles of customers and suppliers in the integration relationship. Further, the discussions of integration ignore organizational goals, culture, and corporate strategies. Finally, different types of internal systems, that is, functional areas, are not identified. As a result, this two-level integration model appears to be too rough to form a good theoretical foundation for successful ERP implementation. A summary of the strengths and weaknesses of the models reviewed in this section is shown in Table 1.

Table 1. Summary of integration models

Models of Integration	Strengths	Weaknesses
Mathew (1988)	MIS, CAD, CAM, integrated DB	Ignores integration between functions, integration between firms, global integration, user integration, temporal integration; shared vision; strategic integration
Burbidge et al. (1987)	Inter business function and intra business function integration	Ignores, integration between firms, global integration, user integration, temporal integration; shared vision; strategic integration
Bullers et al. (1990)	EDP, MIS, DSS, ES, CMS, horizontal, vertical, temporal and physical integration	Ignores, integration between firms, global integration, user integration; shared vision; strategic integration
Meredith et al. (1990)	Level-1: Integration of Standalone hardware; Level-II: standalone hardware connected; Level-III: linking islands of technology	Ignores, integration between firms, global integration, user integration, temporal integration; shared vision; strategic integration
Truman (2000)	B2BEDI; interface integration; internal integration	Ignores, integration between firms, global integration, user integration, temporal integration; shared vision; strategic integration

ERP and Integration

ERP emerged in the late 1980s as a derivative of material requirement planning (MRP) systems that convert master production plans into detailed requirement schedule of raw materials and components. MRP II, an enhanced version of MRP, improves manufacturing system integration by sharing data from several different functional areas, including sales, production, inventory, finance, and accounting. Today's ERP applications are rooted in MRP II (Laframboise, 2005; Markus et al., 2000a) but differ in many ways. They commonly run on client/server architecture instead of MRP II mainframe-based technology. ERP applications support an even broader range of business processes and functional areas than MRP II, and they are used in a variety of industries including manufacturing.

A typical ERP application supports cross-functional business processes by linking the following six primary business functions: (1) accounting and controlling; (2) HR management; (3) production and materials management; (4) project management; (5) quality management and plant maintenance; and (6) sales and distribution (Callaway, 1999; Ward, 2006). Recently, ERP vendors are branching into new areas such as supply chain management (SCM), e-commerce, customer relationship management (CRM), and business intelligence (BI) (Callaway, 2000).

The expected tangible and intangible benefits of implementing ERP include inventory reduction, personnel reduction, improved order management, reduced IT costs, improved responsiveness to customers, standardization of computer platforms, global sharing of information, and Y2K compliance. The primary strategic advantage and the ultimate goal of ERP is enhanced system integration (Bingi et al., 1999). Improve business process integration is the precondition for realizing additional benefits that organizations expect to achieve through ERP implementation.

Integration is the bringing together of related components to form a unified whole. It provides the foundation for coordination, collaboration, and synergy, and it suggests a holistic approach to decision-making, management, and control. We define integration as the collection of related entities, such as computer information systems, manufacturing systems, engineering systems, production systems, management systems, distribution systems, financial systems, accounting systems, and people, to form a unified whole. These entities, when optimally combined, should perform in concert to support and achieve an organization's goals and objectives (Grant, 1995). Entire organizations, not just the manufacturing function, should be well integrated if they are to successfully compete in the global economy. The timely information required for collaboration, coordination, synergy, control, decision-making, and management of organizations will not be realized if companies avoid taking a holistic approach to integration. ERP, if used effectively, can help organizations to achieve improved integration.

The definition of integration is often taken for granted. This has led to conflicting claims by companies of having achieved integration through ERP, but with very different performance outcomes. The problem resides in an older industrial mindset that still dominates many managers, that is, the "technology imperative", which views technology as an exogenous driving force that determines or constrains the behavior of individuals and organizations, which means technology implements itself (Markus & Robey, 1988). Unfortunately, this technology-dictates-itself mindset no longer works in a highly uncertain and competitive post-industrial environment. Clemons and Row (1991) pointed out that, when identical technology is available and applications can be easily duplicated, sustaining technology advantage will not come from whether you have it, but from how effectively it is used. ERP is not a panacea for all performance problems, but rather an enabler for business process integration.

An examination of companies that implemented ERP would reveal that they are at different stages of integration. Main (1990) has questioned whether some firms have achieved it. He thinks there is no universally accepted definition and objective measures of integration. Multiple definitions, subjective measures, and their concomitant interpretations are testaments that integration is neither static nor absolute. Therefore, we need better definitions of integration and a framework that accommodates multiple levels of ERP integration. This may aid in the understanding, managing, and implementing of ERP. Toward this end, we propose a six-level taxonomy of varying degrees of integration exemplified in practice and discussed in the literature. It provides a measure of objectivity for future deliberations on ERP integration.

Proposed Model of ERP Integration

Given the limitations of existing models of integration and the state of ERP implementation practices, we propose a six-level model of ERP integration shown in Figure 1. It is a stage-growth maturity model for achieving integration using ERP (Holland & Light, 2001). Figure 1 depicts the environment as a rectangle and the firm as a circle. The firm is comprised of six interrelated levels of integration. It is connected to the environment via inputs and outputs depicted with the heavy arrows. The smaller arrows depict the connection between various levels of integration. For example, the two rectangles representing the islands of technology integration are connected via a single arrow. The various types of integration that comprise each of the six levels are listed in Table 2.

Figure 1. The firm as a system comprised of six levels of ERP integration

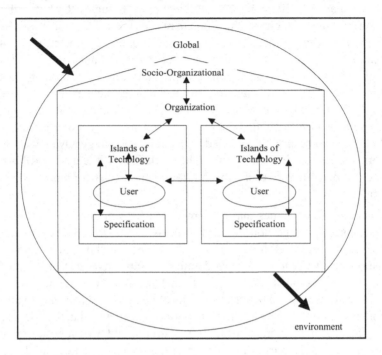

Table 2. Types of integration at each of the six levels

Levels of Integration	Types of integration
Global Integration	Internal horizontal Internal temporal Cultural
Socio-Organizational Integration	External horizontal External vertical External temporal Shared-vision
Organization Integration	Internal vertical Internal horizontal Internal temporal Strategic
Islands of Technology Integration	Horizontal Vertical
System-User Integration	Ergonomic Cognitive
System-Specification Integration	Specification Compatibility

Level-1: System-Specification Integration

System-specification is the lowest level of integration. It is concerned with two types of integration: specification integration and compatibility integration. Specification integration satisfies the system technical design specifications at the software, hardware, and application level of stand-alone equipment. It shares characteristics that are similar to middleware integration by Hasselbring (2000), level-1 integration by Meredith and Hill (1990), and internal integration by Truman (2000). The primary concern is to ensure that the system performs its prescribed function as required by users in the most efficient and effective manner. Compatibility integration addresses the level of compatibility between the various system components. For example, application programs and other software must be compatible with the operating system. Compatibility should also concern itself with the efficient use of human resources (Rotemberg & Saloner, 1991). These two types of integration are closely related because incompatibility will adversely affect specification integration and render the system ineffective. System-specification integration requires the computer hardware to support the minimum specification of the ERP application, and the ERP software compatible with the computer operating system. Since this is the lowest level of integration, most companies experience little difficulty achieving it. Because technology companies specify the system specifications required to run an application, we believe that system-specification integration is widespread.

Level-II: System-User Integration

There is no parallel to this type of integration in the literature reviewed earlier. However, we did find one source where user compatibility integration was briefly discussed (Rotemberg & Saloner, 1991). System-user integration is primarily concerned with ensuring that users are integrated with the technology, and the environment. At this level, there are two types of integration: ergonomic integration and cognitive integration. Ergonomic integration ensures that the system and the environment are ergonomically designed. This means that users' graphical user interface, keyboard, software, and hardware are user-friendly. Cognitive integration ensures that the communication (i.e., error messages, information, etc.) between system and user is intelligible, useful, and consistent with the user's frame of reference. Integration between the user, the technology, and the environment cannot be achieved if the user suffers cognitive dissonance. Therefore, the primary concern of integration is "oneness" and "harmony" between user, technology, and environment. The level of integration that exists between a fighter pilot, his equipment, the information received from his console, and his commanding officers while in the heat of battle, is a good example of system-user integration. Significant amount of user training and further refinement of ERP applications is needed to achieve this level of integration. In fact, a major user complaint about SAP and other ERP applications is the lack of transparency and intuitiveness about where to find information.

Level-III: Islands of Technology Integration

This level attempts to physically link geographically dispersed islands of technology throughout the firm. Integration at this level concerns the ability of these islands to communicate with each other. Islands of technology integration has characteristics similar to internal integration (Truman, 2000), level-II integration (Meredith & Hill, 1990), functional integration (Burbidge et al., 1987), horizontal integration (Bullers & Reid, 1990), data integration (Bhatt, 2000), enterprise integration (Hasselbring, 2000; Mendoza et al., 2006; Rotemberg & Saloner, 1991), and system integration (Rockart & Sbort, 1989). Many companies have invested heavily to integrate islands of technology developed in isolation to solve specific business problems. These islands resulted from ad-hoc development that lacked enterprise-wide integration (Mathew, 2006; Themistocleous & Irani, 2002). Consequently, many of them have been difficult, expensive, and sometimes impossible to integrate. ERP is sometimes a solution to this problem (Truman, 2000) and previous problems (e.g., Y2K problem).

At level-III, two types of integration are required: horizontal integration and vertical integration, both of which are necessary for sharing information between the islands. Horizontal integration is the passing of data between islands to facilitate coordination, collaboration, decision-making, and task performance. Vertical integration is required for the passing of data for management control. The data consist primarily of technical instructions used to monitor and control the technology. Islands of technology integration is typically easy to achieve by an ERP system because the whole package is designed for data compatibility. It may be challenged if it has to integrate with older legacy systems. However, when companies are pressed for time and money, they sometimes implement just a few ERP modules; the result of this is isolated islands of technology. Thus, a carefully planned enterprise-wide rollout of ERP implementation is recommended, but that requires tremendous amount of coordination, resource allocation, change management, and executive management support.

Level-IV: Organization Integration

This level ensures that the company is integrated as a unified whole and not just the technology. The primary focus of organization integration is the ability of islands of technology to support the business goals and objectives across multiple divisions of the company. The lack of organization integration may be reflected in several ways: (1) the poor quality products/services; (2) failure to meet performance expectations; (3) major cost overrun; (4) large number of customer complaints; etc.

This type of integration is concerned with value-chain integration that manages the efforts of various functions across the value-chain (Rockart et al., 1989; Sheu et al., 2003). Functional integration (Al-Mashari & Zairi, 2000; Burbidge et al., 1987; Hammer & Stanton, 1999; Yates & Benjamin, 1991), electronic exchange environments (Truman, 2000), and level-IV integration (Meredith & Hill, 1990), and interrelatedness (Rotemberg & Saloner, 1991) captures part of the essence of organization integration. What they neglected to consider is the ability of the company to achieve its business goals. This is why executives have questioned the value of information systems (IS) when corporate goals are elusive (Ciborra & Jelassi, 1994; Maglitta, 1993). Enterprise-wide implementation of ERP systems in large complex companies is rare (Markus et al., 2000a). This level of integration often requires firms to re-engineer their business processes (Bhatt, 2000), a difficult, disruptive, and painful undertaking. Many ERP failures are due to business problems instead of technical problems (Davenport, 1998; Kumar & Hillegersberg, 2000; Markus et al., 2000). These business problems called "misfits", are the gap between the functionality offered by ERP systems and that required by the adopting company (Sharif, Irani, & Love, 2005; Soh et al., 2000). This may explain why ERP consultants are usually challenged to achieve this level of integration.

There are four types of integration at this level: (1) internal vertical integration, (2) internal horizontal integration, (3) strategic integration, and (4) internal temporal integration. This level of integration is different from level-III because it focuses primarily on the speed, quality, information content, presentation of information, and the ability to analyze and disseminate the information, rather than simple technical data format compatibility. The business intelligence (BI) modules of ERP play an important role here.

Internal vertical integration is the passing of information from strategic management to non-management and vice versa. In the high-performance air cargo industry, vertical integration is the most dominant organizational structure (Foster & Regan, 2001). Companies that exhibit internal vertical integration have effective means of transmitting information up and down the company. This information is important for management control, strategy, and policy formulation. Effective vertical integration may require flattening the management hierarchy and widening the channels of communication. Internal horizontal integration or functional integration (Rockart et al., 1989) is the passing of information between business functions, groups, and individuals to enable collaboration and coordination to take place. Strategic integration measures how well the information systems support the organization's strategic goals, objectives, and critical success factors (CSF). Strategic structural changes may be necessary to capitalize on the intended benefits of ERP (Markus et al., 2000a). It may include strategies to take full advantage of ERP technology. For example, if product quality is a CSF, then the quality management ERP module should be carefully evaluated to see if it improves the product quality. Strategic integration is so important that when companies fail to release major products or services as planned, Wall Street often reacts negatively by temporarily lowering the company's stock price. Internal temporal integration is a measure of the effectiveness that exists between groups, functions, departments, and individuals. It also measures how well the systems that support them coordinate their work activities on a timely basis, and may include the use of historical data for future planning decisions (Bullers & Reid, 1990).

Level-V: Socio-Organizational Integration

Level-V integration extends beyond the brick and mortar of companies to include the social-external (socio) environment. The social-external environment includes industry, government, and civic institutions. It seeks to integrate customer relationship management, supply chain management (Mendoza et al., 2006; Sheu et al., 2003), and the coordination of the task environment (Truman, 2000). Many companies have used electronic data interchange (EDI) as a means of achieving level-V integration referred to by Truman (2000) as interface integration. EDI is a requirement for doing business in several industries (Enunelhainz, 1993) and there is strong evidence for its use (Choudhury, 1997; Hart & Estrin, 1991; Iacovou, Benbasat, & Dexter, 1995; Nygaard-Andersen & Bjorn-Andersen, 1994; Ramamurthy, Premkumar, & Crum, 1999). It has become the standard in the automotive and other industries (Cash, Eccles, Nohria, & Nolan, 1994). E-commerce is another strategy to achieve level-V integration (Scheer et al., 2000). U.S. law enforcement, since the September 11th tragedy, has taken steps to achieve level-V integration across state, federal, and local law enforcement and non-law enforcement institutions such as the Immigration and Naturalization Service and Inland Revenue Service.

Earlier generations of ERP consisted of modules that processed information related to accounting, sales, production, human resource, and quality control (Callaway, 1999). They did not consider the processing of information about markets, competitors, customers, industries, and distribution channels (Li, 1999). However, many firms have realized the importance of inter-organizational integration and demanded that future generations of ERP systems be better equipped. According to Li (1999), these new ERP systems may be called TIS (total information solution) or ELM (external information management). Consequently, we have seen efforts from major ERP software vendors to integrate traditional ERP systems with supply chain management (SCM) systems (Scheer et al., 2000; Zheng, Yen, & Tarn, 2000).

Customer relationship management (CRM) functions are being considered for future ERP applications. Furthermore, several major ERP suites are now Web-enabled for e-business (Callaway, 2000). Even though technology for level-V integration is available, companies that actually achieved this level of integration through ERP implementation are rare because they must satisfy four types of integration.

The four types of integration are: (1) external horizontal, (2) external vertical, (3) external temporal, and (4) shared-vision integration. External horizontal integration is similar to internal horizontal; the difference is that it takes place outside the firm. It measures the level of integration between firms, their customers, and suppliers. External vertical integration measures how well companies are integrated with external control agencies such as city, state, and federal institutions. The term vertical integration describes the hierarchy of control exerted by regulatory institutions that enforce state and federal laws.

External temporal integration is similar to internal temporal integration. The difference is that it is concerned with integration outside the firm. It measures how well companies coordinate their activities with external institutions on a timely basis. External temporal should also consider the effect of doing business in different time zones (Mountain, Pacific, etc.). Shared-vision integration is the sharing of a common vision between business partners. This is extremely important for collaboration, business alliances, and affiliate programs because if a shared vision cannot be developed and effectively communicated, failure is likely to occur. Therefore, it is important that business partners develop a shared, common, and consistent vision acceptable to all stakeholders. For example, if company A buys parts from company B, then both companies should develop a common understanding of acceptable product quality. This is a common occurrence in the automotive industry. Finally, for effective partnership alliances to exist, policies, strategies, rules, and regulations must be mutually beneficial to all partners.

Level-VI: Global Integration

Level-VI is integration across national and cultural boundaries, the highest level of integration (Rochester & Douglass, 1992). This level of integration deals with issues of language, time difference, culture, politics, customs, management style, and so on (Hofstede, 1983; Simchi-Levi, Kaminsky, & Simchi-Levi, 2000; Trompenaars & Hampden-Turner, 1998). According to Barker (1993), companies that are equipped with information technology to do business around the clock and the world will thrive in a rapidly evolving global economy. Global competition has become the rule rather than the exception for many industries (Karimi, Gupta, & Somers, 1996). Deans and Kane (1992) suggest that businesses in the future may be viewed as international with a domestic component. Companies must operate as a single global entity rather than as a series of independent geographic entities (Ein-Dor & Segev, 1993; Fiderio, 1990). Coordinating a firm's activities around the world requires extremely good information sharing and communication.

Global integration must consider three types of integration: (1) international horizontal integration, (2) international temporal integration, and (3) cultural integration. International horizontal and international temporal integration encompasses Sheu et al.'s (2003) idea of international supply chain integration. International horizontal integration is concerned with the effectiveness of doing business across national borders and refers to all data and information that cross them. The four key linkages that facilitate the flow of information include organization, technical, data, and communication (Mandell, 1975). The organization component is concerned with the planning, control, and support of the information systems linkage. The technical component is concerned with hardware and software compatibility between sites. The data component is concerned with data definitions, record layouts, and database specifications. The communication component describes the level and detail of transactions and the type of processing. These pose unique problems, challenges, and opportunities not typically encountered by domestic firms. According to Dean and Kane (1992), the international transfer and management of information systems technology increase in complexity due to the variety of cultures, governments, legal systems, and environments in which the firms operate.

International temporal integration is related to companies to do business in several countries with different time zones. For example, U.S. workers are usually asleep when African and Australian workers are on the job. The problem is how best to address these and other related concerns. Some companies have taken advantage of the time difference by instituting around the clock programming. Cultural integration forces companies to recognize the differences and nuances of other cultures. Different cultures pose unique language, cultural, legal, economic, and political problems. The ability to adjust to these situations dictates the success of global companies. Integration can be a vehicle for dealing with these situations.

Phatak (1989) identified four primary components of the international environment: legal, cultural, economic, and political. Under each of the four, there are several issues to discuss. With respect to culture, consider a team of U.S. and Japanese developers collaborating on a project. Should members from both teams be able to speak a common language, and if so, what language should it be? On the other hand, if data are transmitted back and forth, in what language should the data be written or should computers at the different sites be able to convert English to Japanese and vice versa? How do we deal with words in Japanese that have no English equivalent and vice versa? From a legal perspective, how do companies transfer information and data across national boundaries when there may be legal restrictions on information transfer and the use of specific equipment? For economic and political reasons, foreign companies operating in Europe may have to choose between Q90,

ISO 9000 or IS0 9001 standards. A truly successful ERP implementation should address these relevant issues. While current ERP systems are unable to effectively address such issues, companies like Scala Business Solutions do integrate Internet technology with traditional ERP to make global business simpler (Burdett, 2001). Multi-site ERP implementation has addressed a limited number of the issues but many remain unresolved (Markus et al., 2000a). With all of these issues to consider, truly enterprise-wide implementation of ERP in large complex organizations is the exception rather than the rule (Markus et al., 2000a).

Case Study

The Research Design

To provide empirical evidence of the six levels of integration, we carefully analyzed ERP implementation of six companies using well-known case studies from the MIS literature. The companies in the study include IBM, Cisco, Tecktronic, Vandelay, China Holdings, and APD Manufacturing

Since past research has not addressed the issue of levels of ERP enterprise integration, this analysis is exploratory in nature. We believe the use of case studies is appropriate for exploring and understanding the various levels of integration. We carefully selected case studies of representative companies that use and implement ERP. The size of these companies is medium to large, has multiple geographical locations, and may be multi-national. Such companies likely exhibit each of the six levels of enterprise integration discussed earlier.

The process of selecting the case studies was based on four criteria.

1. Case studies familiar to researchers and practitioners in MIS
2. Case studies with a large number of enterprise integration issues
3. Case studies that exhibit integration issues from several integration levels
4. To find a good mix of case studies that included multi-national and domestic companies

Case Data Analysis

We analyzed each case to identify the presence of levels of enterprise integration (cf. column 3). Each time we found an integration issue or problem, we recorded

Table 3.

Evidence from Tecktronic Case	Levels of Integration Issues	Integration Levels
Global implementation	International horizontal integration	6
International presence	International horizontal integration	6
Lack of technology standards	Incompatibility	3
Problems with IT infrastructure	Islands of technology	3
No commonality among business processes	Lack of functional integration	4
Need for multiple order entry	Incompatibility	3
Need for manual coordination	Re-entry of data	3
Lack of accurate info on company performance (level 3,4,5,6)	Unable to satisfy company objectives	4
Implementing a single world-wide financial and accounting system	Unable to satisfy company objectives	4
Required standardization among Divisions	Unable to satisfy company objectives;	4
	Unable to do business across national borders	6
Improved data integration	Re-entry of data; Lack of visibility	3,4

it in column 1. There was no attempt to eliminate duplicate issues because it was important to get a total tally of how many times a particular issue was mentioned. The issues from column 1 are mapped to specific integration issues (cf. column 2 of table) discussed in the proposed integration model. Column 3 captures the level of integration that was affected. For example, having to re-enter data multiple times (column 1) indicates incompatible systems (column 2), a violation of level-III (column 3). Tables 3-8 capture the individual results of each case study.

Discussions and Implications

In the case of Tecktronic, we found evidence of levels 3,4,6—Vandelay levels 3,4,5,6; IBM levels 3,4,5,6; CISCO levels 1,3,4,5,6; China Holdings levels 3,4,5; and APD levels 2,3,4,5. Across all six companies collectively, we found evidence of the six levels of integration. APD and China Holdings did not exhibit evidence of level-6 (i.e., global integration). It appears that China Holdings and APD are not multi-national corporations and so there were no evidence of global integration

Table 4.

Evidence from Vandelay Case	Levels of Integration Issues	Integration Levels
Global implementation	International horizontal integration	6
International presence	International horizontal integration	6
Widespread business practice changes	BPR changes	4
Inefficient production systems	Lack of internal horizontal and vertical integration	4
Long product lead-times	Lack of internal horizontal integration	4
Time spent on information transfer steps	Reprocessing of information Incompatibility; islands of technology	3
Multiple dissimilar systems and software	Islands of technology	3
Integration across sites is difficult	Lack of strategic integration	4
Manual re-entry of data	Re-entry of data	3
Deluged with customer complaints	Customer complaints; Unable to satisfy company objectives	4
Order taken manually and then rerouted via fax	No electronic means of doing business	4
Incompatible human resource systems	Incompatible systems	3
Manufacturing software not integrated with the site's financial package	Incompatible systems; Lack of strategic integration	3
Varied business practices	BPR	4
Flawed processes	BPR	4
Need for ERP to coordinate organizational functions	Lack of integration across functions	4
Ability to coordinate sites more tightly	Lack of strategic integration	4
Redundant entry and "hand-offs" between application	Re-entry of data	4
Align operations with new business practices	Lack of strategic integration	4

present. The highest level of integration present in these two companies was socio-organizational integration that deals with supply chain and customer-relationship management issues. Tecktronic, Vandelay, IBM, and CISCO are multi-national corporations and evidence of global integration was present.

CISCO was the only company that exhibited clear evidence of level-I integration. Unless something goes drastically wrong at a company, which was the case at CISCO, level-I is seldom an enterprise integration problem. In addition, we expected level-I

Table 5.

Evidence from IBM Case	Levels of Integration Issues	Integration Levels
Linking with customers	CRM	5
Virtual enterprise	Linking with industry partners	5
EDI	EDI	5
Application-to-application integration	Islands of technology	3
Linking 40 facilities around the world	International horizontal integration	6
Problematic order fulfillment and billing	Failure to meet performance expectations	4
Linking facilities in many countries	International horizontal integration	6
Translation between Thai and Hungarian languages	Ability to translate between languages	6
Improve customer responsiveness	Reducing customer complaints	4
Linking sites using a VAN	Technology to support business goals	4
Patchwork of fragmented system	Islands of technology	3
Standards and technology to support a vision	Shared-vision integration	5
Shared vision integration	Shared-vision integration	5
Integrating functions, processes and data	Functional integration	4
External EDI links	EDI	4
Ability to support PC manufacturers (i.e., customers)	CRM integration	5
Application-to-application integration	Horizontal technical integration	3

integration to be easily satisfied. These two reasons may help explain why evidence of level-I is so scant among the six companies. Evidence of level-II integration was missing from all except APD Manufacturing. The issue in the ADP case was user involvement not ergonomic or cognitive as outlined in the model. Some possible explanations for the lack of overwhelming evidence of level-II integration are as follows:

1. Ergonomic and cognitive issues affect individuals differently, and it is customary for users not to complain about cognitive-related problems.

Table 6.

Evidence from CISCO (ERP & Web-enabled) Case	Levels of Integration Issues	Integration Levels
Systems not meeting management requirements	Inability to meet Organization goals	4
Legacy systems failed	Specification requirements	1
Inability of systems to perform	Specification requirements	1
Company shut down for 2 days	Specification requirements	1
Systems on the brink of actual failure	Specification requirements	1
Replace all IT applications and platforms world-wide	Islands of technology integration	3
Investment in Internet and intranet applications	External horizontal integration	5
Business partners and suppliers are linked to the company	External horizontal integration	5
Business processes built on global Internet	International horizontal integration	6
Links to strategic vendor and customers		5
Technical support to customers and resellers delivered electronically	Shared-vision integration	5
Using the internet for full electronic commerce, the biggest in the world	External horizontal integration	5
Implementing applications to support suppliers and customers	External horizontal integration	5
Integrating suppliers into its production systems	External horizontal integration	5
Companies with congruent vision are considered for takeover	External horizontal integration Shared-vision integration	5

2. Users have come to expect error messages and other cognitive expressions from IT to be cryptic and they do not expect a company to undertake a major effort to improve them.

3. Some applications no longer require users to interpret error messages anymore because the application sends information electronically to the software vendor.

4. The design of modern user interfaces has reduced cognitive issues by making them more transparent and user friendly.

5. New generations of IT have improved ergonomically, hence it is no longer a major problem.

Table 7.

Evidence from China Holdings Limited Case	Levels of Integration Issues	Integration Levels
Becoming an e-commerce player	External horizontal integration	5
Integrating all branches and multi-division integration	Internal horizontal and Vertical integration	4
Integrate systems across geographically dispersed sites	Islands of technology integration	3
ERP as a basis for SCM	SCM or External horizontal integration	5
Online TPS linked to ERP	Islands of technology integration	3
Agents in 30 cities ordering online	Internal horizontal integration	4
The need for re-engineering	BRP changes	4
Integrate data across functions	Functional integration	4
Transactions with customers and suppliers conducted online	External horizontal integration	5
Create supply chain management platforms	External temporal or horizontal integration	5

Table 8.

Evidence from APD Manufacturing Plant Case	Levels of Integration Issues	Integration Levels
Information systems becoming less viable	No organization integration Islands of technology	4
Each system unique and unstandardized		3
Updates and maintenance very costly	Major costs overruns	
The need for centralized accounting system	Lack of internal horizontal & vertical integration	4 4
Relatively high accounting expenses	Major costs overruns	
Low manufacturing revenues	Lack of strategic integration	4
Customers' interests not met	Supply chain management	4
Difficulty from the interdependence between manufacturing and other functions	Incompatibility and islands of technology	5 3
Misfit between systems and processes	BPR changes needed	
Lack of user involvement	User integration	4 2

Across all six cases, we found nine observations of level-VI, 19 observations of level-V, 33 observations of level-IV, 17 observations of level-III, two observations of level-II, and four observations of level-I. Levels-IV, V, VI account for 73% of the total observations while levels-I, II, III account for 27%. This is consistent with our expectations because we argued that ERP has difficulty in achieving integration at levels-IV-VI while it does a good job at the levels-I-III. We believe from the outset that there is a marked difference between levels-I-III and levels-IV-VI. Levels-I-III are much easier to achieve than levels-IV-VI and the data support that by the larger percentage of observations coming from levels-IV-VI. The state of the industry seems to be at level-IV since it accounts for 40% of the observations. The dominant issue at level-IV is functional integration. Initially, we had surmised that islands of technology would be the dominant issue. It certainly was the case back in the late 80's. However, the data suggest that the current and dominant issues are related to level-IV followed by level-V with 23%, level-III with 20%, level-VI with 11%, level-I with 5%, and level-II with 1%.

We argue that higher levels of integration build upon the lower levels, therefore the 33 observations at level-IV might suggest that most companies are at level-IV. We believe that higher levels of integration are more difficult to achieve because the issues are process and culture related as opposed to technical. This might explain why, at levels-IV-VI, the higher we go up the integration ladder, the less observations we see. The nine observations at level-VI could also result from two of the six companies operating domestically. This supports our argument that level-VI integration is inappropriate for domestic companies.

At level-VI, the data suggest that companies are mostly concerned with international horizontal integration. It occurred about 75% of the time. At level-V, companies are predominantly concerned with CRM and supply-chain issues. These account for 68% of the observations at this level. At level-IV, companies struggle with the lack of integration across functions and this seems to define that nature of the ERP industry at this time. It accounts for 33% of the observations at level-IV and 33% of all observations. At level-III, the predominant issue is islands of technology integration followed by incompatibility issues. Islands of technology accounted for about 50% of the observations at level-III. Islands of technology and incompatibility together, account for about 82% of observations at level-III. We argued earlier that islands of technology were developed in isolation to address specific organizational problems; consequently, this and the incompatibility issue are intertwined; if one issue is present, we expect to find evidence of the other. The four observations of specification requirements present at level-I came from CISCO.

Because the study is based on six companies, one limitation of it is that the results may not be generalizable. However, Gummesson (1991) argues that applying an approach to one problem at a time increases the stock of theoretical knowledge on a subject by publishing the results in established journals. It then becomes the basis for further investigation and for formulating testable hypotheses (Baskerville, 1996). Baskerville and Lee (1999) and Grant and Ngwenyama (2003) also addressed this issue at length by discussing four types of generalizing in IS research. Galliers (1994) argues that no approach is universally applicable to all problem situations. Yet, it is possible that one or a limited number of case studies can be used to identify general properties (Baskerville, 1996; Fleck, 1979; Galliers, 1994; Gummesson, 1991).

Summary and Future Research Directions

We reviewed and analyzed seminal papers on integration. We then defined ERP and integration. Given the limitations of existing models of integration, we develop our own. Each of the six levels of integration builds upon the lower levels. For example, integration levels I and II are necessary for the successful linking of ERP islands of technology at level-III. This is why companies that claim level-IV integration while level-III remains elusive are really at level-II. Global integration is the highest level but it may be inappropriate for domestic firms.

ERP is very capable of satisfying integration at level-I, but by itself, cannot achieve level-II integration. For this to happen, developers must address the people and ergonomic issues. For example, users require extensive training and technical support on the use of newly implemented ERP systems. Failure to provide it often leads to ERP implementation failure (Gattiker, 2002). According to Bhatt (2000), ERP is a good solution to level-III integration. However, he argues against a piece-meal approach to implementing ERP because it could lead to isolated islands of ERP technologies. Therefore, we recommend an enterprise-wide roll out of ERP (Markus et al., 2000a, 2000b). Success at level-IV is more difficult to achieve because the technology by itself is not enough. It requires additional change management initiatives like BPR. Moreover, successful ERP implementation at level-IV requires satisfying four types of integration. Sharif, Irani, and Love (2005) provided a good case example of failed ERP integration efforts of a renowned industrial products company. They did quite well in achieving level-I through level-III integration due to their strong internal technical capability, but the project ultimately failed due to level-IV organizational integration issues, including problems in change management, lack of cross-divisional communications and collaboration, and a strong silo mentality.

The most difficult type is strategic integration that supports the organization's strategic objectives and mission. Current and earlier versions of ERP do not support level-V integration because they are grossly inadequate with respect to markets, competitors, industries, and distribution-channels support. Another type of integration that must be satisfied at level-V is shared-vision integration. There has been no public announcement that future releases of ERP will satisfy this type of integration (Markus et al., 2000a). We believe that ERP does a satisfactory job at achieving integration at levels-I, II, and III, but is severely challenged at levels-IV-VI.

We are not suggesting that integration is the ultimate goal for all firms because we are quite aware that some firms prefer to operate as autonomous divisions. In addition, level-VI integration may not be appropriate for some firms. In the APD case, it appears that the company had no international component and as a result, we saw no evidence of global integration. Therefore, some firms may pursue level-IV while others may pursue level-V or level-VI. Even autonomous divisions will pursue some level of integration that is required for the smooth functioning of the company. Therefore, each company has to make a decision as to which level of integration is appropriate. Integration is one of several strategies employed to sustain a company long-term success. It is often employed alongside other strategies such as differentiation (Lawrence & Lorsch, 1967), cost leadership and so on.

Future research can extend the current study by using a large-scale survey method. Such an empirical investigation can answer several research questions on the subject.

We can test scientifically, using a much larger sample, if each of the six levels of integration exists in practice. This will help to validate and legitimize the model, and its potential for research and practice. We can also investigate if other levels of integration are missing from the taxonomy. We can then develop measurement criteria to analyze the implementation success of particular levels of integration and the critical success factors for achieving them. One question is what issues, problems, and success factors are associated with each of the six integration levels. This exploratory study provides a starting point for identifying problems and issues at each of the six levels. What are appropriate levels of enterprise integration that companies might pursue? The six levels may aid companies in gauging their level of success concerning integration. We could investigate if different levels of integration require different management philosophies, strategies, training, and education. We can try to understand which management techniques, methods, and frameworks are appropriate for managing the various levels of integration. Lastly, we can investigate what methods are appropriate for justifying IT at the various levels of integration (Meredith & Hill, 1990).

References

Al-Mashari, M., & Zairi, M. (2000). Supply-chain reengineering using enterprise resource planning (ERP) systems: An analysis of a SAP R/3 implementation case. *International Journal of Physical Distribution & Logistics Management, 30*(3), 296-313.

Barker, R. M. (1993). Information systems development in a global environment. *Business Forum*, Winter/Spring, 57-59.

Baskerville, R. (1996). Deferring generalizability: Four classes of generalizing in social inquiry. *Scandinavian Journal of information Systems, 8*(2), 5-28.

Baskerville, R., & Lee, A. (1999). Distinction among different types of generalizing in information systems research. In O. Ngwenyama, I. Introna, M. Myers, & J. I. Degross (Eds.), *New information technologies in organizational processes: Field studies and theoretical reflections on the future of work* (pp. 49-65). New York: Kluwer Academic Publishers.

Bhatt, G. D. (2000). An empirical examination of the effects of information systems integration on business process improvement. *International Journal of Operations & Production Management, 20*(11), 1331-1358.

Bingi, P., Sharma, M. K., & Godla, J. K. (1999). Critical issues affecting an ERP implementation. *Information Systems Management, 16*(3), 7-14.

Bullers, W., & Reid, R. (1990). Towards a comprehensive conceptual framework for computer integrated manufacturing. *Journal of Information and Management, 18*, 57-67.

Burbidge, J. L., Falster, P., Riis, J. O., & Svendsen, O. M. (1987). Integration in Manufacturing. *Computers in Industry, 9*, 297-305.

Burdett, M. (2001). *Scala business solutions: Scala sees solid growth potential in Asia Pacific*. Bath, UK: M2 Communications Ltd.

Callaway, E. (1999). *Enterprise resource planning: Integrating applications and business process across the enterprise*. Charleston, SC: Computer Technology Research Corp.

Callaway, E. (2000). *ERP—the next generation: ERP is Web enabled for e-business*. Charleston, SC: Computer Technology Research Corp.

Cash, J., Eccles, R., Nohria, N., & Nolan, R. (1994). *Building the information-age organization: Structure, control, and information technologies* (3rd ed.). Boston, MA: Irwin.

Chalmeta, C., Campos, C., & Grangel, R. (2001). References architectures for enterprise integration. *The Journal of Systems and Software, 57*, 175-191.

Choudhury, V. (1997). Strategic choices in the development of interorganizational information systems. *Information Systems Research, 8*(1), 1-24.

Clemons, E. K., & Row, M. C. (1991). Sustaining IT advantage: The role of structural differences. *MIS Quarterly, 15*(3), 275-292.

Ciborra, C., & Jelassi, T. (1994). *Strategic information system: A European perspective*. New York: John Wiley.

Davenport, T. (1998). Putting the enterprise into the enterprise system. *Harvard Business Review, 76*(4), 121-131.

Deans, C., & Kane, M. (1992). *International dimensions of information systems technology*. Boston: PWS Kent Publishing Company.

Deutsch, C. (1998). Software that can make a grown company cry. *New York Times*, November 8.

Ein-Dor, P., & Segev, E. (1993). The effect of national culture on IS: Implications for international information systems. *Journal of Global Information Management, 1*(1), 33-44.

Enunelhainz, M. (1993). *EDI: A total management guide* (2nd ed.). New York: Van Nostrand Reinhold.

Fiderio, J. (1990, October). Information must conform in a world without borders. *Computerworld, 24*(40), 91-94.

Fleck, L. (1979). *Genesis and development of a scientific fact*. Chicago: University of Chicago Press.

Foster, P., & Regan, A. (2001). Electronic integration in the air cargo industry: An information processing model of on-time performance. *Transportation Journal, 40*(4), 46-61.

Galliers, R. (1994). *Information systems research: Issues methods and practical guidelines*. London: Alfred Waller Publishers.

Gattiker, T. F. (2002). Anatomy of an ERP implementation gone awry. *Production and Inventory Management Journal*, Third/Fourth Quarter, 96-105.

Grant, D. (1995). *Six levels of integration*. Toronto, Canada: International Association for Computer Information Systems.

Grant, D. (2002). A wider view of business process reengineering. *Communications of the ACM, 45*(2), 85-90.

Grant, D., & Ngwenyama, O. (2003). A report on the use of action research to evaluate a manufacturing information systems development methodology in a manufacturing company. *Information Systems Journal, 13*, 21-35.

Gummesson, E. (1991). *Qualitative methods in management research*. London: Sage Publications.

Hammer, M., & Stanton, S. (1999, November-December). How process enterprises really work. *Harvard Business Review*, 108-118.

Hart, P., & Estrin, D. (1991). Inter-organization networks, computer integration, and shifts in interdependence: The case of the semiconductor industry. *ACM Transactions on Information Systems, 9*(4), 370-398.

Hasselbring, W. (2000). Information system integration. *Communications of the ACM, 43*(6), 32-38.

Hofstede, G. (1983, Fall). The cultural relativity of organizational practices and theories. *Journal of International Business Studies*, 75-89.

Holland, C., & Light, B. (2001). A stage maturity model for ERP systems use. *Data Base for Advances in Information Systems, 32*(2), 34-45.

Iacovou, C., Benbasat, I., & Dexter, A. (1995). Electronic data interchange and small organizations: Adoption and impact of technology. *MIS Quarterly, 19*(4), 465-485.

Jones, M., & Young, R. (2006, March). ERP usage in practice: An empirical investigation. *Information Resource Management Journal, 19*(1), 23-42.

Karimi, J., Gupta, Y. P., & Somers, T. M. (1996). Impact of competitive strategy and information technology maturity on firms' strategic response to globalization. *Journal of Management Information Systems, 12*(4), 55-88.

Kremers, M., & Van Dissel, H. (2000). ERP system migrations. *Communication of the ACM, 43*(4), 52-56.

Kumar, L., & Hillegersberg, J. (2000). ERP experiences and evolution. *Communications of the ACM, 43*(3), 22-26.

Laframboise, K. (2005, Summer). Gaining competitive advantage from integrating enterprise resource planning and TQM. *Journal of Supply Chain Management*, 49-64.

Lawrence, P., & Lorsch, J. (1967). *Organization and environment: Managing differentiation and integration.* Boston, MA: Harvard University Press.

Li, C. (1999). ERP packages: What's next? *Information Systems Management, 16*(3), 31-34.

Mabert, V., Soni, A., & Venkataramanan, M. (2000). Enterprise resource planning survey of U.S. manufacturing firms. *Production and Inventory Management Journal*, 2nd quarter, 52-58.

Madnick, S. (1991). The information technology platform. In M. Scott-Morton (Ed.), *The corporation of the 1990s: Information technology and organizational transformation.* New York: Oxford University Press.

Maglitta, J. (1993, October). Executives: Where's the payback. *Computer World, 27*(42), 15.

Main, J. (1990, September). Computers of the world unite. *Fortune Magazine, 122*(7), 113-116.

Mandell, S. (1975). *Multinational corporate computer-based information system and the parent-subsidiary interface.* PhD dissertation, George Washington University, Washington DC.

Markus, M. L., & Robey, D. (1988). Information technology and organizational change: Causal structure in theory and research. *Management Science, 34*(5), 583-598.

Markus, M. L., & Tanis, C. (2000). Multisite ERP implementations. *Communications of the ACM, 43*(4), 42-46.

Markus, M. L., & Tanis, C. (2000b). The enterprise system experience-form adoption to success. In R. Zmud (Ed.), *Framing the domains of IT research: Glimpsing the future through the pact.* Cincinnati, OH: Publisher, Pinnaflex Educational Resources Inc.

Mathew, P. (1988, August 4-6). *Integration for manufacturing growth.* Presented at the Third International Conference on Manufacturing Engineering, Newcastle.

Mathew, T. (2006). Orchestrating integration strategies. *USBanker*, ISSN 0148-8848, No. 1075612561.

Mendoza, L., Perez, M., & Griman, A. (2006, Spring). Critical success factors for managing systems integration. *Information Systems Management Journal*, 56-75.

Meredith, J., & Hill, M. (1990). Justifying new manufacturing systems: A managerial approach. In A. C. Boynton, & R. W. Zmud (Eds.), *MIS readings and case.* London: Scott, Foresman/Little & Brown Higher Education Publishing.

Nygaard-Andersen, S., & Bjorn-Andersen, N. (1994). To join or not to join: A framework for evaluating electronic data interchange systems. *Journal of Strategic Information Systems, 3*(3), 191-210.

Phatak, A. (1989). *International dimensions of management* (2nd ed.). Boston: PWS-Kent Publishing Company.

Ramamurthy, K., Premkumar, G., & Crum, M. (1999). Organizational and interorganizational determinants of EDI diffusion and organizational performance: A causal model. *Journal of Organizational Computing and Electronic Commerce, 9*(4), 253-285.

Rochester, J. B., & Douglass, D. P. (1992). Redefining computer-integrated manufacturing. *I/S Analyzer, 30*(8), 1-9.

Rockart, J., & Sbort, J. (1989, Winter). IT in the 1990s: Managing organizational interdependence. *Sloan Management Review*, 7-17.

Rotemberg, J., & Saloner, G. (1991). Interfirm competition and collaboration. In M. Scott-Morton (Ed.), *The corporation of the 1990s: Information technology and organizational transformation.* New York: Oxford University Press.

Saccomano, A. (1999). ERP lives. *Traffic World, 259*(10), 38-39.

Sanchez, F. (2006). The SOA approach to integration and transformation. *USBanker 2006,* ISSN 0148-8848, No. 1075612611.

Scalle, C. X., & Cotteler, M. J. (1999). *Enterprise resource planning*. Boston, MA: Harvard Business School Publishing.

Scheer, A., & Habermann, F. (2000). Making ERP a success. *Communications of the ACM, 43*(4), 57-61.

Schulz, J. (2000). Hunt for best practices. *Traffic World, 263*(13), 41-42.

Scott-Morton, M. (1991). *The corporation of the 1990s: Information technology and organizational transformation*. New York: Oxford University Press.

Sharif, A. M., Irani, Z., & Love, P. E. D. (2005). Integrating ERP using EAI: A model for post hoc evaluation. *European Journal of Information Systems, 14*, 162-174.

Sheu, C., Yen, H. R., & Krumwiede, D. W. (2003). The effect of national differences on multinational ERP implementation: An exploratory study. *TQM & Business Excellence, 14*(6), 641-657.

Simchi-Levi, D., Kaminsky, P., & Simchi-Levi, E. (2000). *Designing and managing the supply-chain: Concepts, strategies and case studies*. Boston: Irvin/McGraw Hill.

Soh, C., & Kien, S. (2000). Cultural fits and misfits: Is ERP a universal solution? *Communications of the ACM, 43*(4), 47-51.

Songini, M. (2005). Bungled ERP installation whacks asyst. *Computerworld, 39*(2), 0-1.

Themistocleous, M., & Irani, Z. (2002). *Information systems evaluation and integration group*. 35th Hawaii International Conf. on System Science, January, Island of Hawaii, USA.

Trompenaars, F., & Hampden-Turner, C. (1998). *Riding the waves of culture: Understanding diversity in global business* (2nd ed.). New York: McGraw Hill.

Truman, G. E. (2000). Integration in electronic exchange environments. *Journal of Management Information Systems, 17*(1), 209-244.

Wailgum, T. (2005, May). Big mess on campus: Disastrous ERP implementation have given more than a few universities black eyes. *CIO, 18*(14), 1.

Ward, C. (2006, Spring). ERP: Integrating and extending the enterprise. *The Public Manager, 35*(1), 30-33.

Yates, J., & Benjamin, R. (1991). The past and present as a window on the future. In M. Scott-Morton (Ed.), *The corporation of the 1990s: Information technology and organizational transformation*. New York: Oxford University Press.

Zheng, S., Yen, D. C., & Tarn, J. M. (2000, Fall). The new spectrum of the cross-enterprise solution: The integration of supply chain management and enterprise resource planning systems. *Journal of Computer Information Systems*, 84-93.

Chapter XV

Analyzing Different Strategies to Enterprise System Adoption:
Re-Engineering-Led vs. Quick Deployment

Sue Newell, Bentley College, USA

Jay Cooprider, Bentley College, USA

Gary David, Bentley College, USA

Linda Edelman, Bentley College, USA

Traci Logan, Bentley College, USA

Abstract

The literature on enterprise systems (ES) adoptions suggests that companies use different strategies; some opting to re-engineer business processes up-front, while others employ a quick deployment strategy on the assumption that organizational change will follow. In this chapter, we explore how these two different strategies play out in practice and also consider the factors that influence which approach is taken. We use exploratory data from interviews with consultants from XYZ who have been involved in multiple ES implementations in external companies as well as interviews with project members involved in an internal ES implementation in XYZ. Analysis of the data suggests that some level of re-engineering is an inevitable outcome of ES implementation. However, attempts to re-engineer up-front is difficult and can be problematic. Much of this stems from how the ES is actually used versus its envisioned (or planned) use. The implications for post-implementation exploitation opportunities are explored.

Introduction

Enterprise systems (ES) are being widely adopted by organizations in all types of industry and geographical locations (Robey, Ross, & Boudreau, 2002). The rationale for adoption is that such systems have the potential to allow for the integration of business functions and so facilitate strategic organizational change (Sawyer & Southwick, 2002). However, past research has demonstrated that such systems often do not deliver the hoped-for benefits (Parr & Shanks, 2000; Sauer, Liu, & Johnston, 2001; Scott & Vessey, 2002). Indeed, ERP implementation projects are associated with high levels of failure and user resistance (Aldwani, 2002; Scott & Wagner, 2003). Nevertheless, while failure and project abandonment does occur, most companies persevere to the extent that they get a working information system (Wagner & Newell, 2006b), even though they may be using less of the functionality than anticipated, at least initially, so that they are not fully exploiting the integrating potential of the software (Wagner & Newell, 2006b). It is important, therefore, to consider why companies are able to exploit more or less of the functionality of an ES. In this chapter, we explore this by focusing on different approaches to ES implementation that companies can adopt.

Background Literature

In terms of these different approaches to ES implementation, we can contrast two adoption strategies—a re-engineering-led versus a quick-deployment strategy. In the front-loaded re-engineering model, companies re-design their business processes *before* implementation, with a view to designing new processes that will enable the organization to take maximum advantage of the integrating potential of the technology (Newell, Huang, & Tansley, 2004). On the other hand, the quick-deployment strategy supposedly eliminates this re-engineering phase and focuses on a speedy deployment of the standard "vanilla" ES package (Nah, Zuckweller, & Lau, 2003); that is the package as pre-configured by the software vendor to fit their particular industry and organizational size. In a similar vein, Robey et al. (2002) differentiate between a piece-meal and a concerted approach to ES adoption. With the piece-meal approach, the aim is first to replace legacy systems and then gradually introduce new business processes. Conversely, with the concerted approach, the organization plans to introduce business process changes along with software implementation.

For an organization pursuing a re-engineering-led ES implementation, the project team(s) tasked with implementing the selected ES will need to map existing organizational processes, identify the analogous processes that are embedded in the ES software, and configure the software and the organizational processes to effect some kind of parallel (Soh, Sia, & Tay-Yap, 2000). Companies adopting this approach are, therefore, undertaking a business process re-engineering effort ahead of their ES adoption (Hammer & Champy, 1993). They must define current "as is" processes and then the "to be" processes that ideally are able to take advantage of the integrating functionality of an ES. Thus, while the original proponents of business process re-engineering (Hammer & Champy, 1993) suggested that a firm needs to start with a "blank piece of paper", so ignoring current processes and practice, the reality is that this "history" cannot be ignored (Ciborra & Hanseth, 2000). In this re-engineering-led approach, then, in order to specify the organizational requirements for the system, team members must first understand what workplace activities have been done in the past and why (Soh et al., 2000). This will enable them to determine what needs to be changed to exploit the integrating potential of the ES and the adoption effort will need to concentrate as much on the organizational change effort as the technical implementation effort.

Re-engineering existing processes in this way is very difficult as has been demonstrated by the number of companies where re-engineering projects have failed to deliver the hoped-for benefits (Davenport & Prusak, 2003). If companies want to avoid this effort they can adopt the alternative, quick-adoption strategy, where it is not necessary to fully understand the diversity of existing processes across an organization. Rather, it is sufficient to understand the basic functional requirements and then configure the system to match these requirements, taking the "vanilla" configuration as provided by the software vendor as the starting point, and then making minor configuration adaptations (not customizations, as far as possible, which involve changing the underlying code) to suit the particular work processes in the organization. This approach draws very heavily on the "best practices" that are supposedly embedded in the software (Nah et al., 2003). Given the configurability of an ES, this should enable workers in any area to be able to continue to do things more-or-less as they did before, albeit using a different technology. However, because of the powerful integration capability of an ES, workers will eventually be able to do a lot more than they could do previously. Rather than design this into the implementation strategy, however, in a quick-adoption approach the idea is to get the system up and running, allowing the workers to do what they did before, more or less, and then let them gradually learn to exploit the additional functionality of the ES as they experiment with and come to gradually understand the new IS that they have been given.

Robey et al. (2002) suggest that organizational transformation is more difficult in the piece-meal, quick-adoption strategy because once the system is deployed it may be harder to introduce changes to either the organization or the software. Nah et al. (2003), on the other hand, argue that this latter strategy can make ES implementation much easier and suggest that the transformational potential can be exploited after the system has been implemented, that is, in the post-implementation period.

The purpose of this chapter is to explore how these two different strategies exist in practice, and to consider why organizations adopt one rather than the other. We can state the research questions as follows—can we differentiate, in practice, between a re-engineering-led versus a quick deployment ES implementation strategy; and if yes, under what circumstances and why do organizations adopt a re-engineering-led versus a quick-deployment strategy to ES implementation? The next section of the chapter describes our methodology, and then we present and discuss the data from our consultant interviews as well as from a recent survey that provides additional information about the type of ES adoption strategy that companies are following (Wagner & Newell, 2006a). Finally, we draw conclusions from this exploratory research.

Methodology

We explore the research question through a case study in which the experiences of ES consultants (N=10) working in a large consultancy firm (hereafter called XYZ) were collected. The experience of consultants was chosen because consultants have wide-ranging involvement in a variety of companies which are likely to approach their ES adoptions very differently. Thus, consultants provide a range of experiences that would take many case studies in different organizations to gather. As this was an exploratory study, we wanted to gain access to rich, qualitative data rather than quantitative data that could have been collected by a survey instrument. The main method used was the exploratory interview. In addition to these interviews, we collected documents related to this consultancy firm's implementation methodology. The purpose of collecting data from multiple sources was to enrich the depth of the study, and to triangulate the data to ensure the validity and reliability of the findings (Denzin, 1989).

The data collected in the study is subjected to an interpretive analysis since we had no pre-determined hypotheses or propositions to test. The strengths of the interpretive methodology have been reported in a number of studies, notably Klein and Myers

(1999) and Walsham (1993). The appropriateness of adopting such a paradigm is reflected in the need for not only investigating the influence of the technology implemented, in this case ES, but also the need to take into account the broader context, including the organization and its environment. For example, in the words of Walsham (1993, p. 4-5), interpretive research methods are "aimed at producing an understanding of the context of the information system, and the process whereby the information system influences and is influenced by the context". Further, as suggested by Klein and Myers (1999, p. 69), we wanted to use an interpretive approach that "attempts to understand phenomena through the meanings that people assign to them".

Case Description

XYZ is a very large global organization manufacturing and retailing both PC and high-end computer systems. It has large global consultancy businesses that focus on both general business services and IT-related implementation and support services. They decided to implement Siebel, an enterprise-wide customer-relationship management (CRM) system, in 1999. XYZ had already developed its own CRM systems but the CEO decided they needed to "Web-enable" this application, using an external package. The previously existing CRM systems used a variety of legacy applications, some of which had been developed in very clever ways to support different customer relationship processes. For example, in relation to marketing they had developed their legacy infrastructure based on Lotus Notes:

It was a pretty elaborate Lotus Notes solution. You know, a testament to how big you can scale up Lotus Notes to be frank with you. Because it was never invented for that kind of audience. I mean never ever in a million years was Lotus supposed to get that big.

While these systems were not integrated, working off multiple independent databases, they had been based on a re-engineering analysis that had been undertaken at the time that XYZ was significantly downsizing during the early 1990s. During this re-engineering effort the aim had been to define an international set of common processes and procedures so that the way of interacting with customers was common across all geographies and BUs of XYZ. As a common set of processes had already been defined across BUs, the introduction of Siebel should have been relatively easy since only minimal adjustments to reflect country differences would be necessary. Despite the prediction of an easy implementation, one of the project leaders described the Siebel project as, "Frankly, when I look at the number of hours and the number of people involved in this, it makes putting a man on the moon somewhat trivial".

The case interviews were collected during the fourth year of the project, long after those involved thought the project would have been completed. However, the project was still ongoing as there had been significant delays in implementing some of the modules, as discussed next. This indicates that this project was suffering from the kind of project delays that have been shown to be extremely common in ES implementations (Parr & Shanks. 2000). Moreover, one of the major business rationales for this internal project was that by replacing many customized and independent legacy systems with a single "vanilla" application, maintenance costs would be significantly reduced. With this in mind the project plan had a built-in schedule for "sunsetting" existing applications. Unfortunately, four years on, only one of the scheduled legacy systems had actually been phased out and as one of the project leaders admitted: "We are a little off-track" (PM). The human cost of the project was also very high, especially among the core team, who were described as "burnt-out" by one of the core team members.

A particular problem that they faced on the project, was maintaining resources for the organizational change effort. Thus, any ES implementation impacts the organization both technologically and socially and resources were allocated at XYZ to address these two related sets of issues. That is, some resources were allocated to develop the technical solution while other resources were allocated to facilitate the organizational change and at the outset of the project the change management and relationship issues associated with re-engineering were seen to be central. Yet, very early on, as soon as the project hit some technical problems, funds got diverted from the human to the technical and these resources were never subsequently recovered:

I have this chart that we developed in the first two months of this, which said one of the biggest issues to deal with is people change. We have to focus on that and we really have to make sure that we have that under our belt, and then we promptly forgot about it and we didn't do nearly as much from the people change aspects as we originally had planned to do... The IT side wasn't bedded in, so we gave up funding for people management in the early part, believing that we could put it in later in the season... You can solve the people issues as you go, or theoretically as you go, but you can't solve the IT issues as you go. You need to solve them right now because they stop us.

This interviewee went on to say:

I have yet to see a company, even one that is as enlightened as XYZ on some of this stuff, be able to sustain the dollars for people change.

Thus, overall the CRM project at XYZ had been problematic in a number of ways. We next analyze these problems in terms of the re-engineering-led versus quick-deployment strategy comparison that we have highlighted above.

Re-Engineering-Led vs. Quick Deployment: The Evidence

The Consultants' Ideal: Re-Engineering-Led ES Deployment

Among the ES consultants interviewed, there was general agreement that some degree of re-engineering is essential in an ES implementation in order to achieve the transformational potential:

That's the intent (to get them to re-engineer upfront). To fully utilize the SAP functionality, which is a totally integrated system. To fully utilize the functionality of SAP. And often part of using that means making changes as you know which is why we strongly strongly recommend to try and help facilitate making those changes.

While re-engineering is a high priority among consultants, the consultants noted that often it is not a high priority among companies, many of whom attempt to avoid re-engineering as much as possible. This tension is demonstrated in the following quotation:

I mentioned earlier a lot of times re-engineering and best practices are not always the focal point. They really are not. As much as we would like them to be and we try to drive that, a lot of the time they're not. So they'll look at what standard SAP provides. They'll look at what they have today. And try to go through as least change as possible and that's the way I can describe it. And we, as consultants and as advisors, our challenge is to get them to understand that the answer is not as least change as possible. The answer is take advantage of the opportunity to improve what you have, to re-engineer if that's what you're invested in. Quite frankly that's not always the case. They—human nature as you know probably better than I tend to—I don't want to change. I want to stay with what I have and what's the least painful way that I can do this.

Nevertheless, despite this resistance, they believed that re-engineering was essential in order to ensure that the functionality of the system was fully exploited. Where re-engineering was avoided, the organization would fail to obtain the full benefit from the ES. One specific example that was provided was of a company that was implementing an enterprise-wide procurement module. They implemented a new process, supported by the ES, to send out orders electronically. However, they decided against changing their traditional requisition process, of which there were 27 different variants, because finding a common single process was deemed to be too difficult both technically and organizationally. So they implemented only a small fraction of the procurement module, and according to the consultants gained in return only a small fraction of the potential benefits from the system.

The consultants recognized that re-engineering efforts generally require a large amount of work up-front to document existing processes. The level of pre-implementation work needed can make many organizations wary of such an initiative. However, consultants believed that if organizations did not do the re-engineering up-front, it would be more difficult later:

Any ERP implementation system is very very intense. It's long, although they are becoming shorter duration. Very very intense. And quite frankly people just finally get the system installed and implemented and they made it and they take a breath and they say whew. And they go off by the way and typically will start somewhere else. So they typically will not reflect now let me see how much I'm using, not using.

Moreover, they pointed out that organizations can take advantage of re-engineering in one location and reuse this elsewhere. For example, in large multi-site companies, extensive re-engineering could be done at one site, and then simply take the developed system and processes and apply the "to be" directly to other sites, without doing any prior "as is" analysis:

One of the situations specifically was we did an SAP implementation at a particular major site of geography within a company. That was a major effort, re-engineering, changing the processes they had in place. Spent a lot of time and money to basically do that. When we went to the next geography we didn't go through the exercise again of doing that ... So there was very very little discussion around re-engineering discussions, whether they want to do it this way or not. And when there were exceptions to the baseline we basically set it up so that they had to really justify.

The main problem for achieving re-engineering was described as "legacy thinking". For example, one consultant described a situation where it had been very difficult to get change, because the client project team had been staffed with very experienced employees who had worked for the company for over 35 years:

It was couple of key project team members who were old timers and I am talking of real old-timers; people who had been with the company for 35 years. And after 35 years you can't ask why something is done, because it is just done that way. It has always been done that way. So for me to try and understand why certain things were done in this particular process, I couldn't get there because she was not able to articulate it beyond the fact that it was, you know, there.

We can juxtapose the challenges present when working with an established workforce with the next example, where a consultant recounts an SAP implementation with a workforce that was relatively new with no SAP experience or knowledge whatsoever:

And one of the things we found was we were very very nervous initially because the profile of the people who were going live with SAP was about a year or two experience out of school. No SAP experience. And we were really concerned about it. The more we thought about it, the more we put the plan together, we realized this is going to be the easiest implementation we've ever done. They don't go in there with any predetermined way they want to do it. They found it exciting. ...it was one of the easiest implementations because they had no knowledge of SAP and very little business experience. Now there are other challenges associated with that but that was one of the easiest ones.

So, while re-engineering is endorsed by these consultants, many of the companies they work with do not go through a major re-engineering exercise, preferring instead to adopt a system which simply supports their existing processes. Given this "ideal" as described by the consultants, we can turn to examine what happened in relation to their own ES, CRM implementation project.

The Ideal Re-Engineering-Led Implementation in Practice

On the Siebel project, one of the first stages in their implementation methodology was to undertake a "fit-gap" analysis. Led by the core team, a representative group of people from across the world were brought together for a one-week intensive workshop. For the first module development (the call-centre module), kicked off in

January 2000, the core team walked the selected group of people through the Siebel application screen by screen and challenged them to: "accept it 'as is', out of the box". This would imply that they would need to re-engineer their processes to fit those supported by the software. By taking this group through the Siebel process and comparing this to existing practices, the core team was able to work-flow how these people do their job, with the idea that they would then define what re-engineering was necessary. However, one thing the first team learned from this, which they had not fully anticipated, was that:

There is an interesting difference between the process documents—how they say the job is done and the people at the keyboard actually doing the job—they don't match. You get very clever people who learn their own short-cuts and unless you are a practitioner you don't learn these things.

In other words, even though at the start they had believed that the implementation would be easier because common processes were assumed to have been universally adopted, they found during this fit-gap analysis that the standardized processes only served as a generalized guideline. In reality, groups had developed ad hoc their own collective sets of practices in the course of their carrying out their daily workplace activities.

Mutual discussion during this week among the participants led to the identification of the differences between the way people did, and wanted to continue to do, their job versus how the Siebel tool would enable them to do their job. In this way the first group identified over 600 requirements for customization. However, the decision was made to keep these customizations to the very minimum so that in the first release of the software only eight of the suggested customizations had been enabled. These were mostly related to nomenclature and terminology so that the tool mirrored existing XYZ usage. The rest of the suggested customizations were disregarded as non-essential and the existing processes were modified to suit the configured software.

The "Wicked" Face of Resistance

While the project team were able to get the first call-centre group to go along with the strategy of re-engineering their processes to suit a "vanilla" implementation, this re-engineering approach caused problems when the modules for more powerful groups of employees came to be discussed. More specifically, this discussion about re-engineering led to considerable delay in several of the modules, in particular, the marketing and also the sales module. In these areas people had been more reluctant to accept changes to their existing practices and had held out against this and imposed more modifications on the system:

The sales team basically stuck their tongue out and said screw you; we ain't going to do this unless you do it our way, which has led to a number of compromises in how we actually implemented the package, some of which are good, some of which aren't good.

This had similarly happened in relation to the marketing module. A new manager was eventually brought in to try and resolve this, after a two-year delay, when these problems simply forced the project to stagnate. The previous manager had been attempting to go for a re-engineering-led change, wanting the new system to support what were considered to be "best practices" from the fit-gap analysis. However, this had stalled the project because the decision-makers at the time felt that the system could not actually support these processes:

There was some functionality which the people who were in that decision making position at the time were not happy with...I'm not saying there was a real lack of functionality. It was just the decision makers at the time thought that there was a significant one.

Going for a Quick Deployment

The new manager brought in to resolve the stalemate in the marketing project adopted a very different approach. Rather than attempting a whole re-engineering, this new project manager instead elected to simply develop a quick pilot system and then roll this out gradually to the different European countries, starting with the smaller countries where deployment would be easier. While he recognized that the system would not be perfect, people could find ways to adapt to this in the short-term and if there were some real gaps then functionality could be added at a later point in time:

So there needs to be a little bit of a leap of faith when you're bringing a system like Siebel in... There's always tactical solutions. There's always work a-rounds. They always look at that in a way that says that this is my forever solution and I don't like that. They stand fast and ask for something that is much more sophisticated. And then you get money being chucked at that and time delay.

So his approach was to implement the application and then work to exploit it after it was installed.

*The piloting and working forward I think are the absolute key ingredients because otherwise you can get a committee working and discussing it for **years** and they'll come up with something they think is absolutely perfect and it will fall apart within two weeks of going live because there's so much stuff they didn't know, or the world moved on, or you know it wasn't supposed to be like that, you told me this field was unique, it's not. I thought it was. And suddenly you have all these other issues. So I think getting on and doing it is absolutely important.*

The aim here was to develop the new tool so that it could generate virtually the same benefits as the existing legacy tools did. Asked how this then promoted radical change, the interviewee responded:

That is such a difficult thing to do because you really have to take a lot of effort doing that. You have to have such a—such a hope to change the machine to do that. And I've been involved in projects where we've done that. But you need to be having a very large project team. A lot of people. A lot of money. A lot of time. And I think that carries almost as much risk because of the expense of the project and the time of the project. And you can do it. You can actually do it. You can completely re-engineer the process, completely change the IT people are working on it a totally different way. And you're just going to hang on in there until the change is accepted by the organization and meanwhile the dollars are ticking over. You've got quite a bit of teams that do that. And you can run out of time. You can run out of money as well. And I've been involved in those kind of projects. No I much prefer to increment the change.

His view was that change would happen afterward as people began to exploit the system, resulting in a more "organic" organization change:

People are very good at exploiting (the system); that's people's natural nature when they discover that for example there's a button there and they press it and it actually does something which they couldn't do before, and they go and say, you know this button works... And you don't have to educate people. It just spreads like wildfire. ... So I think the deploying of the enterprise system really is the enabler to massive change. Some change they'll get straight away because they do some things immediately they couldn't do before. Another change they may have to fight for and get the functionality. But they can because the ERP is scaleable in that direction whereas the previous one wasn't. In other cases they simply will discover better ways to exploit their tools which no one ever thought of before.

Even with this "get something in quick" approach, it was obvious that developing the common database and setting up the interfaces with still-to-be-used legacy systems was extremely difficult and time-consuming. For example, to create the common marketing database they had to clean-up data from many different legacy systems:

So you end up with a huge amount of different data formats and different legacy databases... the people are doing the best they can and also people using the fields for something in which it was never intended, either because it was never really closely defined or because tactically they had to do something so they did that.

Each of these legacy systems had grown and developed overtime so that there were many examples of the idiosyncratic use of particular fields. An example was provided of the use of the customer number:

A rather amusing example that is probably XYZ specific; but we had something called the customer number. It's supposed to be a unique identifier for a customer. Which is actually legacy thinking if you think about it because if you've got a customer database that's got separate address lines, customer lines, you don't actually use the proxy which is the customer number. Now the customer number works fine until you end up with duplications because then you end up with more—you have two customer numbers. When you merge them (the files) together which customer number do you use? Well you put them both there with a comma in between. So now we have two customer numbers. In fact I think we have six times as many customer numbers as we have customers and therefore people get confused about which is the correct customer number. I think the most customer numbers we've got on one account, I think there's a university in Paris that has three thousand customer numbers.

This interviewee went on to say that the customer number is obsolete in the new system, so that one way around the problem would simply be to delete all the customer numbers. However, this had not been done because there was resistance from users who had always used customer numbers and could not understand that they would not be needed in the future. So, for the sake of getting user acceptance the customer number (or rather numbers) had been left in. But cleaning up the data so that the databases could be integrated into a single database was a major undertaking, especially because of problems of duplication:

If you've got a duplication of contact or duplication of an account with marketing you can get a major problem with some of the work flows that you've got. And the data quality now is one of the areas where we really started to understand for the first time merging five or six databases together, you really can get not necessarily better data. You can actually end up with a lot of mess which you need to filter, merge, de-duplicate.

Given the numbers of accounts that needed to be integrated onto the common database the problem was enormous. So, for example, in the UK, where they were starting the roll-out there were about 300,000 accounts and over a million contacts to go through. And this was a "small deal" compared to some of the other countries. For example in Germany there were about four million contacts and in Italy over one million accounts.

Discussion

The interviewees recognized the distinction between a re-engineering-led (Newell et al., 2004) and a quick deployment (Nah et al., 2003) ES implementation. Thus, they could recount differences in their consultancy experiences between client organizations that: (a) had wanted the ES to be designed to largely mirror existing practices, with as little change as possible; and (b) client organizations that had undertaken major re-engineering in concert with their ES adoption in order to define process improvements that could leverage the expected advantages of the integrating capability of the ES. With the exception of one of the Siebel interviewees (the new marketing module project manager), they also believed that a re-engineering-led approach was better, as was concluded by Robey et al. (2002). At the same time, the interviewees also pointed out that in many cases re-engineering was very limited, often because of company desires to limit re-engineering. This fits with recent data obtained from a survey of companies that had implemented an ES (Wagner & Newell, 2006a), which showed that only 22% of organizations had modified their organizational and business processes "a great deal" as part of their ES project. The results of our case analysis here help us to understand why this is the case, despite the dominant view from consultants who see upfront re-engineering as essential for exploiting the potential of an ES. Thus, in our discussion we consider two related issues. The first pertains to the difference between these two approaches. The second deals with the exploration of reasons why re-engineering efforts are not as extensive as the consultants might ideally think essential for exploiting the potential of the ES.

In terms of the first issue, analysis of the interviews suggests that the simple dichotomy between a re-engineering-led and a quick deployment ES implementation is over-simplified. The data suggest that all companies engage in some re-engineering, meaning organizational change to existing processes (Hammer & Champy, 1993), albeit in very different ways. This is consistent with the Wagner and Newell (2006a) survey findings, where the majority of adopting organizations indicated that the changes that had been made were undertaken before, during *and* after the ES was implemented, indicating that in reality, elements of a re-engineering-led and quick-deployment strategy co-exist. In general, it is virtually impossible to implement an ES with no organizational change. Two primary reasons for this emerged from the analysis. First, companies recognize the long term benefits of reducing maintenance costs, so there is an inherent desire to adopt the "vanilla" system. While there may be the need for some customization, especially in a large and complex organization like XYZ, most agree with the need to keep these to a minimum. This overarching objective forces some process change in an attempt to fit the standard system. For example, in the Siebel project, the first fit-gap analysis identified 600 ways in which the system would need to be changed to support existing practice. The project team only allowed eight of these changes, at least in the first phase. In the other 592 cases practice had to change to accommodate the new software. Second, there is always going to be some attempt to create more commonality of processes. For example, in the Siebel project, even though the new marketing module leader was going for essentially a quick deployment there were a number of organizational changes that were required, simply because there needed to be convergence of practice across the different geographies if they were going to use the same tool.

While some re-engineering was therefore inevitable, the interviews indicated that there were enormous differences between companies in terms of how much re-engineering was undertaken, a finding that is supported by Wagner and Newell (2006a). First, companies differed in terms of how extensive their definition of an enterprise was. Some companies with whom these consultants had worked had done some re-engineering but at a BU level rather than an enterprise level. Re-engineering within a BU is going to be easier than re-engineering across BUs because there will be less diversity of practice and less required negotiation across reporting structures. Indeed, XYZ in their adoption of SAP had elected to do this at the BU level rather than the corporate level; in the Siebel project they had decided to undertake at the corporate level.

In terms of exploring why more or less upfront re-engineering is undertaken a number of issues seem to influence this. First, there are differences across ES modules. Most ES implementations will involve the adoption of different modules, and there may well be different amounts of re-engineering in each of these. This may reflect the complexity of the tasks within a module, so that more or less configuration and/or customization to the standard template are required. However, the interviews suggested that it may also reflect the relative power of the particular module team in relation to the leadership. So, in the Siebel implementation, the sales and marketing module teams at least initially resisted the insistence that they should change their processes to fit those embedded in the software. They spent time and effort developing separate systems that could interface with the Siebel system in order to provide them with what they saw as essential functionality that was missing from the standard package. In this instance, a new manager reversed this course of action, but in other situations this might not happen.

Second, there are differences within modules. Thus, re-engineering is not necessarily evenly distributed within business modules. Our interviews revealed instances where there was extensive re-engineering to some parts of a process, while other parts of that same process are left unchanged to the point of being supported by legacy, and even paper, systems. Again this may reflect the complexity of different tasks and processes but it may also reflect the ability of the project team to encourage or influence change. The example was provided of a company adopting the procurement module of an ES where they decided not to change the requisition process because it was deemed to be too difficult both technically and organizationally to both understand the existing 27 different systems and agree upon a common framework.

Lastly, there may be more or less re-engineering depending upon whether any previous re-engineering has been done and the timing of it in relation to the ES implementation. In the Siebel project they anticipated a need for relatively less re-engineering because they had already gone through the exercise of agreeing upon common business processes only a short while before. Nevertheless, even in this context it soon became clear that considerable divergence existed in practice, despite this recent common agreement about "best processes". This is because there will always be an emergent quality to any practice (Orlikowski, 1996, 2000) as individuals discover new problem interpretations and solutions and so build-up heuristic knowledge (Collins, 1990). So, while there may be documents and directives that define parts or all of the process, these are likely to bear only a partial relation to actual practice, even when these have been recently agreed, as in the Siebel case.

The data collected in this study point to significant differences, then, in the extent and type of re-engineering undertaken. Given that this was an exploratory study, we can only conclude that these differences exist. They suggest that further study will be useful to understand more fully how the context influences the re-engineering effort during an ES implementation.

While organizations and the people in them differ in terms of their desire for re-engineering, consultants tended to believe that most organizations did less re-engineering than would have been optimal to fully exploit the integrating capability of the system and use the embedded functionality. This concern is well-founded, since Wagner and Newell (2006a) found that only 28% of organizations had fully deployed their ES application functionality. Our case interviews help us understand the reasons why many organizations seem either to consciously avoid or unconsciously limit the amount of re-engineering undertaken. Two core themes were identified from the interview data—problems related to complexity and problems related to commitment.

First, as the Siebel implementation project demonstrated, an ES in a large multi-national organization like XYZ is extremely complex, being compared to landing a man on the moon. And this was in a context where a major re-engineering effort had already been undertaken. In this situation, it is impossible for anyone to understand the whole picture, and so it is inevitable and essential that the project be broken down into smaller pieces, such as by module or geography or BU, and that the pieces are considered independently (Knights & Wilmott, 1997). Even when broken down in this way, it is still very hard to reach consensus on what should be new "best practices", especially if people have been in their jobs for a long period and are therefore unable to envisage working in any other way than the current. Moreover, if an agreement is reached about "best practice", but these are not consistent with those supported by the selected ES, there is likely to be major delays to the project, either to wait for the ES software provider to add the functionality or to customize the software. Moreover, as the implementation of the marketing module of the Siebel project demonstrated, even with a minimal re-engineering effort, there are major obstacles to agreeing and implementing a common database that has "clean" data that will be perceived as valuable by its users, given the diversity and duplication that exists in the existing legacy systems, simply because over time practice diverges from any agreed standard (Orlikowski, 1996).

Second, if a very extensive re-engineering effort is included upfront, it is going to be very time-consuming, and is still likely to encounter operational difficulties when the ES is actually tested and piloted. This is going to delay any visible progress on the project and time delays and a lack of perceived progress are going to make it very difficult to sustain commitment to the project (Markus, Axline, Petrie, & Tanis, 2000). Even without these delays, maintaining the budget for aspects relating to the organizational change associated with any re-engineering is likely to be difficult in the face of inevitable technical challenges inherent in complex ES software development. Thus, in the XYZ project, even though the need to allocate substantial financial resources into the organizational change effort was correctly anticipated, these funds very quickly got diverted to the more pressing technical issues.

Conclusion

The difficulties of implementing an ES are well-known (e.g., Parr & Shanks, 2000; Sauer et al., 2001; Scott & Vessey, 2002) and any executive making a decision to adopt such a system is going to be aware that many companies have struggled with their adoptions and that many such adoptions fail to come in on time, on budget, or deliver the expected benefits. Against this background, it seems that many companies are choosing to try and implement their ES as quickly as possible and with minimal organizational change (Nah et al., 2003). Thus, while some re-engineering is likely for the reasons discussed earlier, many companies are likely to want to minimize this effort, despite the protestations of consultants that they should re-engineer upfront. As discussed, there are good reasons why they should want to do this, including having already undergone extensive re-engineering in the past, or because BUs operate relatively independently. Moreover, there are significant reasons why avoiding re-engineering may actually be beneficial, as when re-engineering might lead to the definition of business processes that are not well-supported by the software (as in the marketing module of Siebel) or more commonly, because re-engineering is likely to be very difficult given the complexity of operations and divergent practices within large organizations. This means that undertaking an extensive re-engineering effort is likely to require extraordinary amounts of stakeholder commitment and unity that are often difficult to sustain in practice given the tendency to divert financial resources earmarked to support organizational changes to address the more immediate and visible need to resolve technical difficulties.

Given this, an approach of minimizing re-engineering upfront and deploying the ES as quickly as possible can be an effective strategy (Nah et al., 2003). Even with this strategy, however, the organizational challenges are substantial, as demonstrated in the Siebel marketing module. Moreover, adopting this strategy will not result in the full exploitation of an ES and much potential functionality will remain dormant, at least initially. That being said, we should not underestimate the improvisational ability of users (Orlikowski, 1996, 2000). As the internally developed CRM applications demonstrate—users can be extremely creative in developing relatively sophisticated applications using tools with limited functionality, as was the case with the Lotus Notes system. We can, therefore, expect that users will over time learn how to exploit at least some of the functionality, especially that which makes their work easier. Indeed, over-specifying practices upfront may actually be detrimental, because it will provide less opportunities for situated learning (Lave & Wenger, 1991), as well as unnecessary because within a short while it is likely that practices will begin to diverge from any agreed process specification, as with the agreed CRM practices in XYZ.

It may be helpful to couple this user-led post-implementation improvisation potential with a strategic post-implementation project focus, so that a team is provided with resources to actually facilitate this emergent exploitation of the system. The danger here, as one of the interviewees commented, is getting organizations to think differently about what post-implementation efforts are meant to accomplish and how to staff and manage them. Unfortunately, given the challenges of such large-scale system implementations, many of the people intimately involved are likely to be "burnt out", as in the Siebel core team, and so want nothing more to do with the ES. Creating a new team may, therefore, be necessary. More generally, the message from the exploratory data analyzed here is that effort put into this post-implementation effort may be as important as the effort put into the implementation project, especially given the tendency for technical issues to trump organizational change during the implementation itself.

References

Aldwani, A. (2002). IT project uncertainty, planning and success: An empirical investigation from Kuwait. *Information, Technology and People*, 15, 210-216.

Ciborra, C., & Hanseth, O. (2000). *From control to drift*. Oxford: Oxford University Press.

Collins, M. H. (1990). *Artificial experts: Social knowledge and intelligent machines*. Cambridge, MA: MIT Press.

Davenport, T., & Prusak, L. (2003). *What's the big idea? Creating and capitalizing on the best management thinking*. Cambridge, MA: Harvard Business School Press.

Denzin, N. (1989). *The research act*. New Jersey: Prentice Hall.

Hammer, M., & Champy, J. (1993). *Reengineering the corporation: A manifesto for business revolution*. New York: Harper Collins.

Klein, H., & Myers, M. (1999) A set of principles for conducting and evaluating interpretive field studies in information systems. *MIS Quarterly*, 23(1), 67-94.

Knights, D., & Wilmott, H. (1997). The hype and hope of interdisciplinary management studies. *British Journal of Management*, 8, 9-22.

Lave, J., & Wenger, E. (1991). *Situated learning: Legitimate peripheral participation*. Cambridge, MA: Cambridge University Press.

Markus, M. L., Axline, S., Petrie, D., & Tanis, C. (2000). Learning from adopters' experiences with ERP: Problems encountered and success achieved. *Journal of Information Technology*, 15, 245-265.

Nah, F., Zuckweller, K., & Lau, J. (2003). ES implementation: Chief information officers' perceptions of critical success factors. *International Journal of Human-Computer Interactions, 16*(1), 5-22.

Newell, S., Huang, J., & Tansley, C. (2004). Social capital and knowledge integration in an ES project team: The importance of bridging and bonding. *British Journal of Management, 15*, 43-57.

Orlikowski, W. (1996). Improvising organizational transformation over time: A situated change perspective. *Information Systems Research, 7*(1), 63-92.

Orlikowski, W. (2000). Using technology and constituting structures: A practice lens for studying technology in organizations. *Organization Science, 11*(4), 404-428.

Parr, A., & Shanks, G. (2000). A model of ES project implementation. *Journal of Information Technology,* 15, 289-303.

Robey, D., Ross, J., & Boudreau, M.-C. (2002). Learning to implement enterprise systems: An exploratory study of the dialectics of change. *Journal of Management Information Systems, 19*(1), 17-46.

Sauer, C., Liu, L., & Johnston, K. (2001). Where project managers are kings. *Project Management Journal, 32*(4), 39-49.

Sawyer, S., & Southwick, R. (2002). Temporal issues in information and communication technology-enabled organizational change. *Information Society,* 18, 263-280.

Scott, J., & Vessey, I. (2002). Managing risks in enterprise systems implementations. *Communications of the ACM, 45*(4), 74-81.

Scott, S., & Wagner, E. (2003). Networks, negotiations and new times: The implementation of ERP into an academic administration. *Information and Organization,* 13, 285-313.

Soh, C., Sia, S. K., & Tay-Yap, J. (2000). Cultural fits and misfits: Is ES a universal solution? *Communications of the ACM,* 43, 47-51.

Wagner, E., & Newell, S. (2006a). Does best practice makes perfect? Fitting off-the-shelf applications to meet your needs. *Cutter Benchmark Review, 6*(9), 5-12.

Wagner, E., & Newell, S. (2006b). Repairing ERP: Producing social order to create a working information system. *Journal of Applied Behavioral Research, 42*(1), 40-57.

Walsham, G. (1993) *Interpreting information systems in organization.* Chichester, UK: Wiley.

About the Authors

Angappa Gunasekaran is a professor of operations management and the chairperson of the Department of Decision and Information Sciences at the Charlton College of Business, University of Massachusetts Dartmouth (USA). He has a PhD in industrial engineering and operations research from the Indian Institute of Technology (Bombay). Dr. Gunasekaran has held academic positions at Brunel University (UK), Monash University (Australia), the University of Vaasa (Finland), the University of Madras (India), and the University of Toronto, Laval University, and Concordia University (Canada). He has over 200 articles published/forthcoming in 40 different peer-reviewed journals. He has presented about 50 papers and published 60 articles in conferences and given a number of invited more talks in about 20 countries. Dr. Gunasekaran is on the editorial board of over 20 peer-reviewed journals. He is involved with several national and international collaborative projects that are funded by both private and government agencies. He has organized several international workshops and conferences in the emerging areas of operations management and information systems. Dr. Gunasekaran is currently interested in researching e-procurement, competitiveness of SMEs, information technology/systems evaluation, performance measures and metrics in new economy, logistics, and supply chain management. Dr. Gunasekaran is also the director of Business Innovation Research Center (BIRC).

*   *   *   *   *

M. Ruhul Amin is a professor of management and director of the Center for Management Development (CMD) at Bloomsburg University (USA). During the last 21 years of his academic career at Bloomsburg, Dr. Amin also held many administrative positions including assistant vice president and dean of graduate studies and research, chair of management department and MBA coordinator. He teaches undergraduate and graduate management courses. He has authored and co-authored numerous publications in the area of benchmarking, organizational behavior, and small business management.

Nafeez Amin is an entrepreneur and the owner of an automotive service facility in Allentown, Pennsylvania (USA). He graduated from Bloomsburg University (2002) and served on a research project on Benchmarking Outcomes of Undergraduate Business Curriculum. He has a strong interest in applied business research involving e-tailing and financial markets. He co-authored several publications in the area of benchmarking and small business management.

Nijaz Bajgoric is an associate professor of business computing and information technology management in the School of Economics and Business at the University of Sarajevo (Bosnia-Herzegovina). He has a PhD from the University of Sarajevo. He teaches and conducts research in information technology, business computing, information technology management, and operating systems. He has published papers in the following peer-reviewed journals: *International Journal of Enterprise Information Systems*, *Kybernetes*, *Information Management and Computer Security*, *Information Systems Management*, *Industrial Management and Data Systems*, *International Journal of Production Research*, *European Journal of Operational Research*, *International Journal of Agile Management Systems*, *Journal of Concurrent Engineering*, *International Journal of Agile Manufacturing*, and has authored and co-authored chapters in edited books published by: Elsevier Science, Kluwer Academic Publishers, CRC Press, and Auerbach Publications. His current areas of research include continuous computing technologies, business continuity, enterprise information systems, and information technology management.

C. Richard Baker is a professor of accounting in the School of Business at Adelphi University, Garden City, New York (USA). Prior to joining Adelphi, he served as professor and chair of the Accounting Department in the Charlton College of Business at the University of Massachusetts Dartmouth. He has also held academic positions at Columbia University and Fordham University in New York City. His research interests concentrate on the regulatory, legal, and ethical aspects of accounting and auditing. He is the author of over 90 academic papers, research books, and other publications. He holds a PhD from the Anderson School of Management at UCLA, and he is a certified public accountant in New York.

Dirk Baldwin is an associate professor of management information systems and the Department Chair of Business at the University of Wisconsin-Parkside (USA). Professor Baldwin conducts research related to multiple view systems, decision support systems, and document management. He has published in journals such as the *Journal of MIS* and *IEEE Transactions on System, Man, and Cybernetics*. He has co-authored books on MS Access. Professor Baldwin is chair of the Information Technology Practice Center and was named Wisconsin Idea fellow by the University of Wisconsin Board of Regents.

David H. Brown is the chair of Strategy and Information Systems and director of the Lancaster China Management Centre at Lancaster University Management School (UK). His research interests have two separate but linked strands: first, strategic studies including strategic information systems and e-business; and, second, the application of these strands internationally, especially Asia. Current research, funded by EU and EPSRC research grants, includes SMEs and relevant e-business models; e-science and e-management; and e-business and innovation in China and Laos. The majority of his work is strongly organizationally-based and includes action research and soft systems methodology. He has published many articles on information systems, e-business, and strategy formulation, and co-authored three books on management transition in China. He is a fellow professor in management science at Renmin University, Beijing.

Suresh Chalasani is an associate professor of management information systems at the University of Wisconsin-Parkside (USA). Professor Chalasani specializes in supply chain management systems, e-commerce technologies, parallel computing, and bioinformatics applications. Prior to joining the University of Wisconsin-Parkside, Professor Chalasani was a faculty member at the University of Wisconsin-Madison. He is a member of IEEE and IASTED. He published extensively in IEEE journals and conference proceedings in the area of information systems. He served on the program committees for numerous symposia and conferences. Professor Chalasani was a recipient of multiple research and instructional grants from the National Science Foundation and the University of Wisconsin System.

Jay Cooprider (PhD) is an associate trustee teaching professor of computer information systems at Bentley College in Waltham, Massachusetts (USA). He is the author of numerous articles dealing with management and information technology issues in such journals as *Information Systems Research, MIS Quarterly,* and the *IBM Systems Journal*, and has consulted widely in the use of information technology in building organizational relationships, knowledge management, and high performing workgroups. He received his SB in computer science from the Massachusetts Institute of Technology and PhD in management with an information technology specialization from the Sloan School of Management at M.I.T. He was formerly a faculty member and associate director of the Information Systems Management Program in the Graduate School of Business at the University of Texas at Austin.

Gary David is an associate professor of sociology at Bentley College (USA) (BS in sociology and psychology; MA in sociology, Central Michigan University; PhD in sociology, Wayne State University). Dr. David's research focuses on the role that interpersonal interactions play in the formation of intergroup relations, as well as ethnographic studies of the workplace. He has conducted research primarily in workplace settings where intercultural/intergroup interactions take place on a regular basis. Past studies include the analysis of interactions between workers and customers in Arab-owned convenience stores in Metropolitan Detroit. Present projects include examining globally-distributed collaborative software development teams, focusing on the role of information and communication technologies. Other workplace research includes examinations of enterprise system design and implementation. Dr. David also specializes in Arab-American studies and ethnic identity research. Recent publications and presentations include topics on Muslim American communities, Arab-owned convenience stores, images of Arabs in the West, Arab-American identity, theories of immigrant entrepreneurship, and intercultural service encounters. He is also the administrator of an online discussion group devoted to Arab-American studies.

Linda Edelman is an assistant professor of strategic management at Bentley College (USA). Previously, she was a research fellow at the Warwick Business School in Coventry (UK), and is currently a member of the ikon (innovation, knowledge, organizational networks) research team. She received her MBA and her DBA from Boston University. She is the author of six book chapters and over 25 scholarly articles. Her current research examines the resources, cognitive strategies, and networks of new ventures as well as the innovation and learning strategies of project groups and teams. Her work has appeared in journals such as the *Journal of Business Venturing, Academy of Management Learning and Education, Journal of Small Business Management, Organization Studies, Management Learning,* and *British Journal of Management.*

Delvin Grant is an associate professor of management information systems and the undergraduate MIS program coordinator at the School of Commerce at DePaul University (USA). He received his bachelor's degree from NY Institute of Technology in mechanical engineering and his MBA and PhD from the State University of New York at Binghamton. He has worked for IBM, Merrill Lunch, and Techumseh. He has published in academic journals including *Communications of the ACM, Information Systems Journal, Information Technology and People, International Journal* *of Computer Integrated Manufacturing, Computers and Industrial Engineering, International Journal of Enterprise Information Systems, Information Technology and People*, and *Total Quality Management.* His research interests include system development methods for information systems and manufacturing, action research, and TQM.

Christopher S. Hoffer has a BS in accounting, MBA, and MS in information systems from Penn State Harrisburg (USA). He is employed as a business analyst for an S&P 500 company.

S. C. Lenny Koh is the director of the Logistics and Supply Chain Management Research Group and an associate professor/senior lecturer in Operations Management at the University of Sheffield Management School (UK). She holds a doctorate in operations management and a first-class honours degree in industrial and manufacturing systems engineering. Her research interests are in the areas of production planning and control (ERP and ERPII), uncertainty management, modern operations management practices, logistics and supply chain management, e-business, e-organisations, knowledge management, sustainable business, and eco-logistics. Dr. Koh has 180 publications in journal papers, books, edited books, edited proceedings, edited special issues, book chapters, conference papers, technical papers, and reports. She is the editor-in-chief of the *International Journal of Enterprise Network Management, International Journal of Value Chain Management*, and the *International Journal of Logistics Economics and Globalisation.* She is the associate editor of the *International Journal of Systems Science, Enterprise Information Systems*, and the *International Journal of Operational Research.*

Chuck C. H. Law is an assistant professor and director of the Center of Information Technology Development at the Department of Information Management, Chaoyang University of Technology (Taiwan). Before the current academic endeavor, he served as senior consultant, director of information systems, and chief information officer with Big 6 consultancies and multi-nationals in North America, and the Asia/Pacific region. His research interest is in IT productivity paradox issues, business process redesign, ERP systems, e-commerce, knowledge management, and RFID technologies. His research has been presented in international conferences, and published or accepted by several international journals.

Frank Lefley is a research fellow at Royal Holloway, University of London (UK). He received his MSc in management systems and sciences from the University of Hull, his MPhil in accounting and financial management from the University of Buckingham (which involved a joint project with the University of Texas at Arlington, USA), and his PhD from the University of London. He is an alumnus of Imperial College, London. His published research has appeared in a recent book and a number of academic and professional journals. He is a qualified accountant and also a fellow of the Institute of Chartered Secretaries and Administrators, and the Royal Society of Art.

Allen R. Lias is presently a professor and department head of mathematics at Robert Morris University, Pittsburgh, Pennsylvania (USA). He is a co-principal investigator for a National Science Foundation Comprehensive Grant to improve K-16 mathematics and science education. He holds a PhD in mathematics education from the University of Pittsburgh.

Nigel J. Lockett is the business development manager for InfoLab21 Knowledge Business Centre (KBC) at Lancaster University (UK), which involves managing a small team whose primary objective is supporting engagement between academic staff and businesses. He holds a PhD in management science, and his current research interests include e-business, in particular by SMEs, and knowledge transfer. Recent EPSRC-funded research projects include the "Lancaster Centre for e-Management and e-Science" and the "InfoLab21 Knowledge Transfer Study". He is a knowledge transfer and information management specialist with experience gained in both leading academic and dynamic commercial environments. He has a proven track record in managing enterprises, with 15 years senior management experience.

Traci Logan is the vice president for Information Technology and vice provost for Academic Affairs at Bentley College (USA). In this dual role, she oversees the divisions of Information Technology and Academic Services, reflecting the college's belief that IT is at the heart of innovation and business process, and inextricably linked with the goals of higher education administration and business education. She has spent the last 22 years in higher education administration. She has extensive experience in strategic planning, security and privacy, business continuity and recovery, IT assessment, systems integration, high-tech facility design, business process management, contract management, enterprise-wide system implementation, educational technology, and financial operations. Ms. Logan's division is wide-ranging and includes the traditional IT functions: systems, networks, telecommunications, management information systems, technology planning and deployment, and client computing services as well as critical academic functions that rely heavily on IT—academic technology and curriculum innovation, faculty research services, library, registrar, and academic administrative operations which includes business and finance and contract administration. She collaborates with faculty and the external business community in the evaluation of emerging applications, in defining cooperative applied research initiatives, and in the development and evolution of application specific, IT intensive learning environments to ensure Bentley remains a leader in capturing in the curricula the impact of IT on business practice.

Charles Møller is teaching and researching the management of enterprise information systems in a supply chain context. His current interest is business process innovation, and the purpose of his work is to develop methods and tool for developing effective enterprise systems in industry. His publications exceed 100 papers, and he is the first author on more than 80 papers. His publications include 18 papers in Danish and international journals, 36 refereed conference papers, and 25 chapters or books. He was recently awarded the Emerald Literati Network 2006 Highly Commended Award. He is a member of the editorial board for *Enterprise Information Systems* and has served as "ad hoc" reviewer for the *Journal of Information Technology, Journal of Strategic Information Systems, European Journal of Information Systems, Production Planning and Control, International Journal of Integrated Supply Management, Behaviour & Information Technology, IRMA, IDEA* and *Ledelse & Erhvervsøkonomi*. He is a workshop organizer at the International Conference on Enterprise Information Systems and served at program committees for IFIP 8.6, ICESAcc, CONFENIS, and TIGeBR. He served on PhD committees at the Technical University of Denmark, Aalborg University, and at the University of Southern Denmark, where he is also employed as an external associate professor.

Sue Newell is the Cammarata Professor of Management, Bentley College (USA), and a part-time professor of information management at Warwick University (UK). She has a BSc and PhD from Cardiff University (UK). Sue is currently the PhD director at Bentley. Her research focuses on understanding the relationships between innovation, knowledge and organisational networking (ikon)—primarily from an organisational theory perspective. She was one of the founding members of ikon, a research centre based at Warwick University. She has been involved in many of the ikon projects and is currently working on a project titled "The Evolution of Biomedical Knowledge: Interactive Innovation in the UK and US". She is also involved in research which focuses on exploring the implementation and use of packaged information systems, for example, to support distributed project work or health records. Her research emphasises a critical, practice-based understanding of the social aspects of innovation, change, knowledge management, and inter-firm networked relations. She has published over 70 journal articles in the areas of organization studies, management and information systems, as well as numerous books and book chapters.

Eric W. T. Ngai is currently an associate professor in the Department of Management and Marketing at The Hong Kong Polytechnic University (PR China). His research interests are in the areas of e-commerce, decision support systems, supply chain systems, and knowledge management systems. He has published in a number of journals including *IEEE Transactions on Systems, Man and Cybernetics, Information and Management, Expert Systems and Applications, Expert Systems, International Journal of Operations and Production Management, Omega, European Journal of Marketing, European Journal of Operational Research* and others. Dr. Ngai serves on the editorial board of *International Journal of Production Research.*

Joseph Sarkis is a professor of operations management within Clark University's Graduate School of Management (USA). He was previously at the University of Texas at Arlington. He earned his PhD in management sciences from the University of Buffalo. He has published over 200 articles in a wide variety of outlets on a broad spectrum of interdisciplinary topics and issues. He is the editor of *Management Research News.*

Farooq M. Sheikh is an assistant professor of operations management at SUNY Geneseo (USA). He earned his PhD from Smeal College of Business at Penn State University under the guidance of Dr. Kalyan Chatterjee. His dissertation was a study of modular products in regard to interface choices (proprietary versus standard) and rate of innovation. His research interest is in problems of operations management that lend to economic modeling and game theoretic analysis. He also takes active interest in interdisciplinary research problems within and outside business areas of study. His current research is focused on coordination, quality and innovation issues in supply chain management, auctions, and pricing on Internet channel.

Alan D. Smith is presently a university professor of operations management at Robert Morris University, located in Pittsburgh, Pennsylvania. Previously he was the chair of the Department of Quantitative and Natural Sciences and coordinator of Engineering Programs at the same institution, as well as an associate professor of business administration at Eastern Kentucky University. He holds concurrent PhDs in engineering systems/education from The University of Akron and in business administration from Kent State University. He is the author of numerous articles and book chapters.

Girish H. Subramanian is an associate professor of information systems in the School of Business at Penn State Harrisburg (USA). He obtained his PhD in computer and information systems from Temple University. His work has appeared in *Communications of the ACM, Decision Sciences, Journal of Management Information Systems, Journal of Systems & Software, Journal of Computer Information Systems* as well as several other journals. His research interests are in computer-aided software engineering, data warehousing, object-oriented development metrics, capability maturity model and software process improvement, and global software development.

Qiang Tu is an associate professor of management information systems at the College of Business of Rochester Institute of Technology (USA). He received his Bachelor's degree in management engineering and master's degree in systems engineering from Jiaotong University (China). He holds a PhD from the College of Business Administration of University of Toledo. He has published in academic journals including *Information Systems Research, Decision Sciences, Journal of Operations Management, OMEGA: The International Journal of Management Science, Journal of Strategic Information Systems*, and *Information Resources Management Journal*. His research interests include information systems strategy, manufacturing strategy, technology management, and behavioral issues in information systems and manufacturing management.

Dothang Truong is an assistant professor of information systems and operations management at Fayetteville State University (USA). He received his PhD in manufacturing management from the University of Toledo and a MBA from Asian Institute of Technology. Before joining Fayetteville State University in 2003, he has taught for two years at the University of Toledo and for three years at Hanoi University of Technology. He teaches operations management, e-commerce, quantitative methods for business, microcomputer applications for business, and data analysis for business. He has a number of publications in various academic journals such as *Electronic Markets, International Journal of Enterprise Information Systems, Behavior and Information Technology Journal, Industrial Marketing Management*, and the *Journal of Academy of Business and Economics*. In addition, he has an extensive number of proceeding publications in conferences such as: Decision Sciences Institute (DSI), Institute for Operations Research and the Management Sciences (INFORMS), Institute for Supply Management (ISM), and International Institute of Informatics and Systemics (IIIS). His research interests include e-commerce, business-to-business e-marketplaces, radio frequency identification, and e-supply chain management. He received The Best Research Paper Award by International Academy of Business and Public Administration Disciplines (2006), honorable mention award for dissertation competition by Decision Sciences Institute (DSI) Conference (2005), The Student Pacemaker of the Year Award (2004), and many other awards.

Alexander Y. Yap is an associate professor at Elon University, North Carolina (USA). He has served as an information systems and business consultant in the private sector. He holds a PhD in management information systems from Copenhagen Business School (Denmark), an MBA in international management from Exeter

University (UK), and a master's degree in development economics from Williams College (USA). He has won the Best Paper Award at the highly prestigious International Conference on Information Systems (ICIS). He currently teaches e-business and Web development. His research papers have been published in the *Journal of Global Information Management*, the *Journal of E-Commerce Research*, *Journal of Electronics Market*, and the *Journal of Enterprise Information Systems*, among others. He has also published and presented several papers in prestigious information systems conferences, which include the ICIS, ECIS, ACM and ISECON.

Index